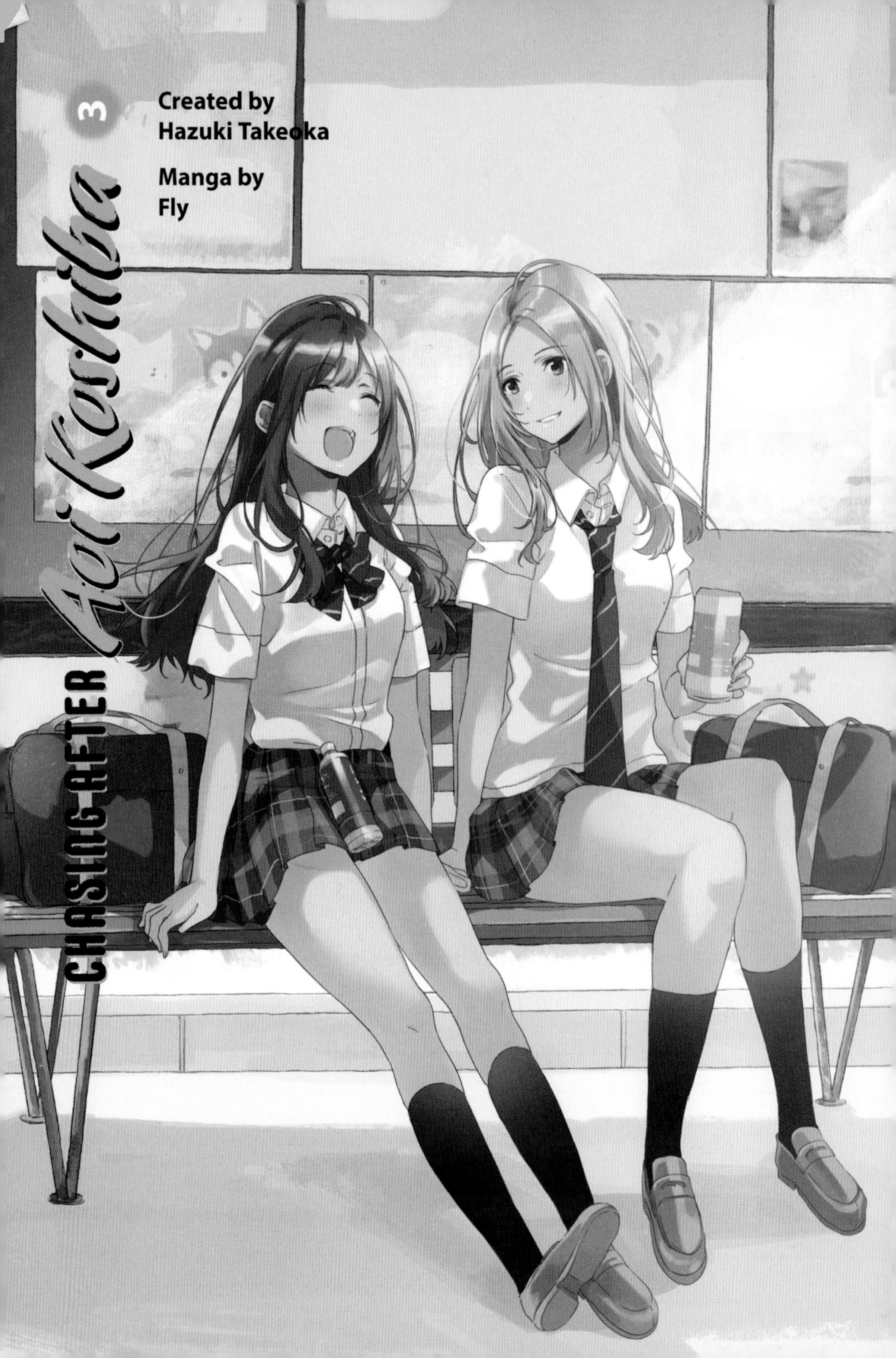
CHASING AFTER
Aoi Koshiba
3
Created by
Hazuki Takeoka
Manga by
Fly

contents

Chapter 17: Connecting the Stars

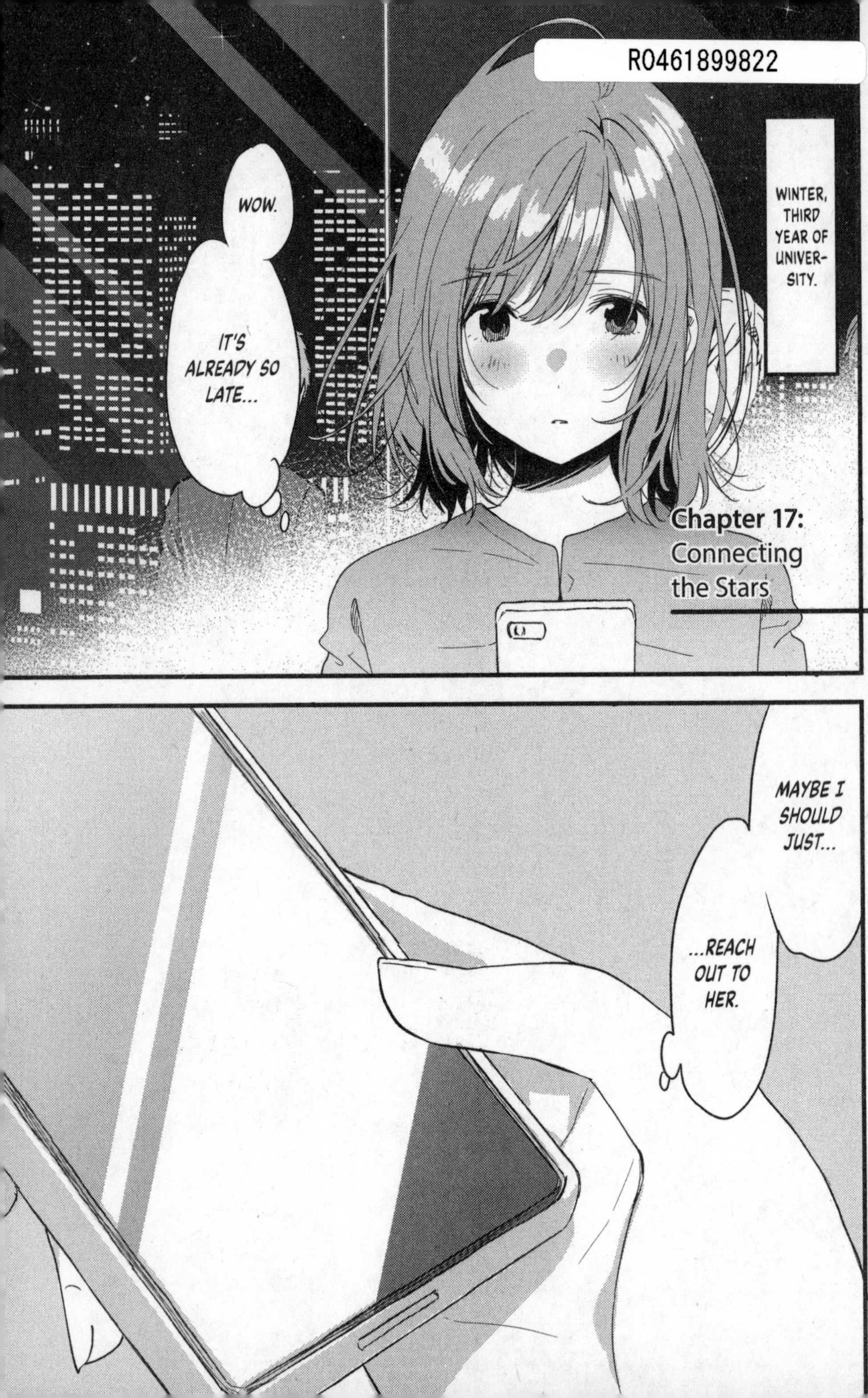
WINTER, THIRD YEAR OF UNIVERSITY.
WOW.
IT'S ALREADY SO LATE...
MAYBE I SHOULD JUST...
...REACH OUT TO HER.

Chapter 17:
Connecting the Stars

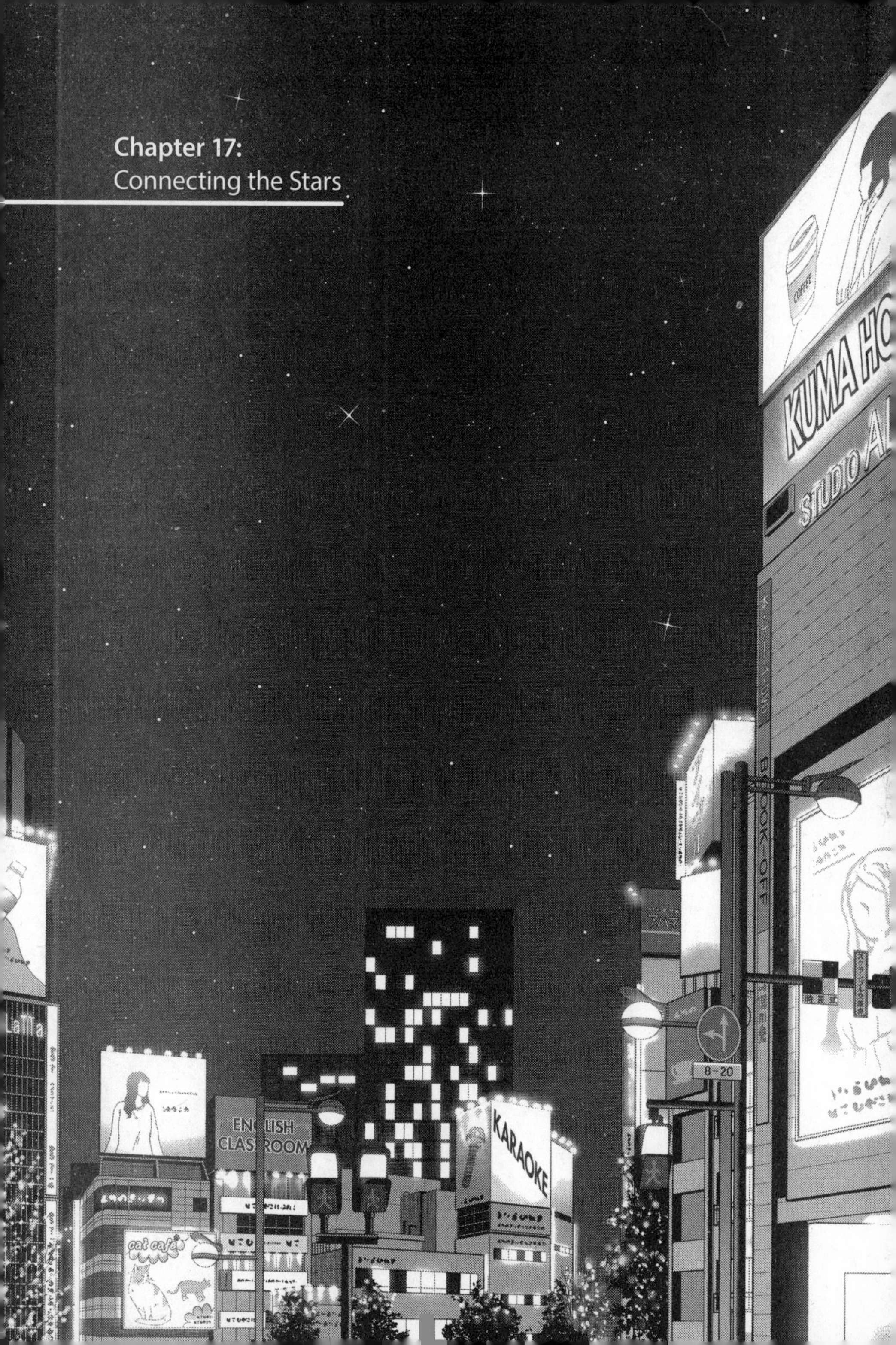
COFFEE
KUMA HO
STUDIO A
BOOK-OFF
8-20
KARAOKE
ENGLISH
CLASSROOM
cat cafe

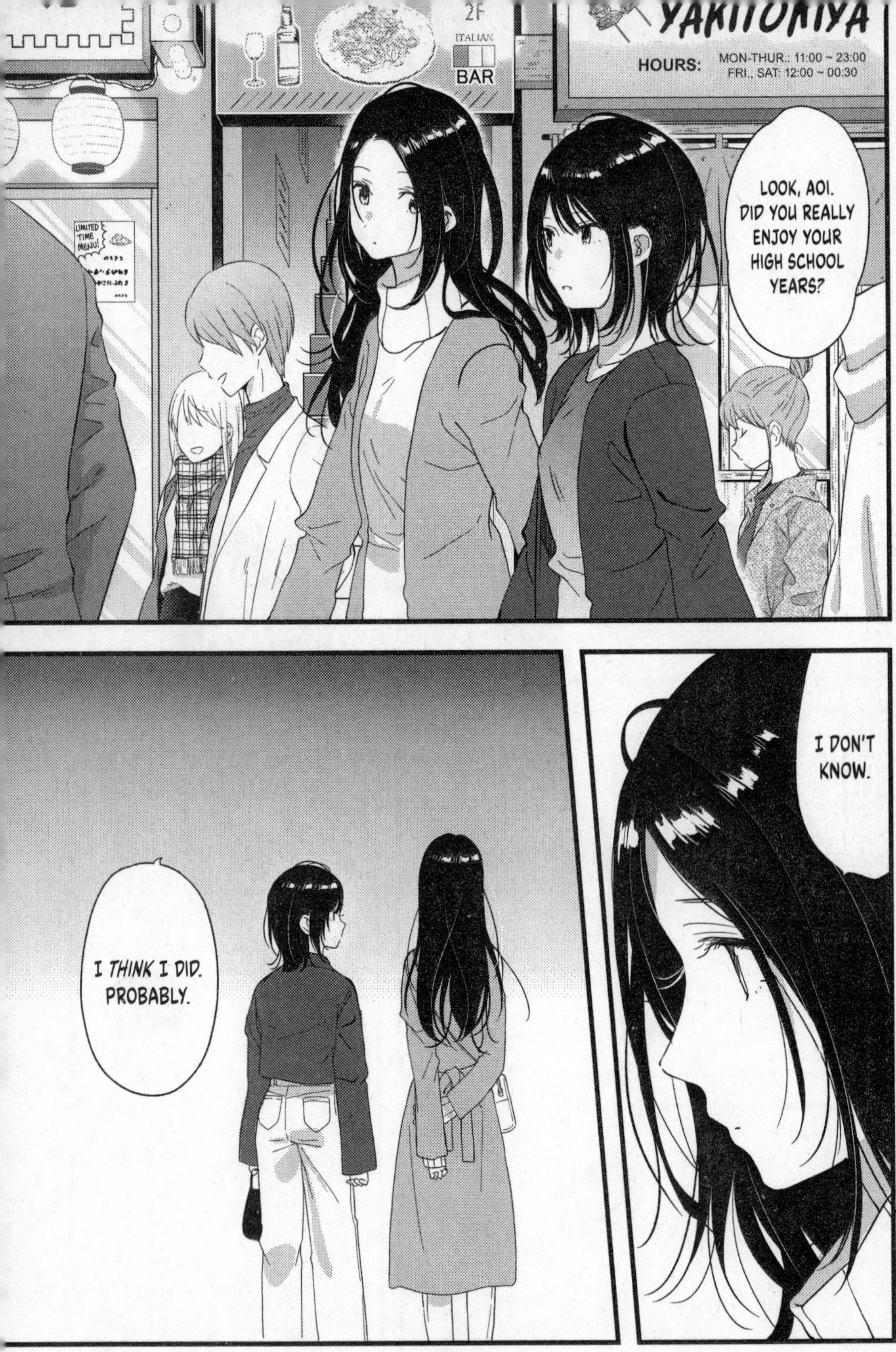
YAKITORIYA
HOURS: MON-THUR.: 11:00 ~ 23:00
FRI., SAT: 12:00 ~ 00:30
2F
ITALIAN
BAR
LIMITED TIME MENU!
LOOK, AOI. DID YOU REALLY ENJOY YOUR HIGH SCHOOL YEARS?
I DON'T KNOW.
I *THINK* I DID. PROBABLY.

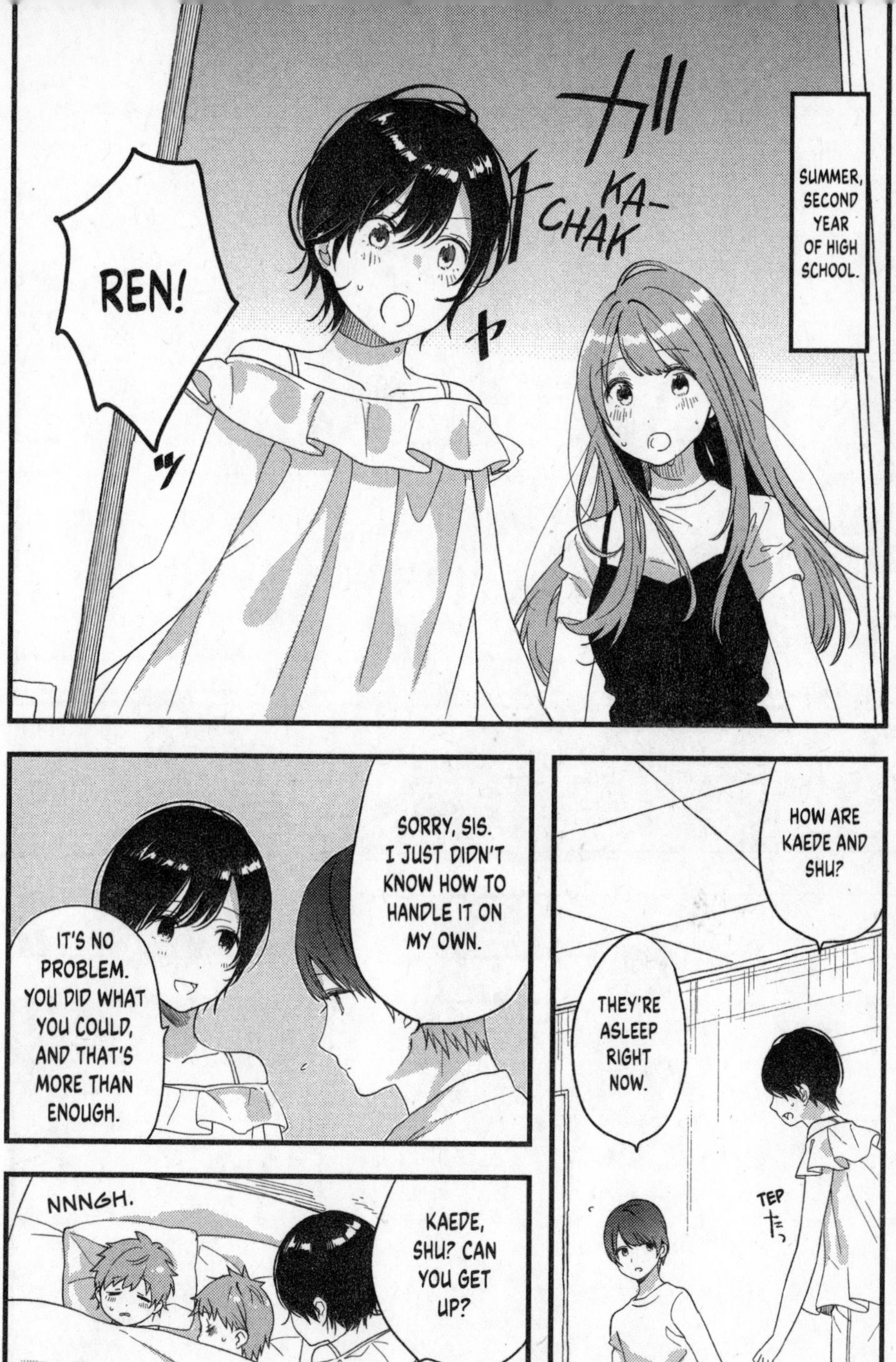
SUMMER, SECOND YEAR OF HIGH SCHOOL.
KA-CHAK
REN!
HOW ARE KAEDE AND SHU?
THEY'RE ASLEEP RIGHT NOW.
TEP
SORRY, SIS. I JUST DIDN'T KNOW HOW TO HANDLE IT ON MY OWN.
IT'S NO PROBLEM. YOU DID WHAT YOU COULD, AND THAT'S MORE THAN ENOUGH.
KAEDE, SHU? CAN YOU GET UP?
NNNGH.

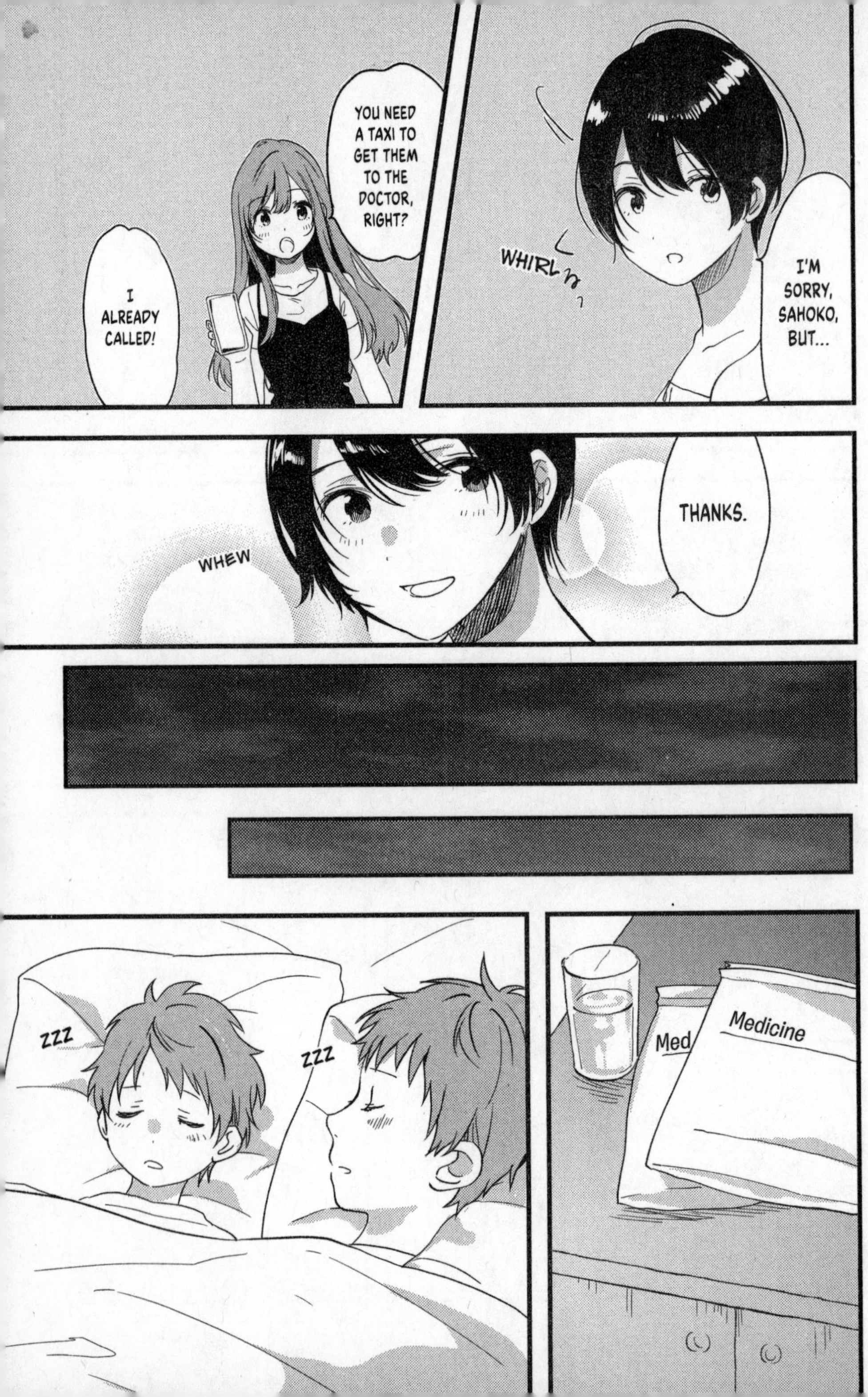

WHIRL
I'M SORRY, SAHOKO, BUT...
YOU NEED A TAXI TO GET THEM TO THE DOCTOR, RIGHT?
I ALREADY CALLED!
THANKS.
WHEW
Medicine
Med
ZZZ
ZZZ

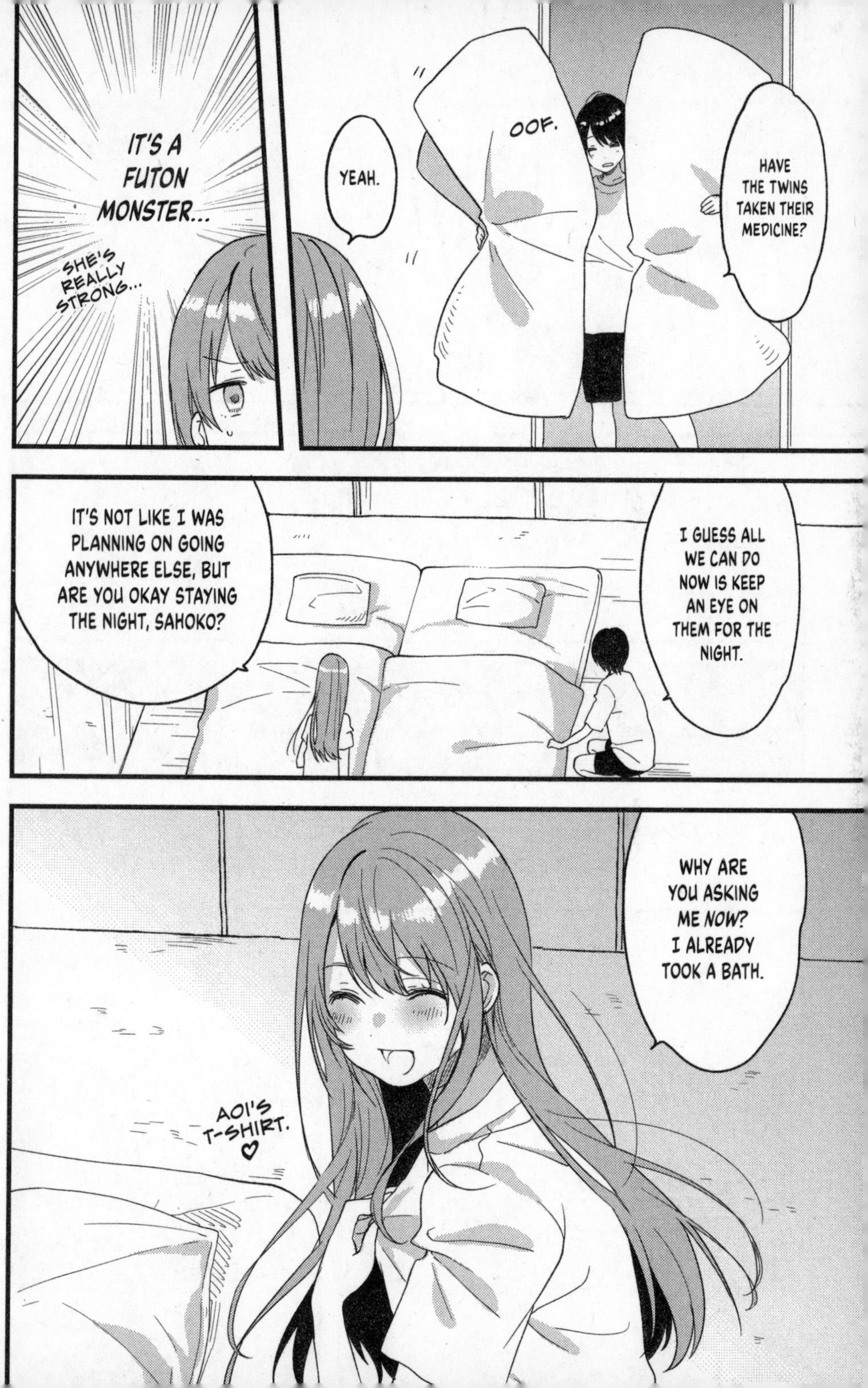
HAVE THE TWINS TAKEN THEIR MEDICINE?
OOF.
YEAH.
IT'S A FUTON MONSTER...
SHE'S REALLY STRONG...
I GUESS ALL WE CAN DO NOW IS KEEP AN EYE ON THEM FOR THE NIGHT.
IT'S NOT LIKE I WAS PLANNING ON GOING ANYWHERE ELSE, BUT ARE YOU OKAY STAYING THE NIGHT, SAHOKO?
WHY ARE YOU ASKING ME *NOW*? I ALREADY TOOK A BATH.
AOI'S T-SHIRT. ♥

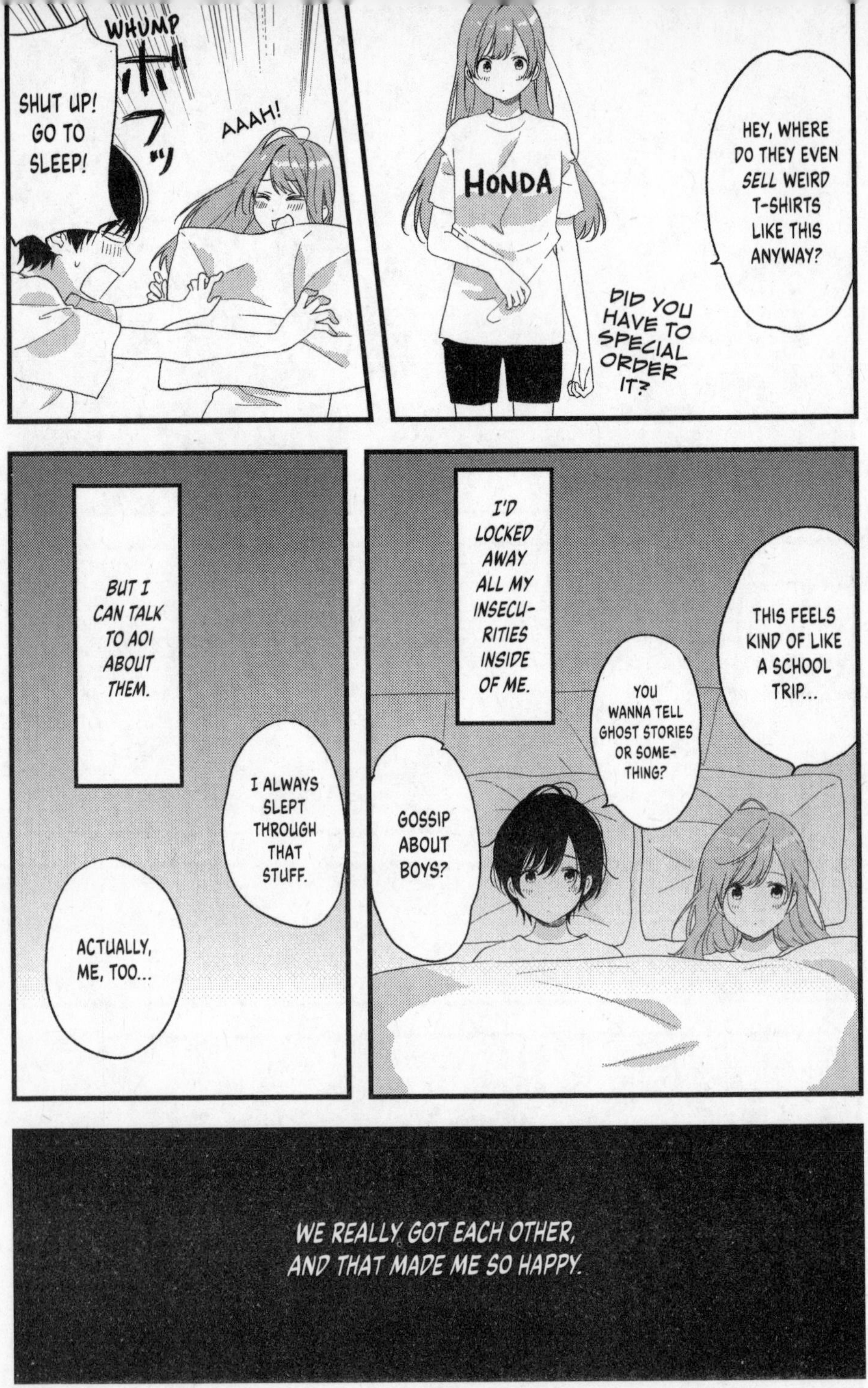
HONDA
HEY, WHERE DO THEY EVEN SELL WEIRD T-SHIRTS LIKE THIS ANYWAY?
DID YOU HAVE TO SPECIAL ORDER IT?
WHUMP
SHUT UP! GO TO SLEEP!
ボフッ
AAAH!
THIS FEELS KIND OF LIKE A SCHOOL TRIP...
I'D LOCKED AWAY ALL MY INSECURITIES INSIDE OF ME.
YOU WANNA TELL GHOST STORIES OR SOME-THING?
GOSSIP ABOUT BOYS?
BUT I CAN TALK TO AOI ABOUT THEM.
I ALWAYS SLEPT THROUGH THAT STUFF.
ACTUALLY, ME, TOO...
WE REALLY GOT EACH OTHER, AND THAT MADE ME SO HAPPY.

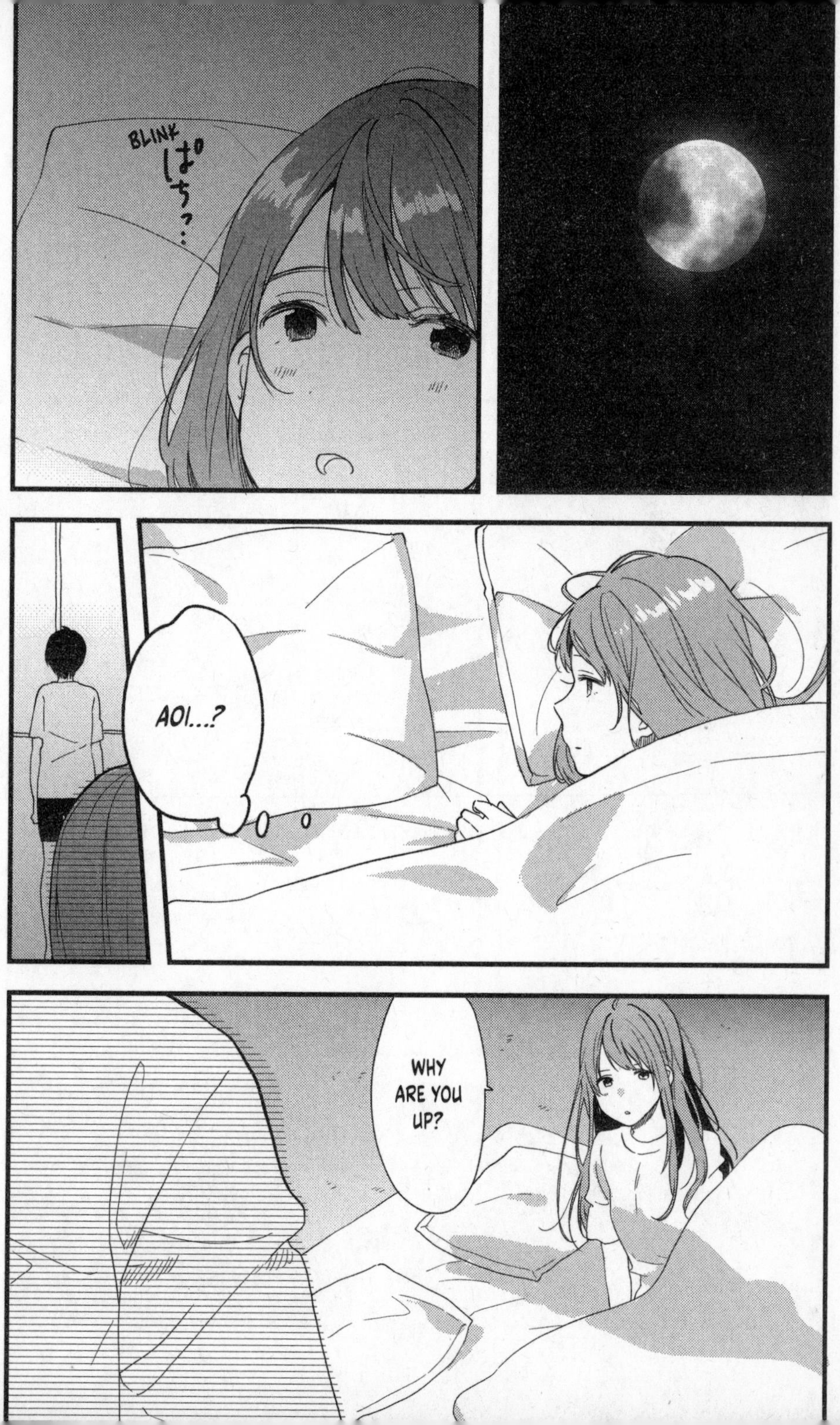
BLINK
ぱちっ…
AOI...?
WHY ARE YOU UP?

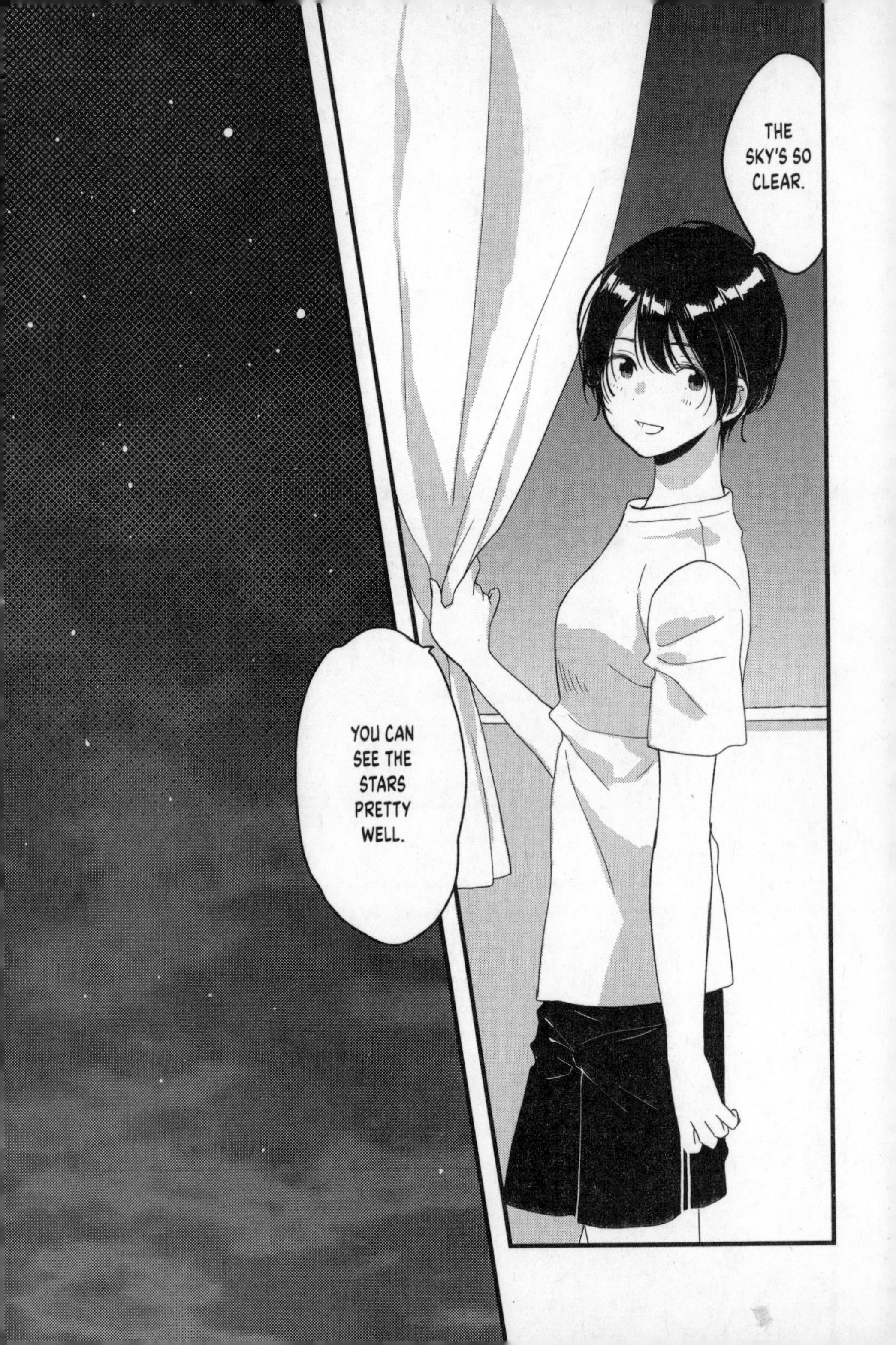
THE SKY'S SO CLEAR.
YOU CAN SEE THE STARS PRETTY WELL.

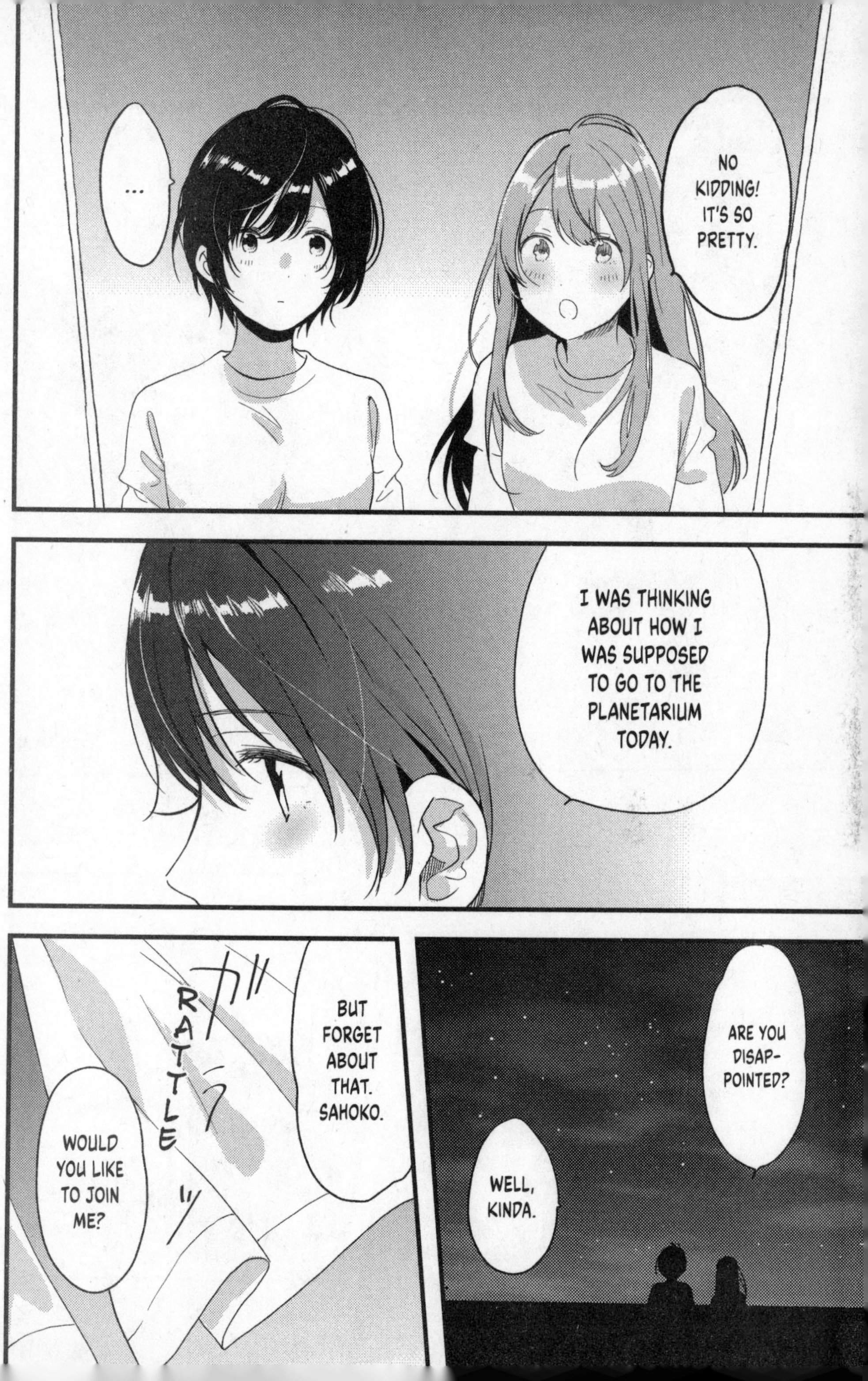
NO KIDDING! IT'S SO PRETTY.
...
I WAS THINKING ABOUT HOW I WAS SUPPOSED TO GO TO THE PLANETARIUM TODAY.
ARE YOU DISAP-POINTED?
WELL, KINDA.
BUT FORGET ABOUT THAT. SAHOKO.
RATTLE
WOULD YOU LIKE TO JOIN ME?

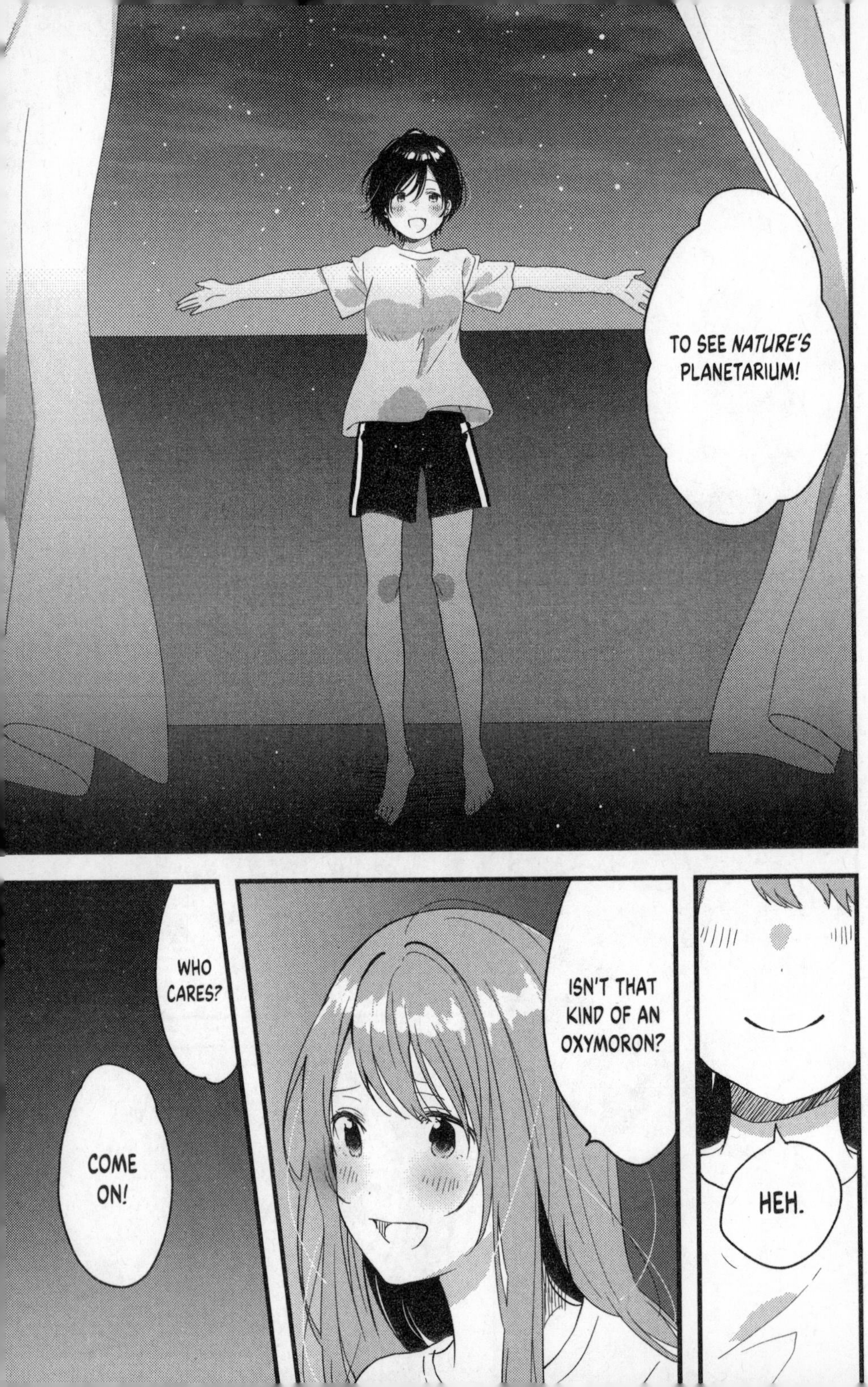
TO SEE *NATURE'S* PLANETARIUM!
HEH.
ISN'T THAT KIND OF AN OXYMORON?
WHO CARES?
COME ON!

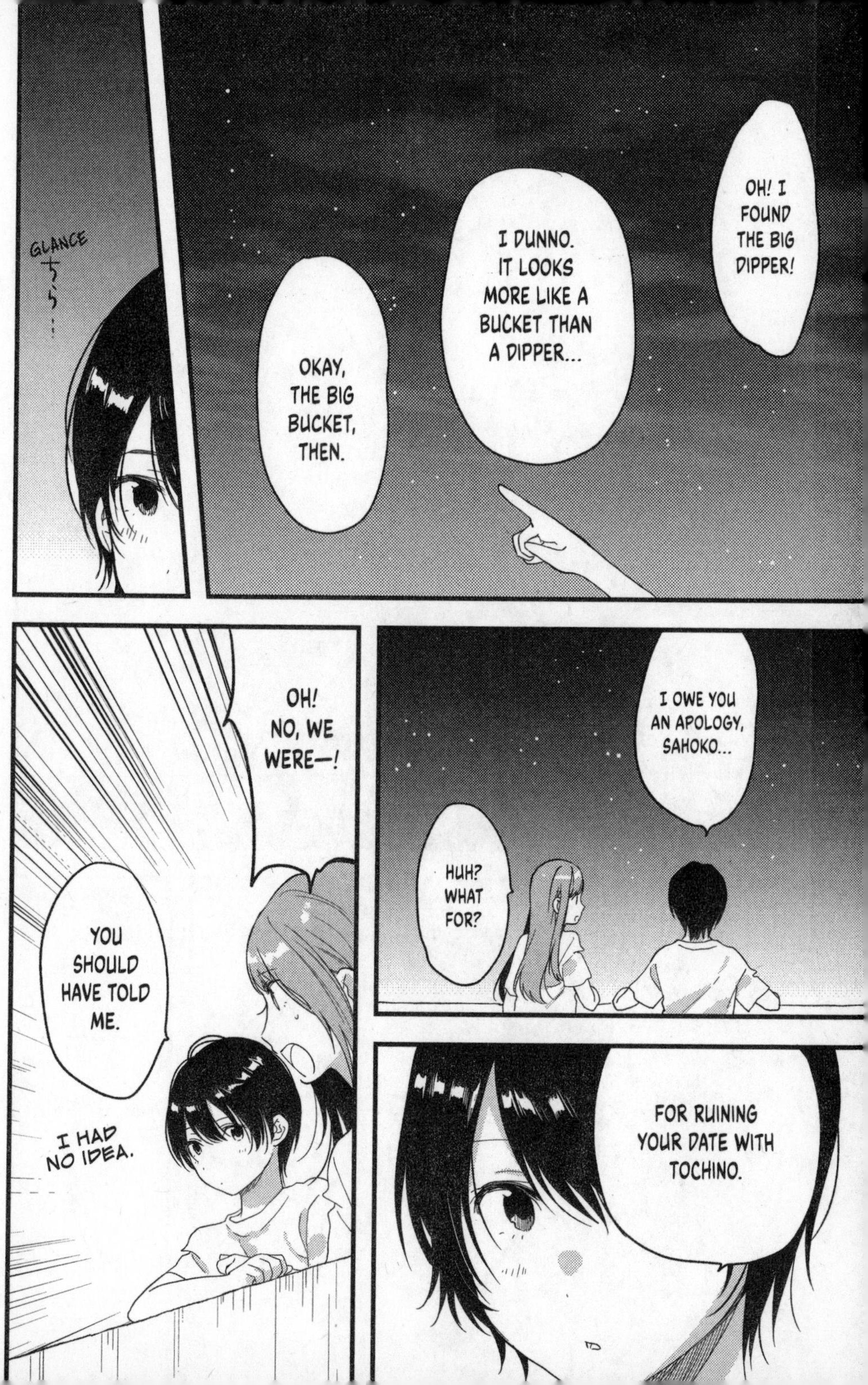
OH! I FOUND THE BIG DIPPER!
I DUNNO. IT LOOKS MORE LIKE A BUCKET THAN A DIPPER...
OKAY, THE BIG BUCKET, THEN.
GLANCE
ちら…
I OWE YOU AN APOLOGY, SAHOKO...
HUH? WHAT FOR?
FOR RUINING YOUR DATE WITH TOCHINO.
OH! NO, WE WERE—!
YOU SHOULD HAVE TOLD ME.
I HAD NO IDEA.

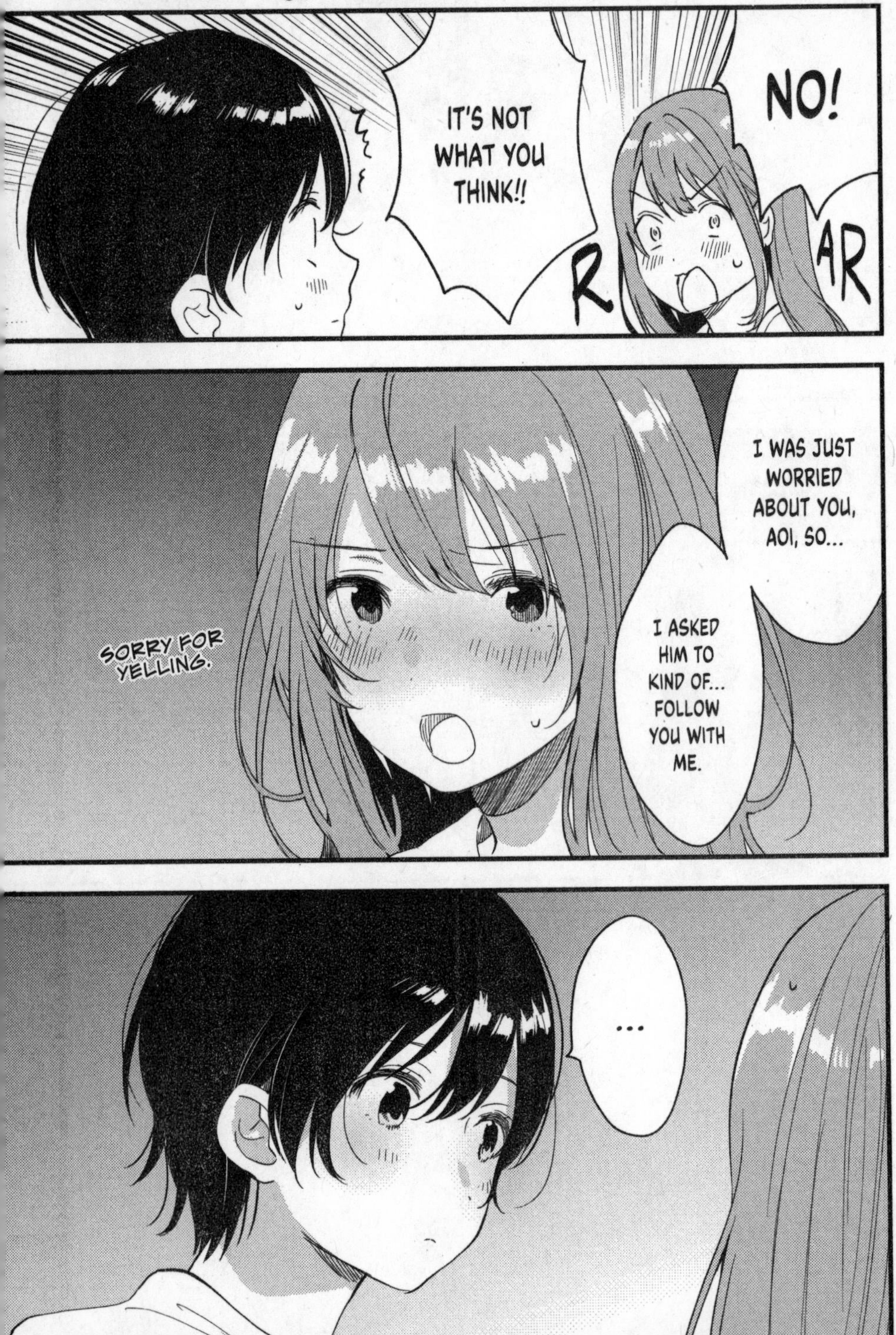
NO!
IT'S NOT WHAT YOU THINK!!
R
AR
I WAS JUST WORRIED ABOUT YOU, AOI, SO...
I ASKED HIM TO KIND OF... FOLLOW YOU WITH ME.
SORRY FOR YELLING.
...

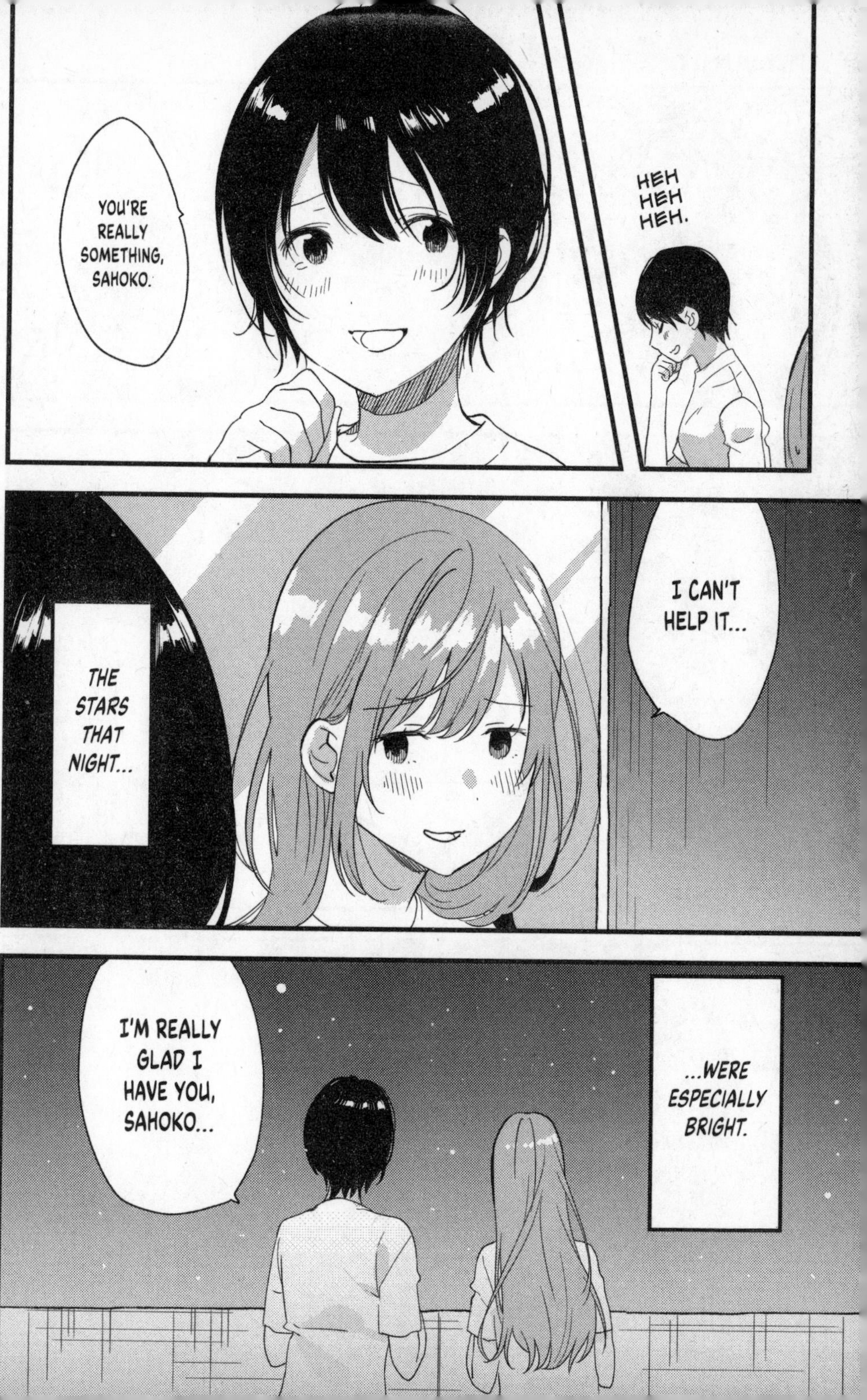
HEH HEH HEH.
YOU'RE REALLY SOMETHING, SAHOKO.
I CAN'T HELP IT...
THE STARS THAT NIGHT...
...WERE ESPECIALLY BRIGHT.
I'M REALLY GLAD I HAVE YOU, SAHOKO...

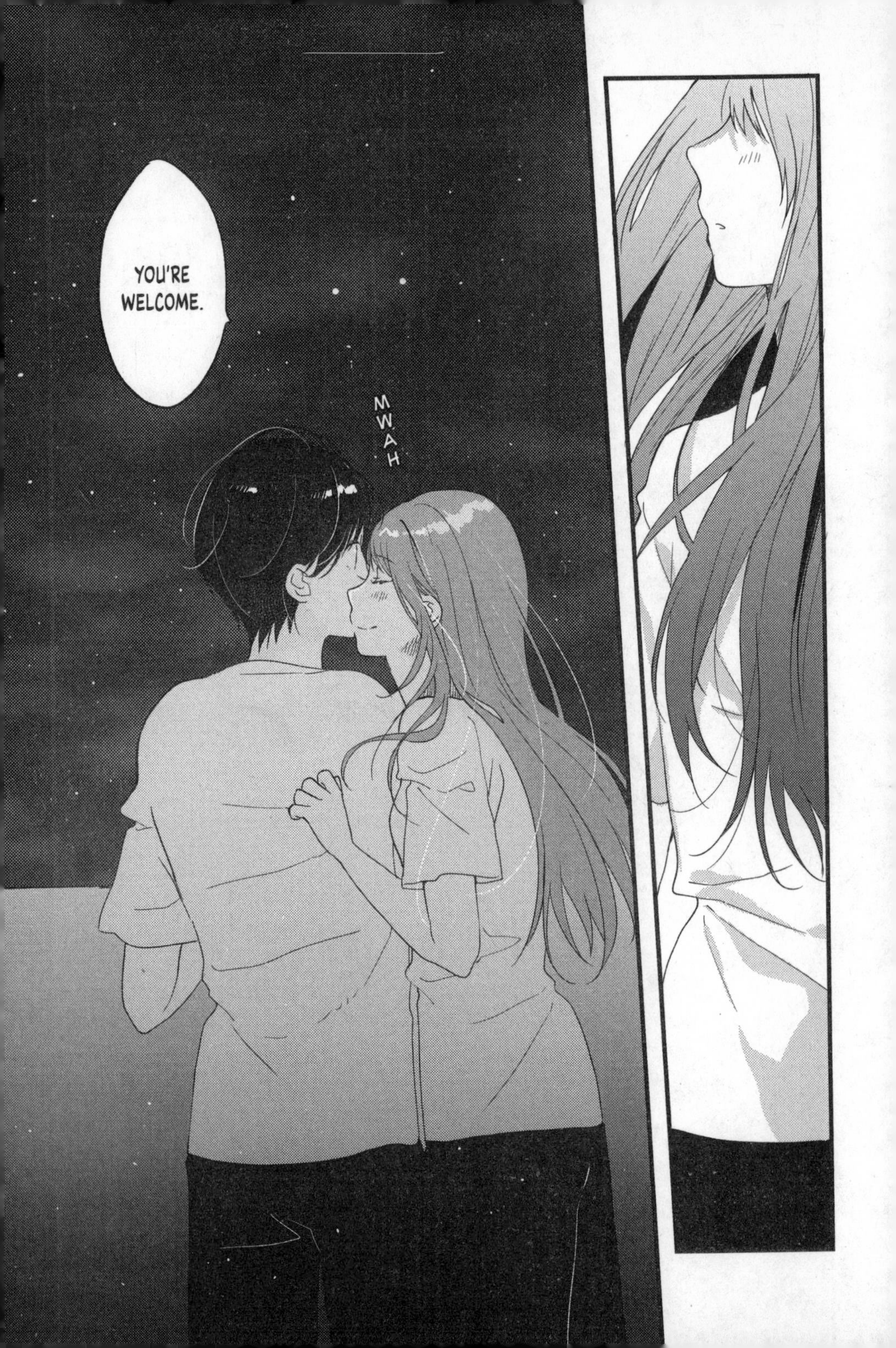
YOU'RE WELCOME.
MWAH

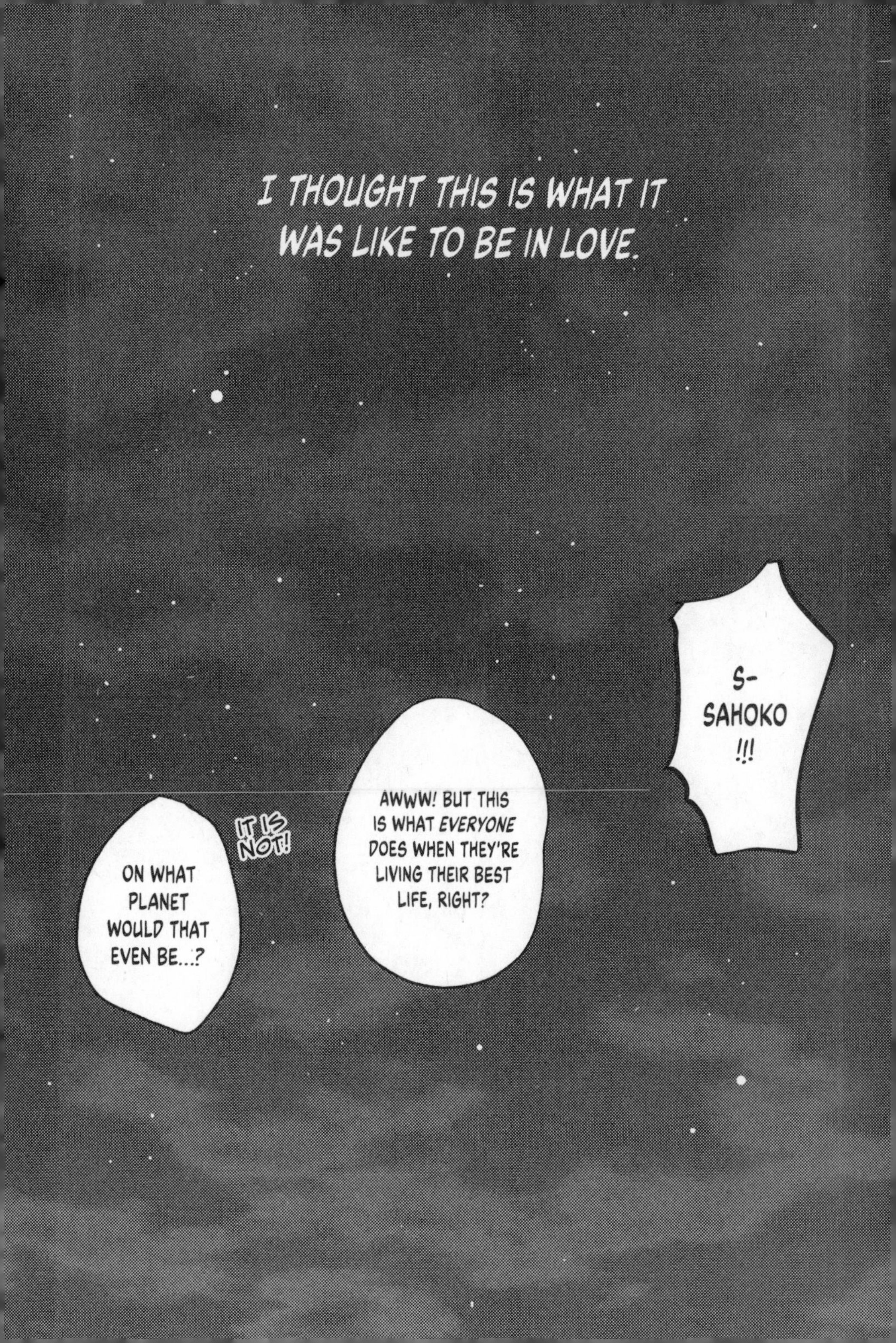
I THOUGHT THIS IS WHAT IT WAS LIKE TO BE IN LOVE.
S-SAHOKO!!!
AWWW! BUT THIS IS WHAT *EVERYONE* DOES WHEN THEY'RE LIVING THEIR BEST LIFE, RIGHT?
IT IS NOT!
ON WHAT PLANET WOULD THAT EVEN BE...?

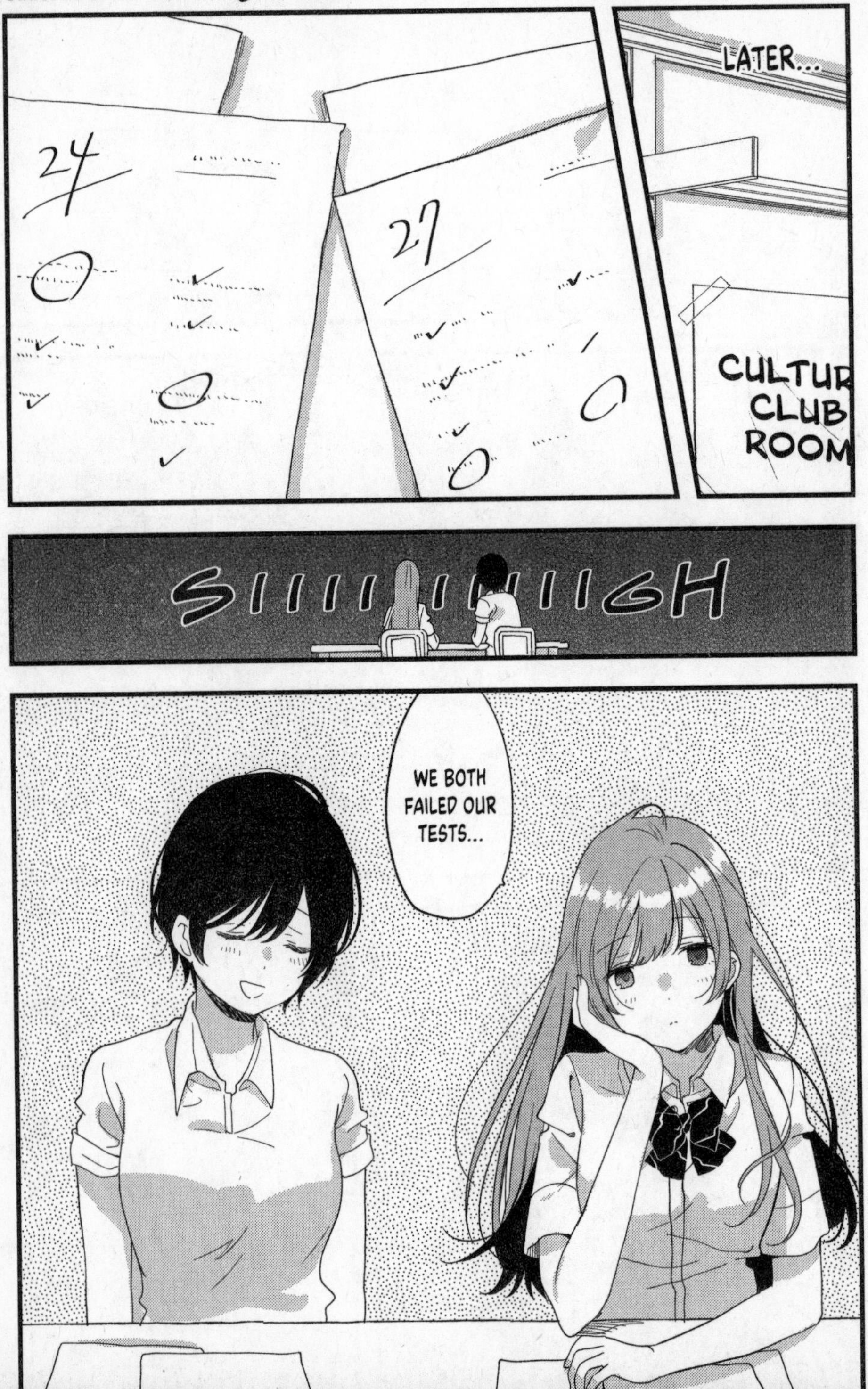
LATER...
CULTUR CLUB ROOM
24
27
SIIIIIIIIIIGH
WE BOTH FAILED OUR TESTS...

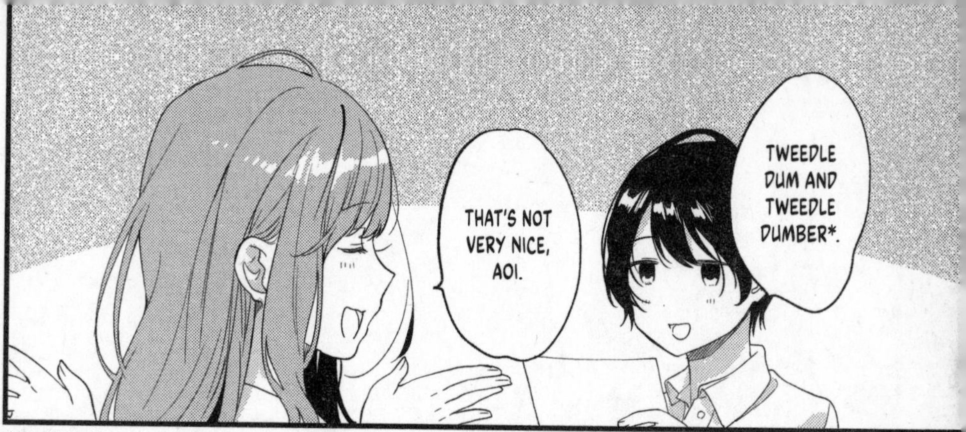
TWEEDLE DUM AND TWEEDLE DUMBER*.
THAT'S NOT VERY NICE, AOI.

*SEE PAGE 162.

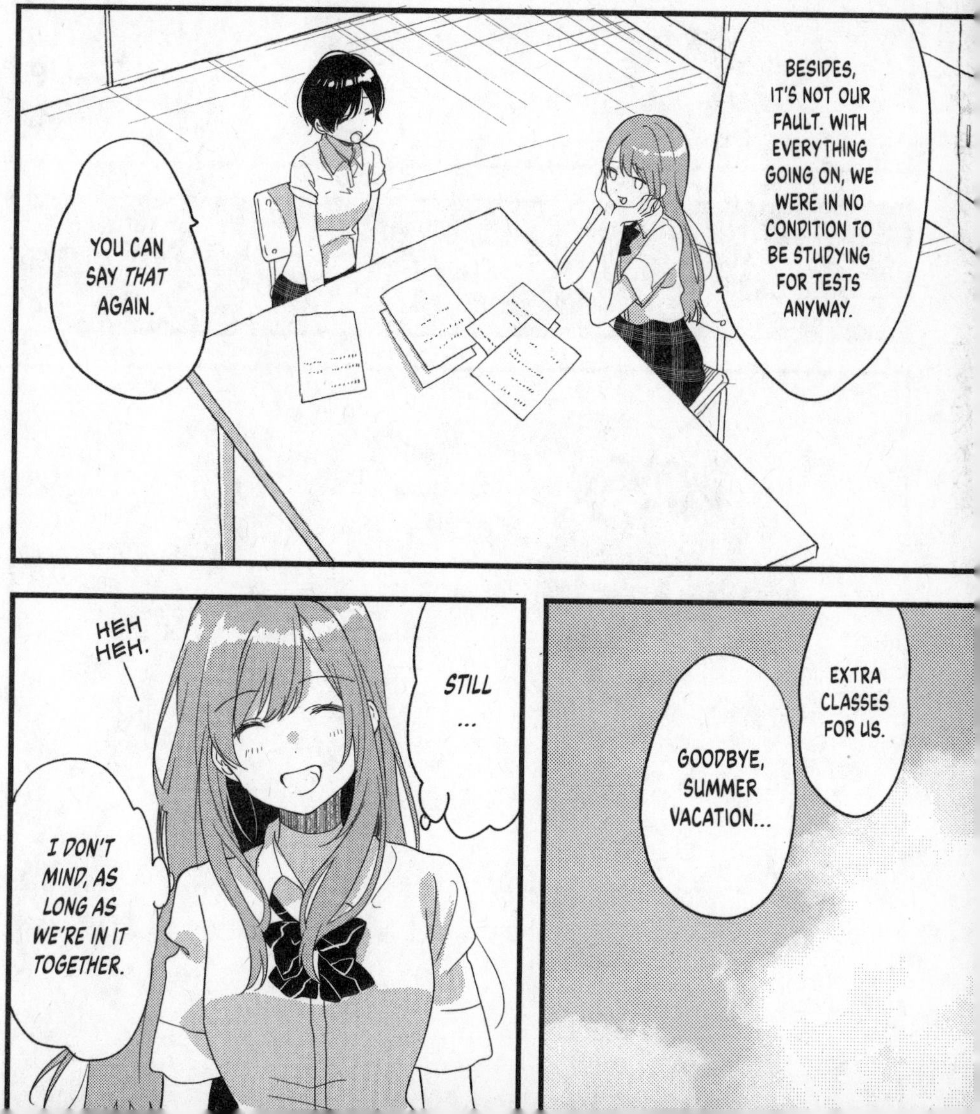
BESIDES, IT'S NOT OUR FAULT. WITH EVERYTHING GOING ON, WE WERE IN NO CONDITION TO BE STUDYING FOR TESTS ANYWAY.
YOU CAN SAY *THAT* AGAIN.
EXTRA CLASSES FOR US.
GOODBYE, SUMMER VACATION...
STILL ...
HEH HEH.
I DON'T MIND, AS LONG AS WE'RE IN IT TOGETHER.

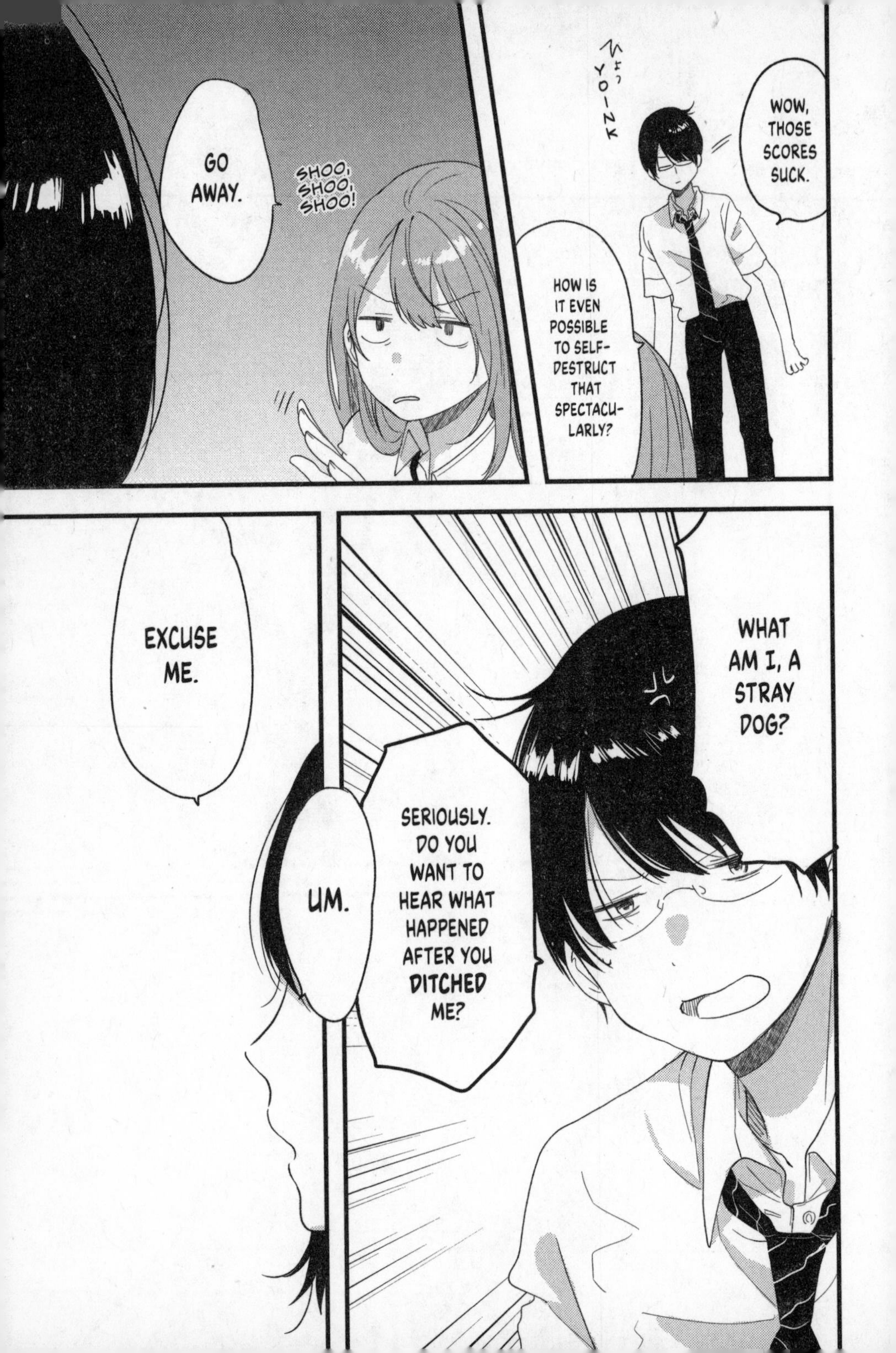
YO-INK
WOW, THOSE SCORES SUCK.
HOW IS IT EVEN POSSIBLE TO SELF-DESTRUCT THAT SPECTACULARLY?
SHOO, SHOO, SHOO!
GO AWAY.
WHAT AM I, A STRAY DOG?
SERIOUSLY. DO YOU WANT TO HEAR WHAT HAPPENED AFTER YOU DITCHED ME?
UM.
EXCUSE ME.

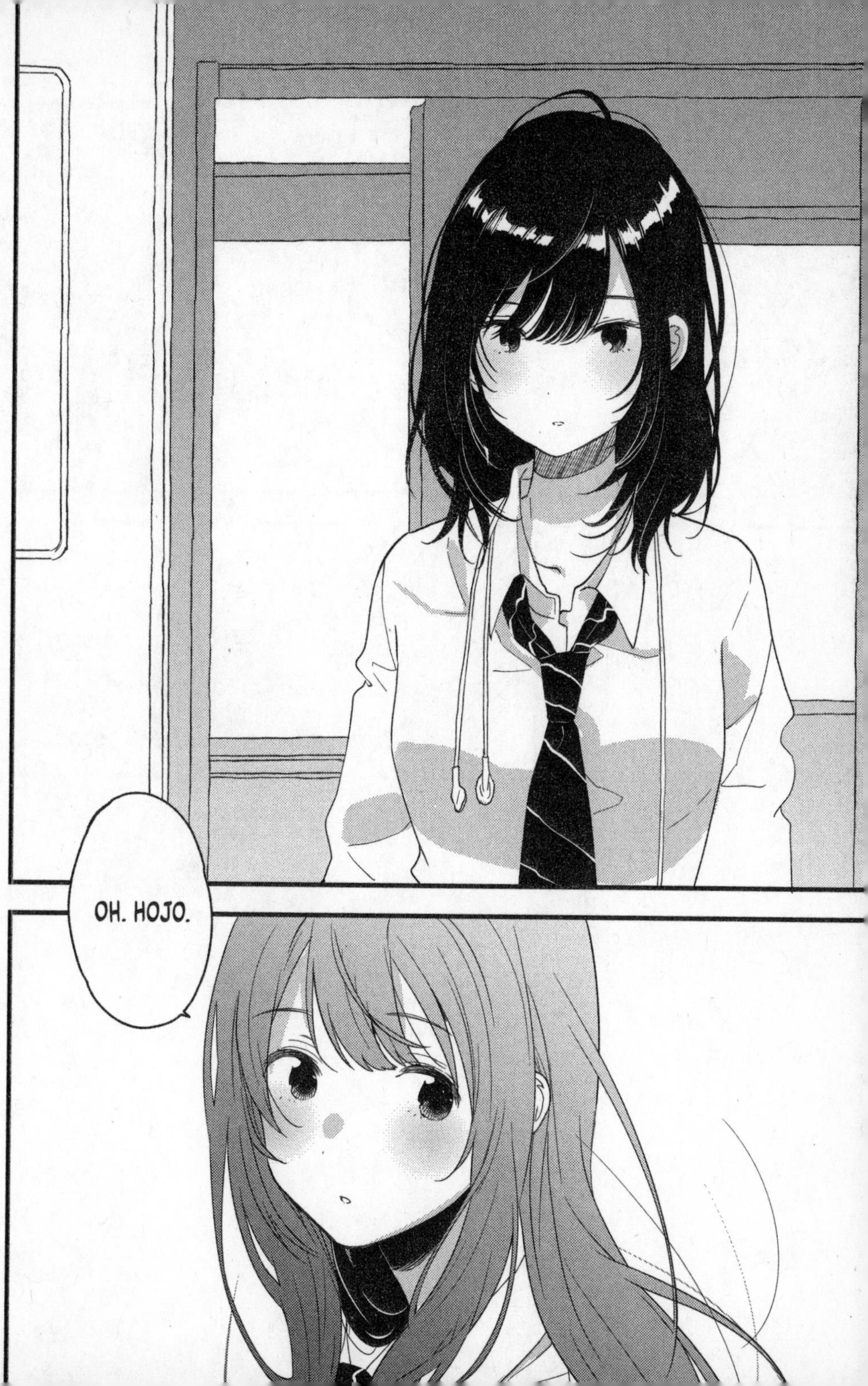
OH. HOJO.

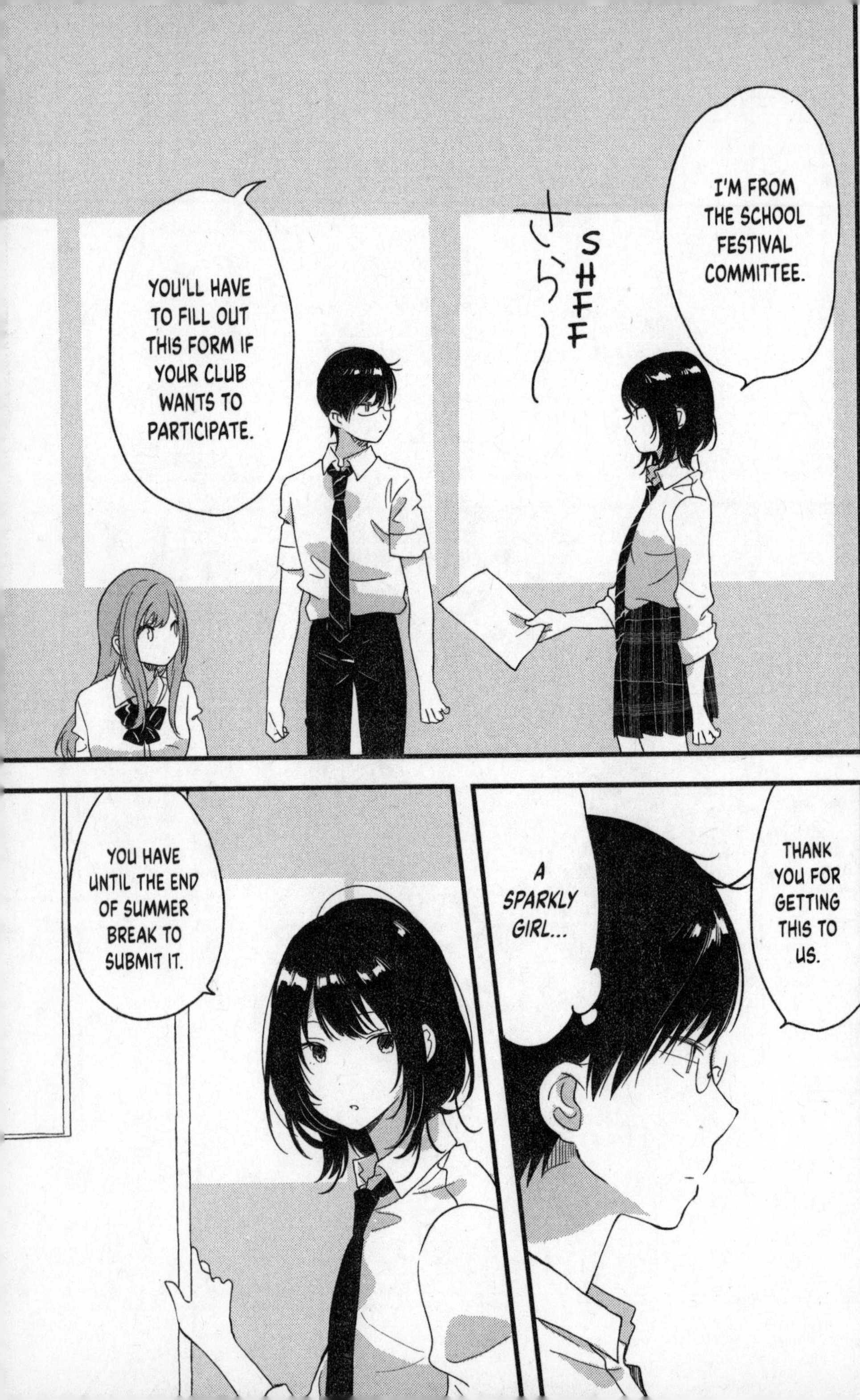
I'M FROM THE SCHOOL FESTIVAL COMMITTEE.
さら～
SHFF
YOU'LL HAVE TO FILL OUT THIS FORM IF YOUR CLUB WANTS TO PARTICIPATE.
THANK YOU FOR GETTING THIS TO US.
A SPARKLY GIRL...
YOU HAVE UNTIL THE END OF SUMMER BREAK TO SUBMIT IT.

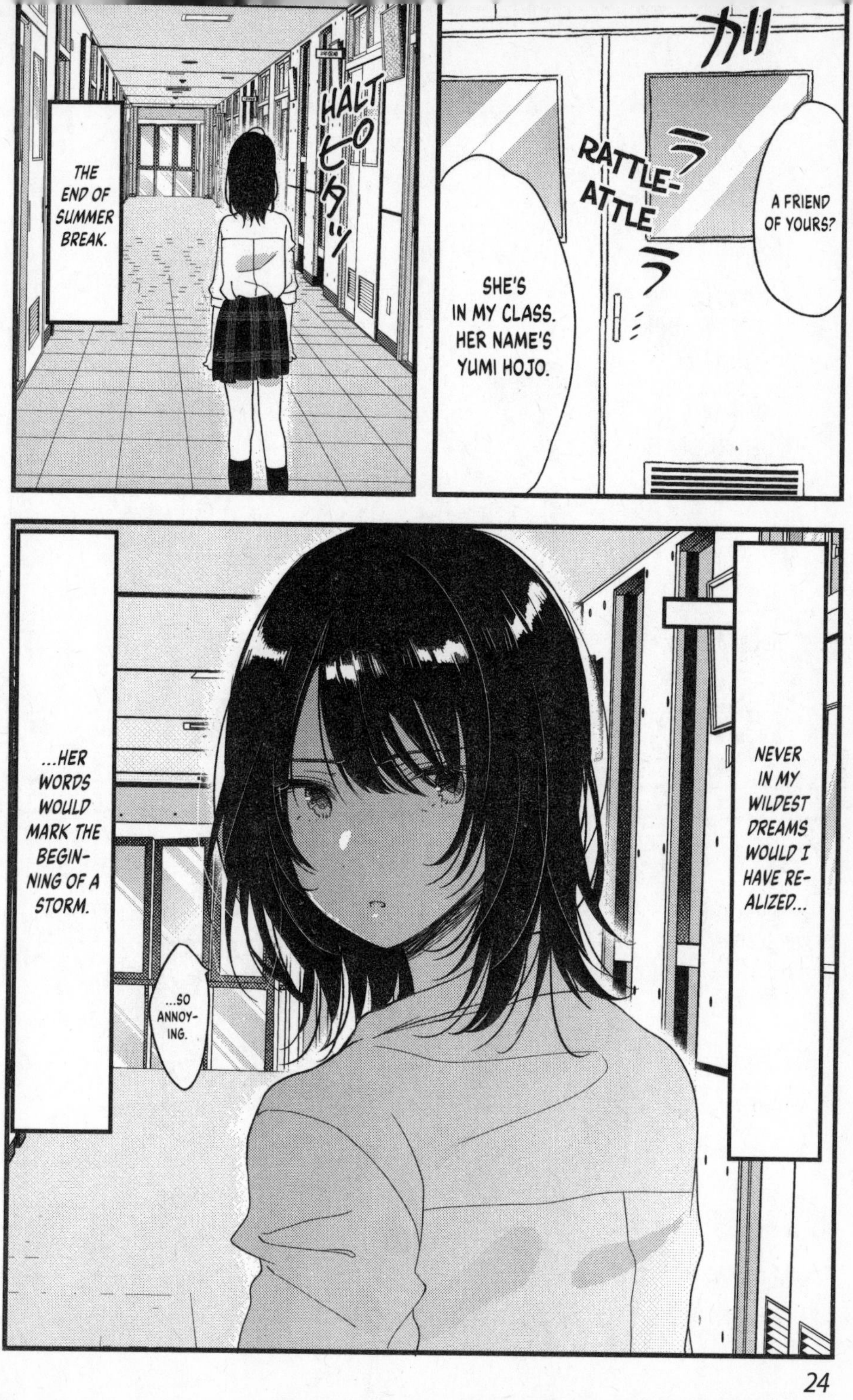
カリ
A FRIEND OF YOURS?
RATTLE-ATTLE
ラ
ラ
SHE'S IN MY CLASS. HER NAME'S YUMI HOJO.
HALT
ピタッ
THE END OF SUMMER BREAK.
NEVER IN MY WILDEST DREAMS WOULD I HAVE RE-ALIZED...
...SO ANNOY-ING.
...HER WORDS WOULD MARK THE BEGIN-NING OF A STORM.

CHASING AFTER *Aoi Koshiba*

Summer, Second Year of High School

Chapter 18:
The Way of the Anti-Fan (Part 1)

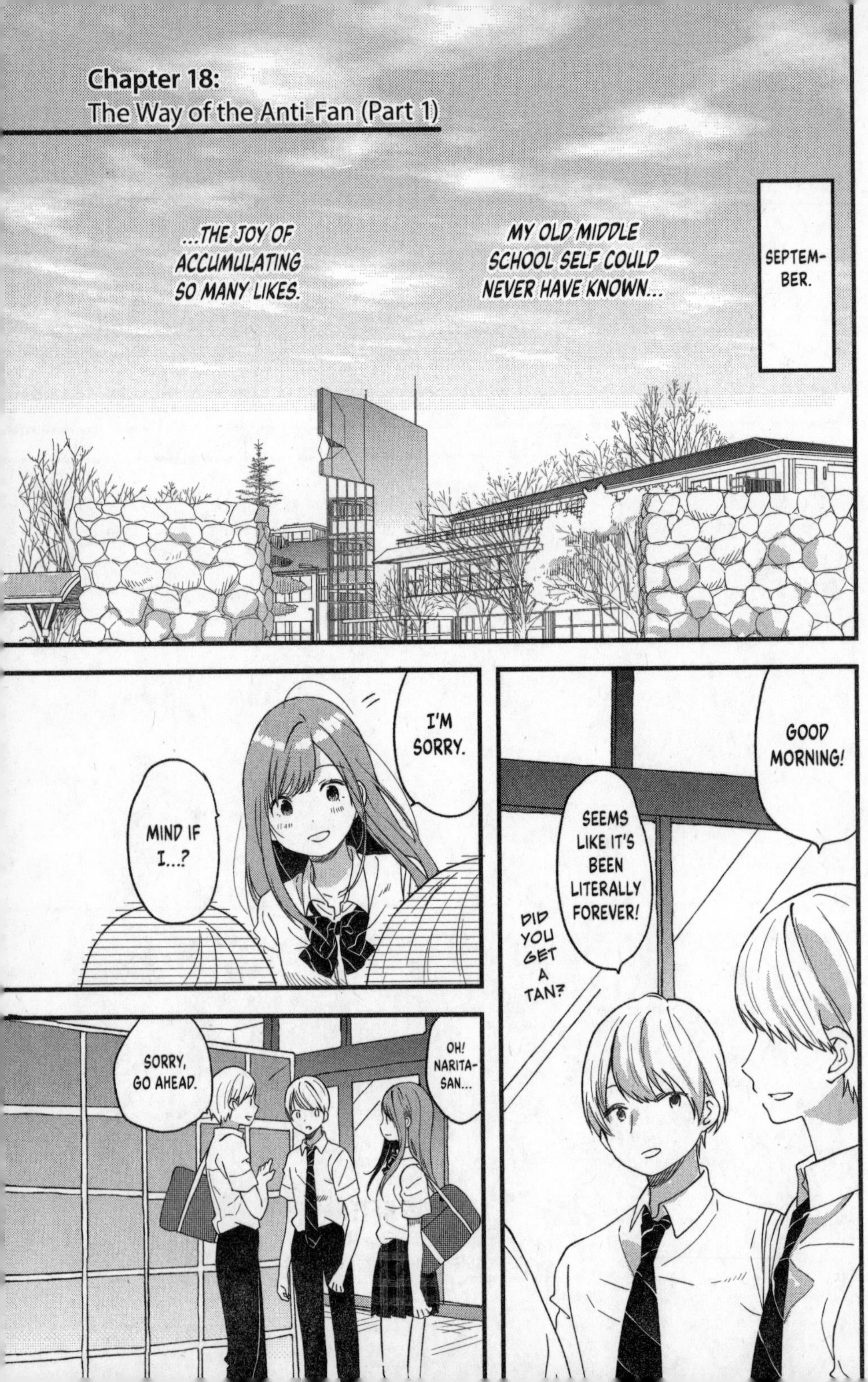
SEPTEMBER.
MY OLD MIDDLE SCHOOL SELF COULD NEVER HAVE KNOWN...
...THE JOY OF ACCUMULATING SO MANY LIKES.
GOOD MORNING!
SEEMS LIKE IT'S BEEN LITERALLY FOREVER!
DID YOU GET A TAN?
I'M SORRY.
MIND IF I...?
OH! NARITA-SAN...
SORRY, GO AHEAD.

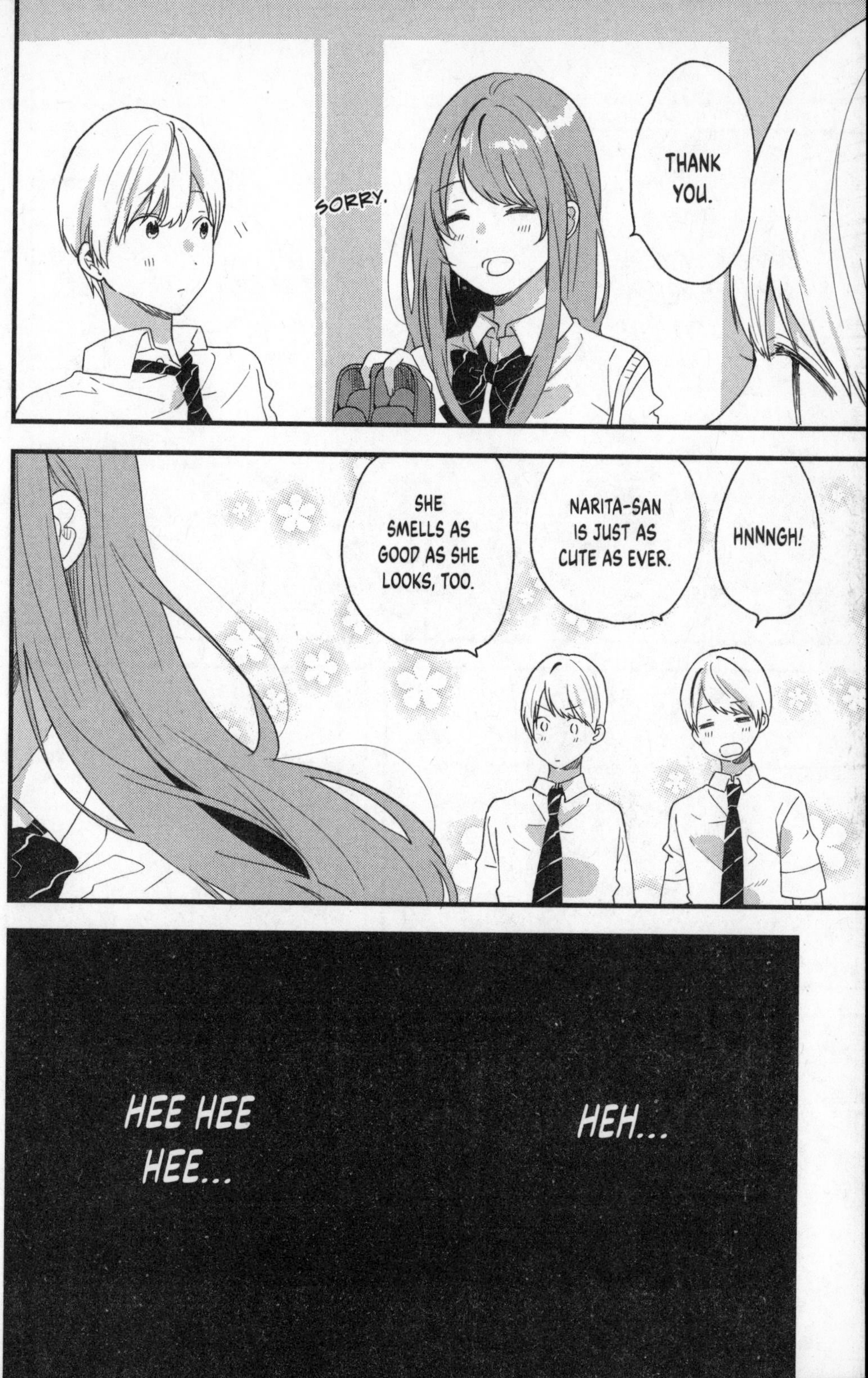
THANK YOU.
SORRY.
HNNNGH!
NARITA-SAN IS JUST AS CUTE AS EVER.
SHE SMELLS AS GOOD AS SHE LOOKS, TOO.
HEH...
HEE HEE HEE...

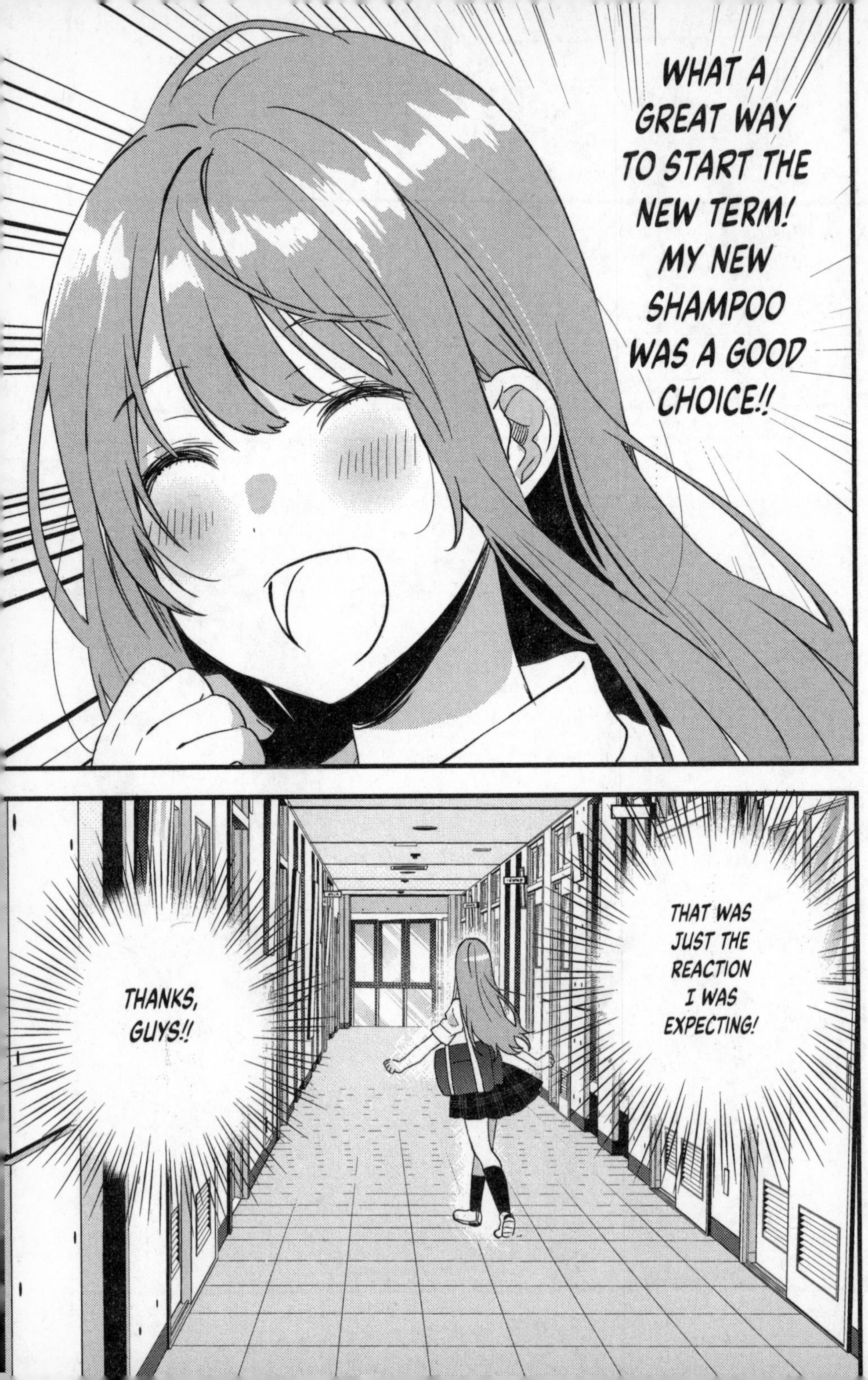
WHAT A GREAT WAY TO START THE NEW TERM! MY NEW SHAMPOO WAS A GOOD CHOICE!!
THAT WAS JUST THE REACTION I WAS EXPECTING!
THANKS, GUYS!!

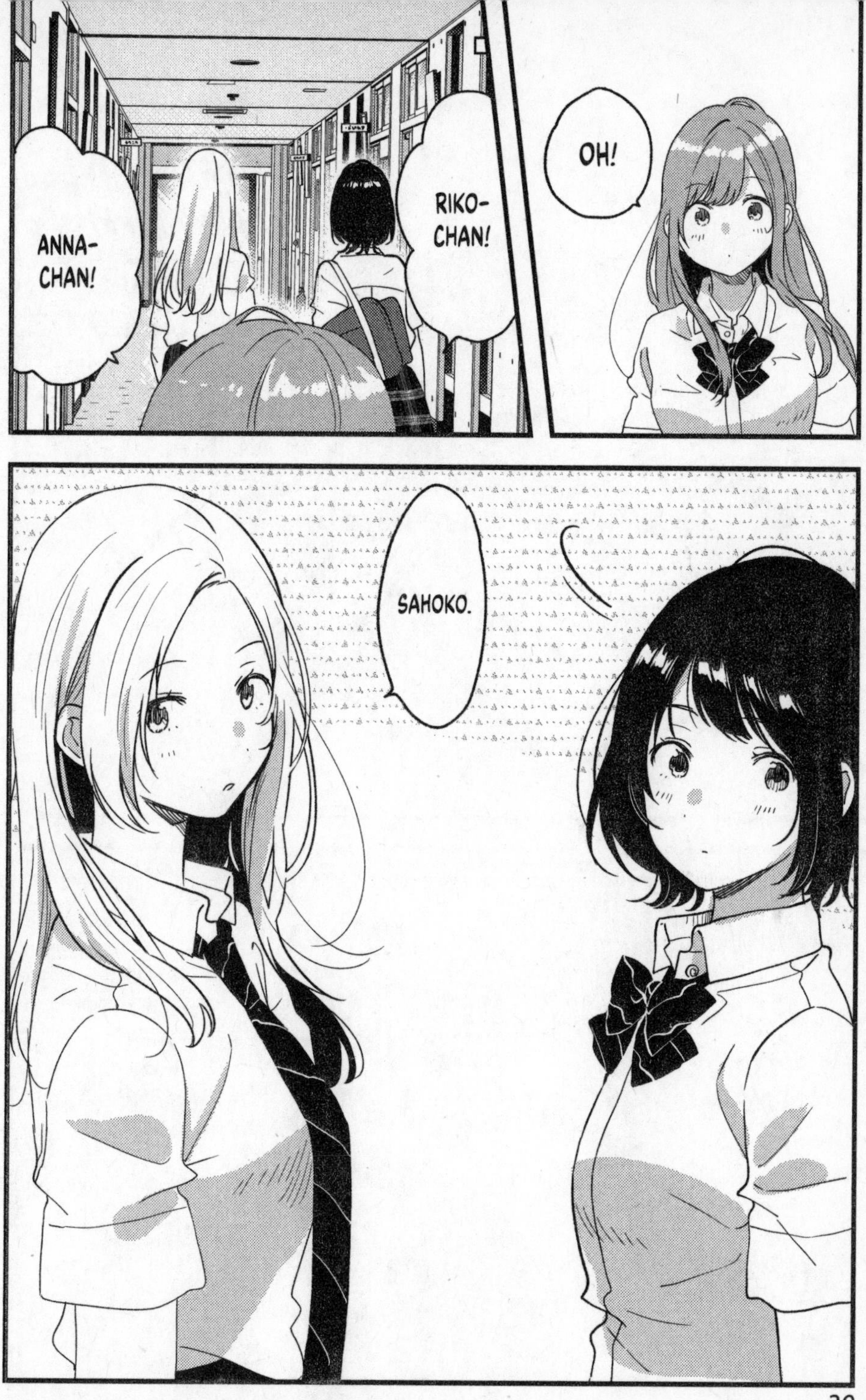
OH!
RIKO-CHAN!
ANNA-CHAN!
SAHOKO.

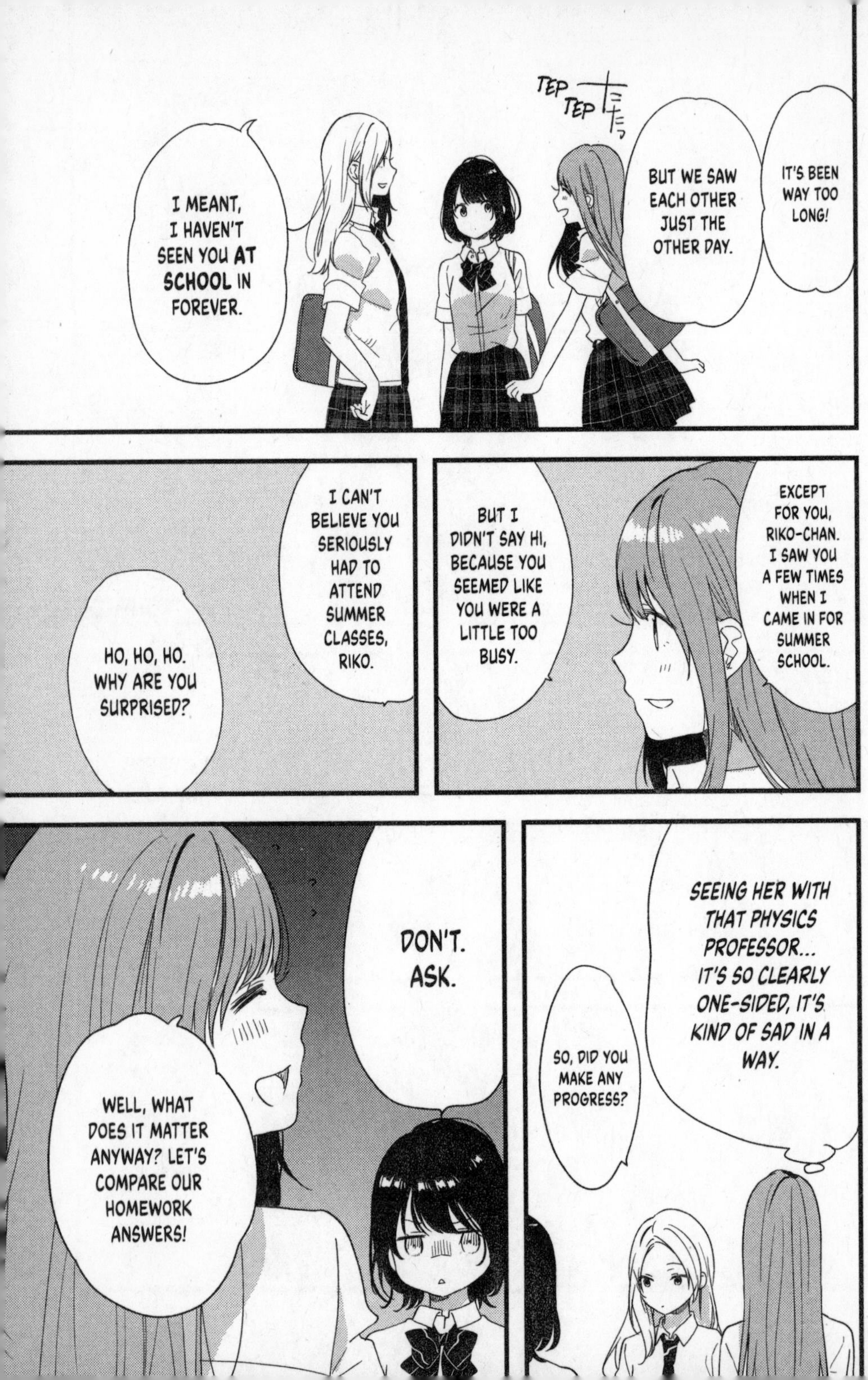
TEP TEP
IT'S BEEN WAY TOO LONG!
BUT WE SAW EACH OTHER JUST THE OTHER DAY.
I MEANT, I HAVEN'T SEEN YOU AT SCHOOL IN FOREVER.
EXCEPT FOR YOU, RIKO-CHAN. I SAW YOU A FEW TIMES WHEN I CAME IN FOR SUMMER SCHOOL.
BUT I DIDN'T SAY HI, BECAUSE YOU SEEMED LIKE YOU WERE A LITTLE TOO BUSY.
I CAN'T BELIEVE YOU SERIOUSLY HAD TO ATTEND SUMMER CLASSES, RIKO.
HO, HO, HO. WHY ARE YOU SURPRISED?
SEEING HER WITH THAT PHYSICS PROFESSOR... IT'S SO CLEARLY ONE-SIDED, IT'S KIND OF SAD IN A WAY.
SO, DID YOU MAKE ANY PROGRESS?
DON'T. ASK.
WELL, WHAT DOES IT MATTER ANYWAY? LET'S COMPARE OUR HOMEWORK ANSWERS!

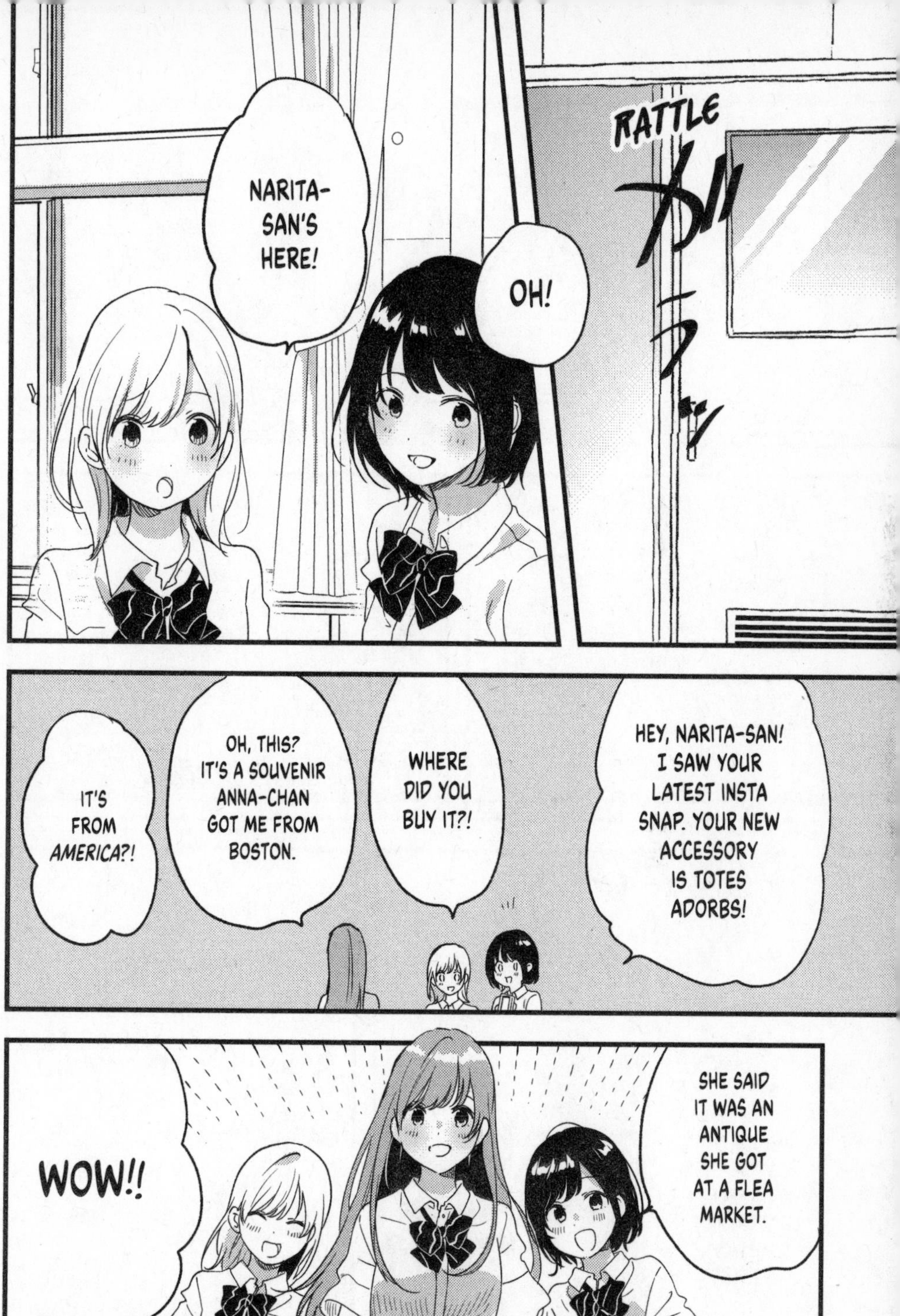
RATTLE
NARITA-SAN'S HERE!
OH!
HEY, NARITA-SAN! I SAW YOUR LATEST INSTA SNAP. YOUR NEW ACCESSORY IS TOTES ADORBS!
WHERE DID YOU BUY IT?!
OH, THIS? IT'S A SOUVENIR ANNA-CHAN GOT ME FROM BOSTON.
IT'S FROM *AMERICA*?!
SHE SAID IT WAS AN ANTIQUE SHE GOT AT A FLEA MARKET.
WOW!!

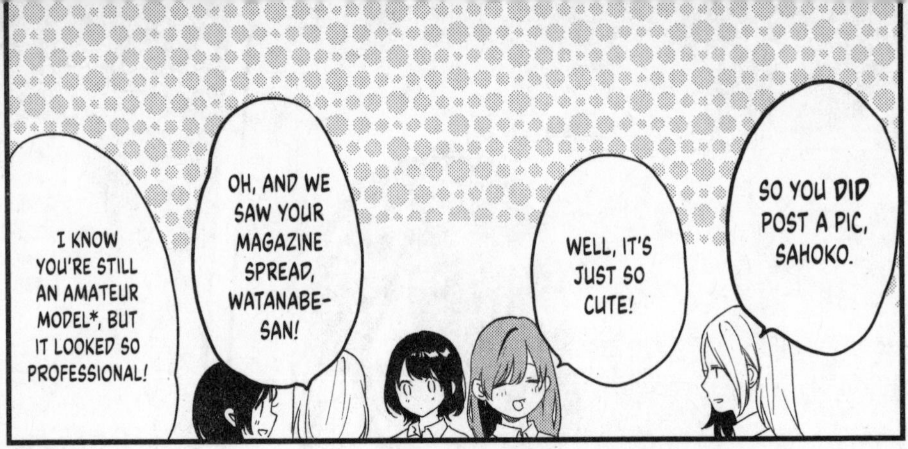
SO YOU **DID** POST A PIC, SAHOKO.
WELL, IT'S JUST SO CUTE!
OH, AND WE SAW YOUR MAGAZINE SPREAD, WATANABE-SAN!
I KNOW YOU'RE STILL AN AMATEUR MODEL*, BUT IT LOOKED SO PROFESSIONAL!

*SEE PAGE 162.

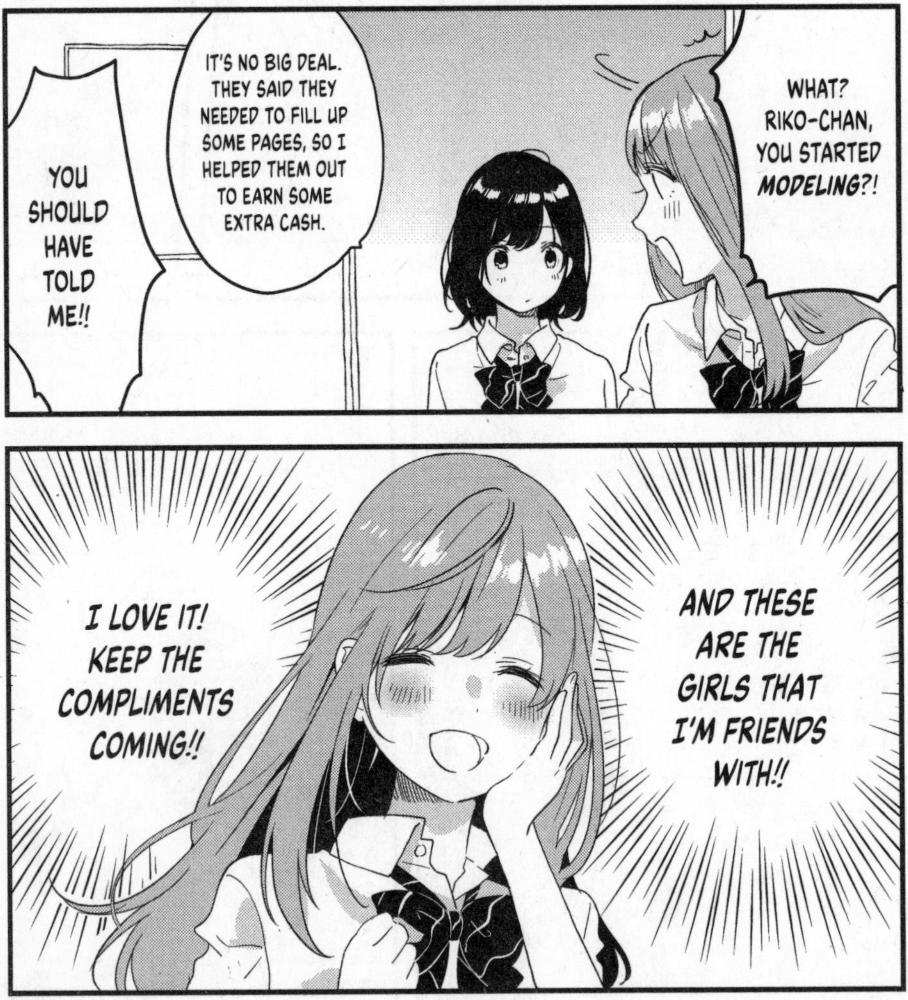
WHAT? RIKO-CHAN, YOU STARTED *MODELING?!*
IT'S NO BIG DEAL. THEY SAID THEY NEEDED TO FILL UP SOME PAGES, SO I HELPED THEM OUT TO EARN SOME EXTRA CASH.
YOU SHOULD HAVE TOLD ME!!
AND THESE ARE THE GIRLS THAT I'M FRIENDS WITH!!
I LOVE IT! KEEP THE COMPLIMENTS COMING!!

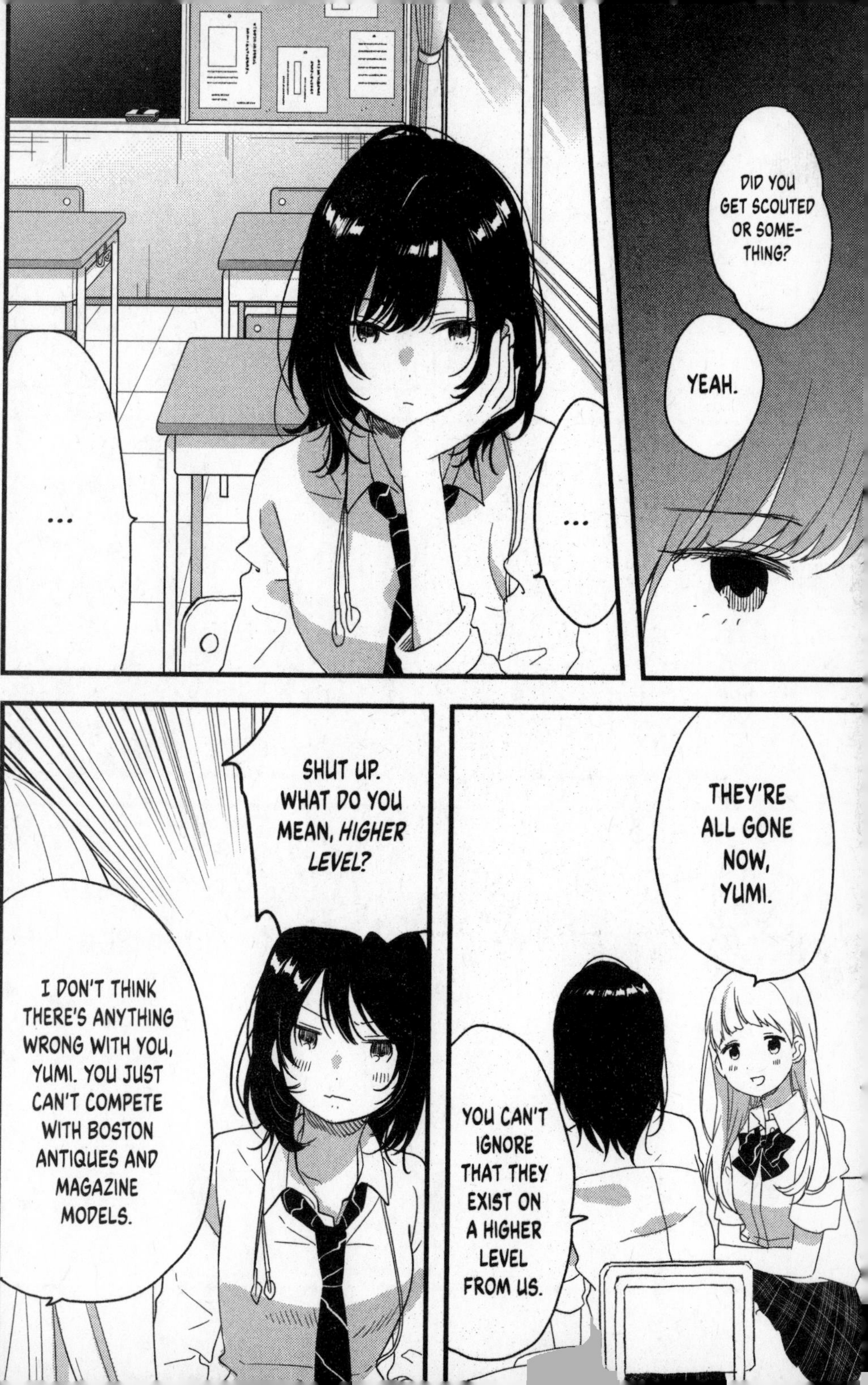
DID YOU GET SCOUTED OR SOME-THING?
YEAH.
...
...
THEY'RE ALL GONE NOW, YUMI.
YOU CAN'T IGNORE THAT THEY EXIST ON A HIGHER LEVEL FROM US.
SHUT UP. WHAT DO YOU MEAN, *HIGHER LEVEL?*
I DON'T THINK THERE'S ANYTHING WRONG WITH YOU, YUMI. YOU JUST CAN'T COMPETE WITH BOSTON ANTIQUES AND MAGAZINE MODELS.

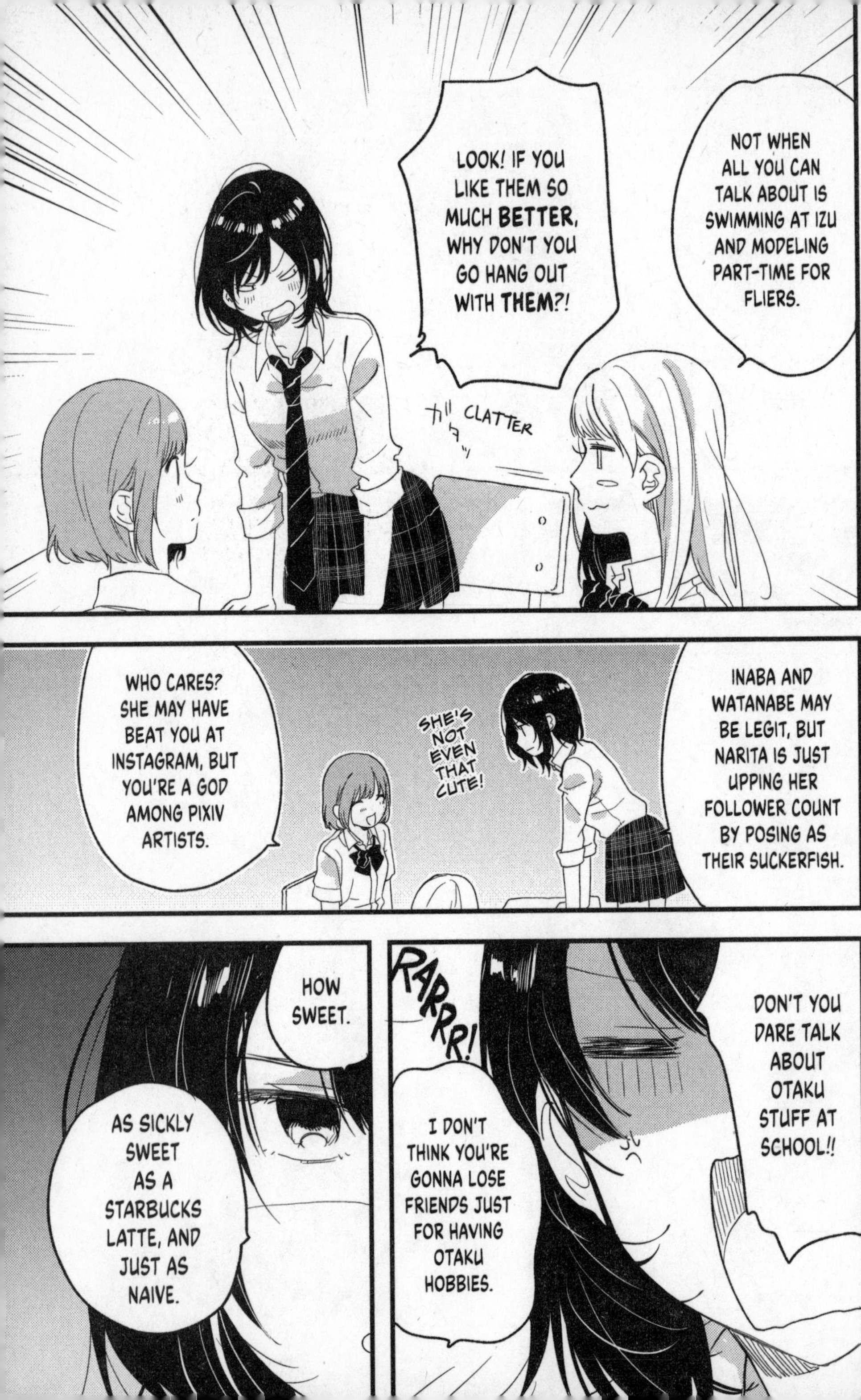
NOT WHEN ALL YOU CAN TALK ABOUT IS SWIMMING AT IZU AND MODELING PART-TIME FOR FLIERS.
LOOK! IF YOU LIKE THEM SO MUCH **BETTER**, WHY DON'T YOU GO HANG OUT WITH **THEM**?!
ガタッ CLATTER
INABA AND WATANABE MAY BE LEGIT, BUT NARITA IS JUST UPPING HER FOLLOWER COUNT BY POSING AS THEIR SUCKERFISH.
SHE'S NOT EVEN THAT CUTE!
WHO CARES? SHE MAY HAVE BEAT YOU AT INSTAGRAM, BUT YOU'RE A GOD AMONG PIXIV ARTISTS.
DON'T YOU DARE TALK ABOUT OTAKU STUFF AT SCHOOL!!
RARRRR!
I DON'T THINK YOU'RE GONNA LOSE FRIENDS JUST FOR HAVING OTAKU HOBBIES.
HOW SWEET.
AS SICKLY SWEET AS A STARBUCKS LATTE, AND JUST AS NAIVE.

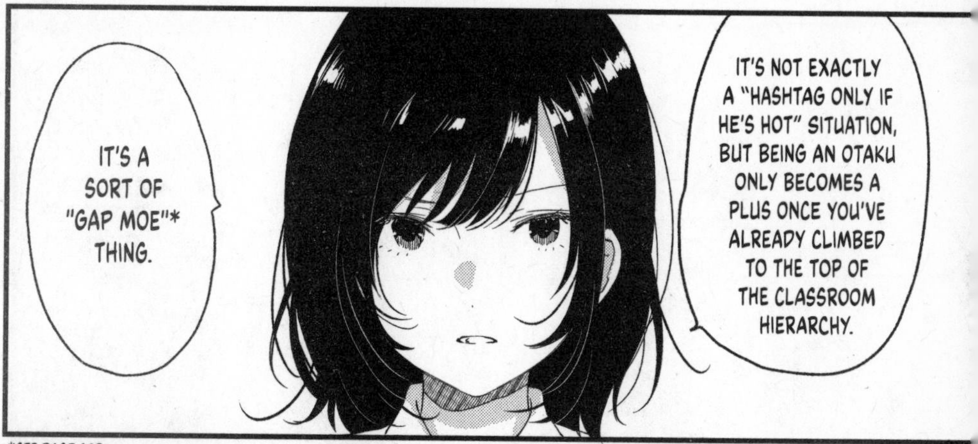
IT'S NOT EXACTLY A "HASHTAG ONLY IF HE'S HOT" SITUATION, BUT BEING AN OTAKU ONLY BECOMES A PLUS ONCE YOU'VE ALREADY CLIMBED TO THE TOP OF THE CLASSROOM HIERARCHY.
IT'S A SORT OF "GAP MOE"* THING.

*SEE PAGE 162.

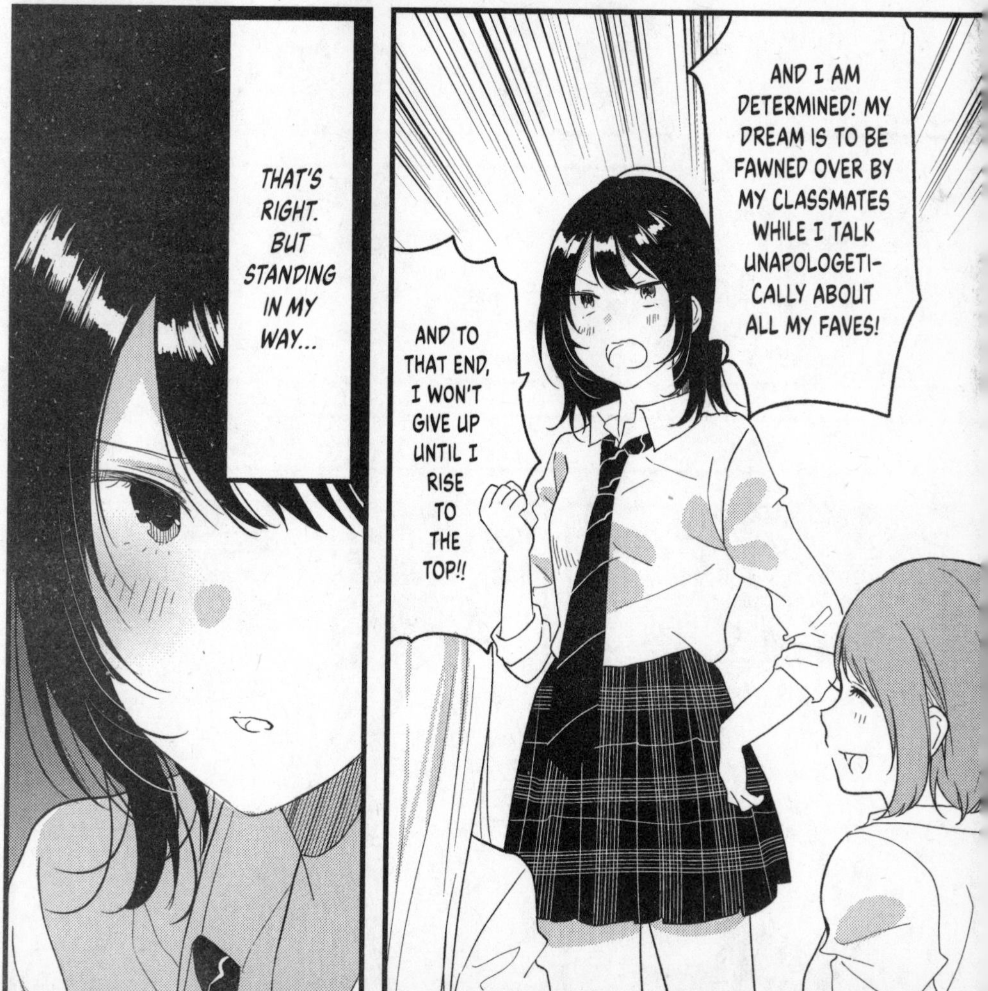
AND I AM DETERMINED! MY DREAM IS TO BE FAWNED OVER BY MY CLASSMATES WHILE I TALK UNAPOLOGETI-CALLY ABOUT ALL MY FAVES!
AND TO THAT END, I WON'T GIVE UP UNTIL I RISE TO THE TOP!!
THAT'S RIGHT. BUT STANDING IN MY WAY...

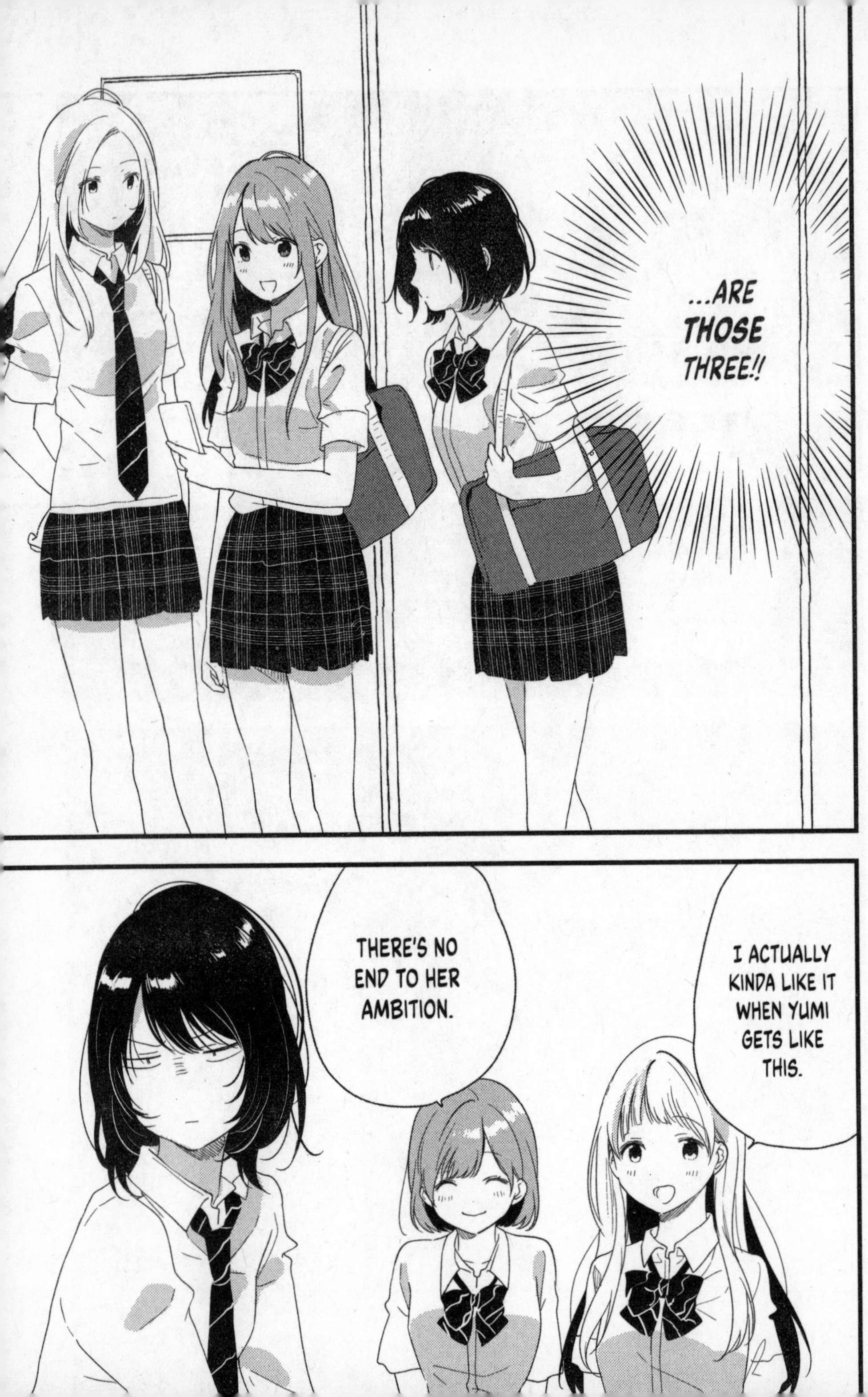
...ARE THOSE THREE!!
I ACTUALLY KINDA LIKE IT WHEN YUMI GETS LIKE THIS.
THERE'S NO END TO HER AMBITION.

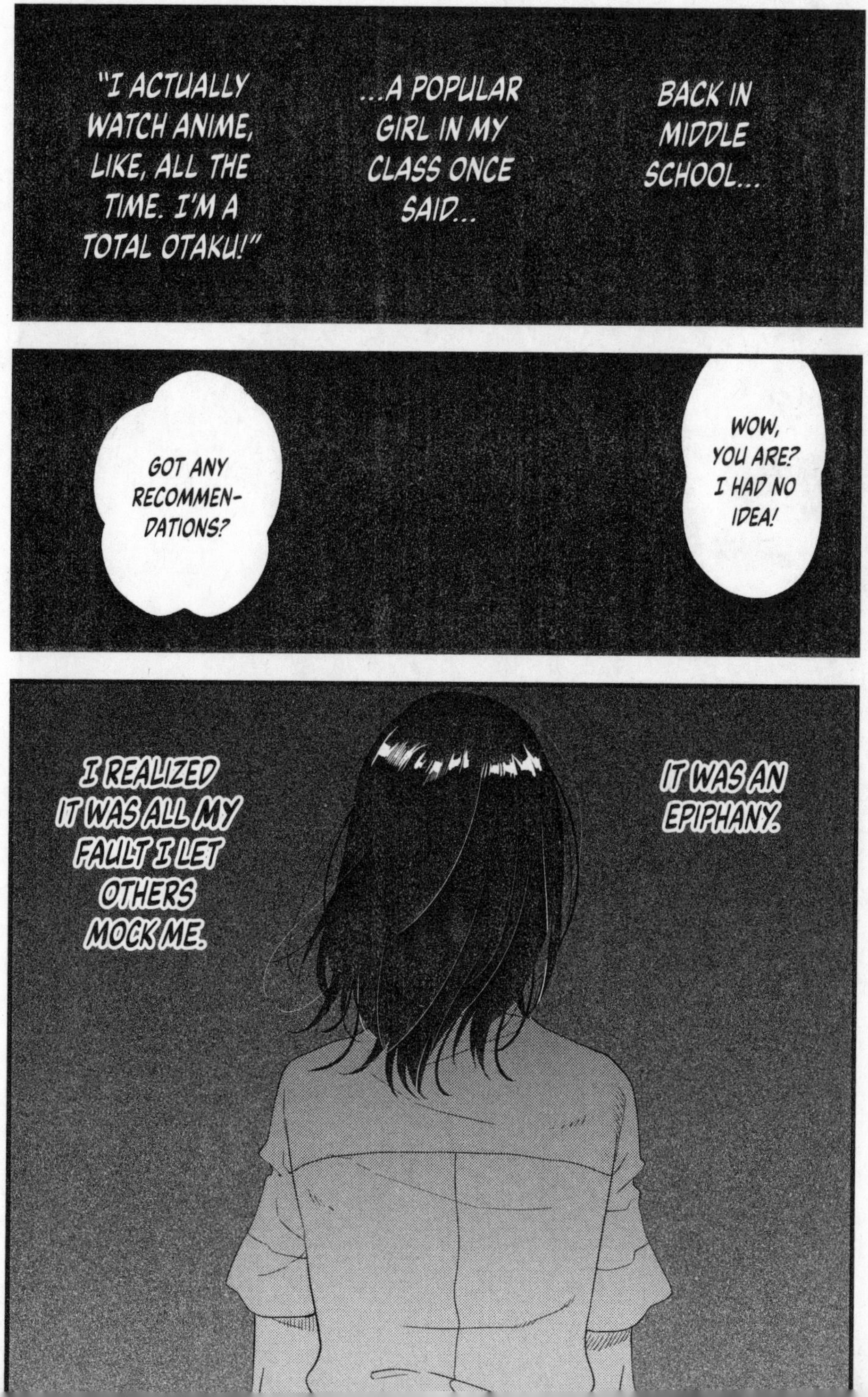
BACK IN MIDDLE SCHOOL...
...A POPULAR GIRL IN MY CLASS ONCE SAID...
"I ACTUALLY WATCH ANIME, LIKE, ALL THE TIME. I'M A TOTAL OTAKU!"
WOW, YOU ARE? I HAD NO IDEA!
GOT ANY RECOMMEN-DATIONS?
IT WAS AN EPIPHANY.
I REALIZED IT WAS ALL MY FAULT I LET OTHERS MOCK ME.

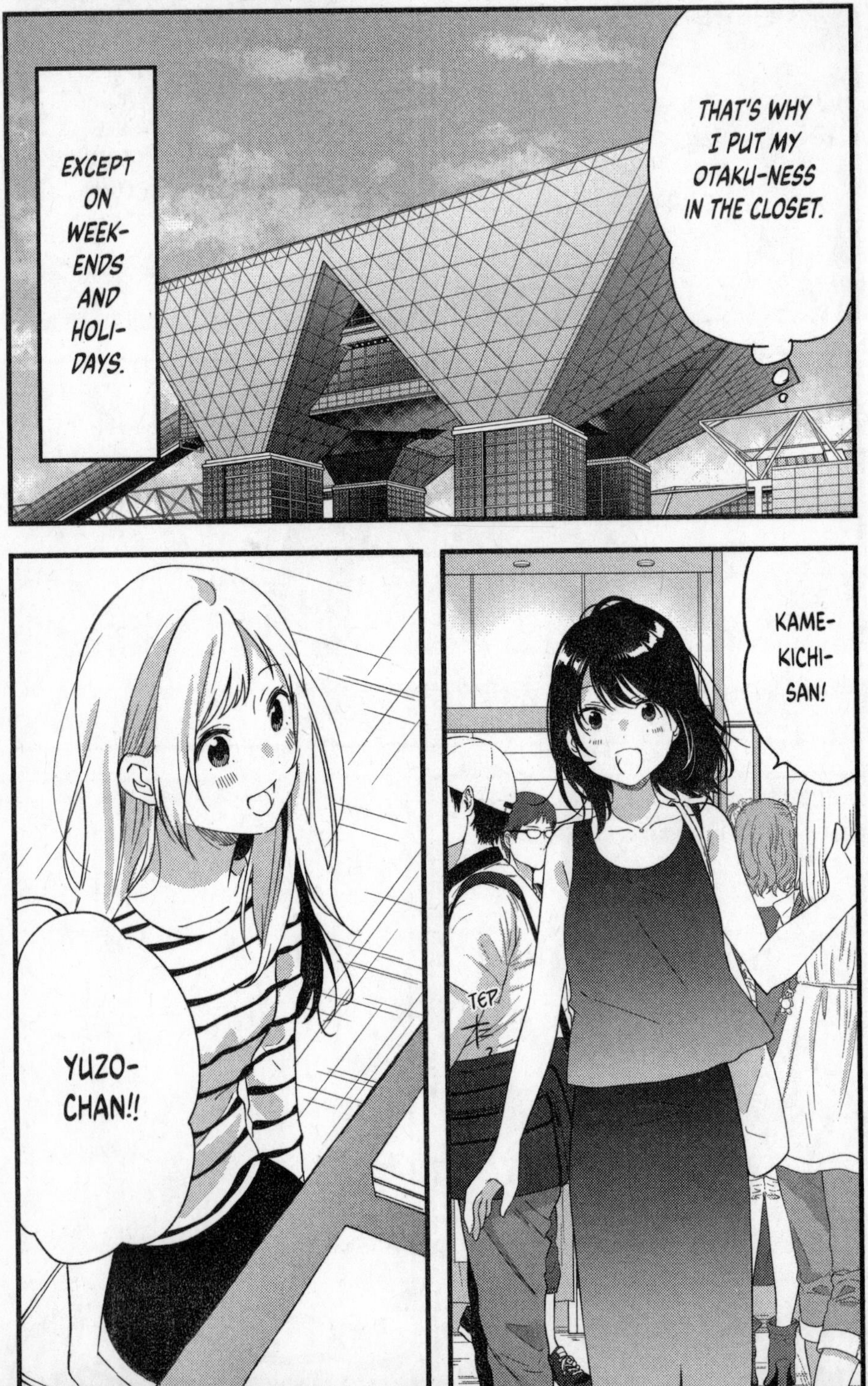
THAT'S WHY I PUT MY OTAKU-NESS IN THE CLOSET.
EXCEPT ON WEEK-ENDS AND HOLI-DAYS.
KAME-KICHI-SAN!
TEP
YUZO-CHAN!!

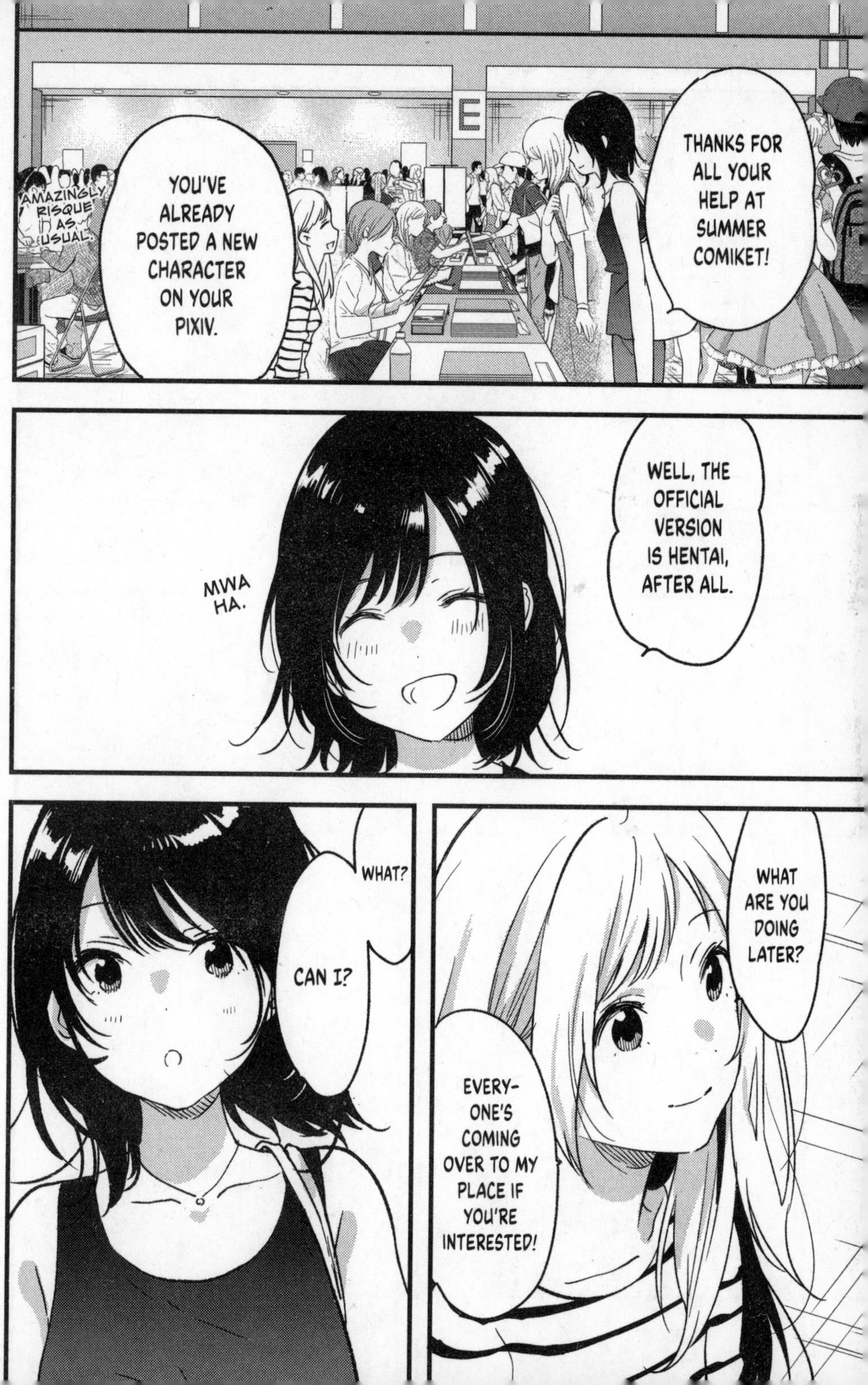
THANKS FOR ALL YOUR HELP AT SUMMER COMIKET!
YOU'VE ALREADY POSTED A NEW CHARACTER ON YOUR PIXIV.
AMAZINGLY RISQUE AS USUAL.
WELL, THE OFFICIAL VERSION IS HENTAI, AFTER ALL.
MWA HA.
WHAT ARE YOU DOING LATER?
EVERY-ONE'S COMING OVER TO MY PLACE IF YOU'RE INTERESTED!
WHAT?
CAN I?

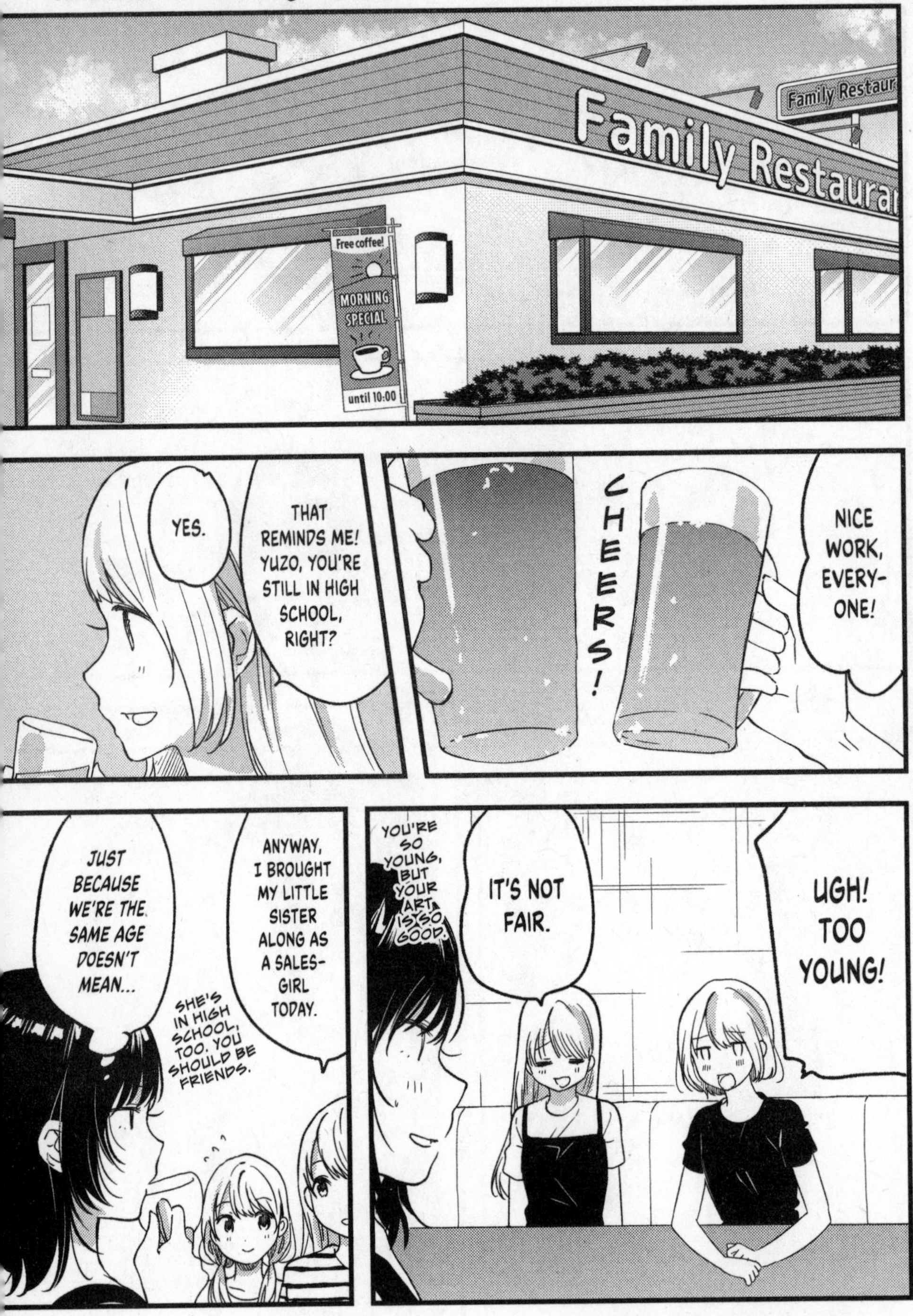
Family Restaurant
Family Restaur
Free coffee!
MORNING SPECIAL
until 10:00
NICE WORK, EVERY-ONE!
CHEERS!
THAT REMINDS ME! YUZO, YOU'RE STILL IN HIGH SCHOOL, RIGHT?
YES.
UGH! TOO YOUNG!
IT'S NOT FAIR.
YOU'RE SO YOUNG, BUT YOUR ART IS SO GOOD.
ANYWAY, I BROUGHT MY LITTLE SISTER ALONG AS A SALES-GIRL TODAY.
SHE'S IN HIGH SCHOOL, TOO. YOU SHOULD BE FRIENDS.
JUST BECAUSE WE'RE THE SAME AGE DOESN'T MEAN...

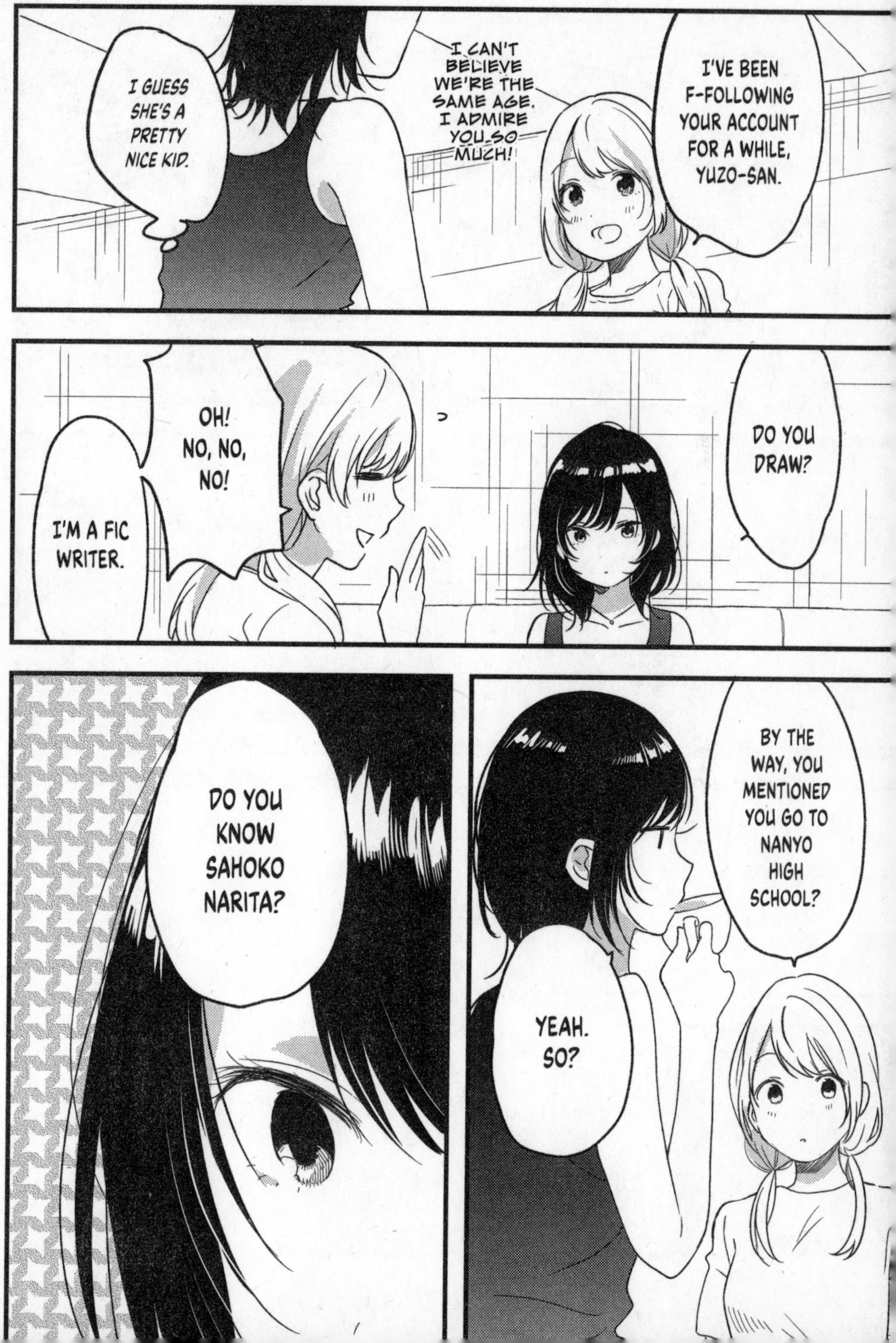
I'VE BEEN F-FOLLOWING YOUR ACCOUNT FOR A WHILE, YUZO-SAN.
I CAN'T BELIEVE WE'RE THE SAME AGE. I ADMIRE YOU SO MUCH!
I GUESS SHE'S A PRETTY NICE KID.
DO YOU DRAW?
OH! NO, NO, NO!
I'M A FIC WRITER.
BY THE WAY, YOU MENTIONED YOU GO TO NANYO HIGH SCHOOL?
YEAH. SO?
DO YOU KNOW SAHOKO NARITA?

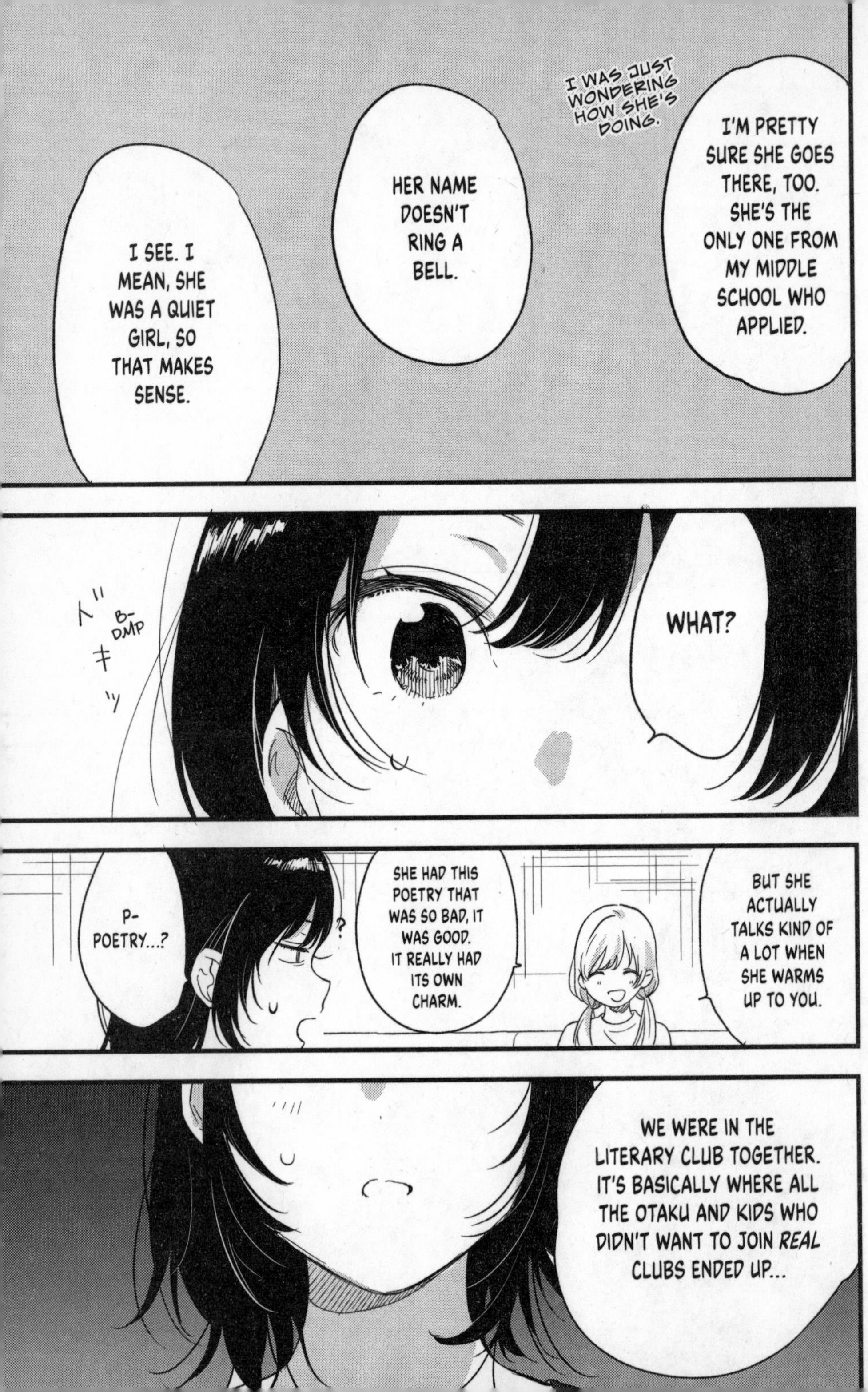
I'M PRETTY SURE SHE GOES THERE, TOO. SHE'S THE ONLY ONE FROM MY MIDDLE SCHOOL WHO APPLIED.
I WAS JUST WONDERING HOW SHE'S DOING.
HER NAME DOESN'T RING A BELL.
I SEE. I MEAN, SHE WAS A QUIET GIRL, SO THAT MAKES SENSE.
WHAT?
ドキッ
B-DMP
BUT SHE ACTUALLY TALKS KIND OF A LOT WHEN SHE WARMS UP TO YOU.
SHE HAD THIS POETRY THAT WAS SO BAD, IT WAS GOOD. IT REALLY HAD ITS OWN CHARM.
P-POETRY...?
WE WERE IN THE LITERARY CLUB TOGETHER. IT'S BASICALLY WHERE ALL THE OTAKU AND KIDS WHO DIDN'T WANT TO JOIN *REAL* CLUBS ENDED UP...

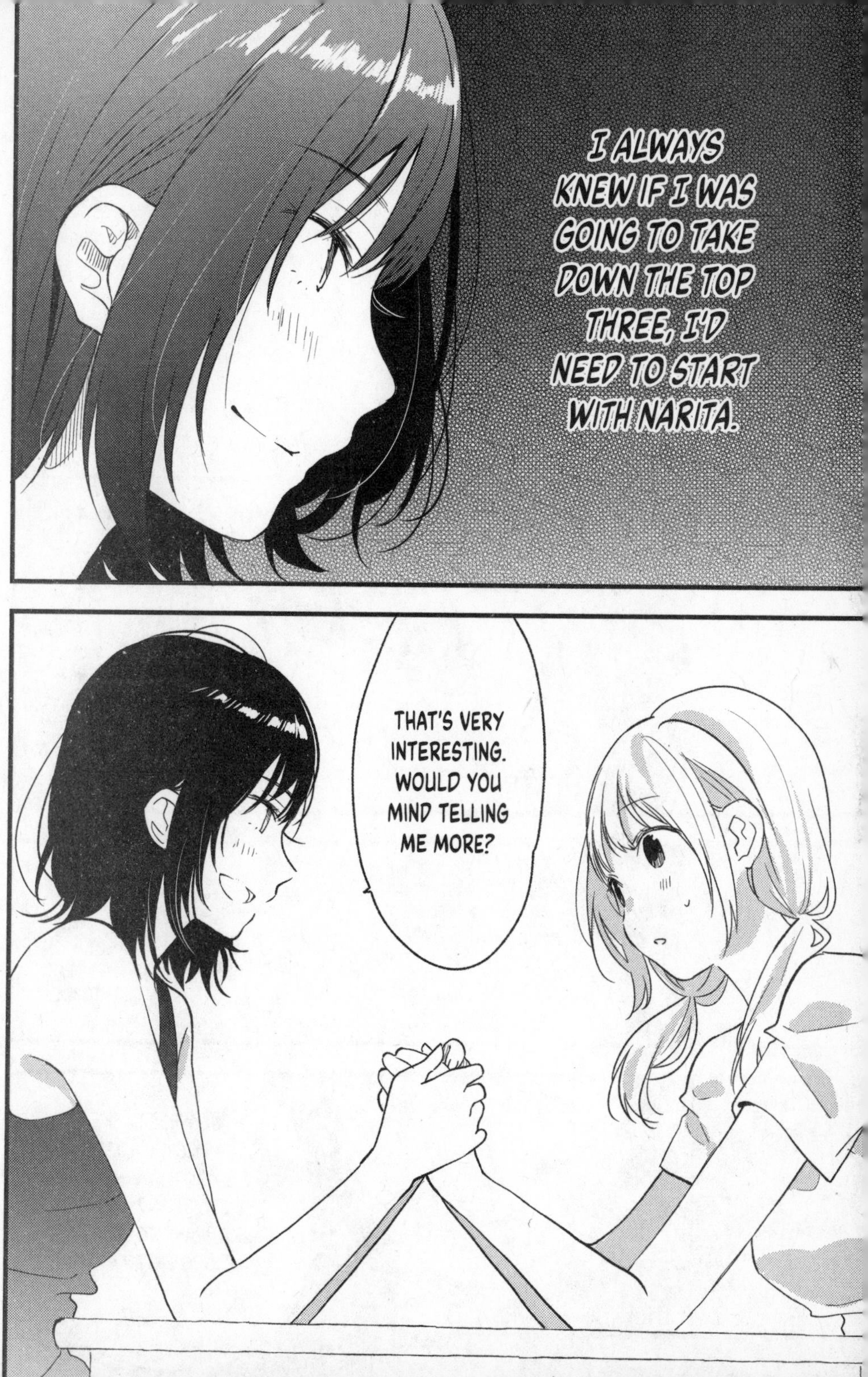
I ALWAYS KNEW IF I WAS GOING TO TAKE DOWN THE TOP THREE, I'D NEED TO START WITH NARITA.
THAT'S VERY INTERESTING. WOULD YOU MIND TELLING ME MORE?

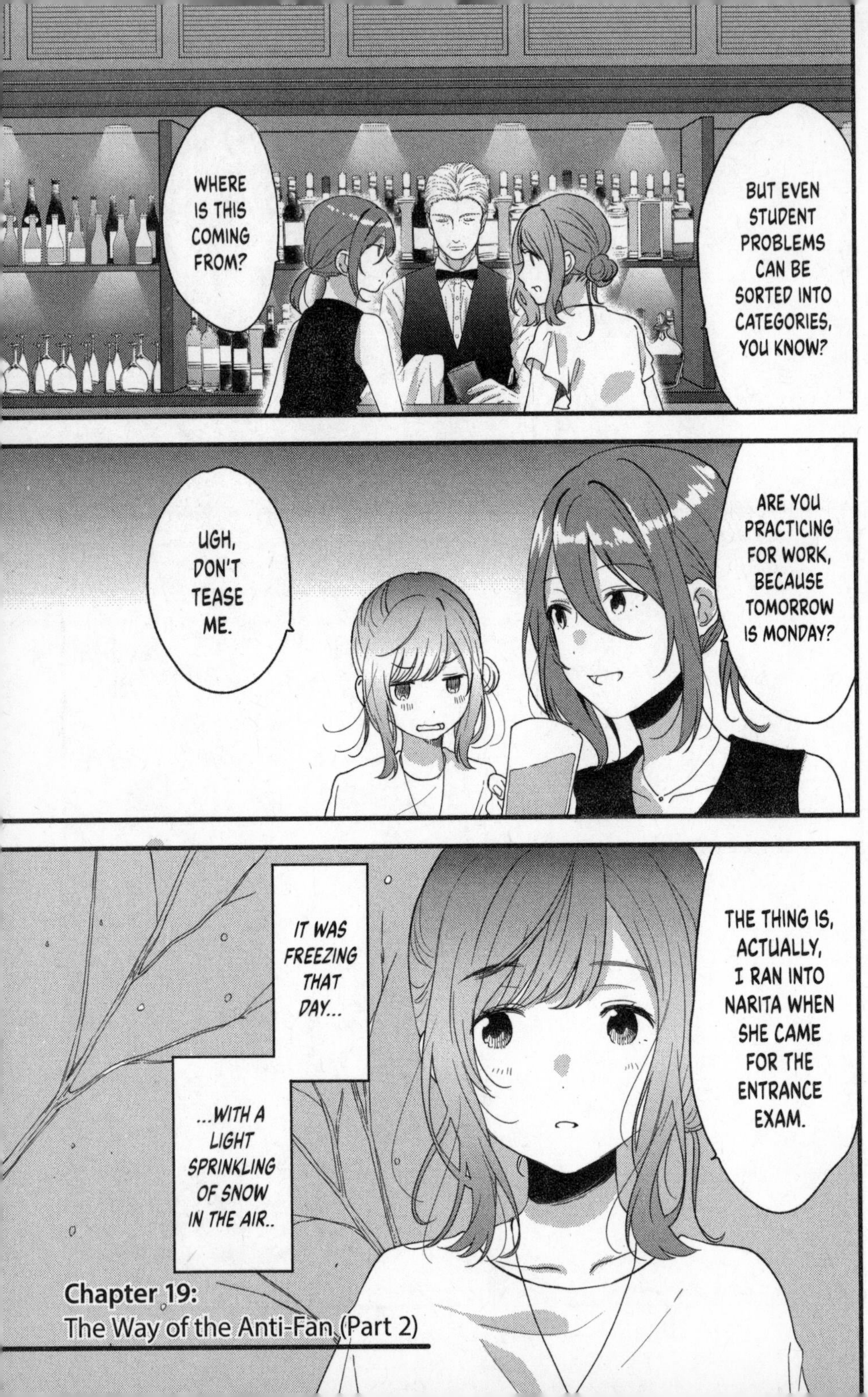
BUT EVEN STUDENT PROBLEMS CAN BE SORTED INTO CATEGORIES, YOU KNOW?
WHERE IS THIS COMING FROM?
ARE YOU PRACTICING FOR WORK, BECAUSE TOMORROW IS MONDAY?
UGH, DON'T TEASE ME.
THE THING IS, ACTUALLY, I RAN INTO NARITA WHEN SHE CAME FOR THE ENTRANCE EXAM.
IT WAS FREEZING THAT DAY...
...WITH A LIGHT SPRINKLING OF SNOW IN THE AIR..

Chapter 19:
The Way of the Anti-Fan (Part 2)

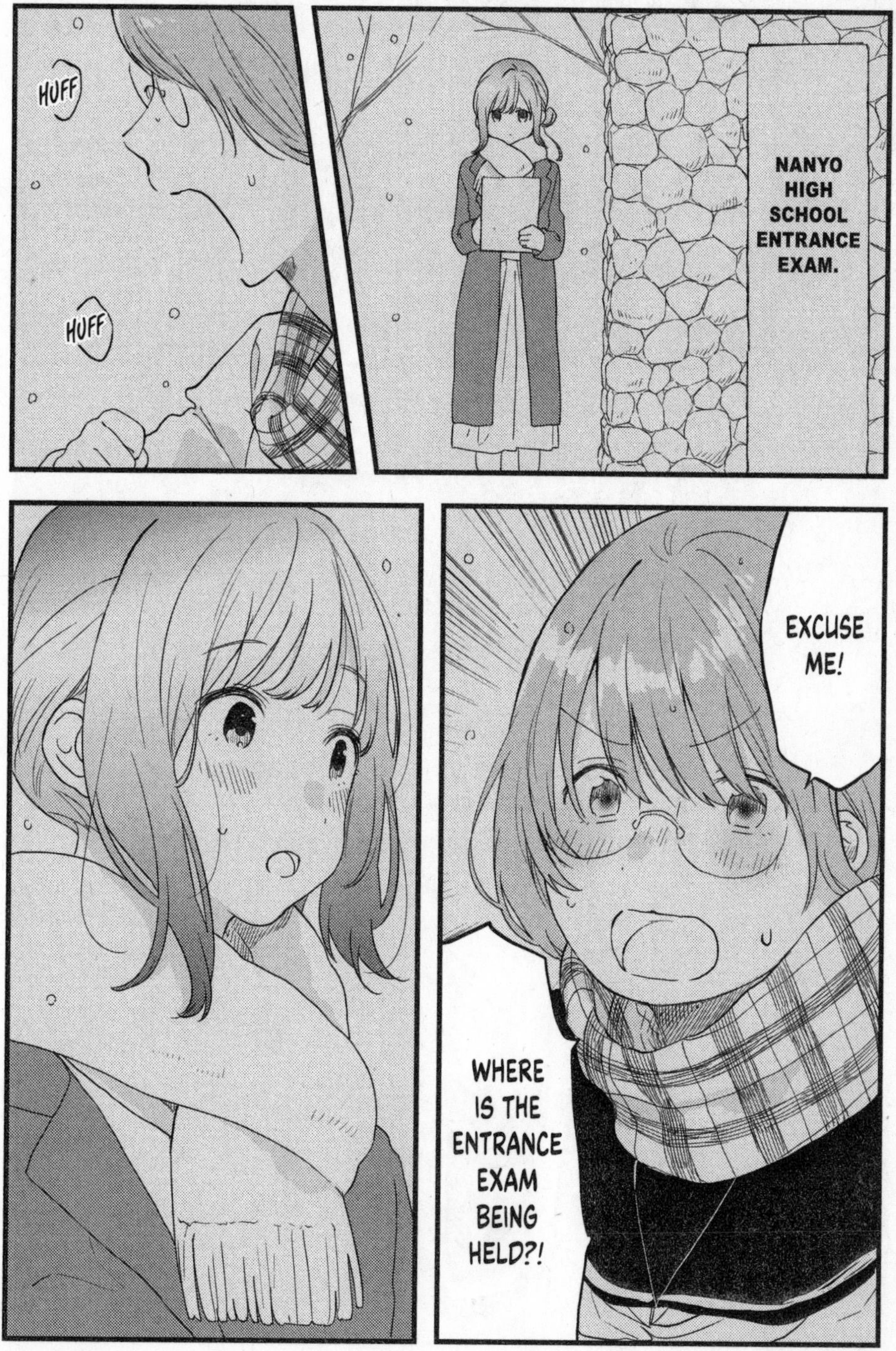
NANYO HIGH SCHOOL ENTRANCE EXAM.
HUFF
HUFF
EXCUSE ME!
WHERE IS THE ENTRANCE EXAM BEING HELD?!

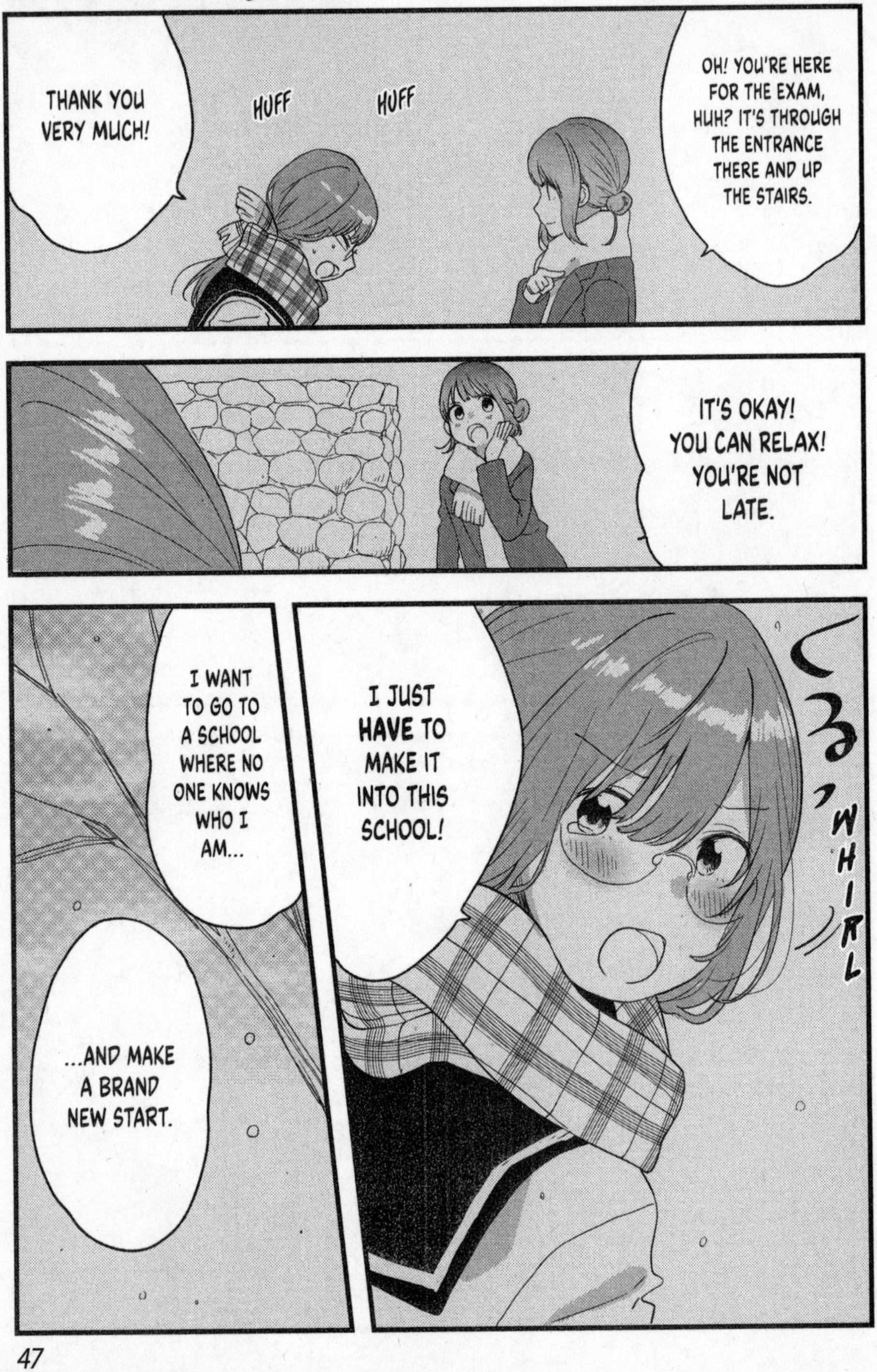
OH! YOU'RE HERE FOR THE EXAM, HUH? IT'S THROUGH THE ENTRANCE THERE AND UP THE STAIRS.
HUFF
HUFF
THANK YOU VERY MUCH!
IT'S OKAY! YOU CAN RELAX! YOU'RE NOT LATE.
くるっ
WHIRL
I JUST **HAVE** TO MAKE IT INTO THIS SCHOOL!
I WANT TO GO TO A SCHOOL WHERE NO ONE KNOWS WHO I AM...
...AND MAKE A BRAND NEW START.

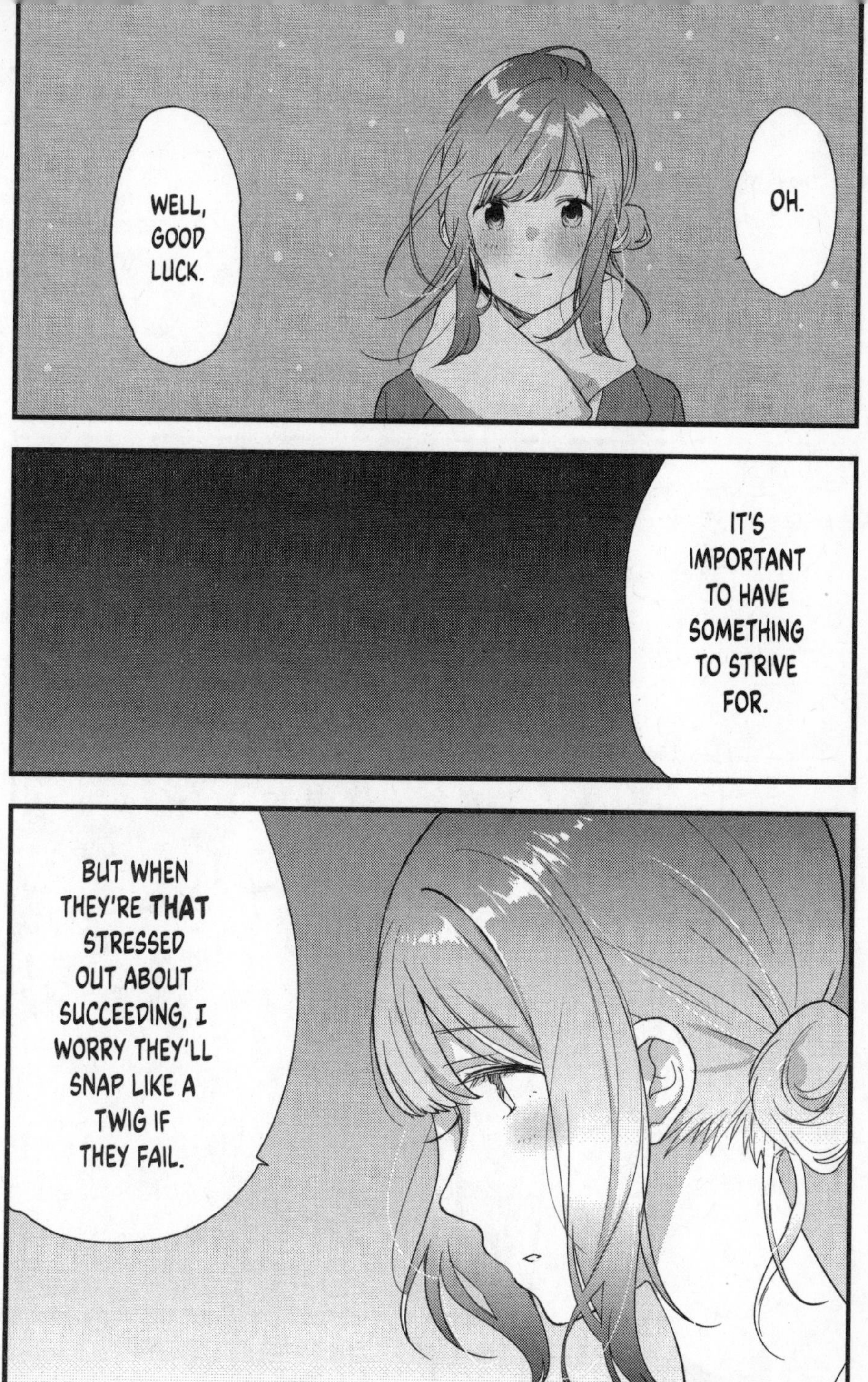
OH.
WELL, GOOD LUCK.
IT'S IMPORTANT TO HAVE SOMETHING TO STRIVE FOR.
BUT WHEN THEY'RE **THAT** STRESSED OUT ABOUT SUCCEEDING, I WORRY THEY'LL SNAP LIKE A TWIG IF THEY FAIL.

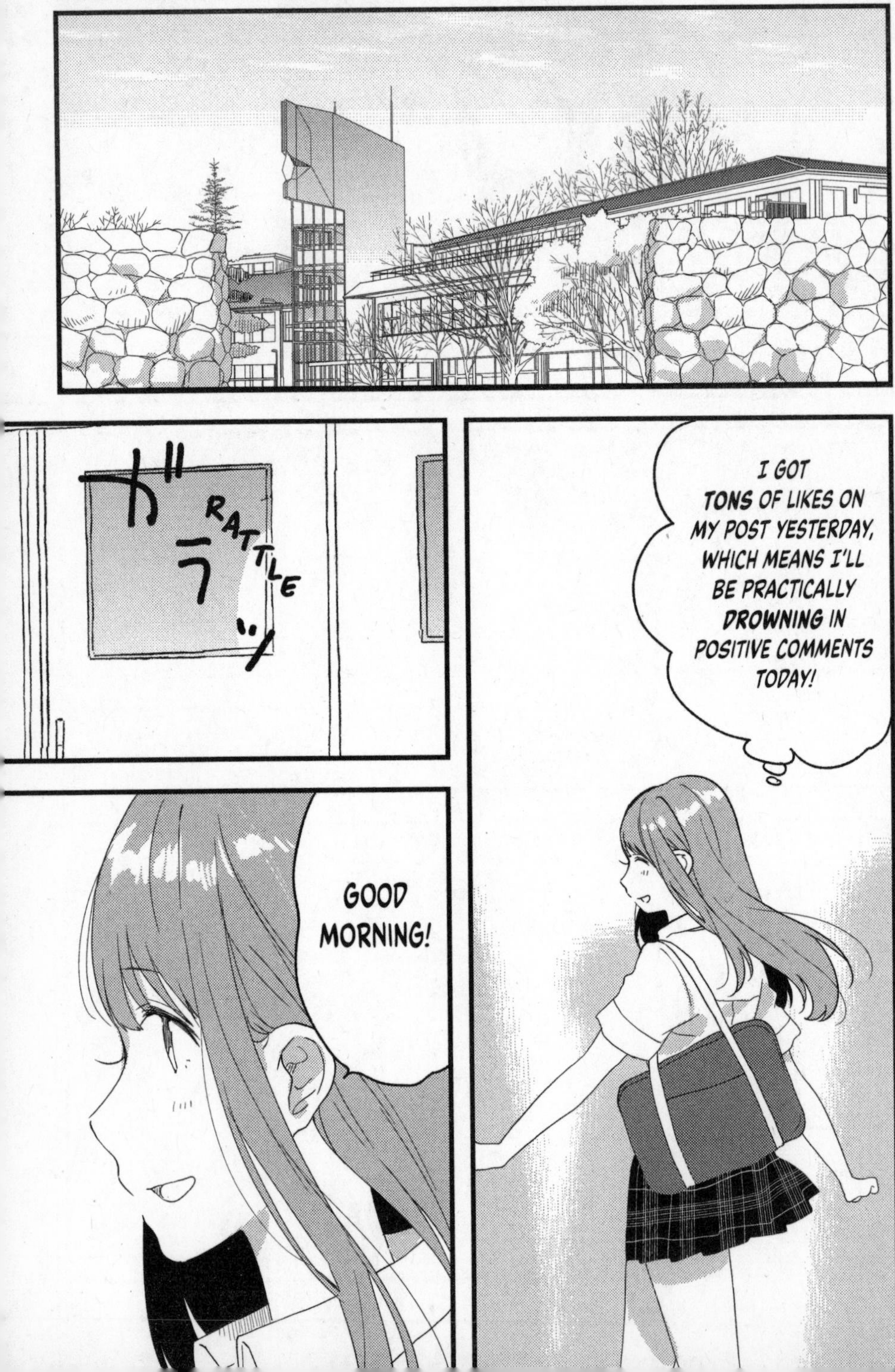
I GOT TONS OF LIKES ON MY POST YESTERDAY, WHICH MEANS I'LL BE PRACTICALLY DROWNING IN POSITIVE COMMENTS TODAY!
ガラッ
RATTLE
GOOD MORNING!

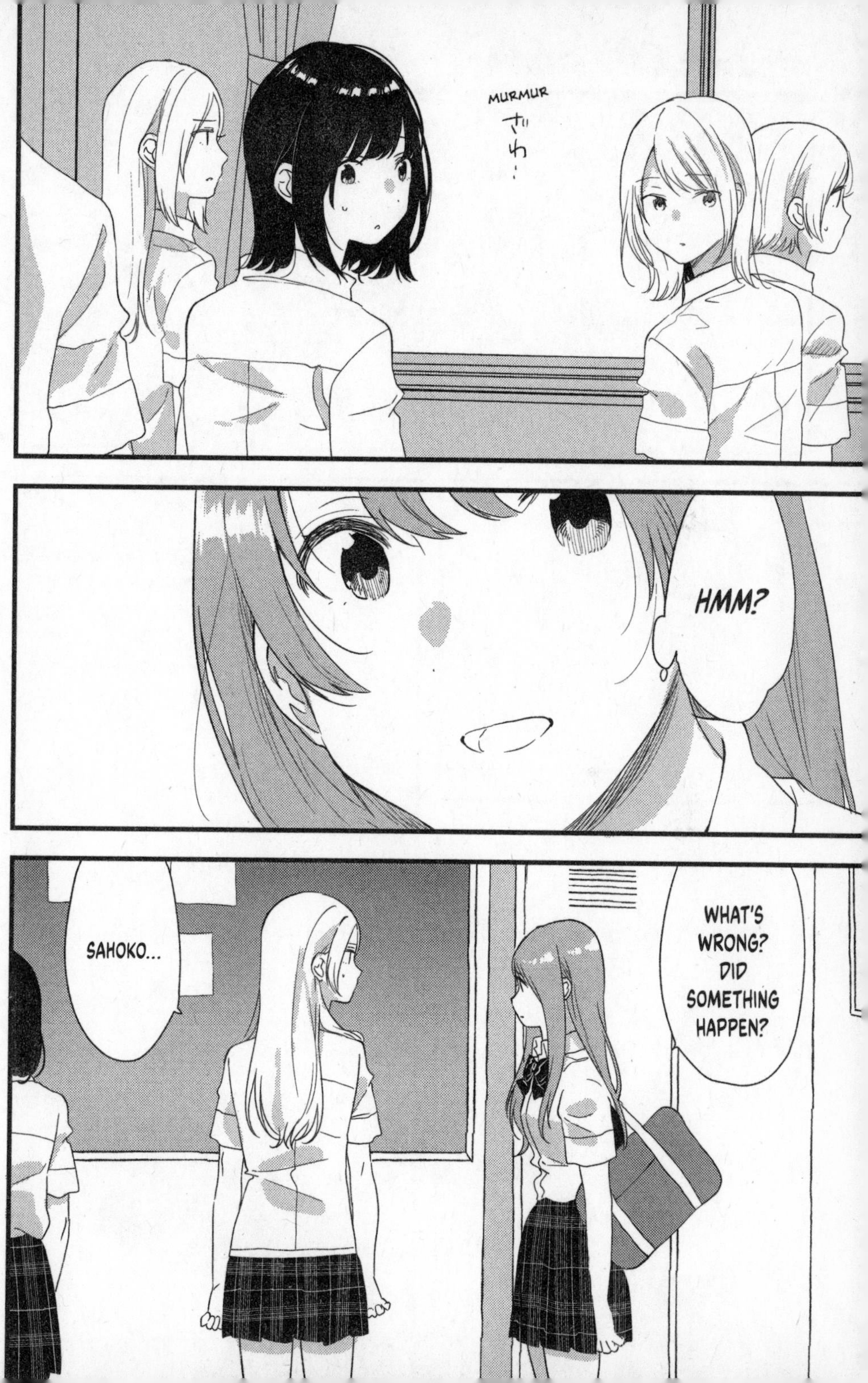
MURMUR
ざわ…
HMM?
WHAT'S WRONG? DID SOMETHING HAPPEN?
SAHOKO...

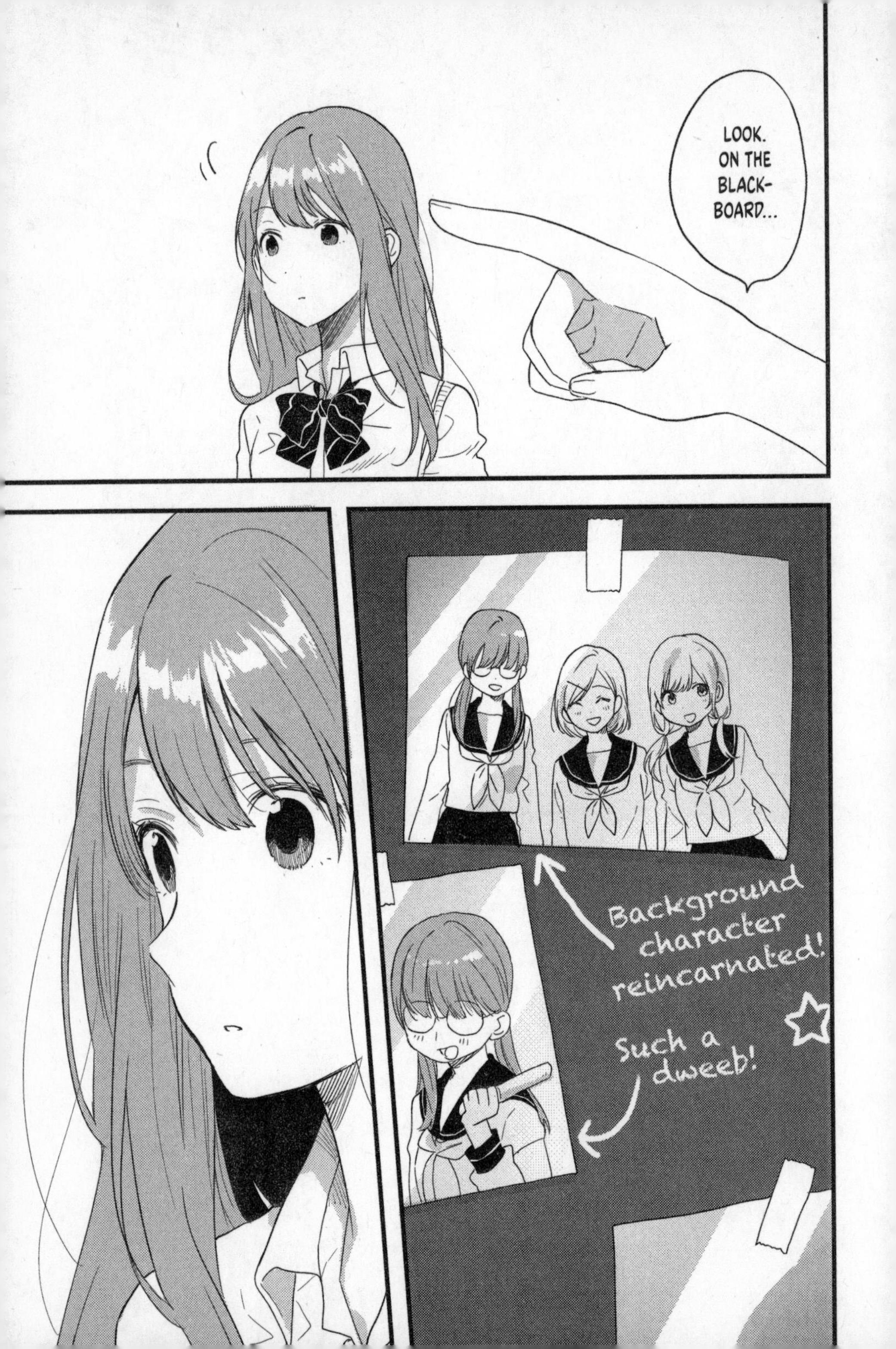
LOOK. ON THE BLACK-BOARD...
Background character reincarnated!
Such a dweeb!

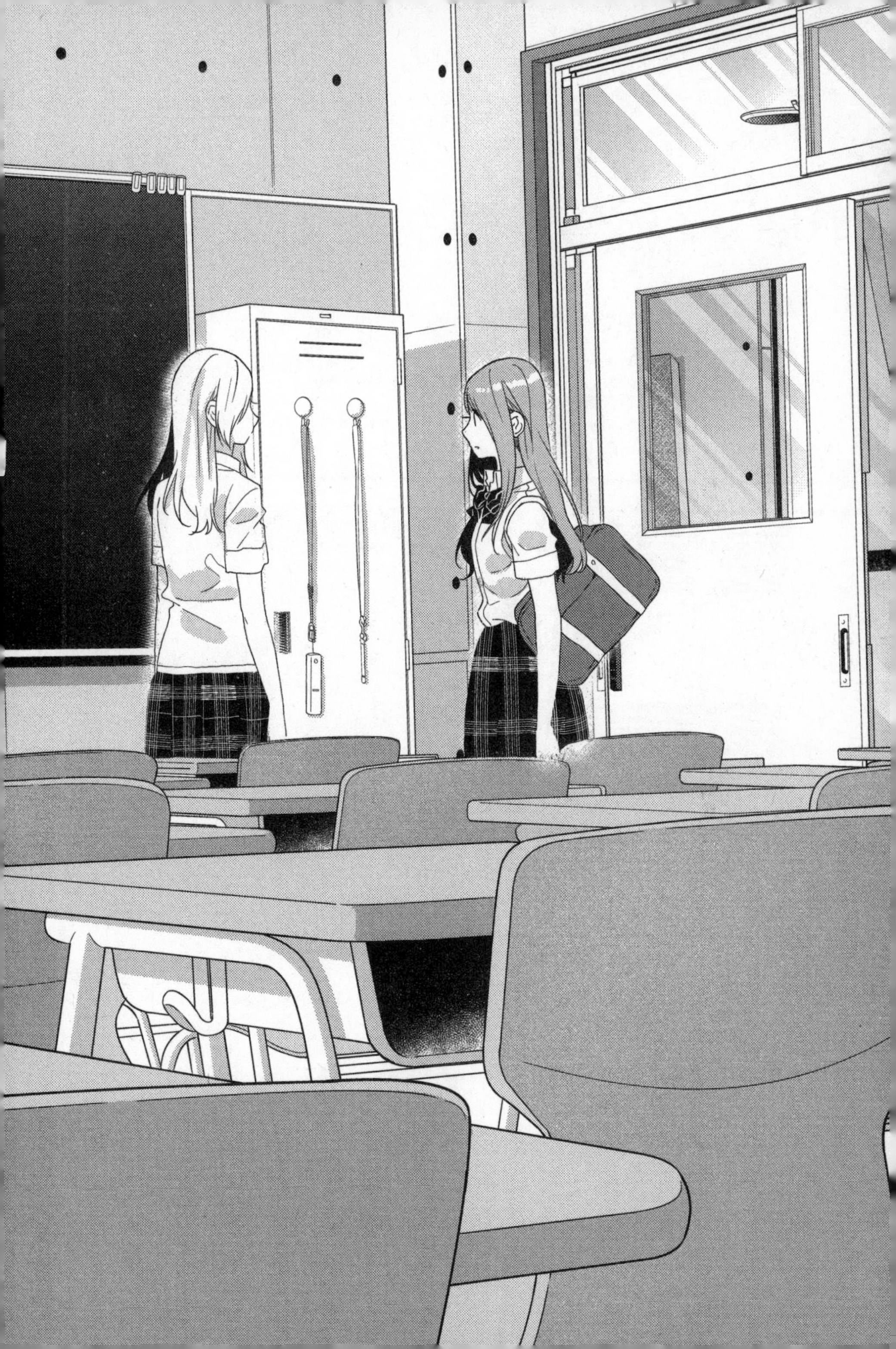

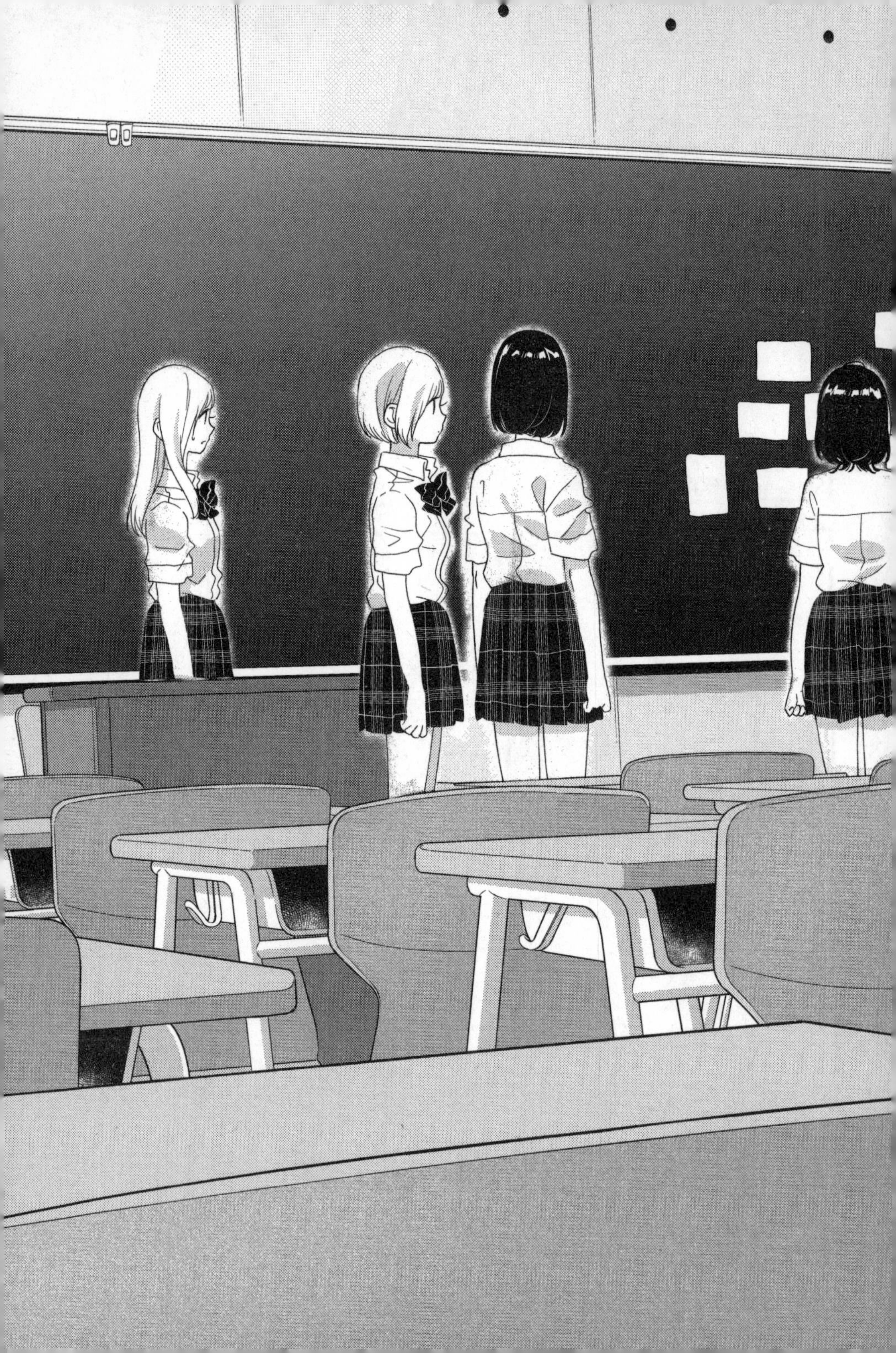

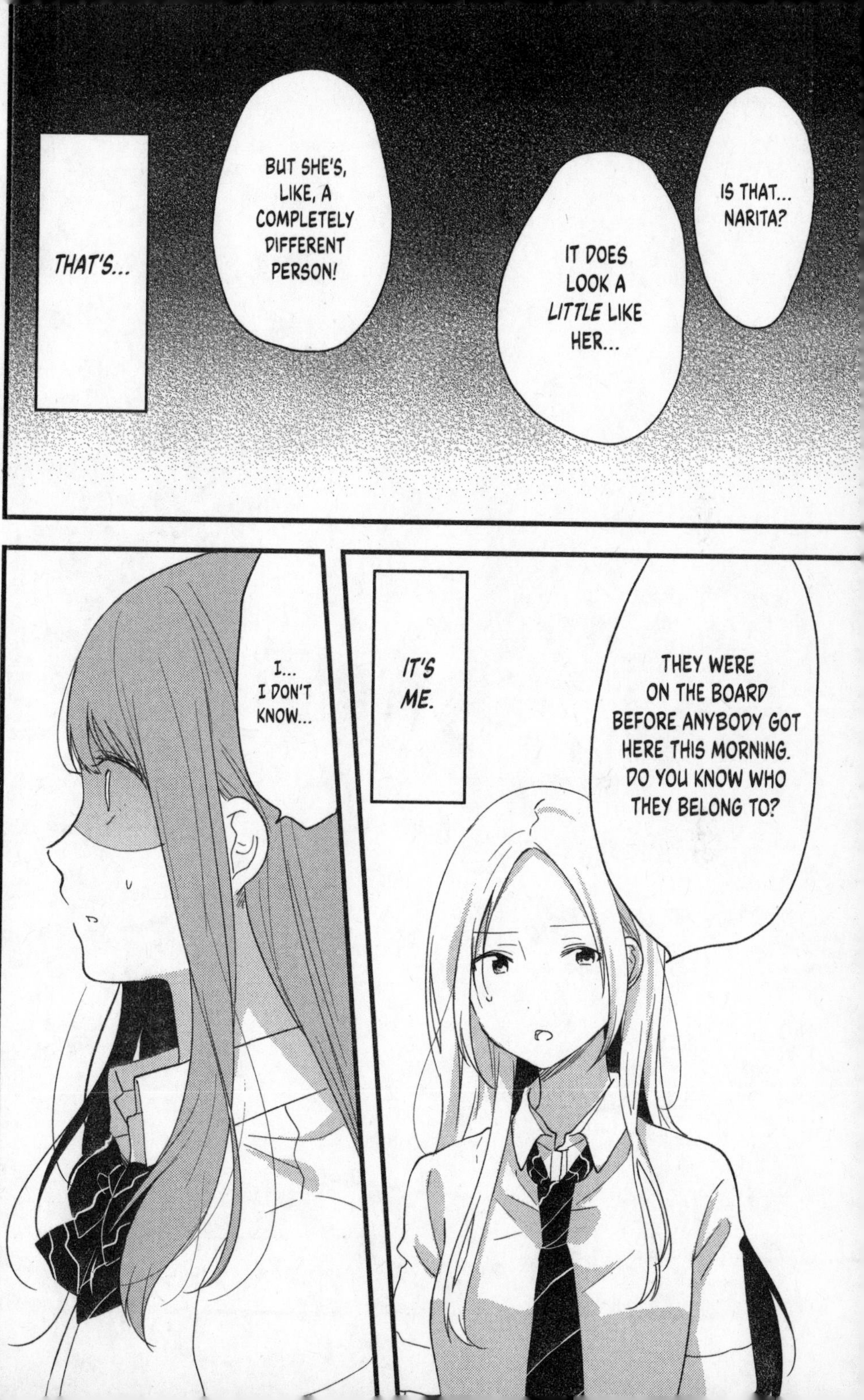
IS THAT... NARITA?
IT DOES LOOK A *LITTLE* LIKE HER...
BUT SHE'S, LIKE, A COMPLETELY DIFFERENT PERSON!
THAT'S...
THEY WERE ON THE BOARD BEFORE ANYBODY GOT HERE THIS MORNING. DO YOU KNOW WHO THEY BELONG TO?
IT'S ME.
I... I DON'T KNOW...

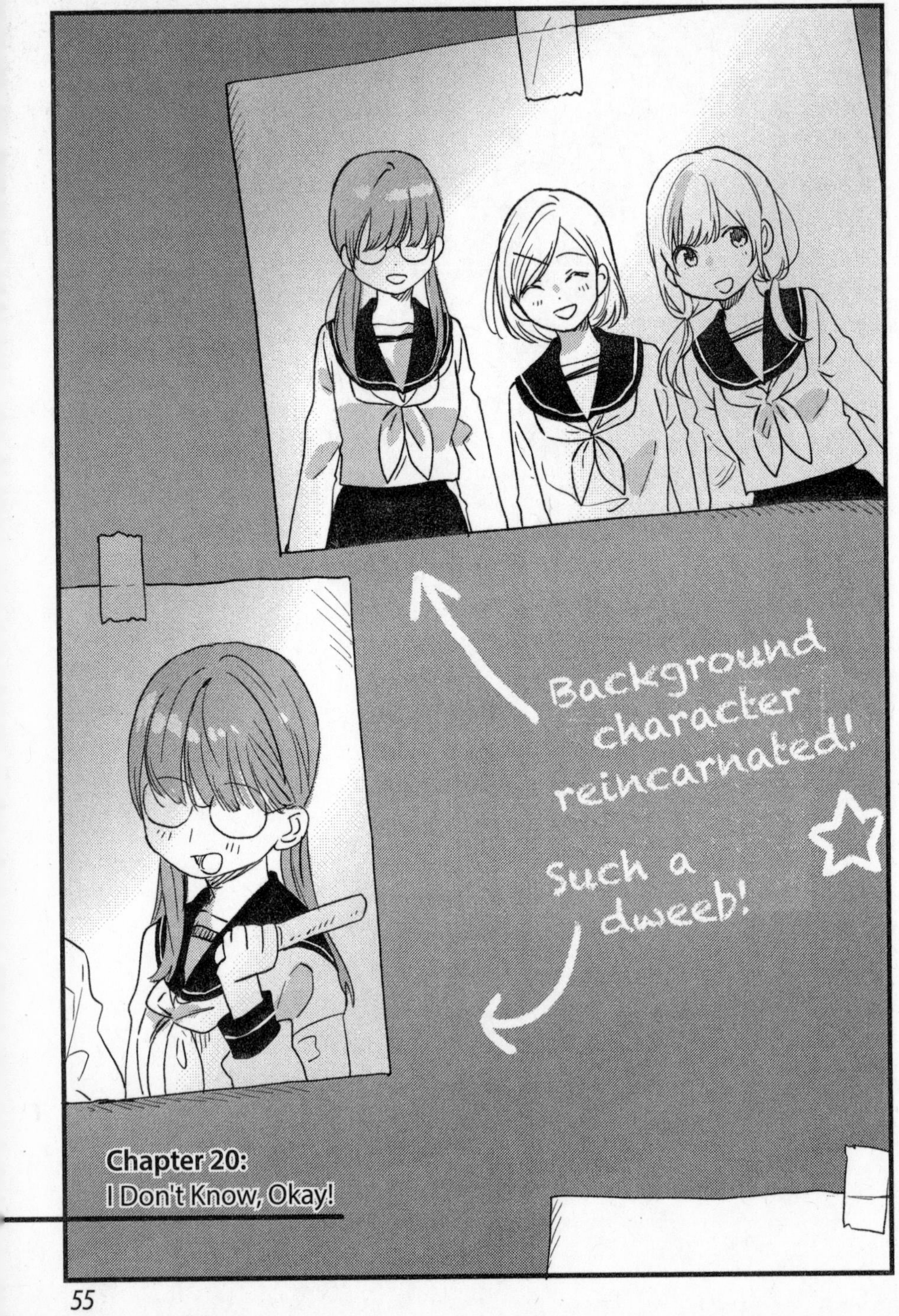
Background character reincarnated!
Such a dweeb!
Chapter 20:
I Don't Know, Okay!

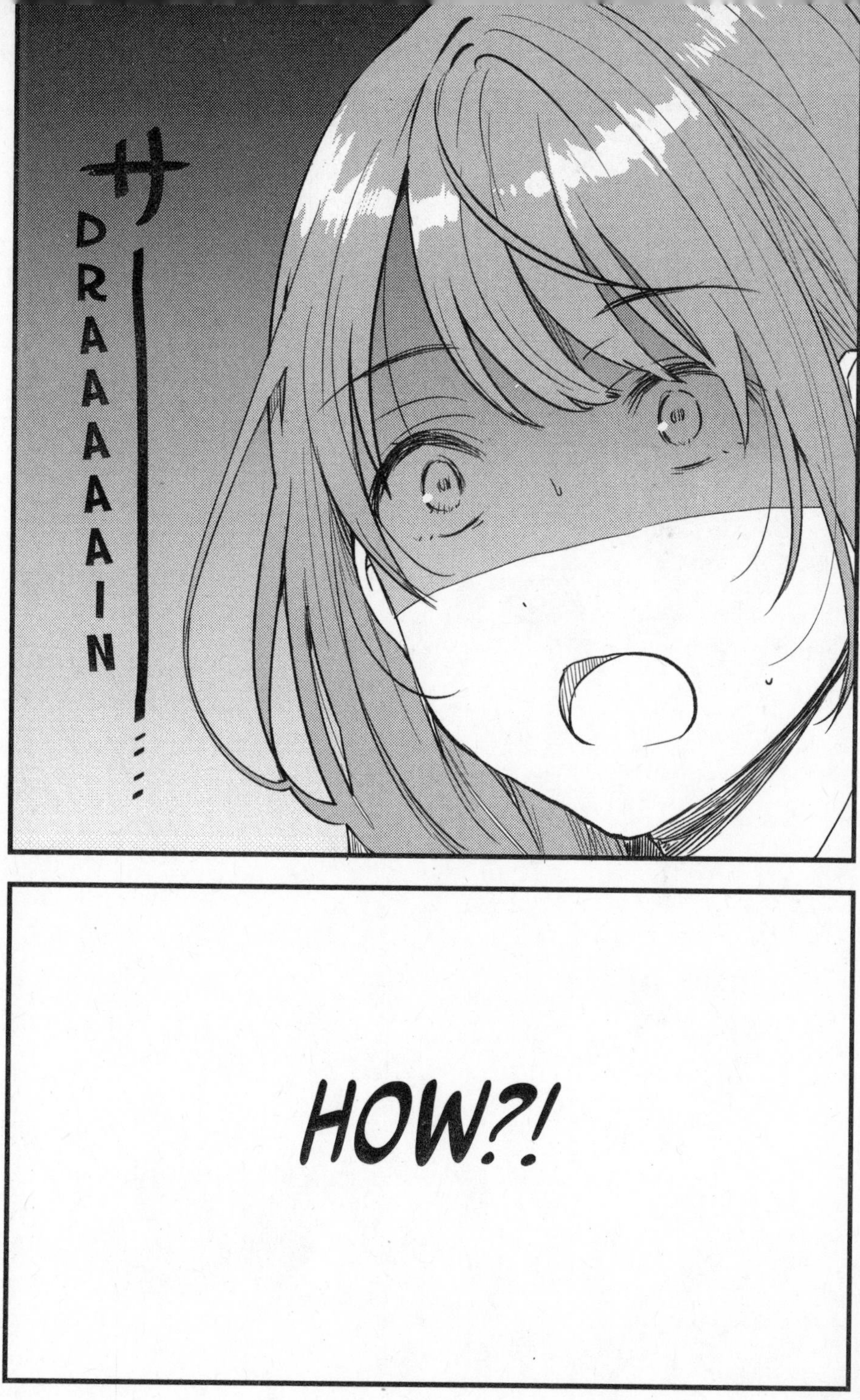
サー…
DRAAAAAIN
HOW?!

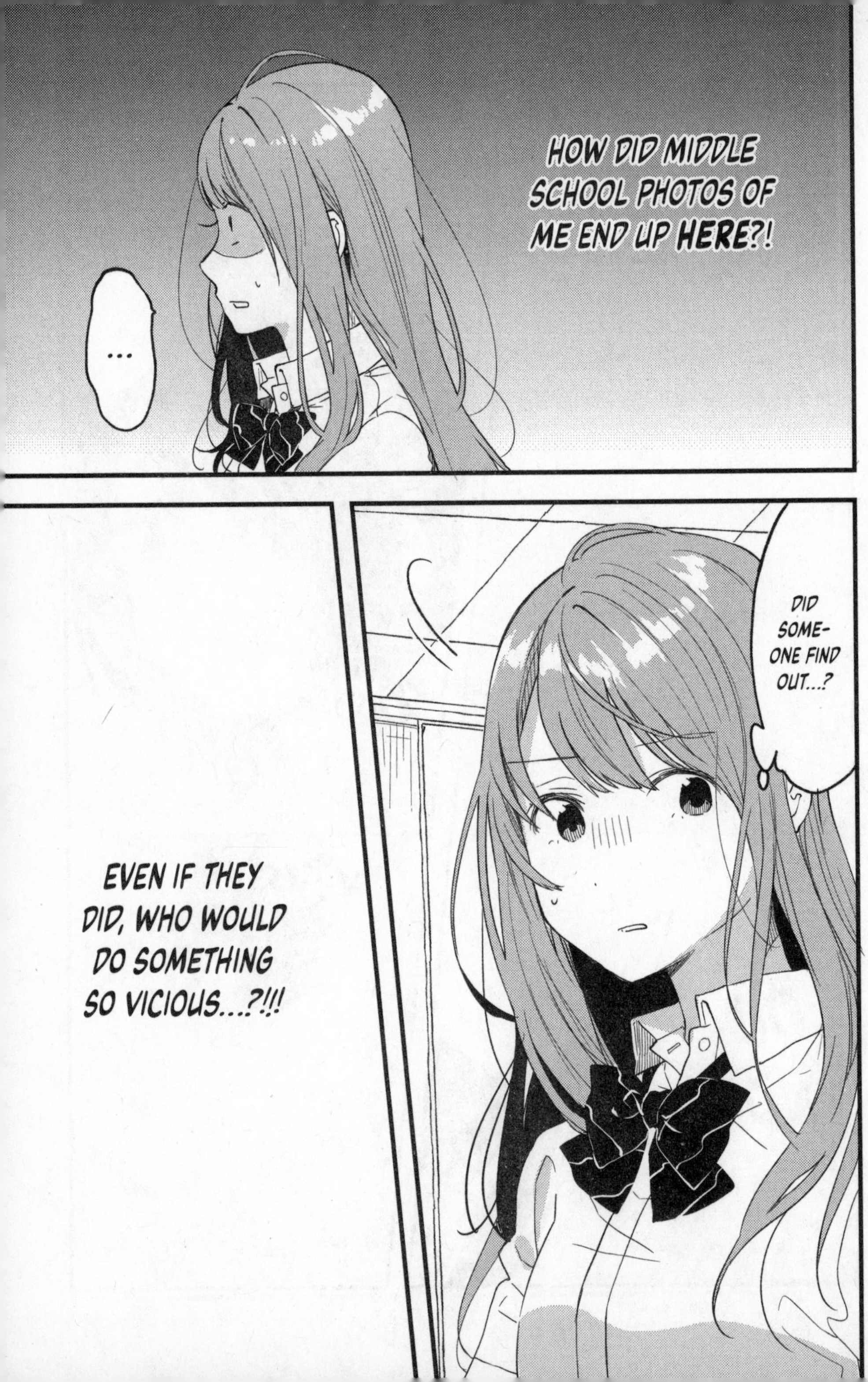
HOW DID MIDDLE SCHOOL PHOTOS OF ME END UP HERE?!
...
DID SOME-ONE FIND OUT...?
EVEN IF THEY DID, WHO WOULD DO SOMETHING SO VICIOUS...?!!!

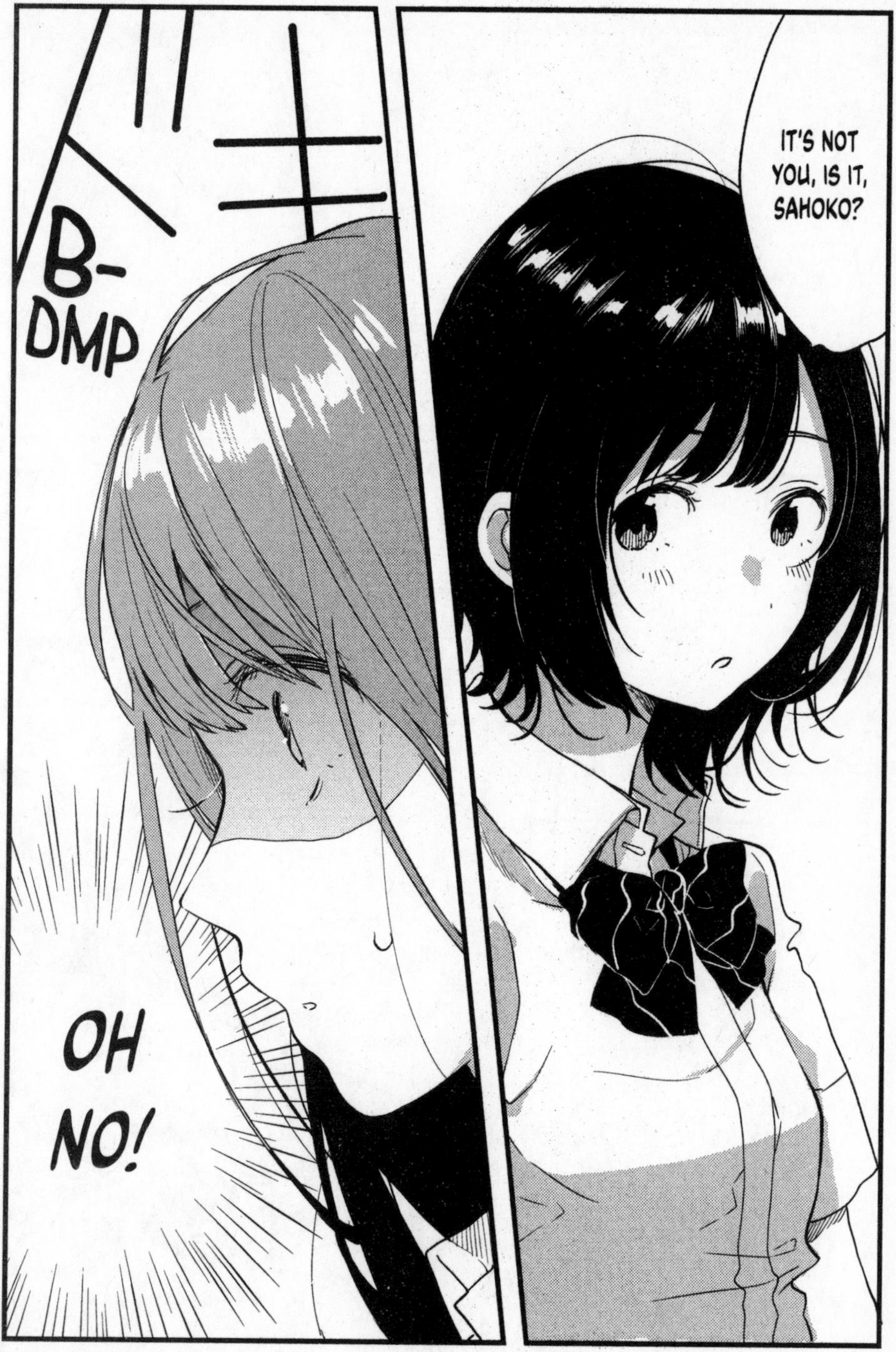
IT'S NOT YOU, IS IT, SAHOKO?
B-DMP
OH NO!

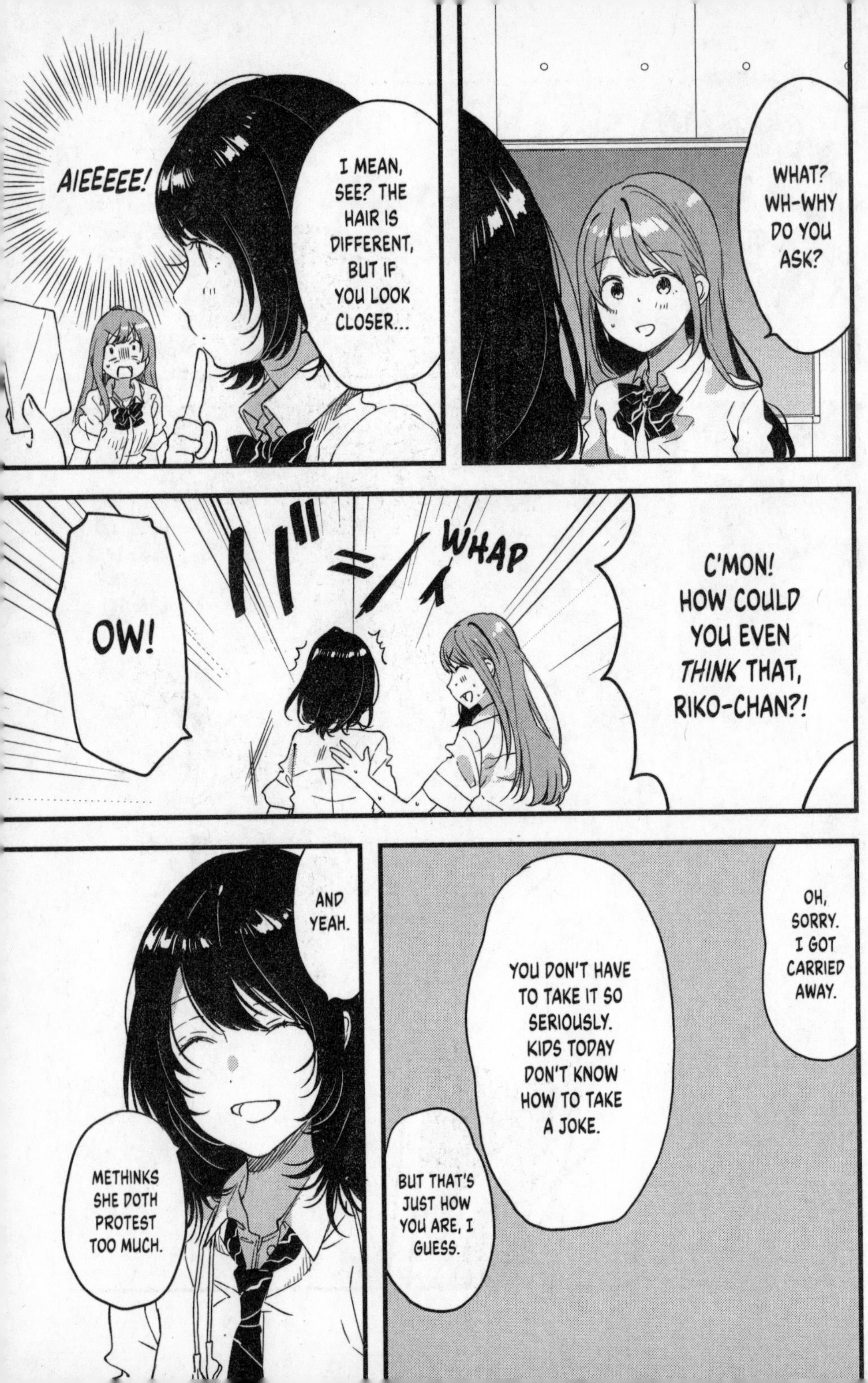
WHAT? WH-WHY DO YOU ASK?
I MEAN, SEE? THE HAIR IS DIFFERENT, BUT IF YOU LOOK CLOSER...
AIEEEEE!
C'MON! HOW COULD YOU EVEN *THINK* THAT, RIKO-CHAN?!
WHAP
OW!
OH, SORRY. I GOT CARRIED AWAY.
YOU DON'T HAVE TO TAKE IT SO SERIOUSLY. KIDS TODAY DON'T KNOW HOW TO TAKE A JOKE.
BUT THAT'S JUST HOW YOU ARE, I GUESS.
AND YEAH.
METHINKS SHE DOTH PROTEST TOO MUCH.

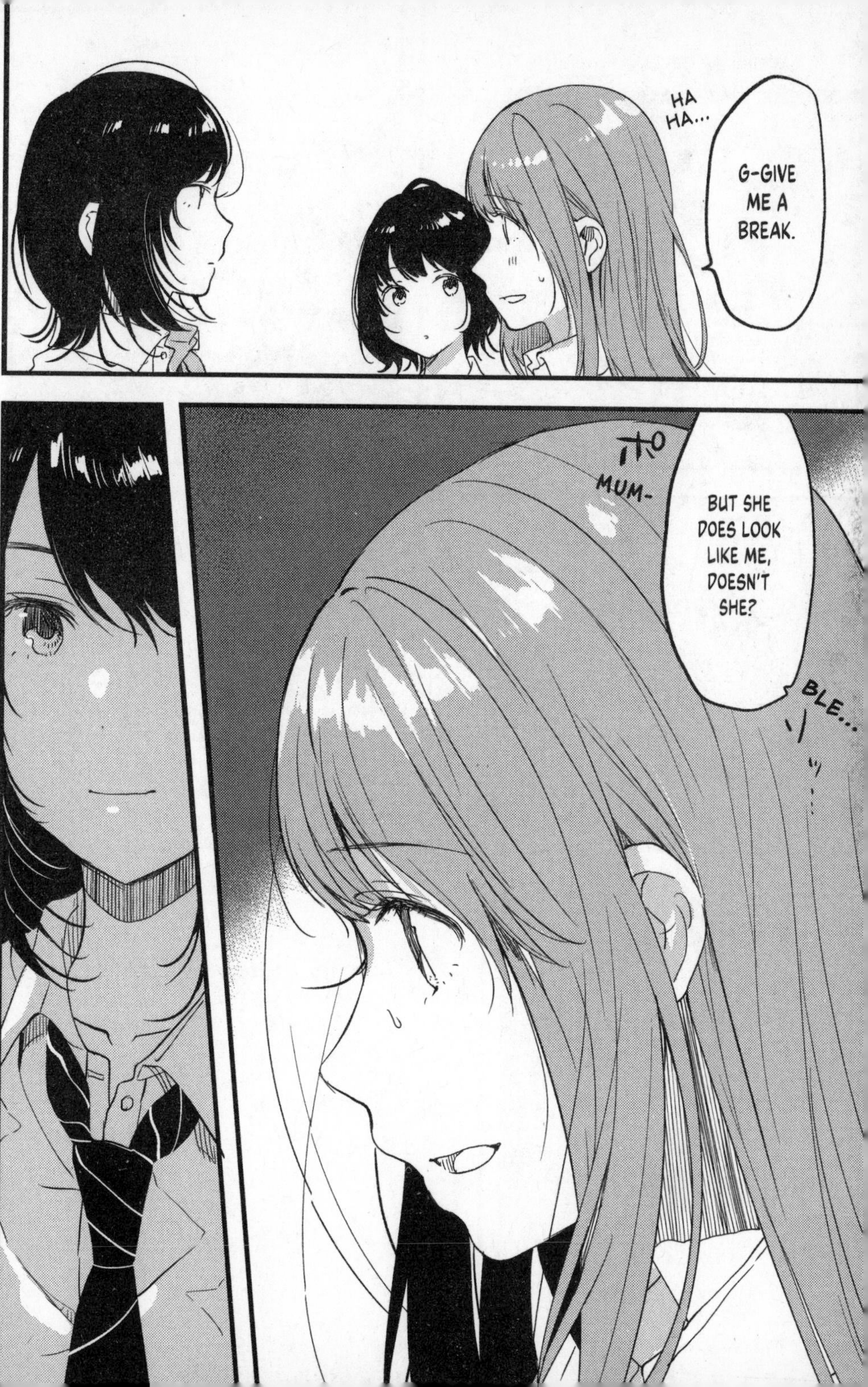

G-GIVE ME A BREAK.
HA HA...
BUT SHE DOES LOOK LIKE ME, DOESN'T SHE?
MUM-
BLE...

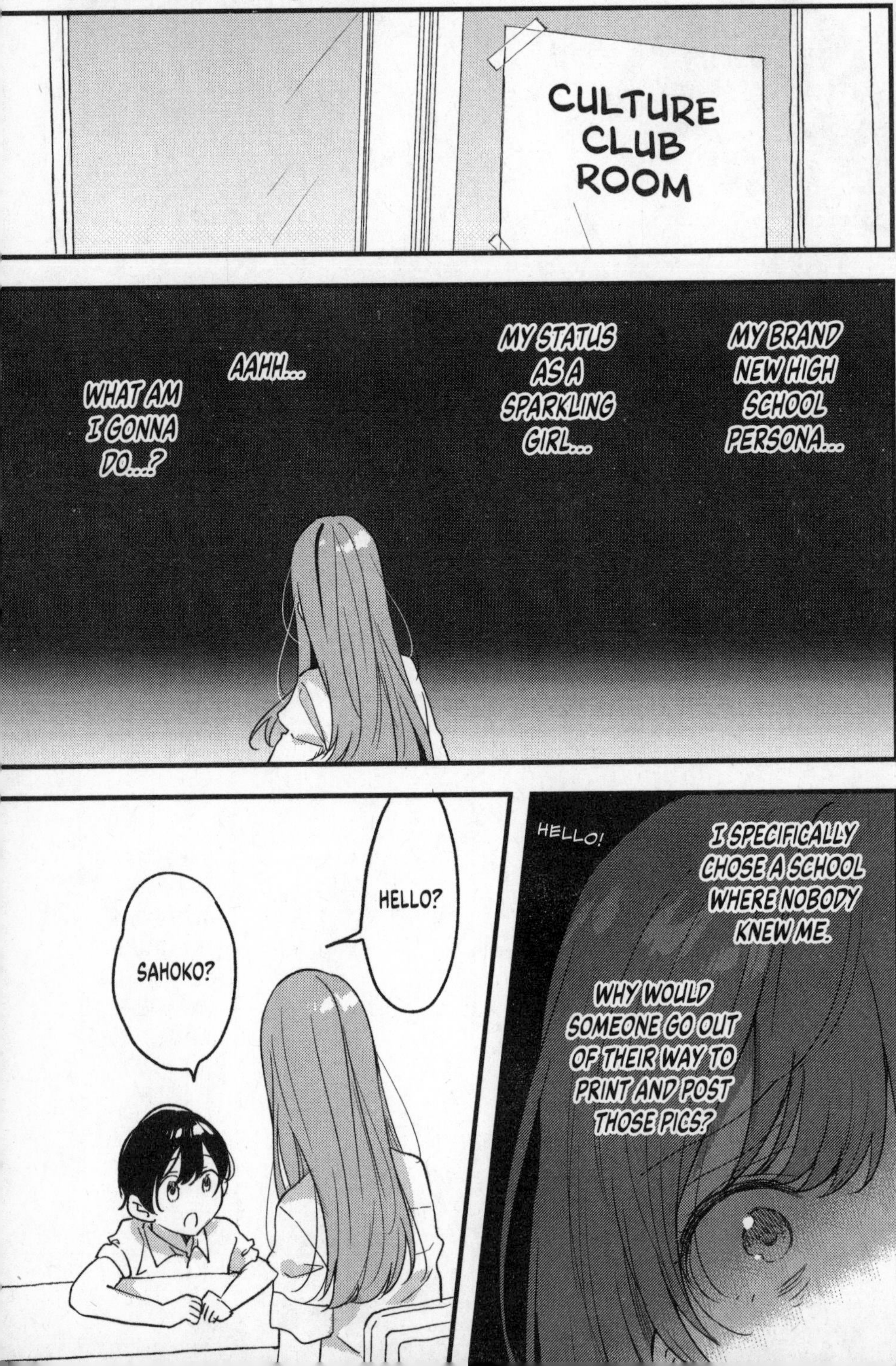
CULTURE CLUB ROOM
MY BRAND NEW HIGH SCHOOL PERSONA...
MY STATUS AS A SPARKLING GIRL...
AAHH...
WHAT AM I GONNA DO...?
I SPECIFICALLY CHOSE A SCHOOL WHERE NOBODY KNEW ME.
WHY WOULD SOMEONE GO OUT OF THEIR WAY TO PRINT AND POST THOSE PICS?
HELLO!
HELLO?
SAHOKO?

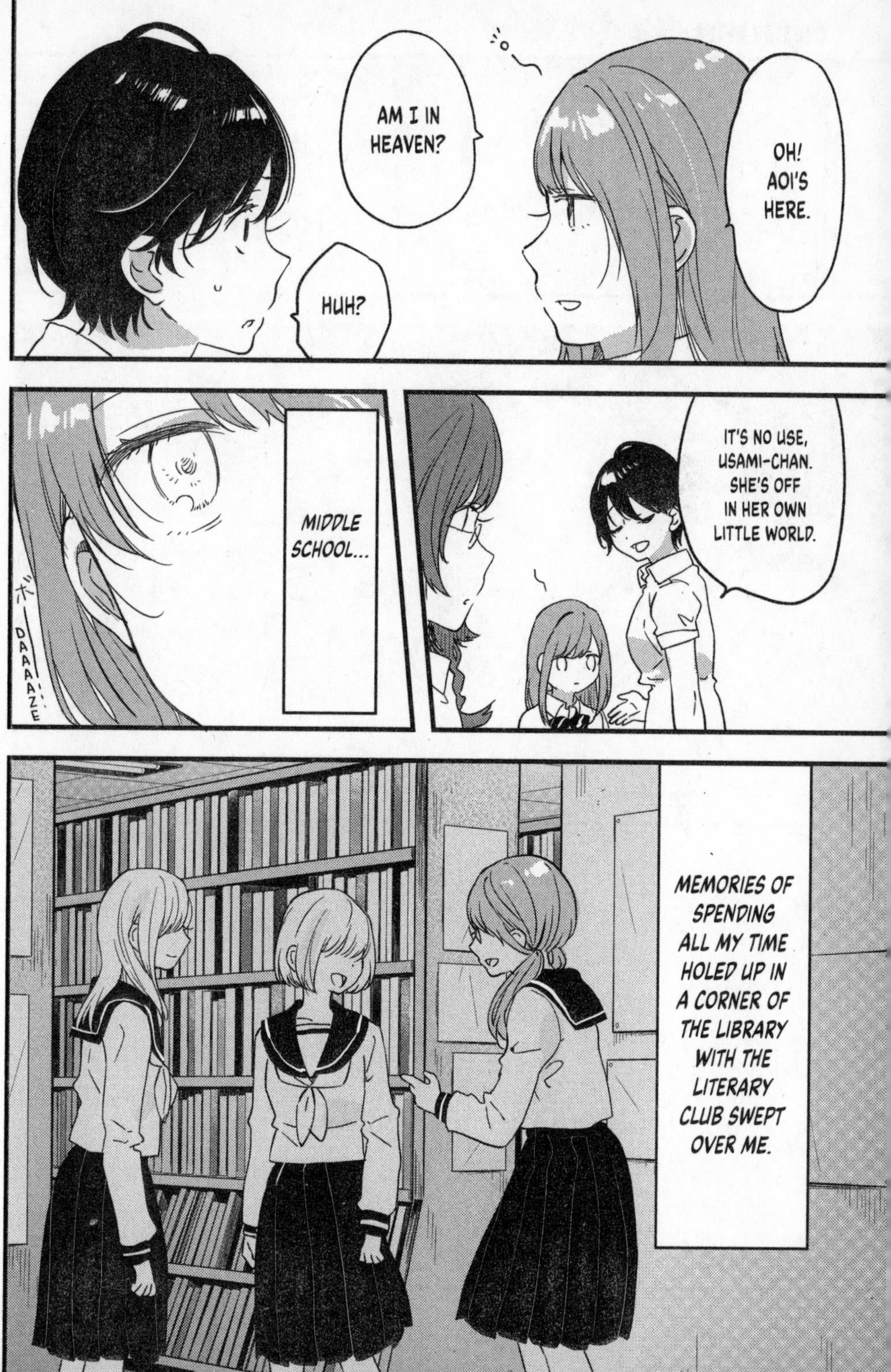
OH! AOI'S HERE.
AM I IN HEAVEN?
HUH?
IT'S NO USE, USAMI-CHAN. SHE'S OFF IN HER OWN LITTLE WORLD.
MIDDLE SCHOOL...
ボー DAAAAAZE
MEMORIES OF SPENDING ALL MY TIME HOLED UP IN A CORNER OF THE LIBRARY WITH THE LITERARY CLUB SWEPT OVER ME.

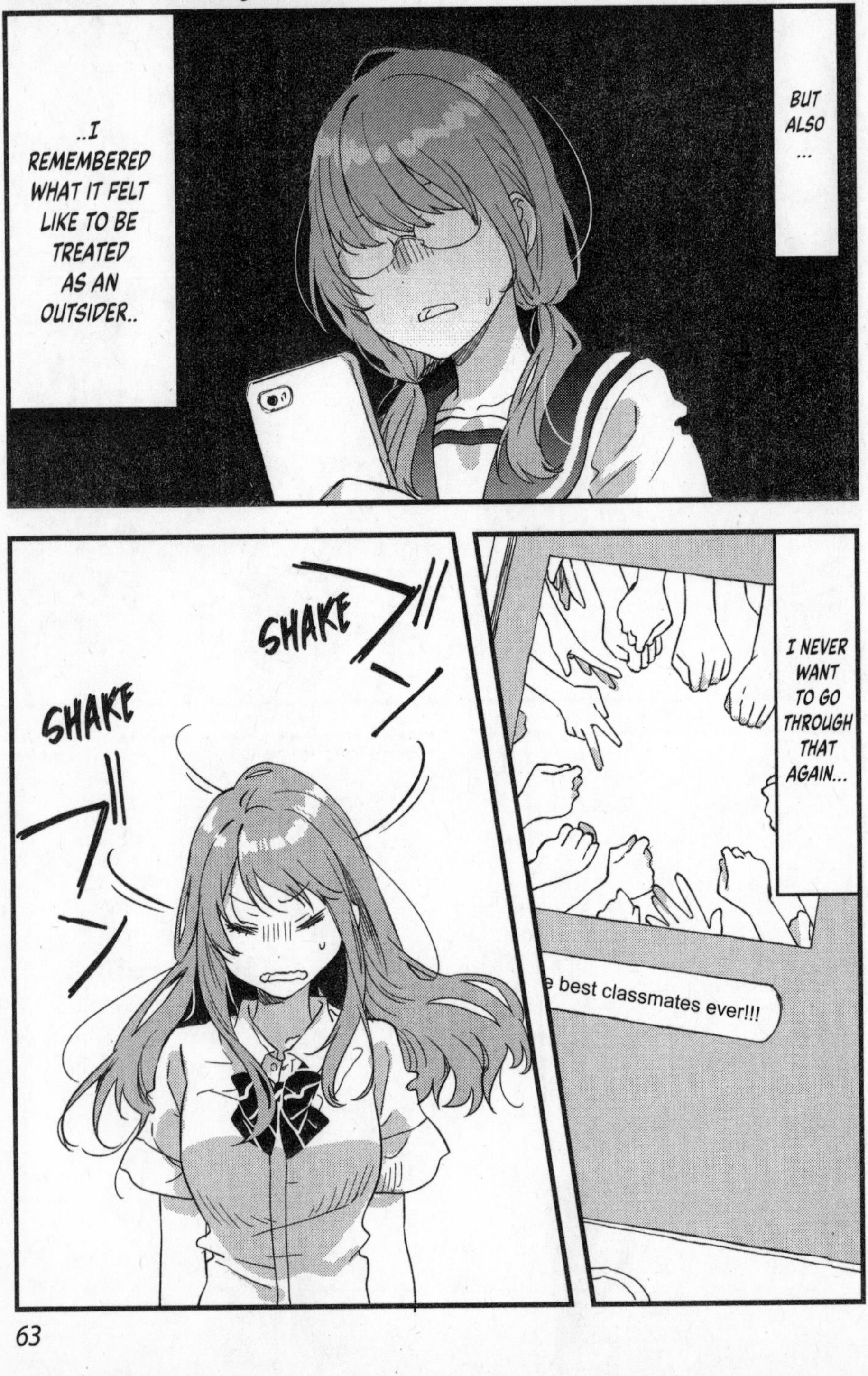
BUT ALSO ...
..I REMEMBERED WHAT IT FELT LIKE TO BE TREATED AS AN OUTSIDER..
I NEVER WANT TO GO THROUGH THAT AGAIN...
e best classmates ever!!!
SHAKE
SHAKE

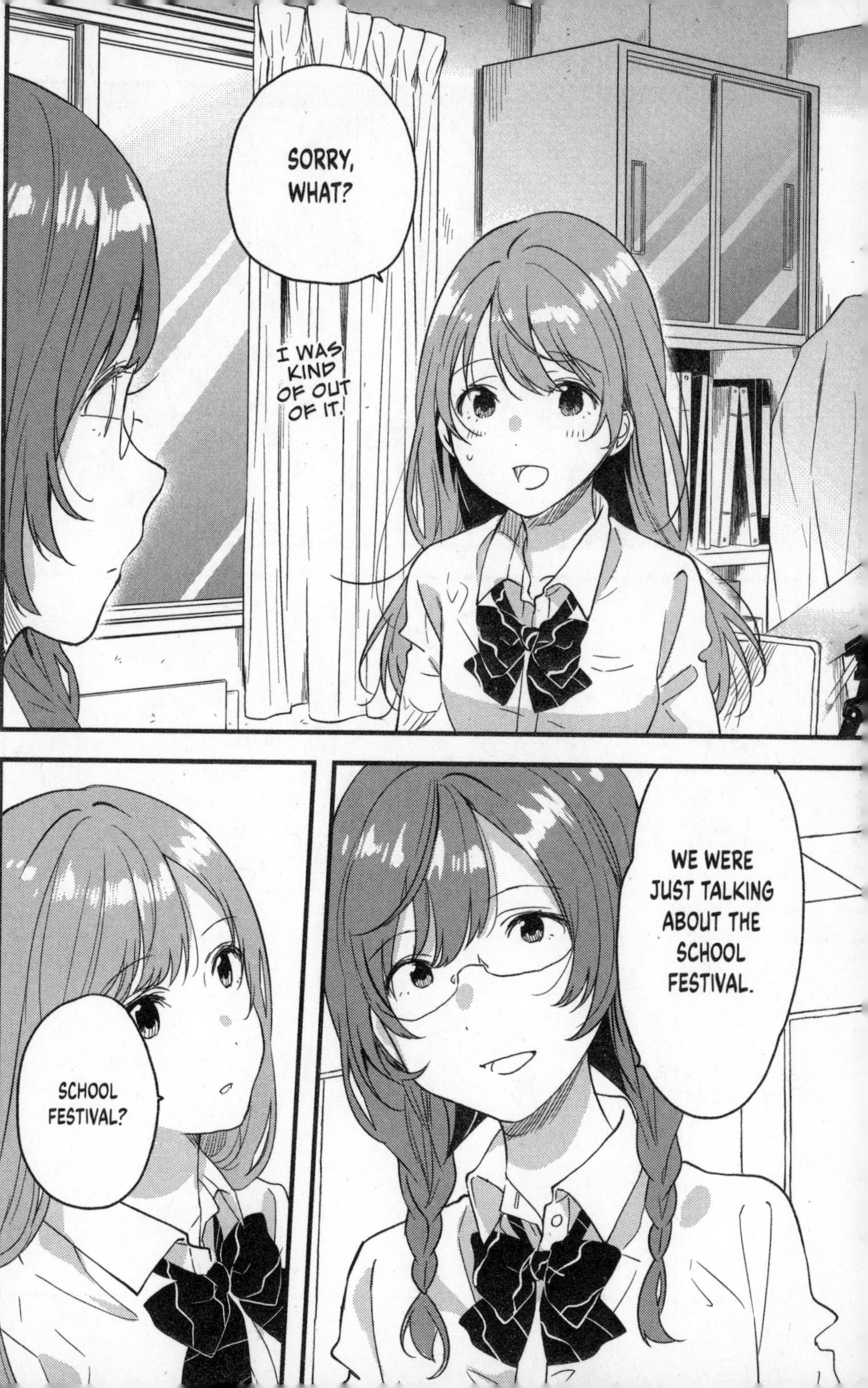
SORRY, WHAT?
I WAS KIND OF OUT OF IT.
WE WERE JUST TALKING ABOUT THE SCHOOL FESTIVAL.
SCHOOL FESTIVAL?

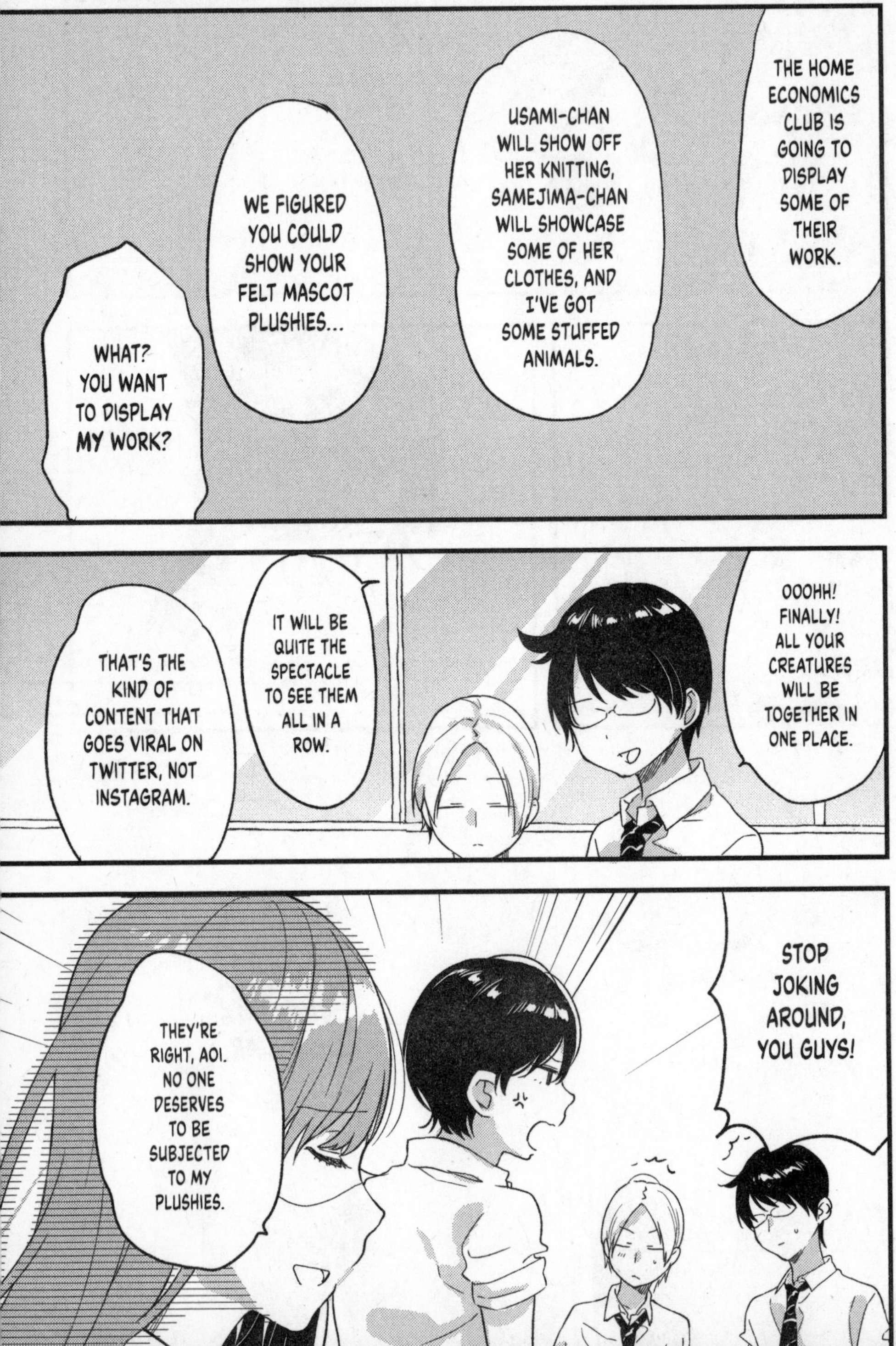
THE HOME ECONOMICS CLUB IS GOING TO DISPLAY SOME OF THEIR WORK.
USAMI-CHAN WILL SHOW OFF HER KNITTING, SAMEJIMA-CHAN WILL SHOWCASE SOME OF HER CLOTHES, AND I'VE GOT SOME STUFFED ANIMALS.
WE FIGURED YOU COULD SHOW YOUR FELT MASCOT PLUSHIES...
WHAT? YOU WANT TO DISPLAY MY WORK?
OOOHH! FINALLY! ALL YOUR CREATURES WILL BE TOGETHER IN ONE PLACE.
IT WILL BE QUITE THE SPECTACLE TO SEE THEM ALL IN A ROW.
THAT'S THE KIND OF CONTENT THAT GOES VIRAL ON TWITTER, NOT INSTAGRAM.
STOP JOKING AROUND, YOU GUYS!
THEY'RE RIGHT, AOI. NO ONE DESERVES TO BE SUBJECTED TO MY PLUSHIES.

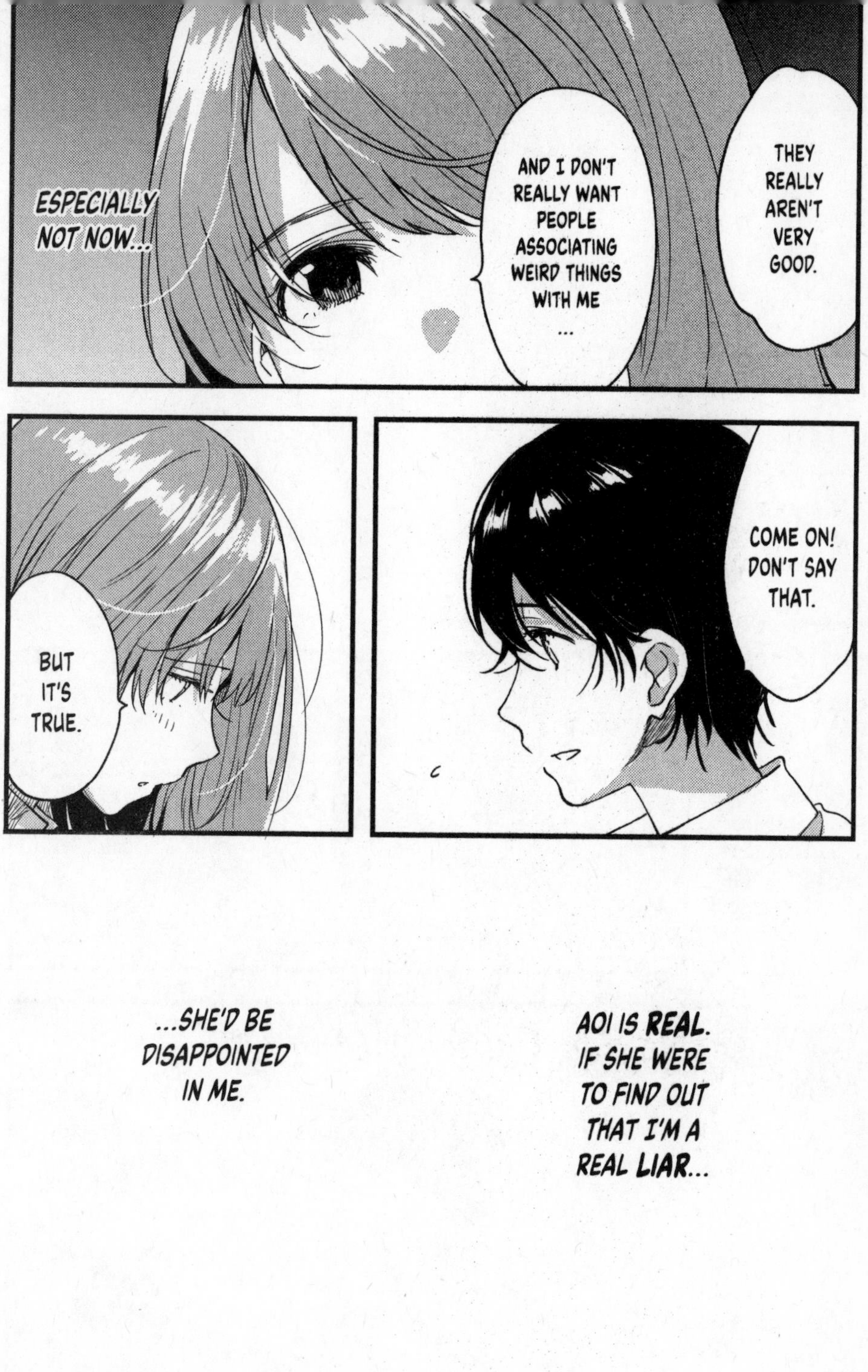
THEY REALLY AREN'T VERY GOOD.
AND I DON'T REALLY WANT PEOPLE ASSOCIATING WEIRD THINGS WITH ME ...
ESPECIALLY NOT NOW...
COME ON! DON'T SAY THAT.
BUT IT'S TRUE.
AOI IS REAL. IF SHE WERE TO FIND OUT THAT I'M A REAL LIAR...
...SHE'D BE DISAPPOINTED IN ME.

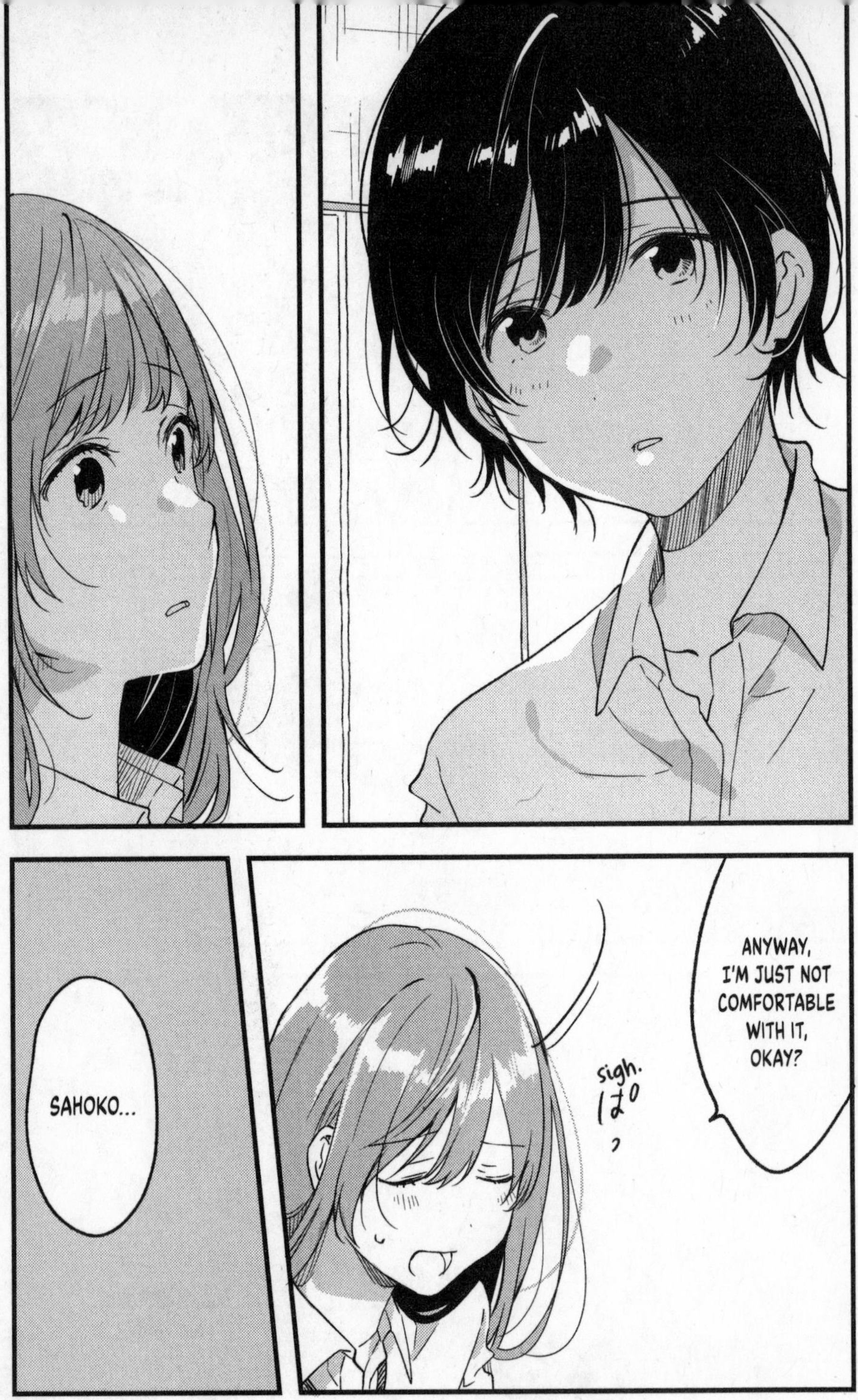
ANYWAY, I'M JUST NOT COMFORTABLE WITH IT, OKAY?
sigh.
SAHOKO...

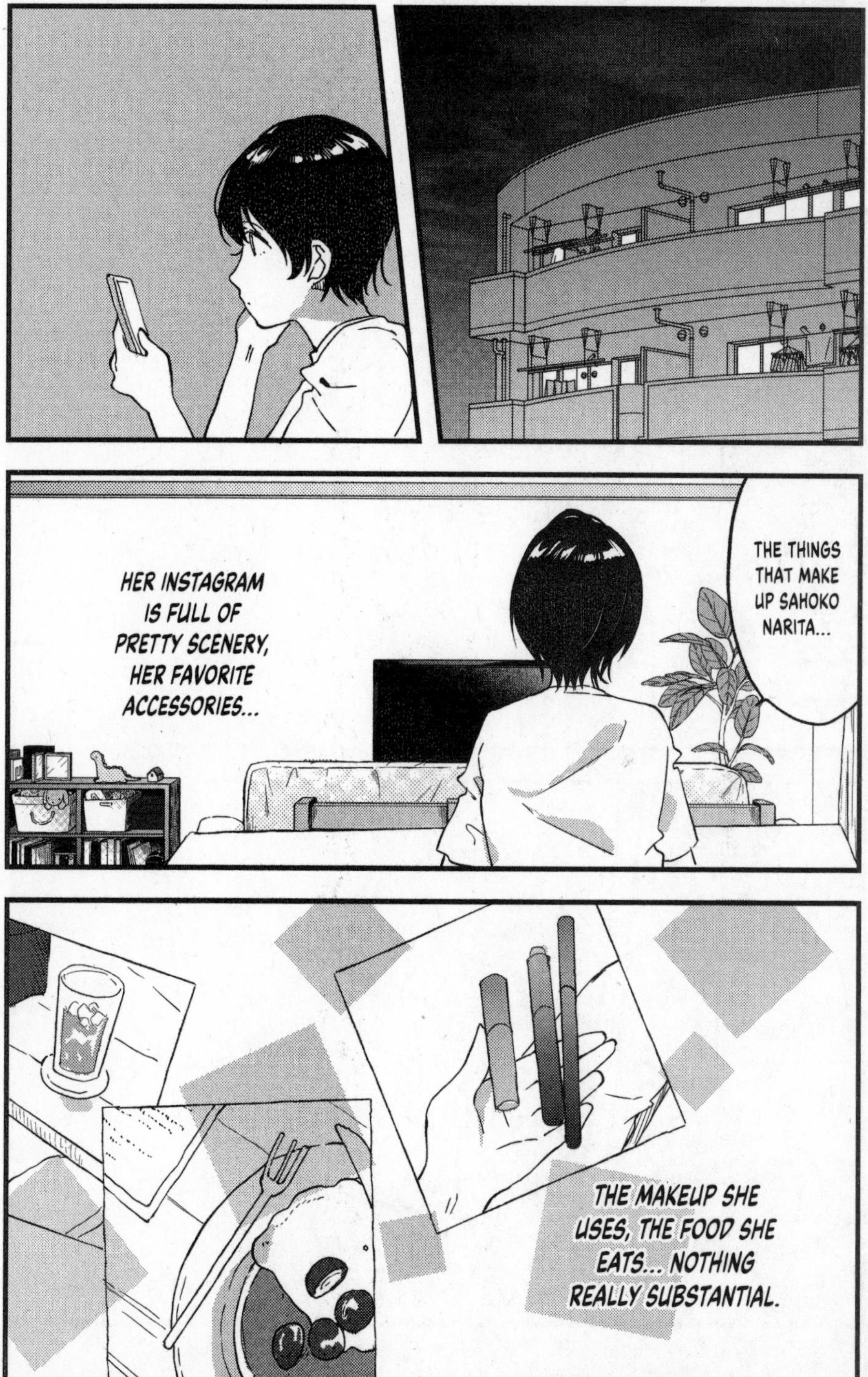
THE THINGS THAT MAKE UP SAHOKO NARITA...
HER INSTAGRAM IS FULL OF PRETTY SCENERY, HER FAVORITE ACCESSORIES...
THE MAKEUP SHE USES, THE FOOD SHE EATS... NOTHING REALLY SUBSTANTIAL.

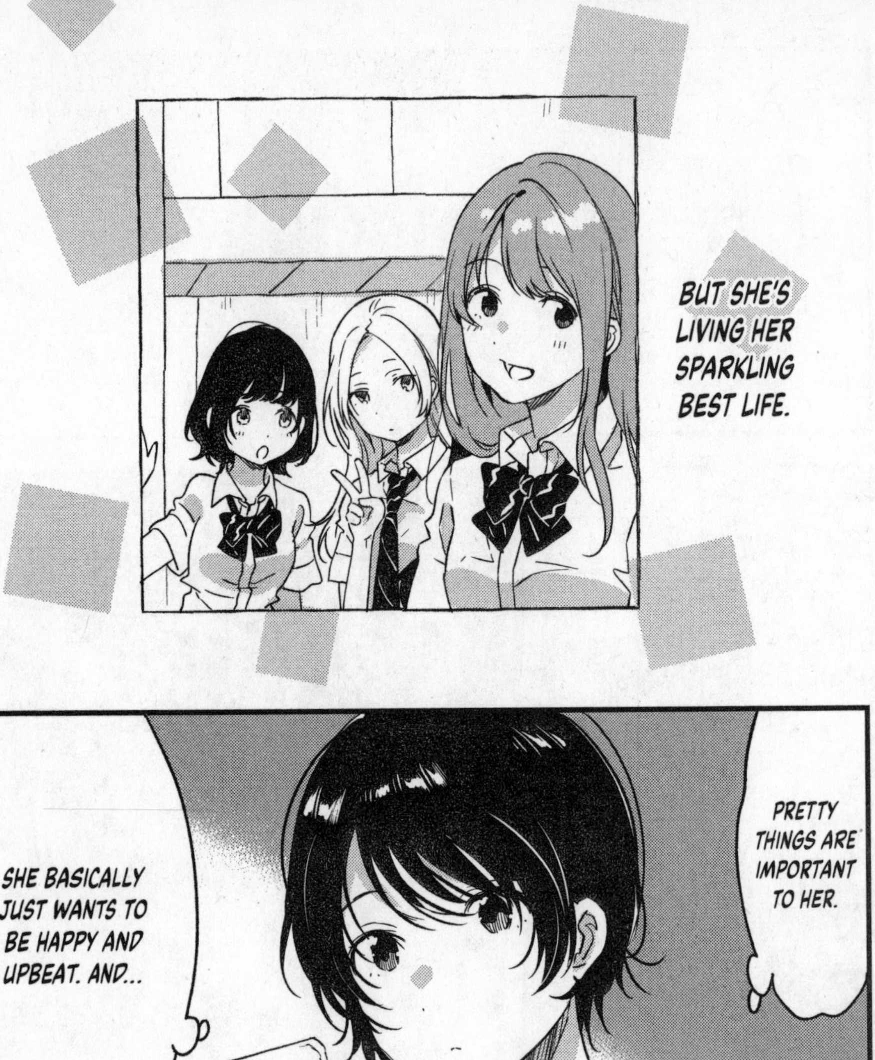
BUT SHE'S LIVING HER SPARKLING BEST LIFE.
PRETTY THINGS ARE IMPORTANT TO HER.
SHE BASICALLY JUST WANTS TO BE HAPPY AND UPBEAT. AND...

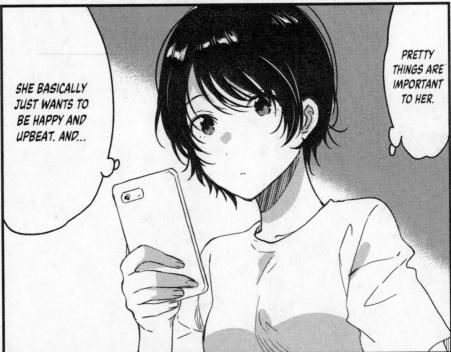

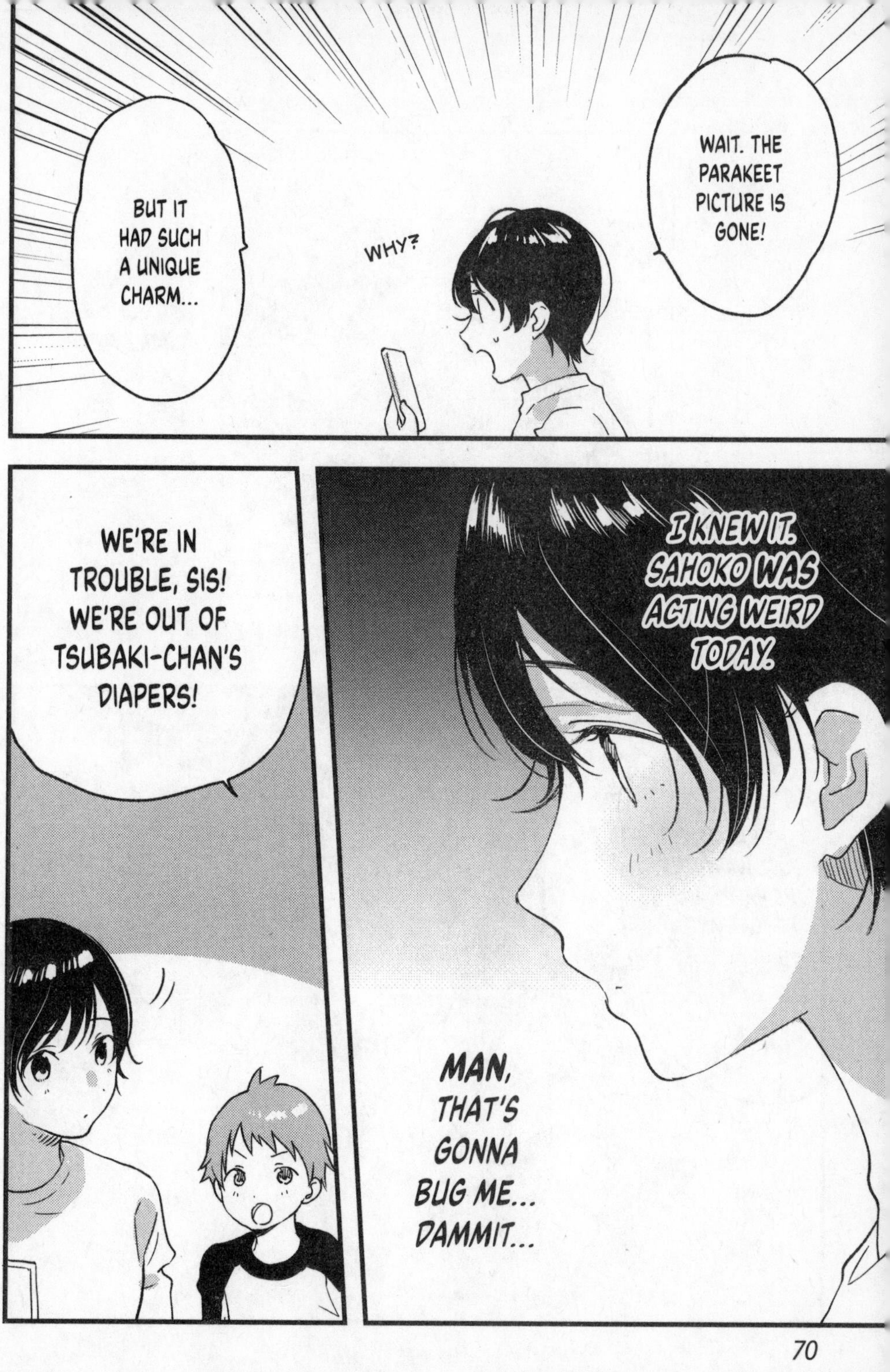
WAIT. THE PARAKEET PICTURE IS GONE!
WHY?
BUT IT HAD SUCH A UNIQUE CHARM...
I KNEW IT. SAHOKO WAS ACTING WEIRD TODAY.
MAN, THAT'S GONNA BUG ME... DAMMIT...
WE'RE IN TROUBLE, SIS! WE'RE OUT OF TSUBAKI-CHAN'S DIAPERS!

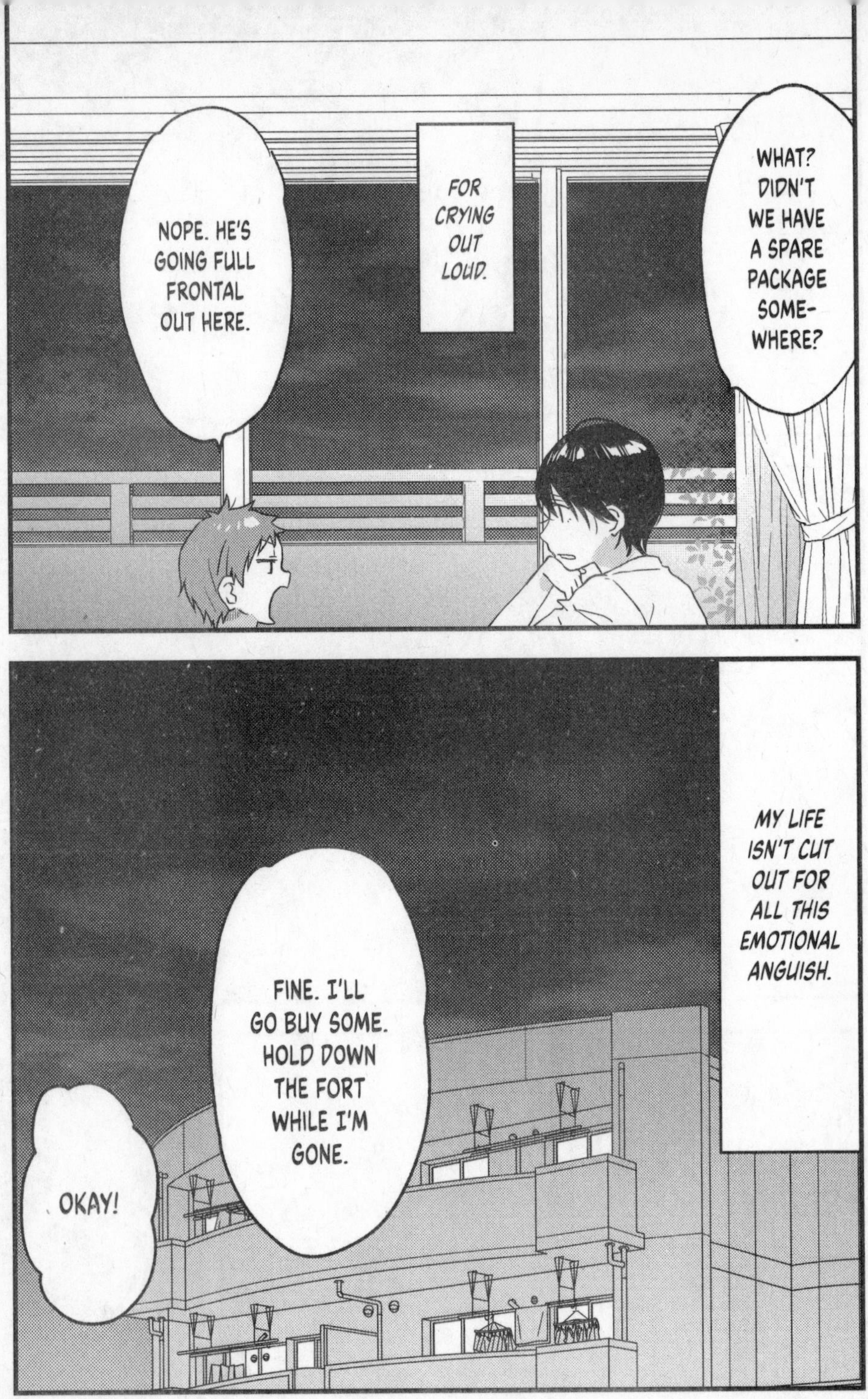
WHAT? DIDN'T WE HAVE A SPARE PACKAGE SOME-WHERE?
FOR CRYING OUT LOUD.
NOPE. HE'S GOING FULL FRONTAL OUT HERE.
MY LIFE ISN'T CUT OUT FOR ALL THIS EMOTIONAL ANGUISH.
FINE. I'LL GO BUY SOME. HOLD DOWN THE FORT WHILE I'M GONE.
OKAY!

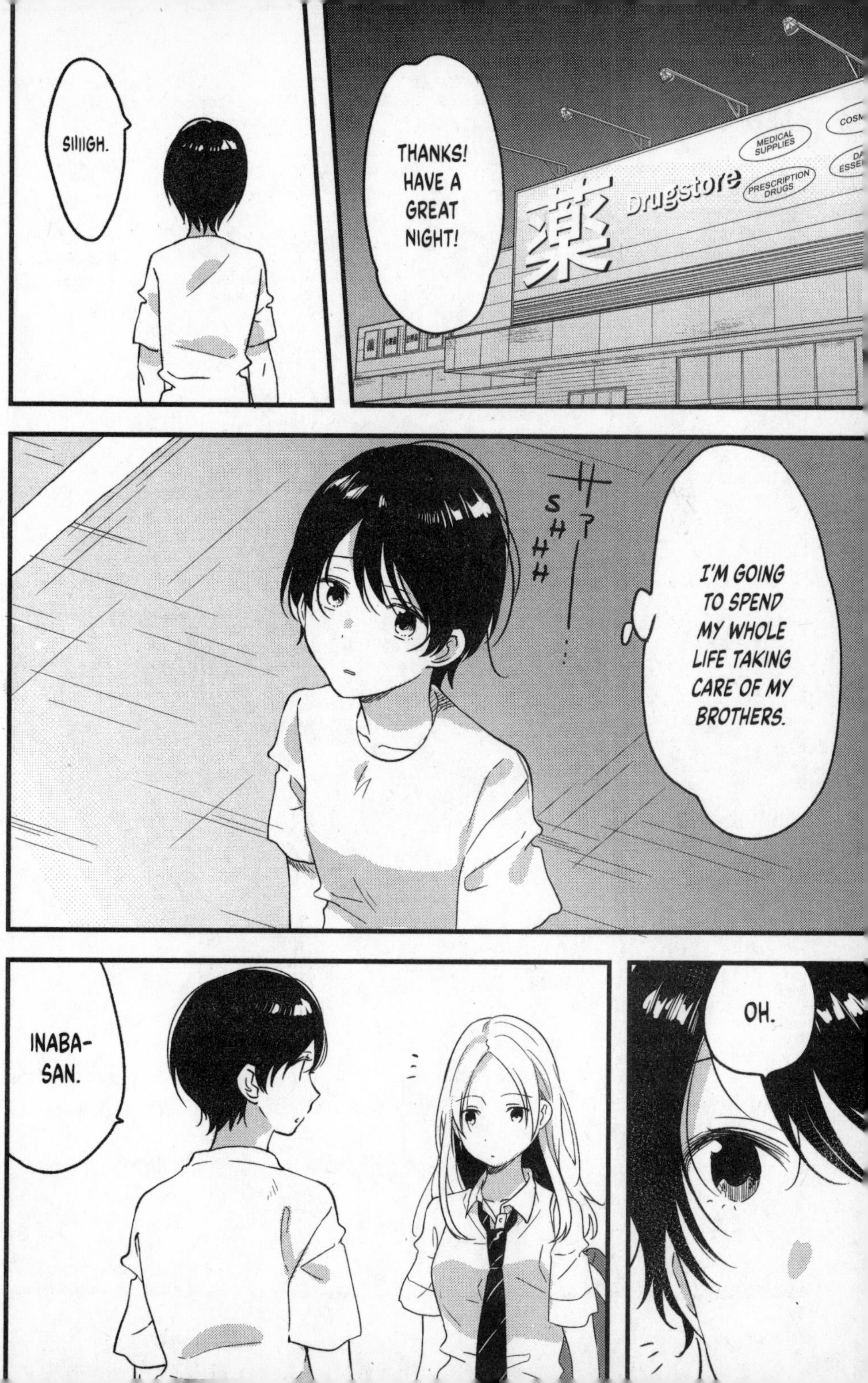
THANKS! HAVE A GREAT NIGHT!
薬 Drugstore
MEDICAL SUPPLIES
PRESCRIPTION DRUGS
SIIIGH.
I'M GOING TO SPEND MY WHOLE LIFE TAKING CARE OF MY BROTHERS.
SHHH
OH.
INABA-SAN.

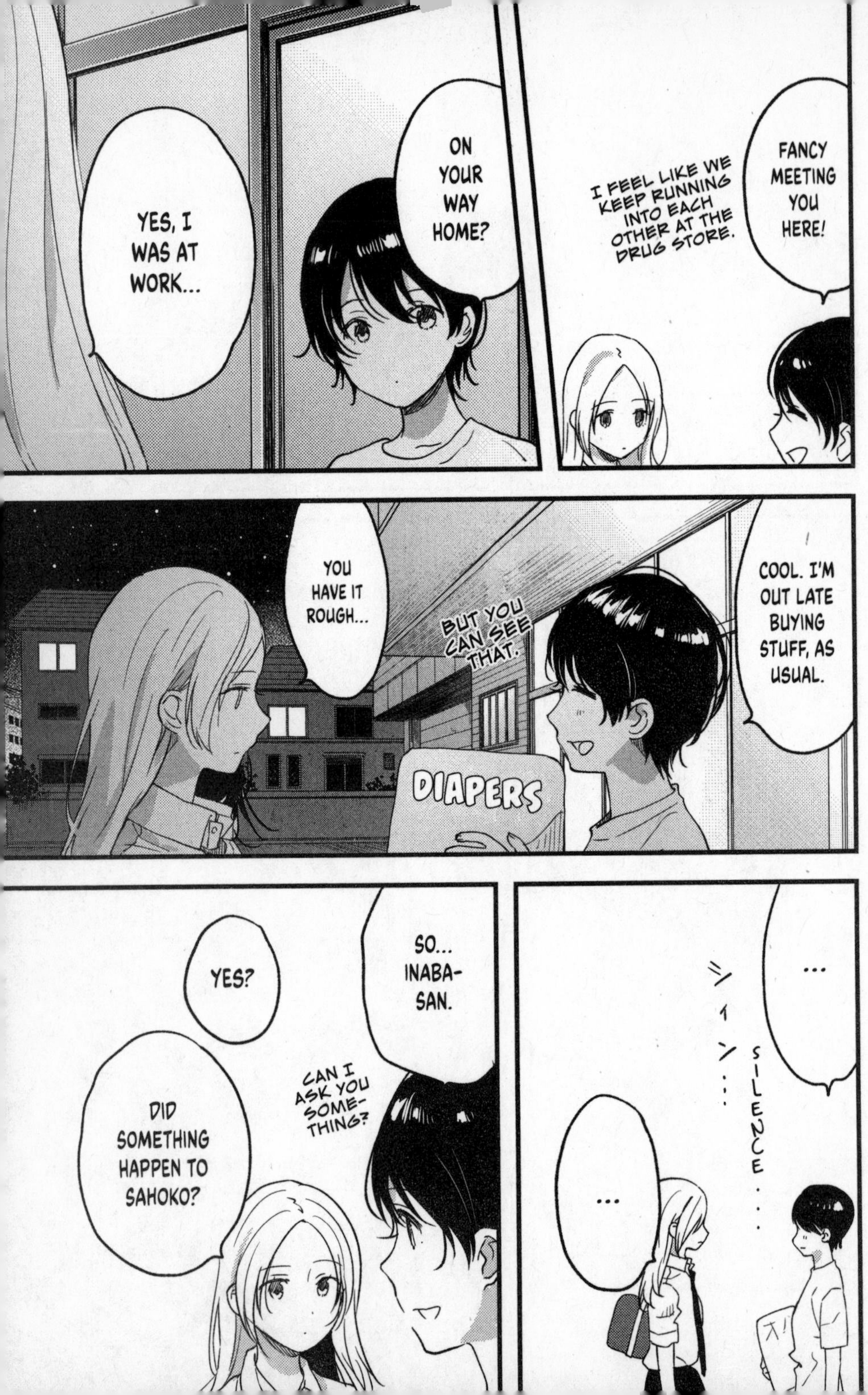
FANCY MEETING YOU HERE!
I FEEL LIKE WE KEEP RUNNING INTO EACH OTHER AT THE DRUG STORE.
ON YOUR WAY HOME?
YES, I WAS AT WORK...
COOL. I'M OUT LATE BUYING STUFF, AS USUAL.
BUT YOU CAN SEE THAT.
DIAPERS
YOU HAVE IT ROUGH...
...
シィン…
SILENCE . . .
...
SO... INABA-SAN.
YES?
CAN I ASK YOU SOMETHING?
DID SOMETHING HAPPEN TO SAHOKO?

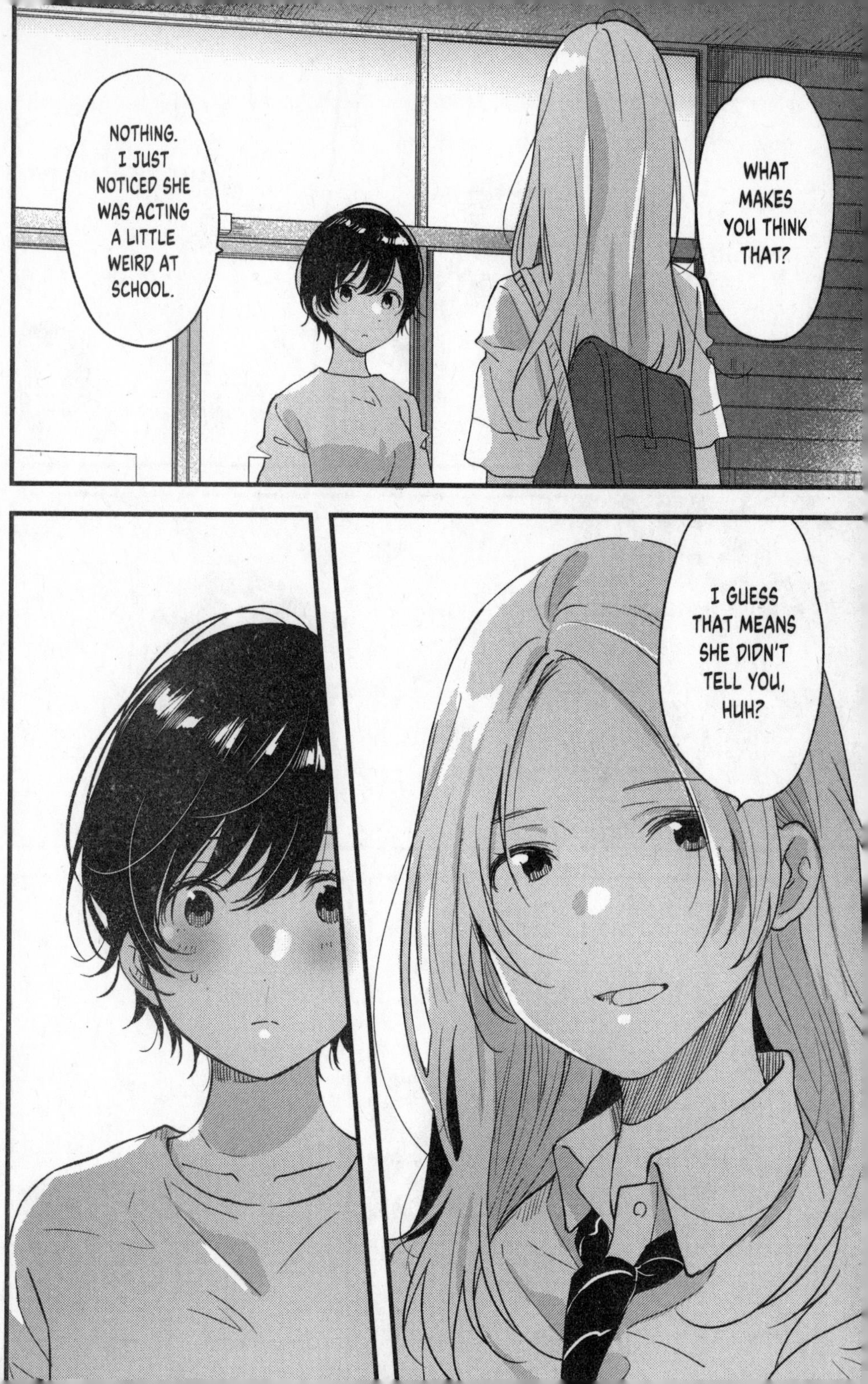
WHAT MAKES YOU THINK THAT?
NOTHING. I JUST NOTICED SHE WAS ACTING A LITTLE WEIRD AT SCHOOL.
I GUESS THAT MEANS SHE DIDN'T TELL YOU, HUH?

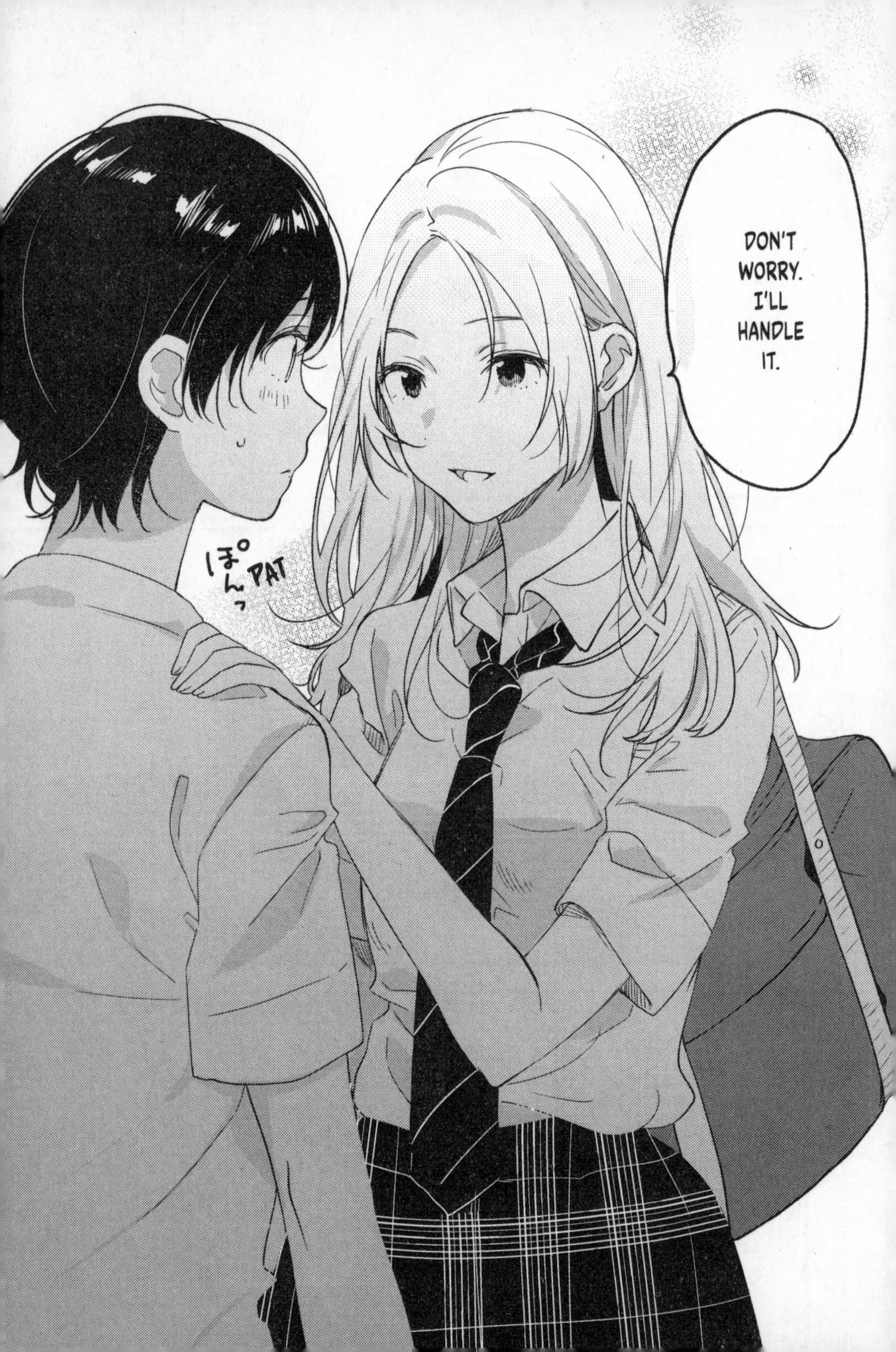
DON'T WORRY. I'LL HANDLE IT.
ぽんっ PAT

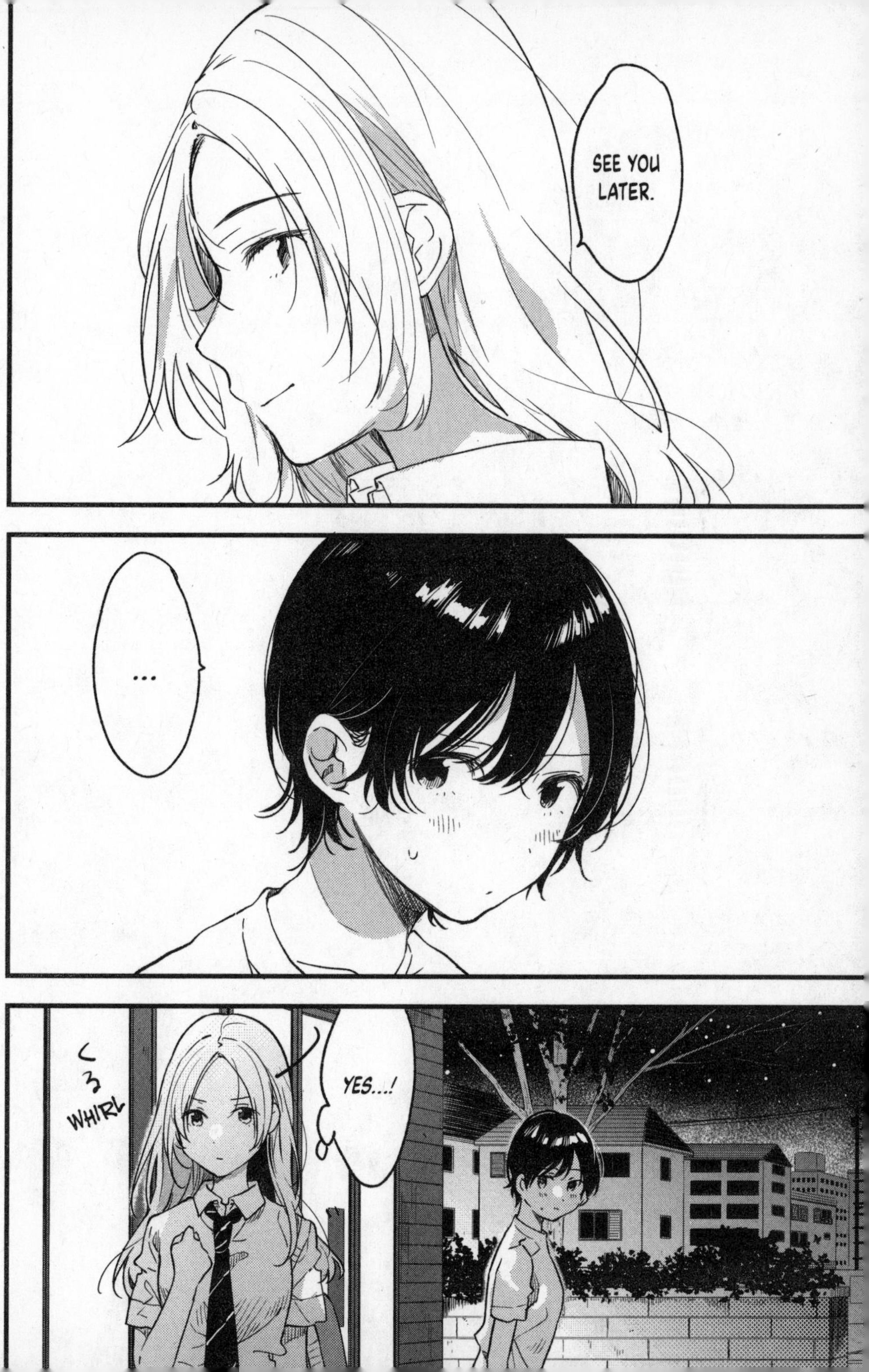
SEE YOU LATER.
...
YES...!
くる
WHIRL

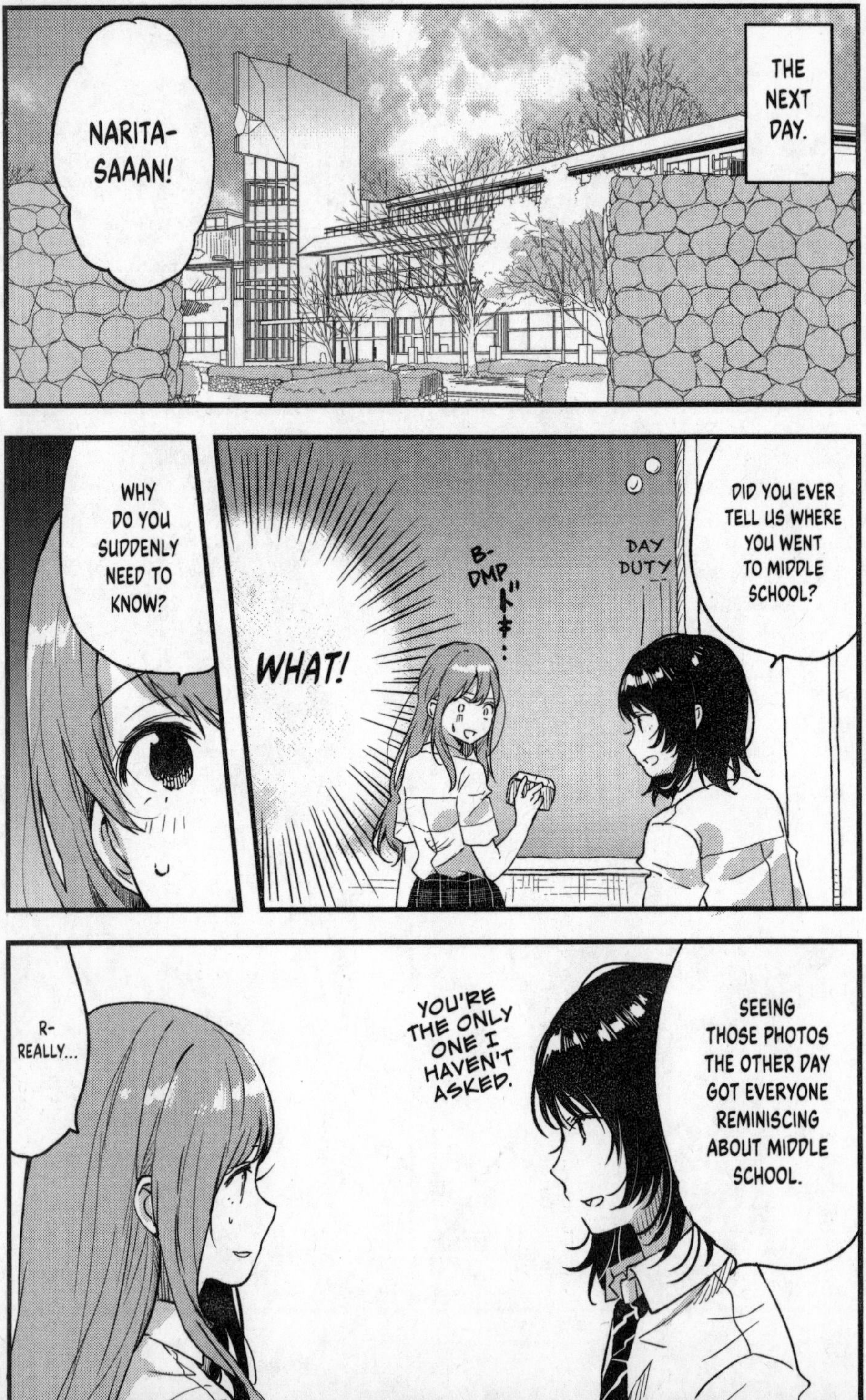
THE NEXT DAY.
NARITA-SAAAN!
DID YOU EVER TELL US WHERE YOU WENT TO MIDDLE SCHOOL?
DAY DUTY
B-DMP
ドキ
WHAT!
WHY DO YOU SUDDENLY NEED TO KNOW?
SEEING THOSE PHOTOS THE OTHER DAY GOT EVERYONE REMINISCING ABOUT MIDDLE SCHOOL.
YOU'RE THE ONLY ONE I HAVEN'T ASKED.
R-REALLY...

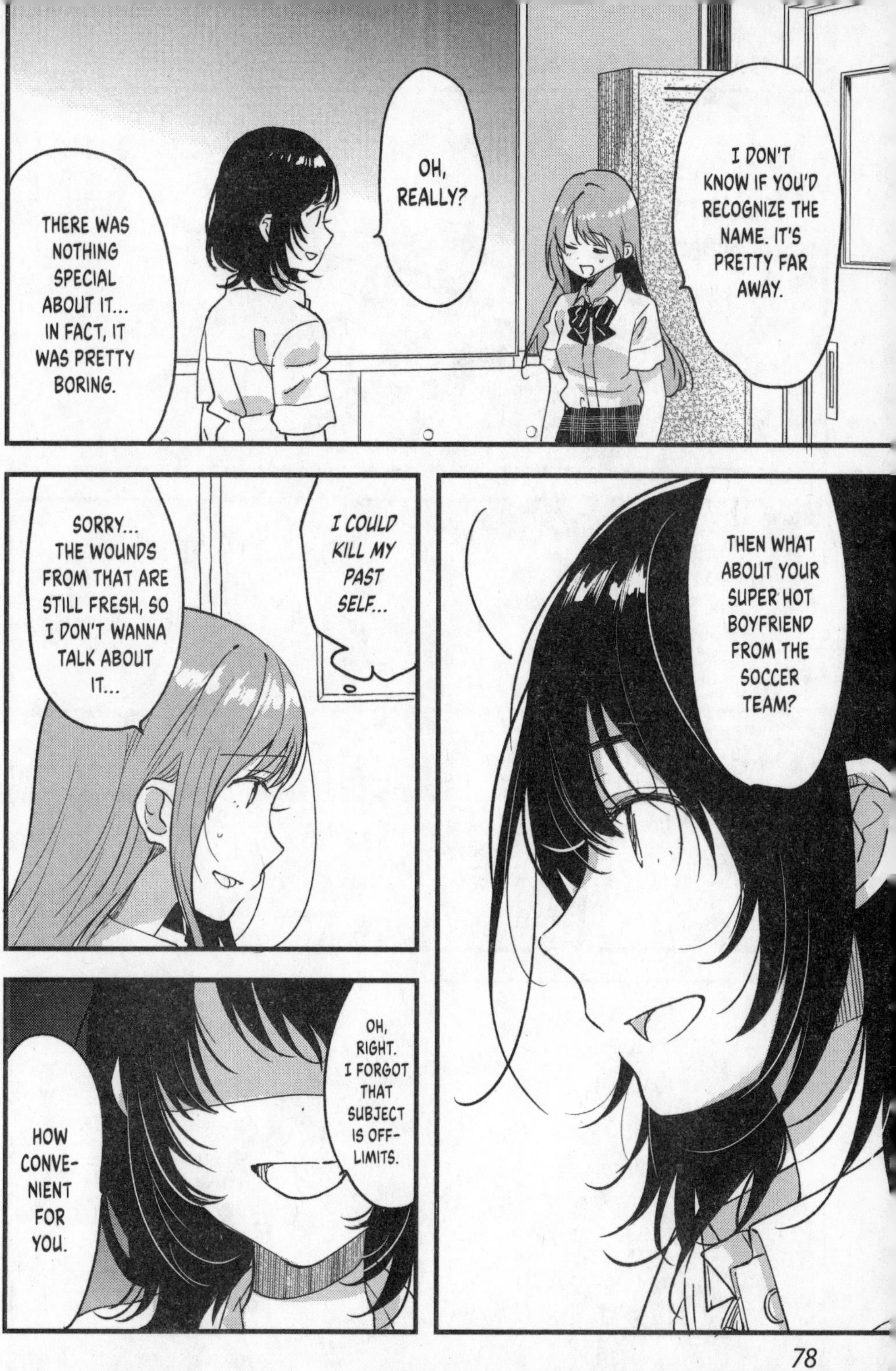
I DON'T KNOW IF YOU'D RECOGNIZE THE NAME. IT'S PRETTY FAR AWAY.
OH, REALLY?
THERE WAS NOTHING SPECIAL ABOUT IT... IN FACT, IT WAS PRETTY BORING.
THEN WHAT ABOUT YOUR SUPER HOT BOYFRIEND FROM THE SOCCER TEAM?
I COULD KILL MY PAST SELF...
SORRY... THE WOUNDS FROM THAT ARE STILL FRESH, SO I DON'T WANNA TALK ABOUT IT...
OH, RIGHT. I FORGOT THAT SUBJECT IS OFF-LIMITS.
HOW CONVE-NIENT FOR YOU.

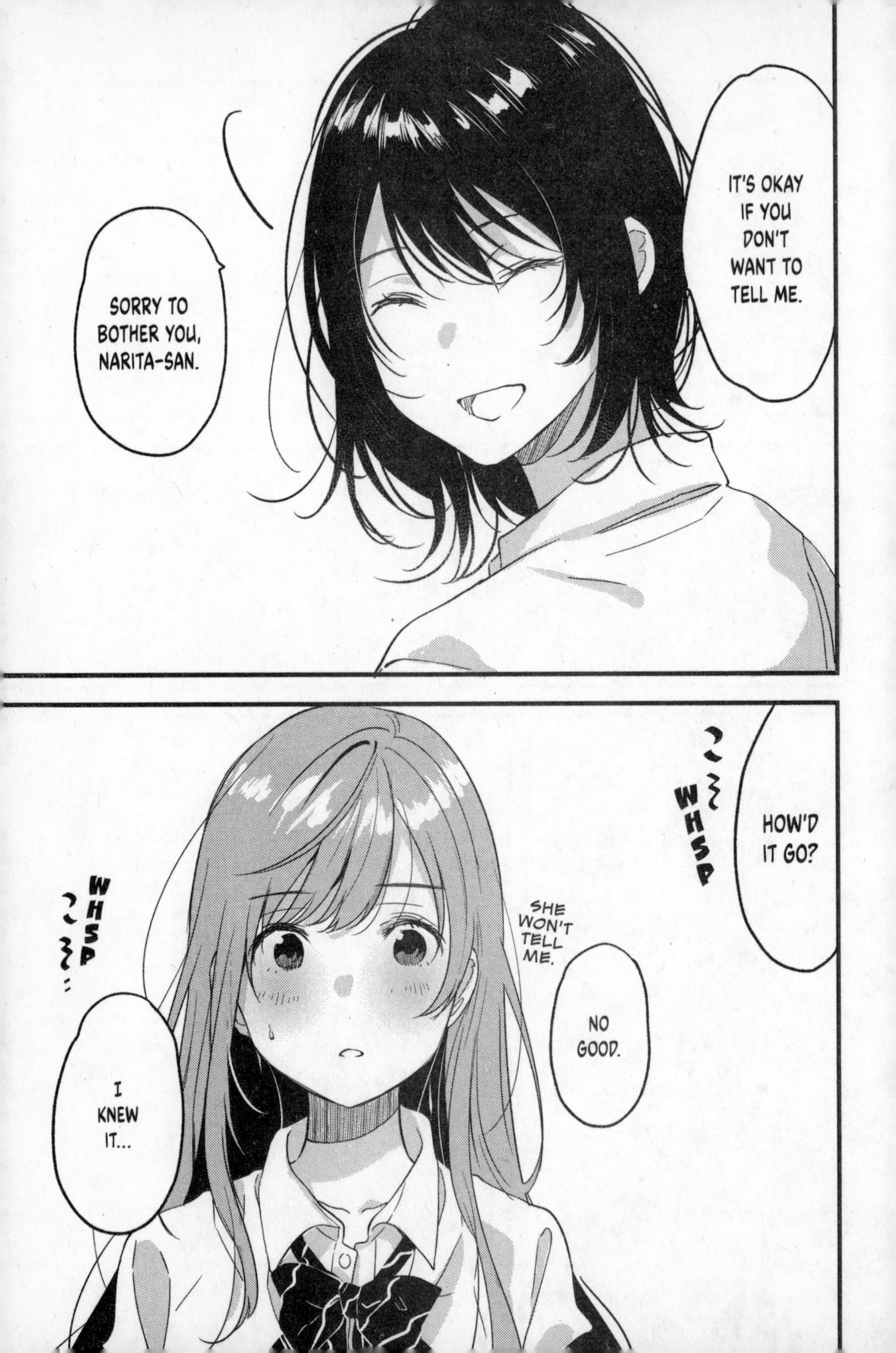
IT'S OKAY IF YOU DON'T WANT TO TELL ME.
SORRY TO BOTHER YOU, NARITA-SAN.
WHSP
HOW'D IT GO?
SHE WON'T TELL ME.
NO GOOD.
WHSP
I KNEW IT...

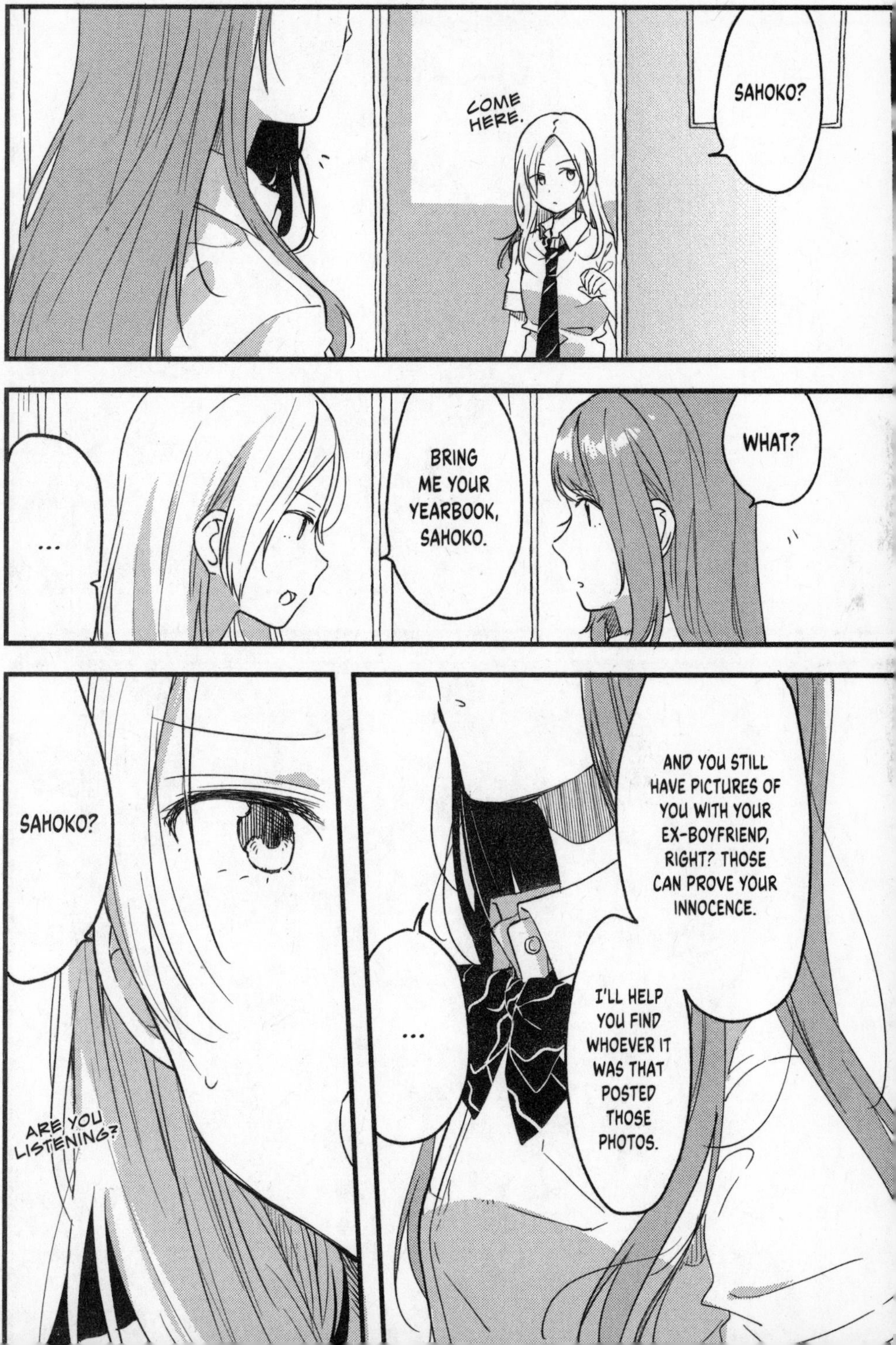
SAHOKO?
COME HERE.
WHAT?
BRING ME YOUR YEARBOOK, SAHOKO.
...
AND YOU STILL HAVE PICTURES OF YOU WITH YOUR EX-BOYFRIEND, RIGHT? THOSE CAN PROVE YOUR INNOCENCE.
I'LL HELP YOU FIND WHOEVER IT WAS THAT POSTED THOSE PHOTOS.
...
SAHOKO?
ARE YOU LISTENING?

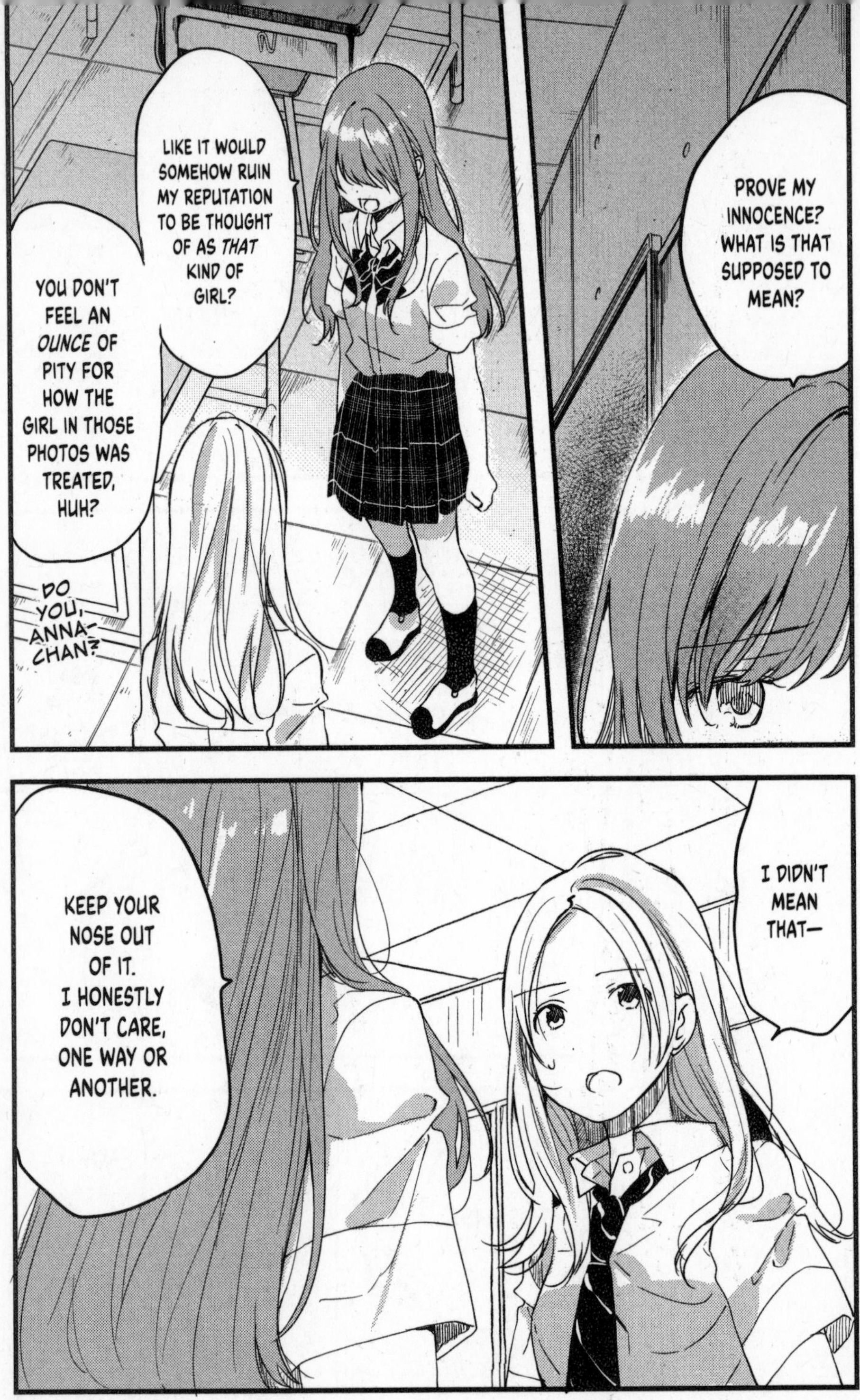
PROVE MY INNOCENCE? WHAT IS THAT SUPPOSED TO MEAN?
LIKE IT WOULD SOMEHOW RUIN MY REPUTATION TO BE THOUGHT OF AS *THAT* KIND OF GIRL?
YOU DON'T FEEL AN *OUNCE* OF PITY FOR HOW THE GIRL IN THOSE PHOTOS WAS TREATED, HUH?
DO YOU, ANNA-CHAN?
I DIDN'T MEAN THAT—
KEEP YOUR NOSE OUT OF IT. I HONESTLY DON'T CARE, ONE WAY OR ANOTHER.

WINCE

JUST LEAVE ME ALONE!

I'M SORRY, ANNA-CHAN...

I DIDN'T MEAN IT LIKE THAT. I'M SORRY.

I GUESS I'LL GO.

ANYWAY.

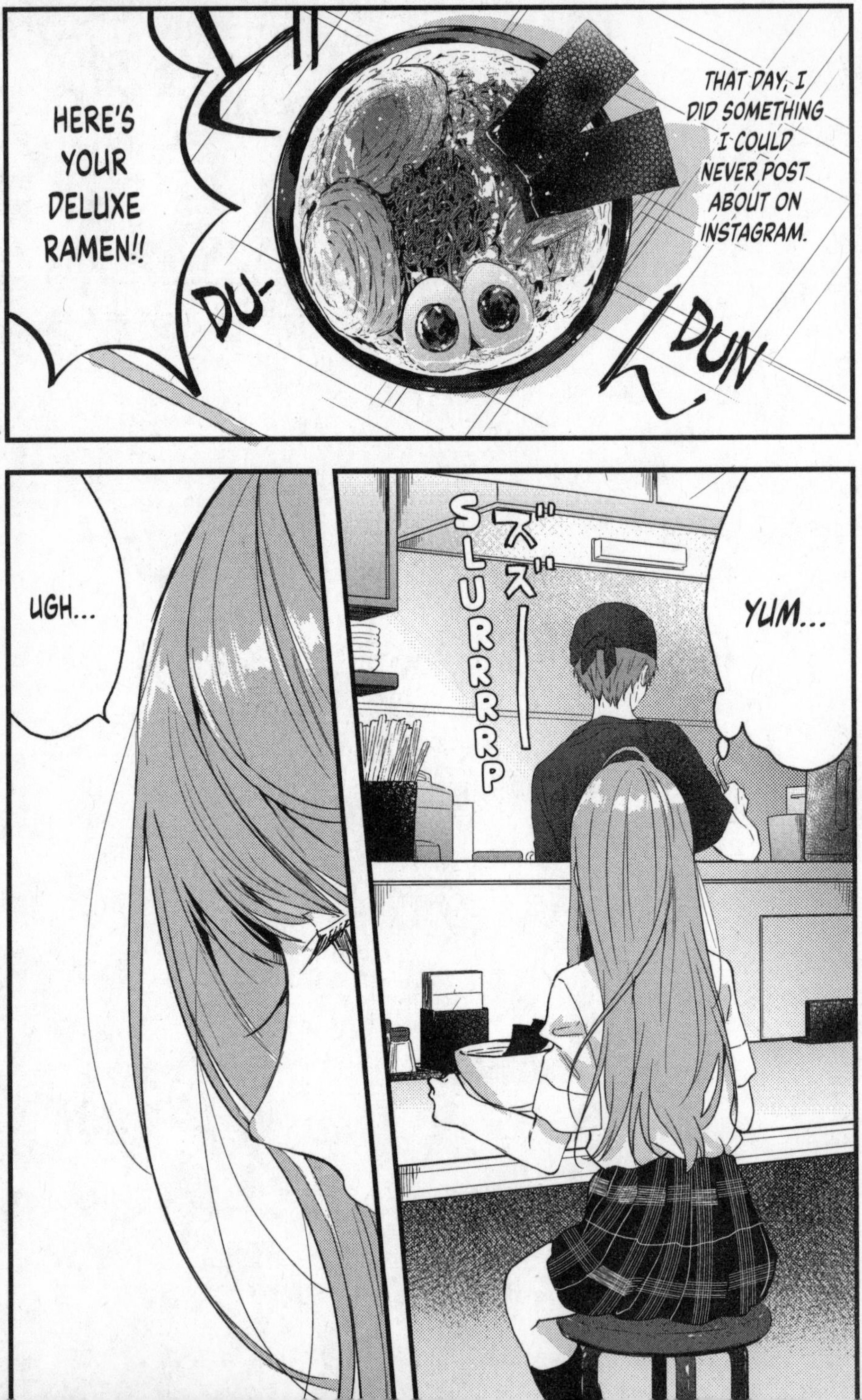
THAT DAY, I DID SOMETHING I COULD NEVER POST ABOUT ON INSTAGRAM.
HERE'S YOUR DELUXE RAMEN!!
DU-
DUN
ズズー
SLURRRRP
YUM...
UGH...

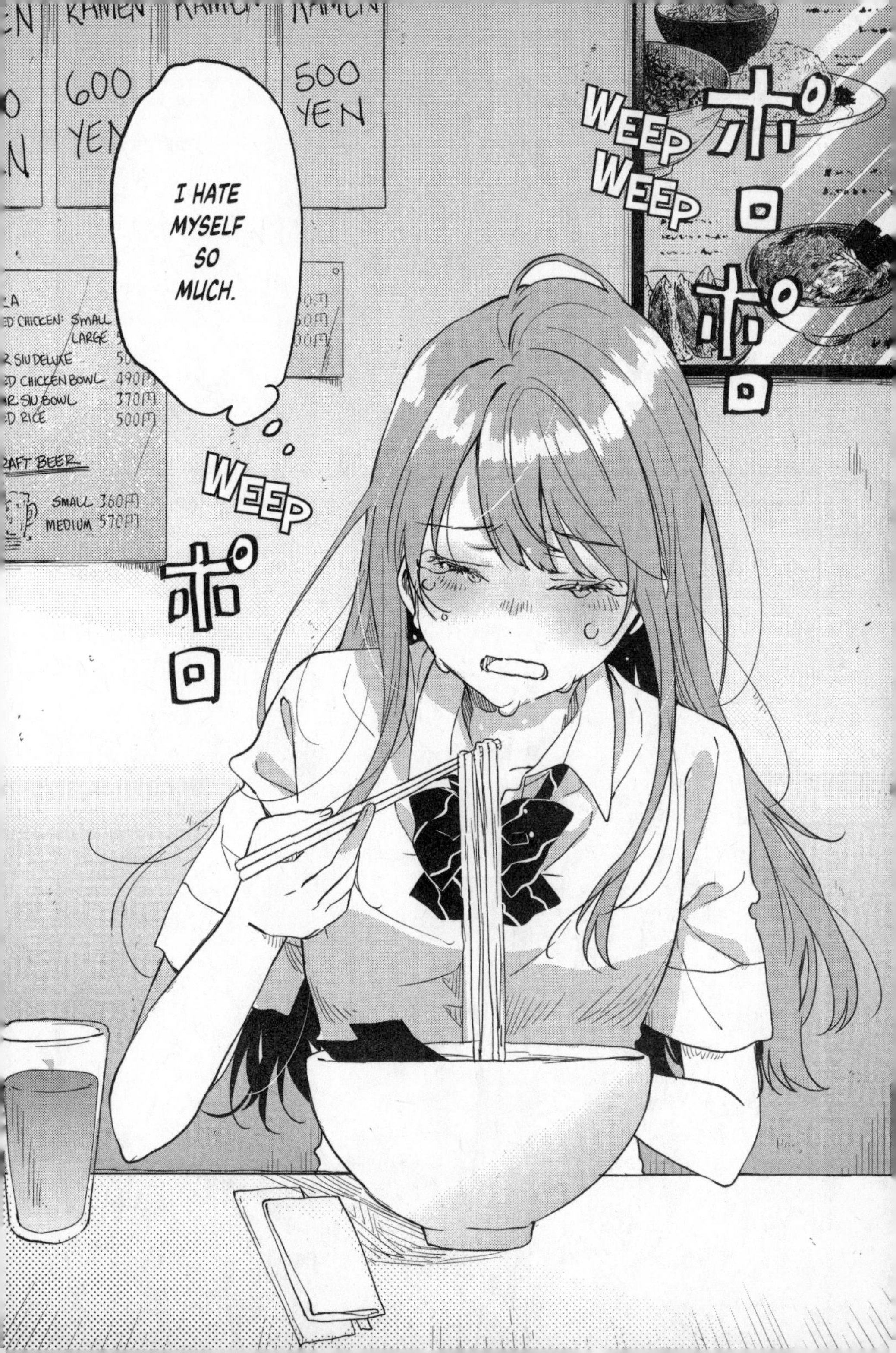

WEEP WEEP
ポロポロ
I HATE MYSELF SO MUCH.
WEEP
ポロ
600 YEN
500 YEN
SMALL 360円
MEDIUM 570円

Chapter 21:
Now It's My Turn (Part 1)

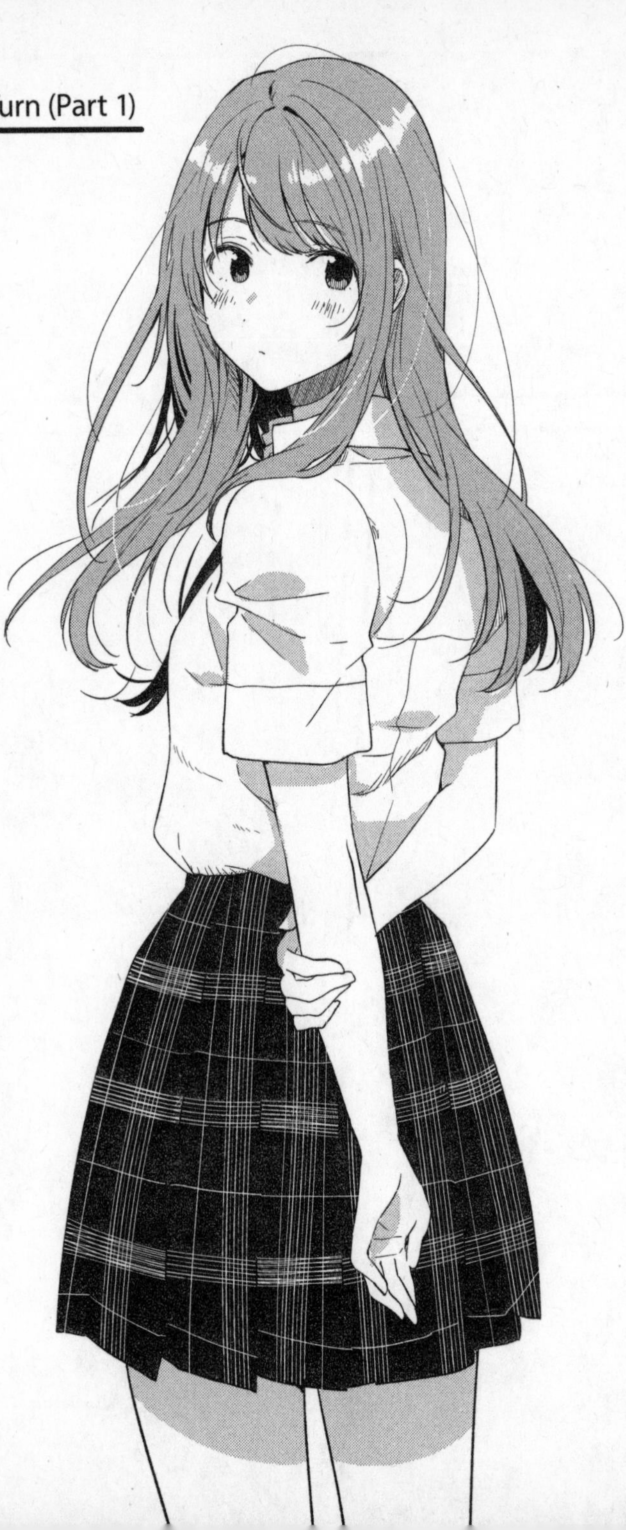

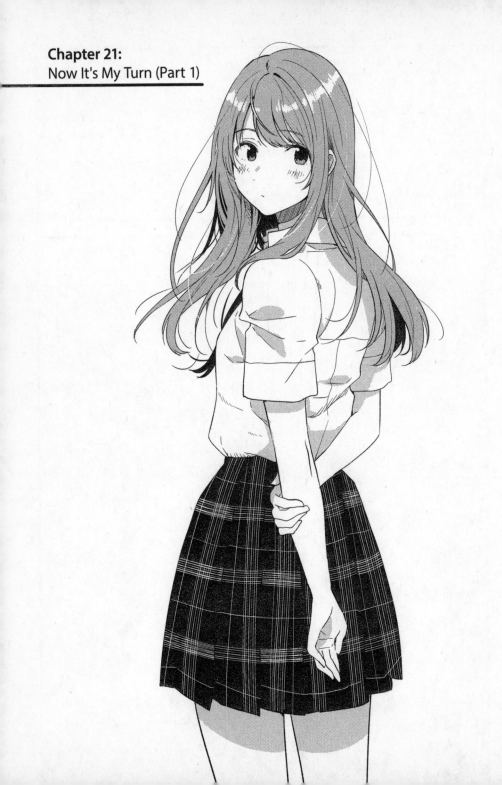

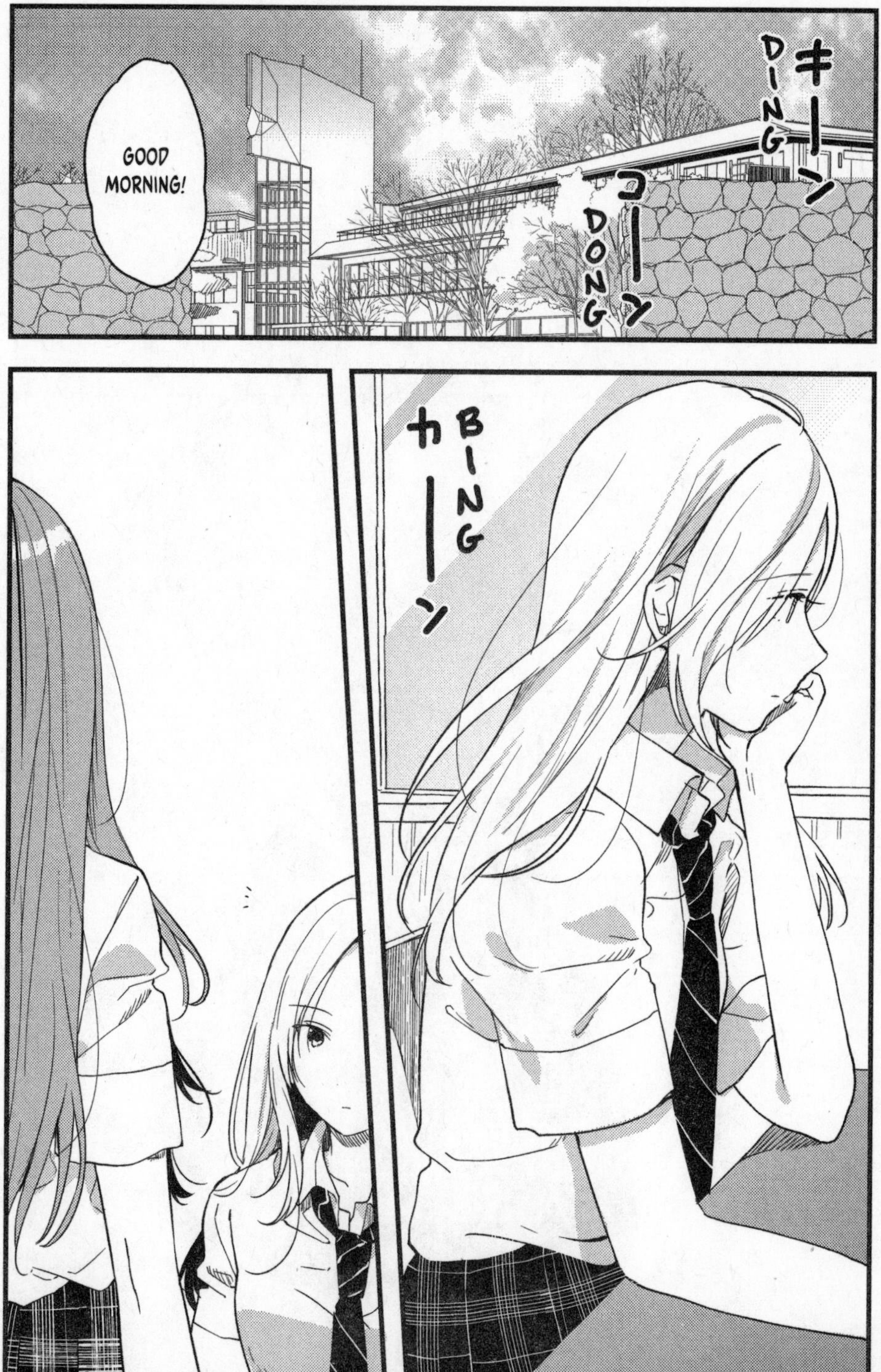

キーン
DING
コーン
DONG
GOOD MORNING!
カーン
BING

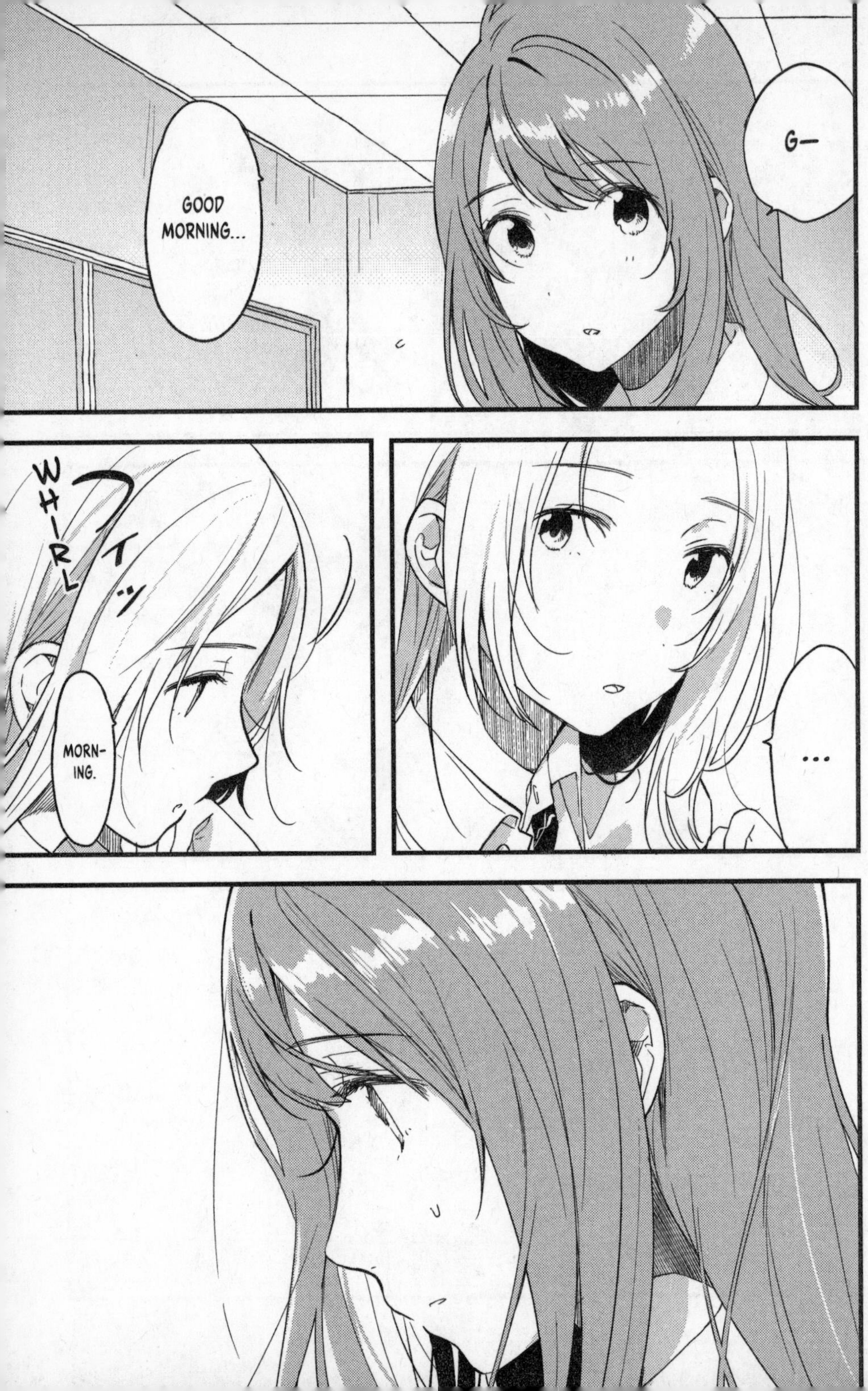
G—
GOOD MORNING...
...
WHIRL
フイッ
MORN-ING.

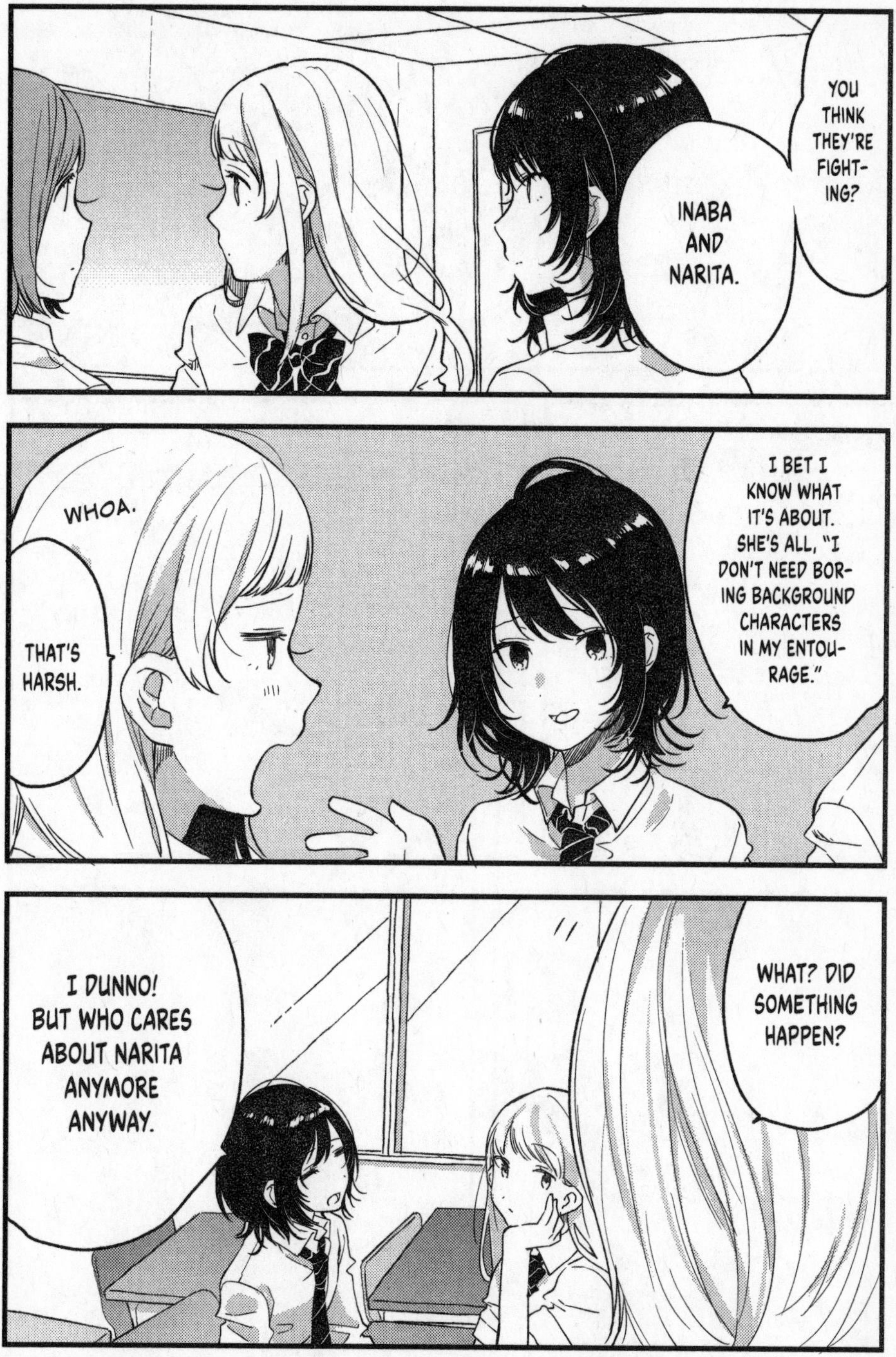
YOU THINK THEY'RE FIGHTING?
INABA AND NARITA.
I BET I KNOW WHAT IT'S ABOUT. SHE'S ALL, "I DON'T NEED BORING BACKGROUND CHARACTERS IN MY ENTOURAGE."
WHOA.
THAT'S HARSH.
WHAT? DID SOMETHING HAPPEN?
I DUNNO! BUT WHO CARES ABOUT NARITA ANYMORE ANYWAY.

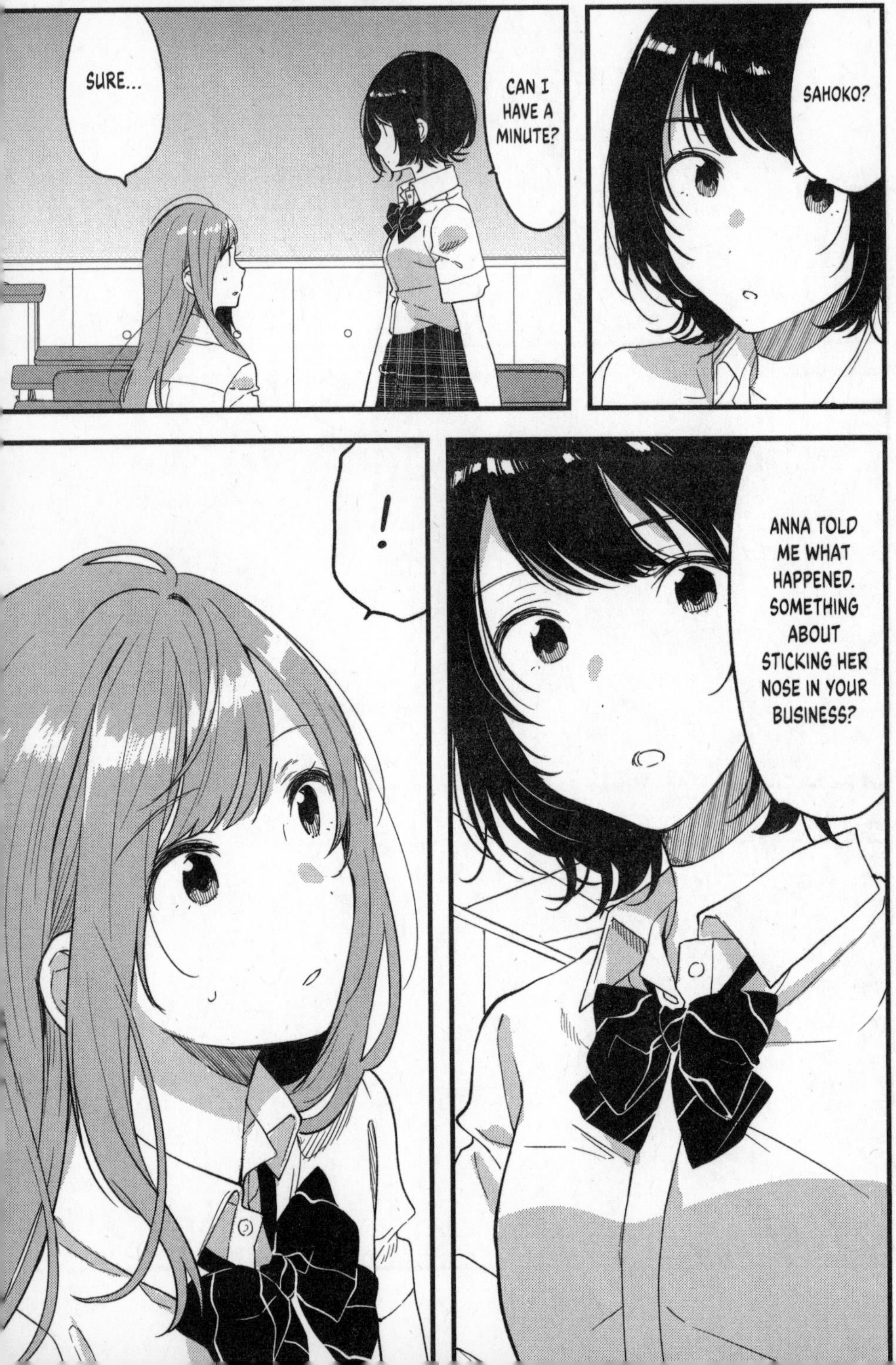
SAHOKO?
CAN I HAVE A MINUTE?
SURE...
ANNA TOLD ME WHAT HAPPENED. SOMETHING ABOUT STICKING HER NOSE IN YOUR BUSINESS?
!

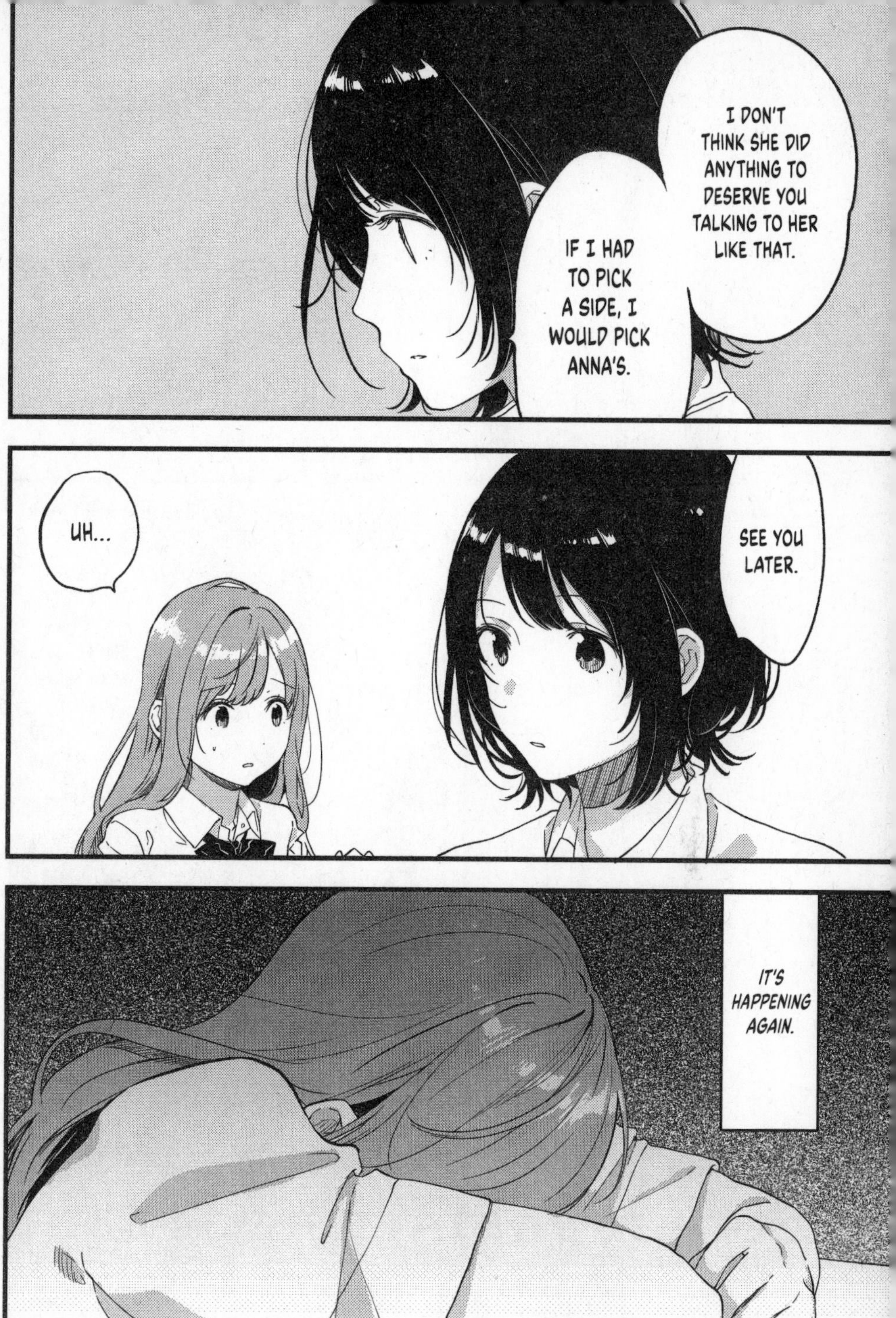
I DON'T THINK SHE DID ANYTHING TO DESERVE YOU TALKING TO HER LIKE THAT.
IF I HAD TO PICK A SIDE, I WOULD PICK ANNA'S.
SEE YOU LATER.
UH...
IT'S HAPPENING AGAIN.

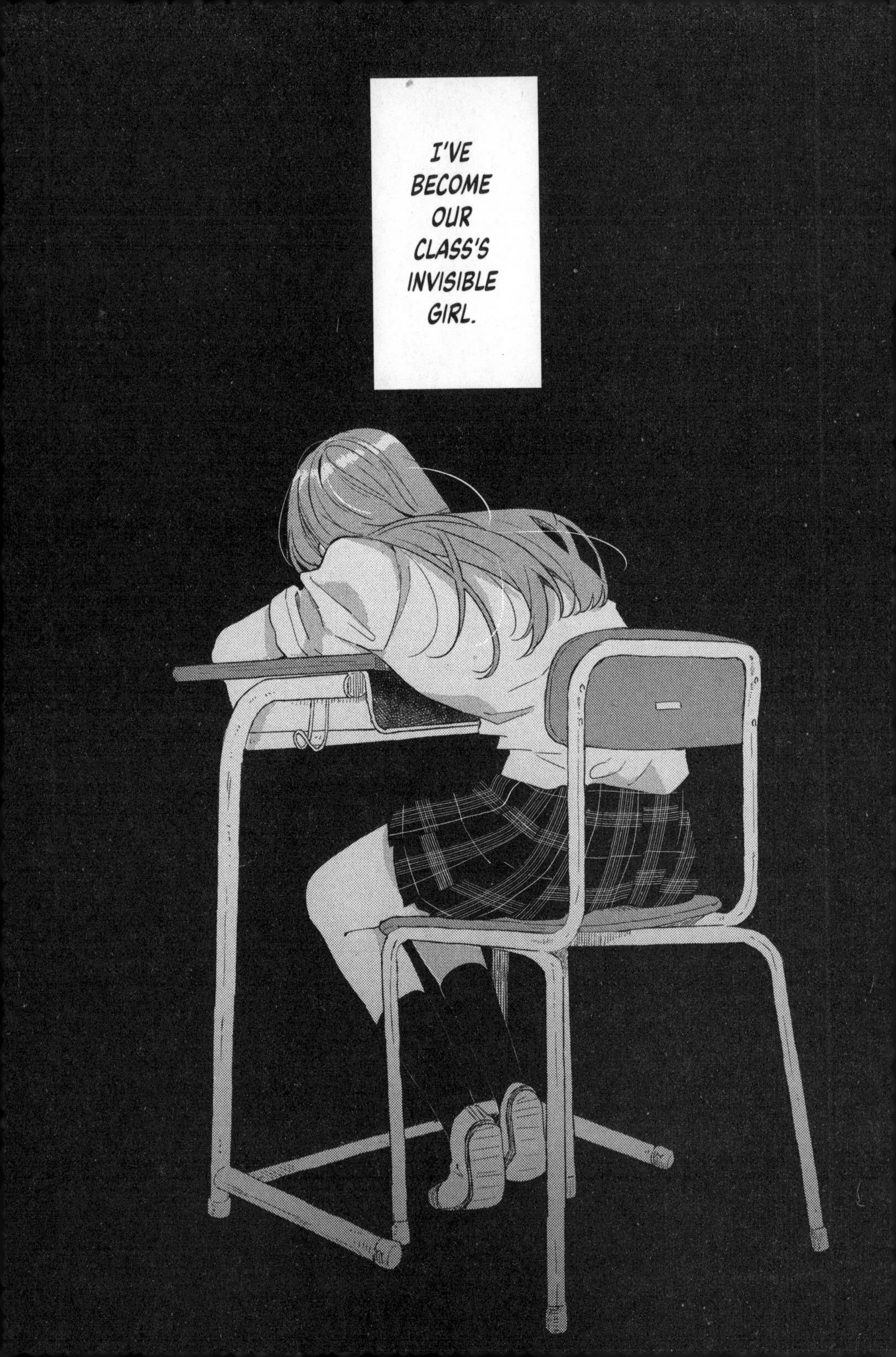
I'VE BECOME OUR CLASS'S INVISIBLE GIRL.

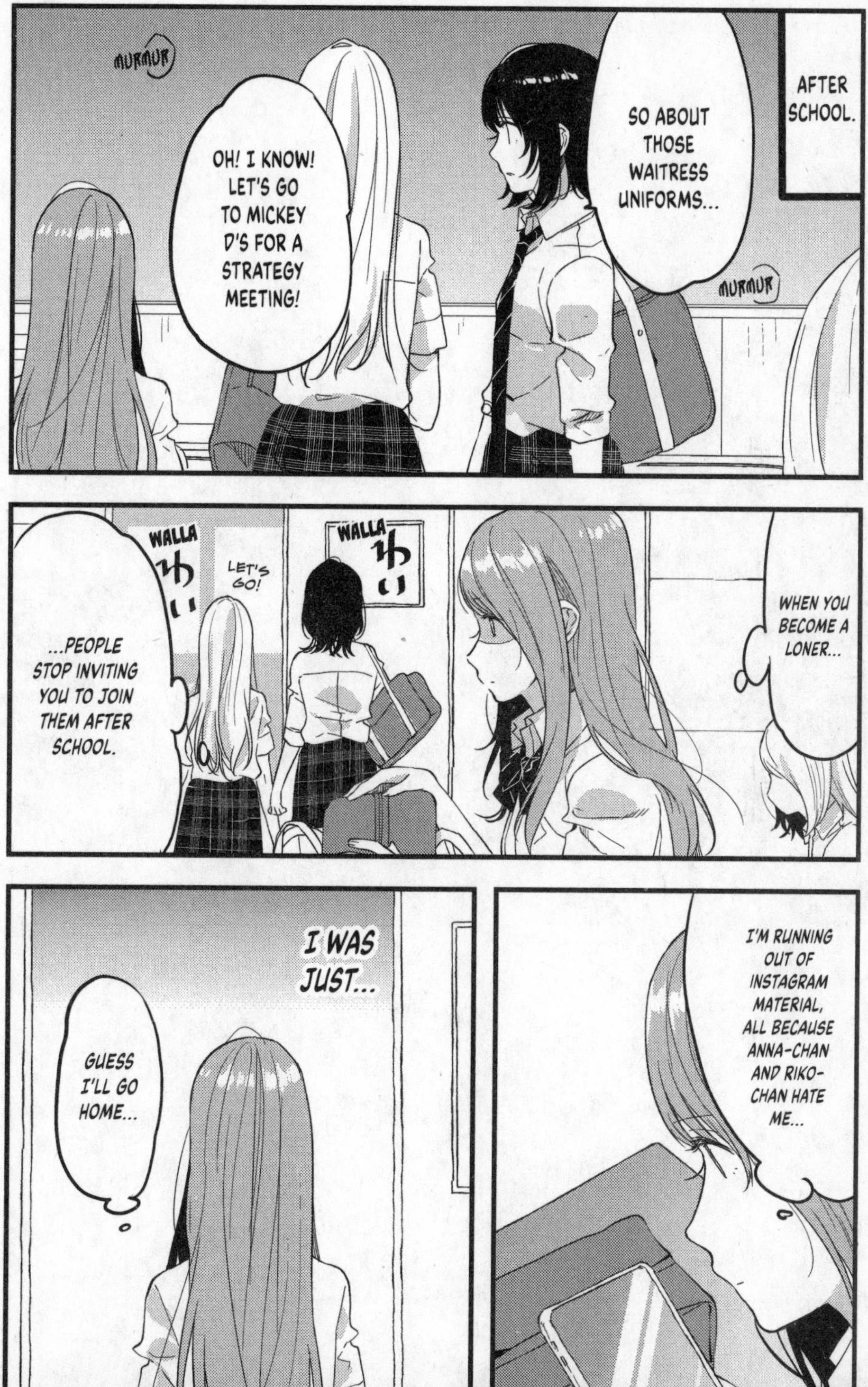
AFTER SCHOOL.
SO ABOUT THOSE WAITRESS UNIFORMS...
MURMUR
OH! I KNOW! LET'S GO TO MICKEY D'S FOR A STRATEGY MEETING!
MURMUR
WHEN YOU BECOME A LONER...
WALLA わい
LET'S GO!
WALLA わい
...PEOPLE STOP INVITING YOU TO JOIN THEM AFTER SCHOOL.
I'M RUNNING OUT OF INSTAGRAM MATERIAL, ALL BECAUSE ANNA-CHAN AND RIKO-CHAN HATE ME...
I WAS JUST...
GUESS I'LL GO HOME...

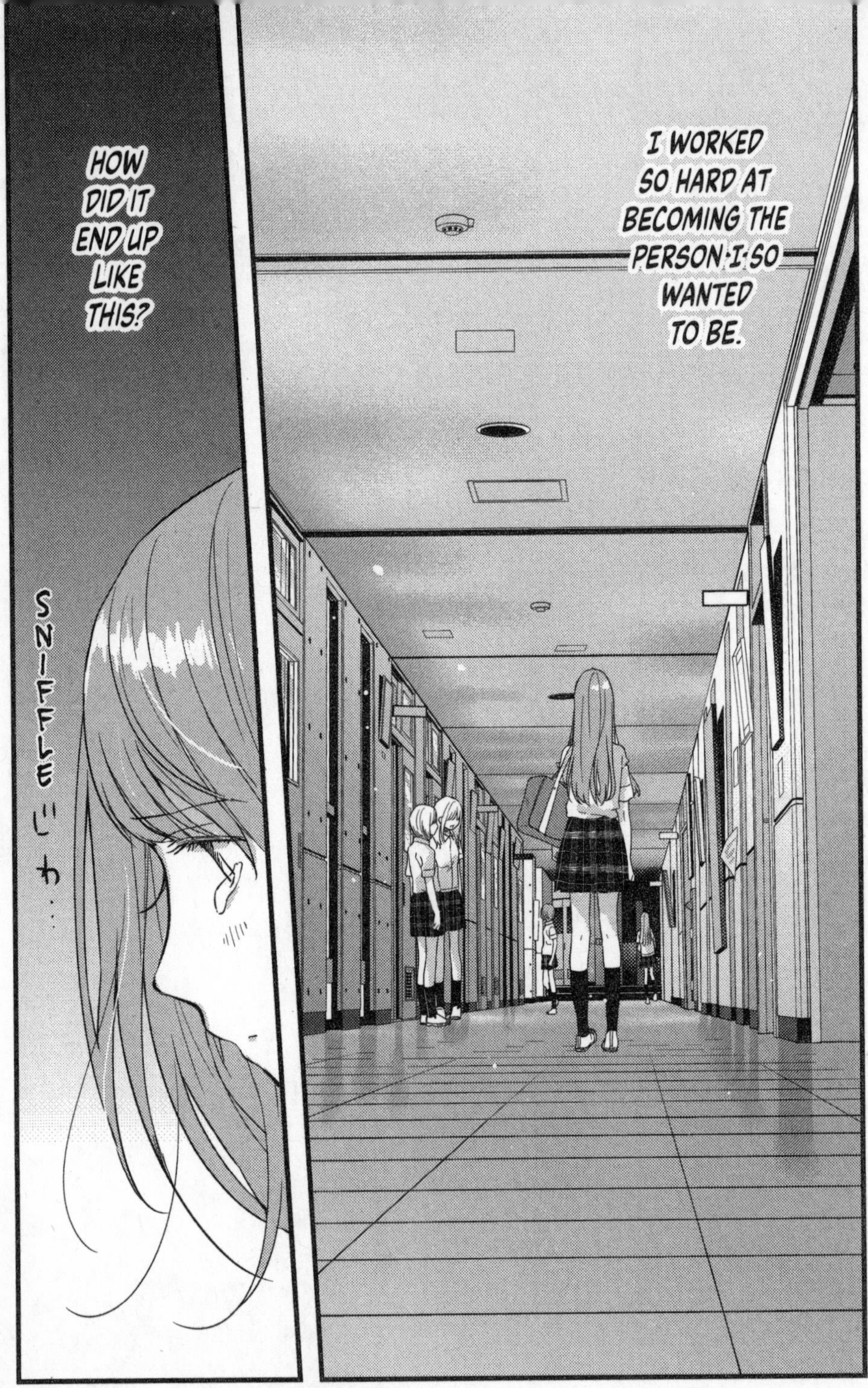
I WORKED SO HARD AT BECOMING THE PERSON I SO WANTED TO BE.
HOW DID IT END UP LIKE THIS?
SNIFFLE
じわ…

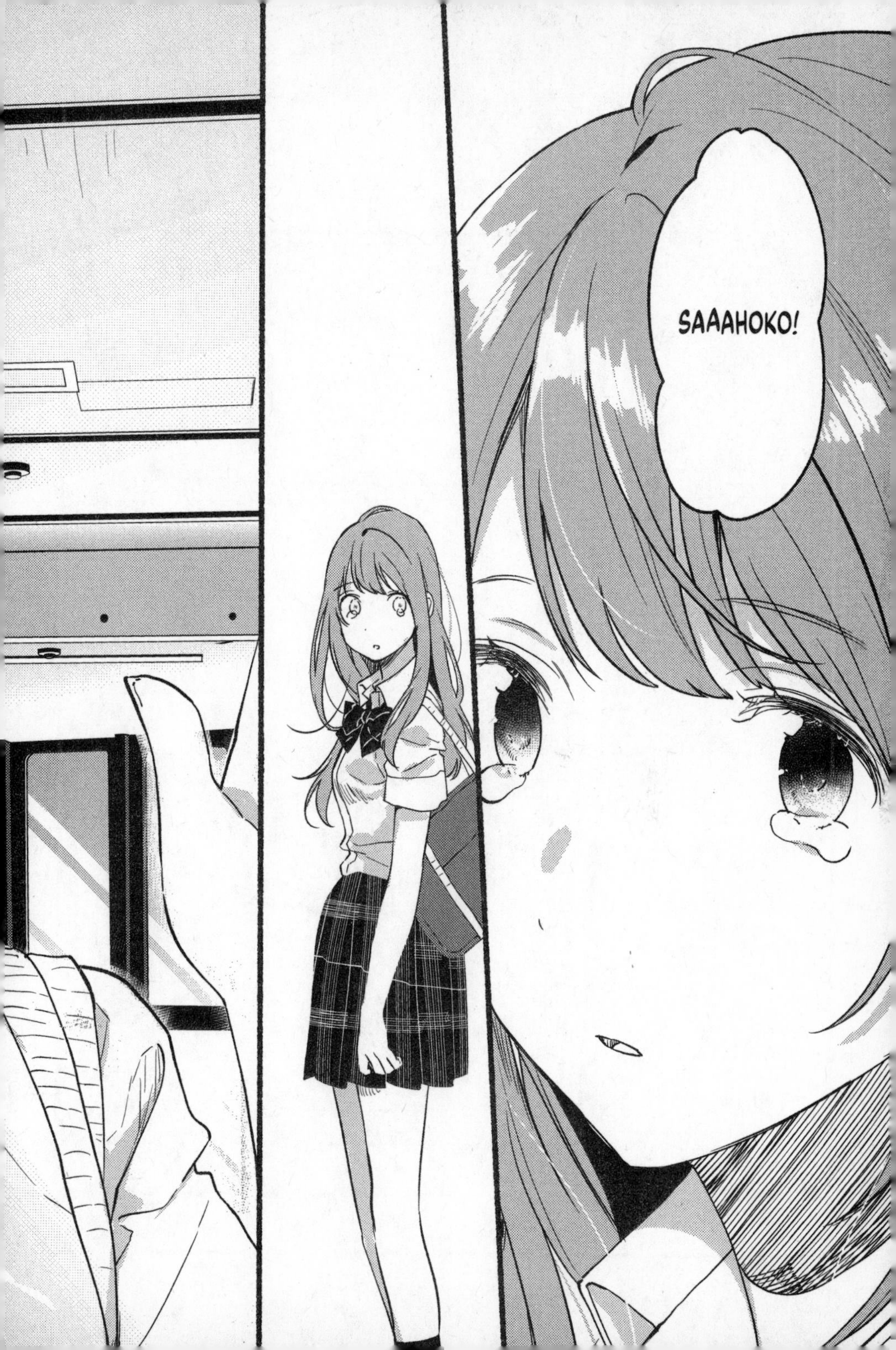
SAAAHOKO!

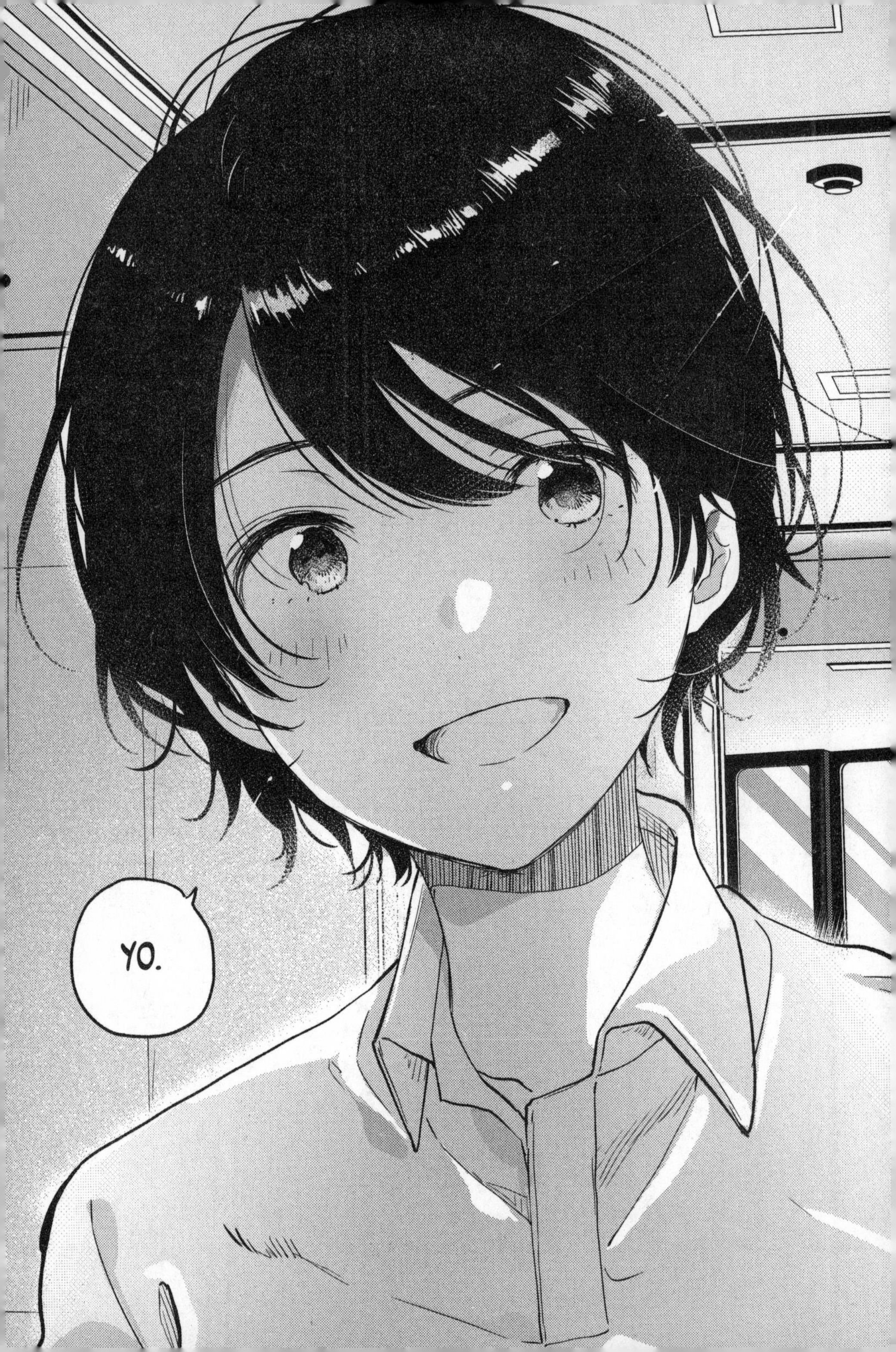
YO.

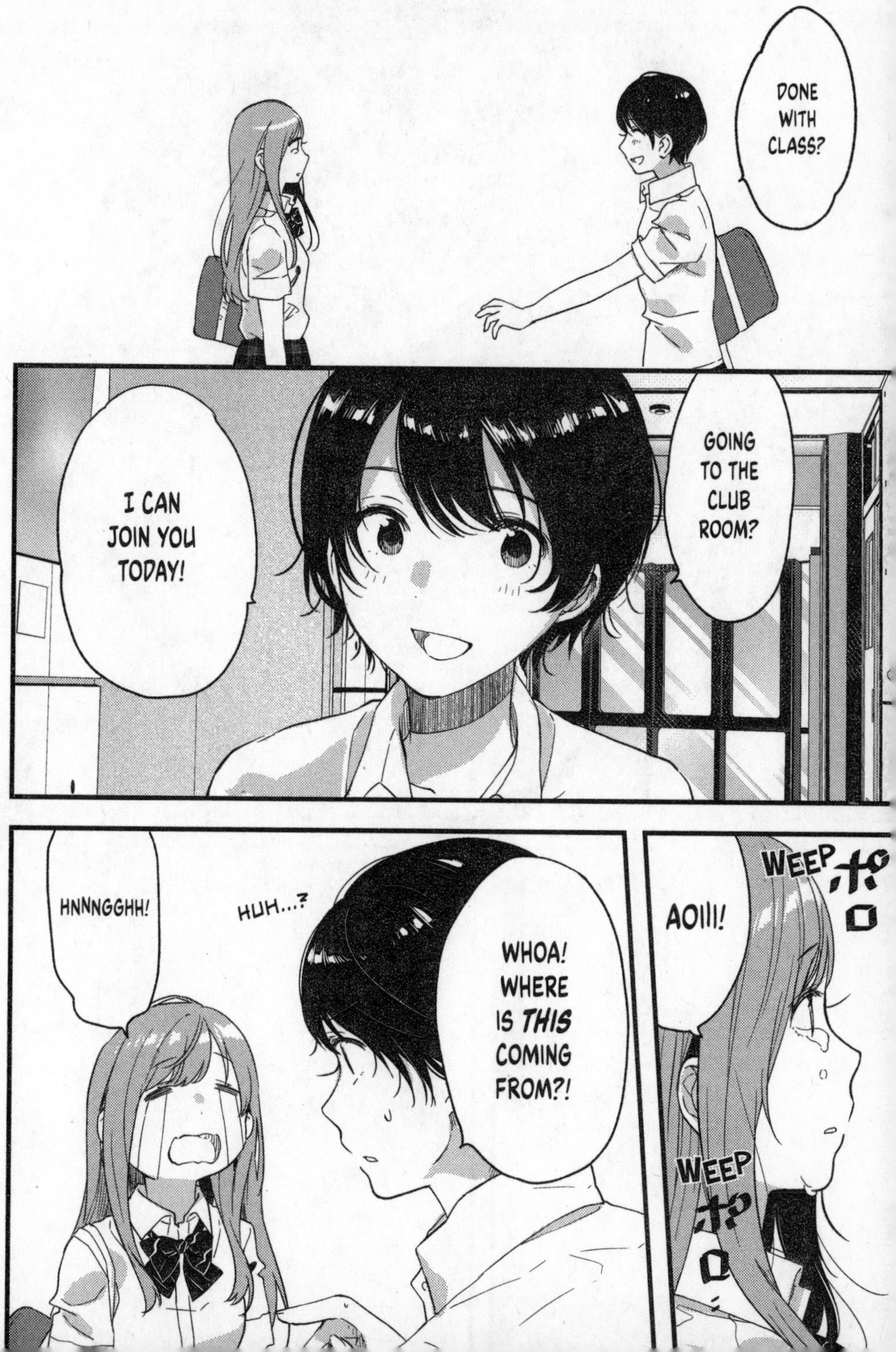
DONE WITH CLASS?
GOING TO THE CLUB ROOM?
I CAN JOIN YOU TODAY!
WEEP
AOIII!
WEEP
WHOA! WHERE IS *THIS* COMING FROM?!
HUH...?
HNNNGGHH!

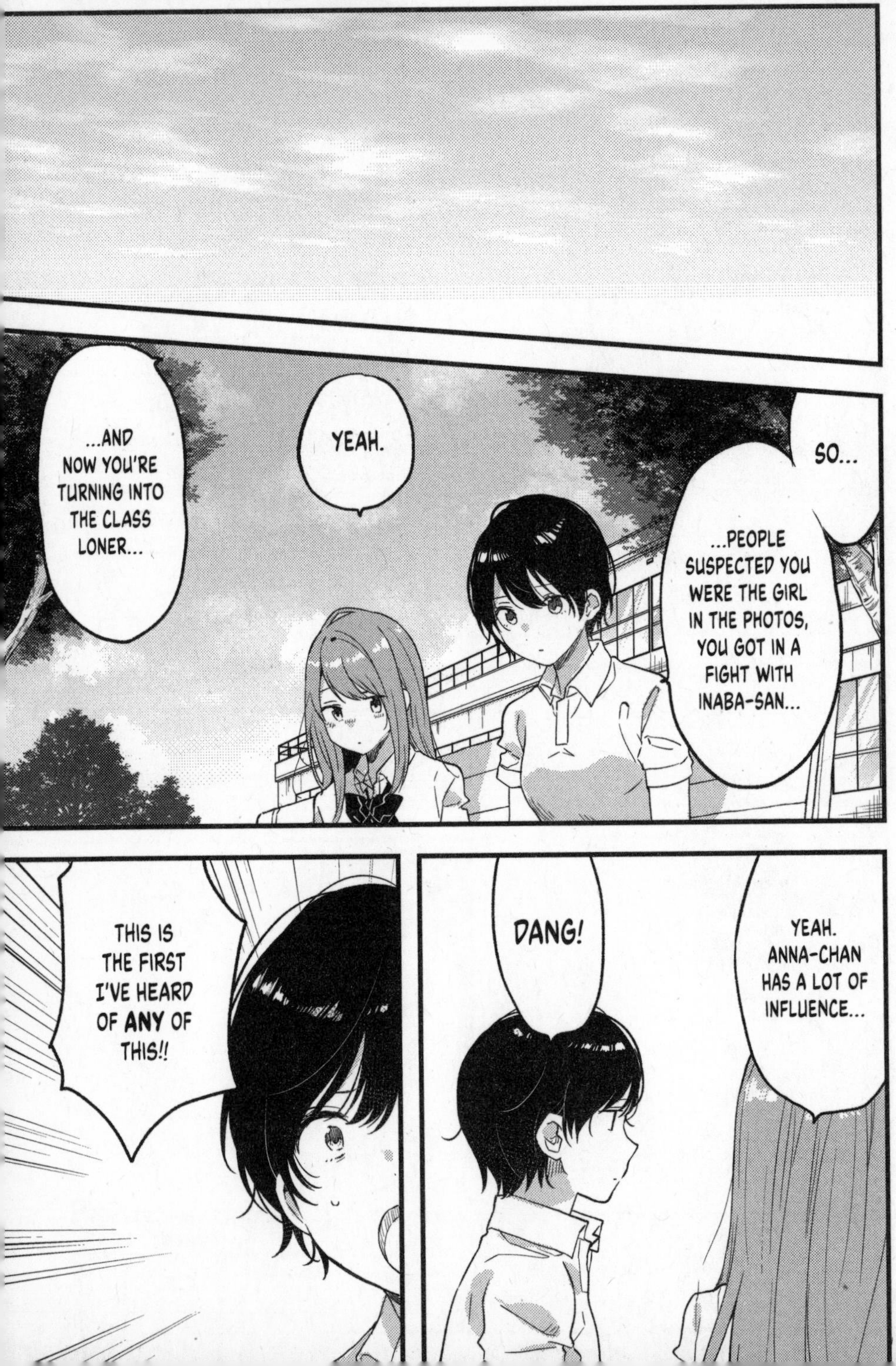
SO...
...PEOPLE SUSPECTED YOU WERE THE GIRL IN THE PHOTOS, YOU GOT IN A FIGHT WITH INABA-SAN...
YEAH.
...AND NOW YOU'RE TURNING INTO THE CLASS LONER...
YEAH. ANNA-CHAN HAS A LOT OF INFLUENCE...
DANG!
THIS IS THE FIRST I'VE HEARD OF **ANY** OF THIS!!

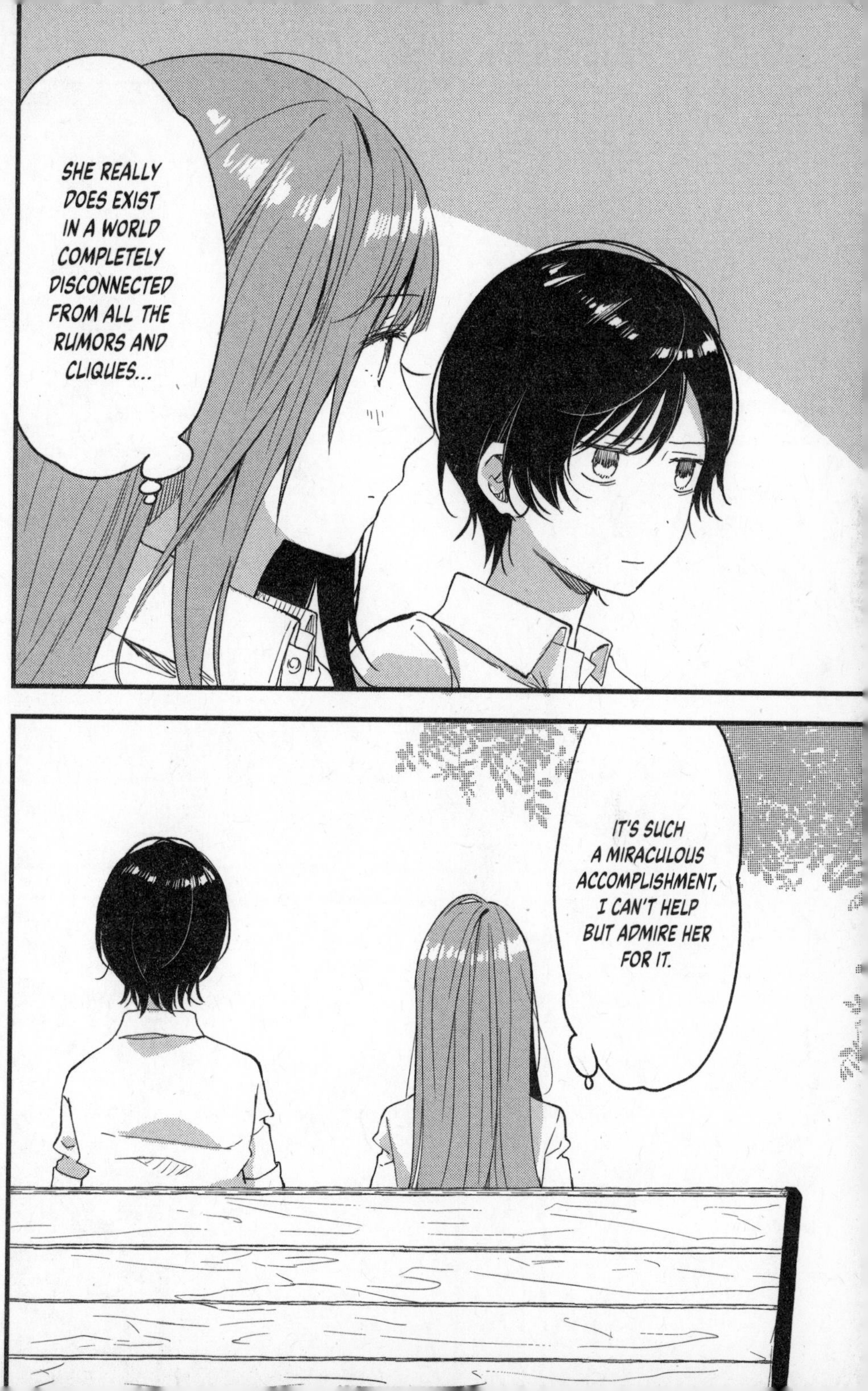
SHE REALLY DOES EXIST IN A WORLD COMPLETELY DISCONNECTED FROM ALL THE RUMORS AND CLIQUES...
IT'S SUCH A MIRACULOUS ACCOMPLISHMENT, I CAN'T HELP BUT ADMIRE HER FOR IT.

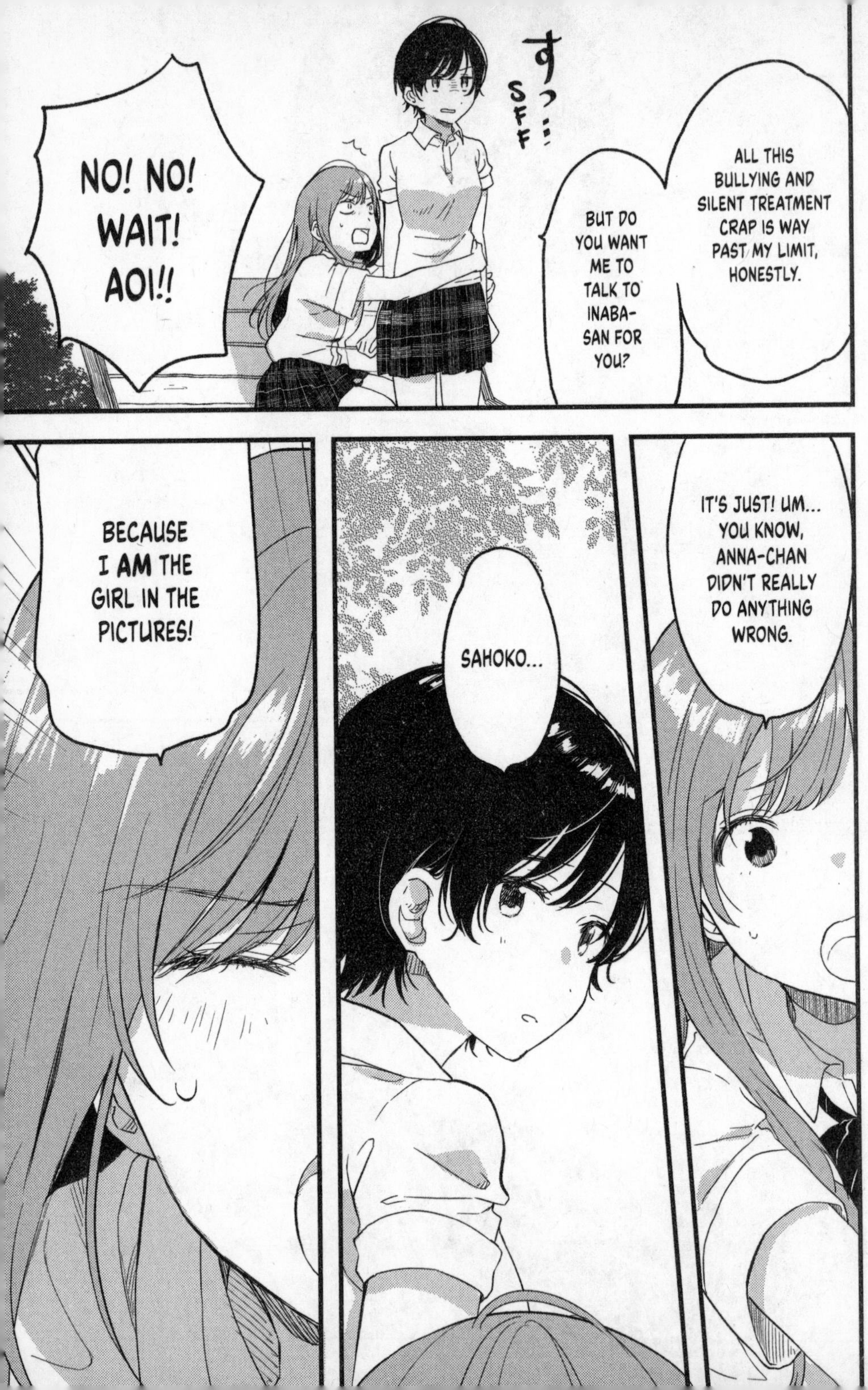
ALL THIS BULLYING AND SILENT TREATMENT CRAP IS WAY PAST MY LIMIT, HONESTLY.
BUT DO YOU WANT ME TO TALK TO INABA-SAN FOR YOU?
すっ
SFF
NO! NO! WAIT! AOI!!
IT'S JUST! UM... YOU KNOW, ANNA-CHAN DIDN'T REALLY DO ANYTHING WRONG.
SAHOKO...
BECAUSE I **AM** THE GIRL IN THE PICTURES!

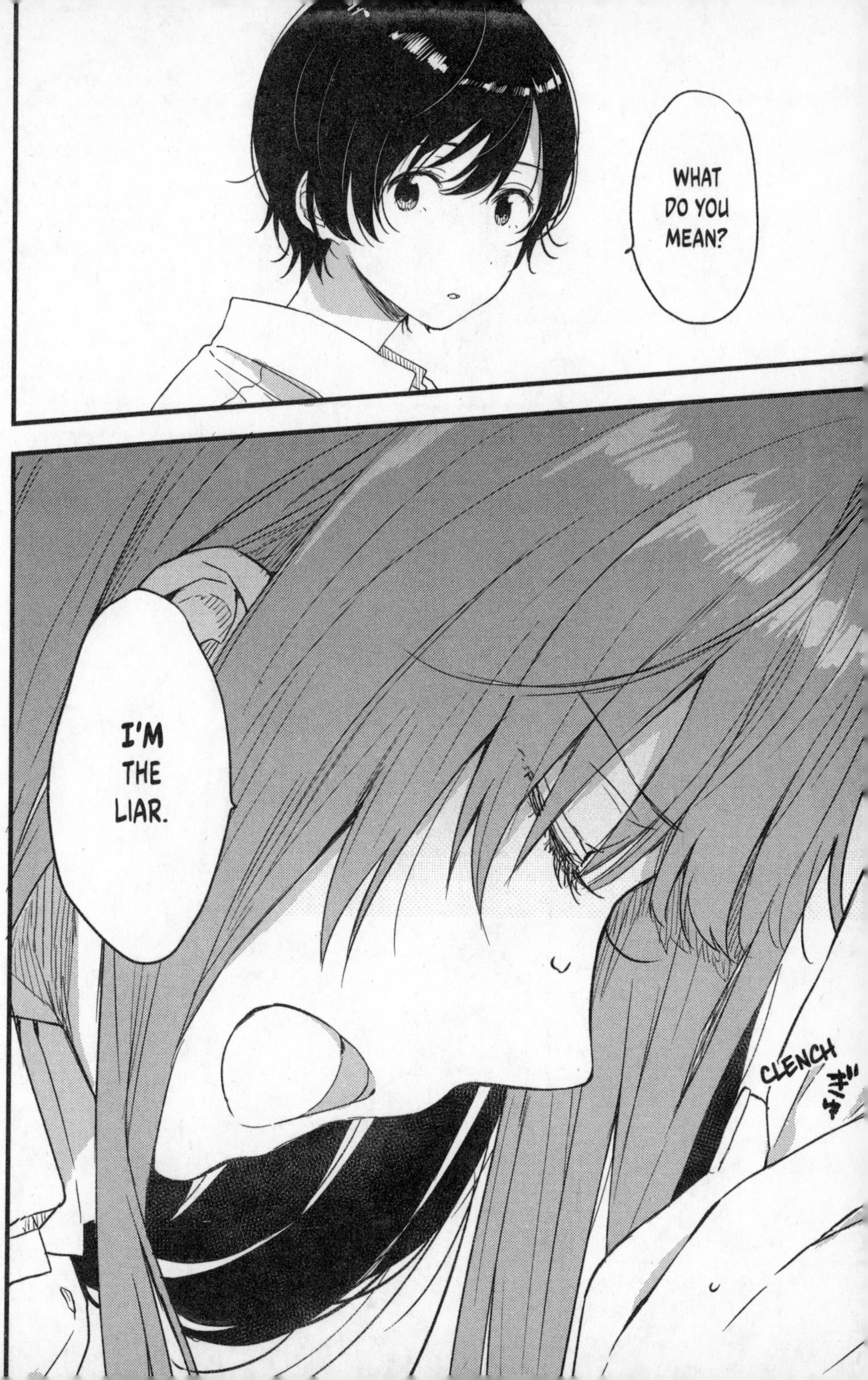
WHAT DO YOU MEAN?
I'M THE LIAR.
CLENCH
ぎゅ

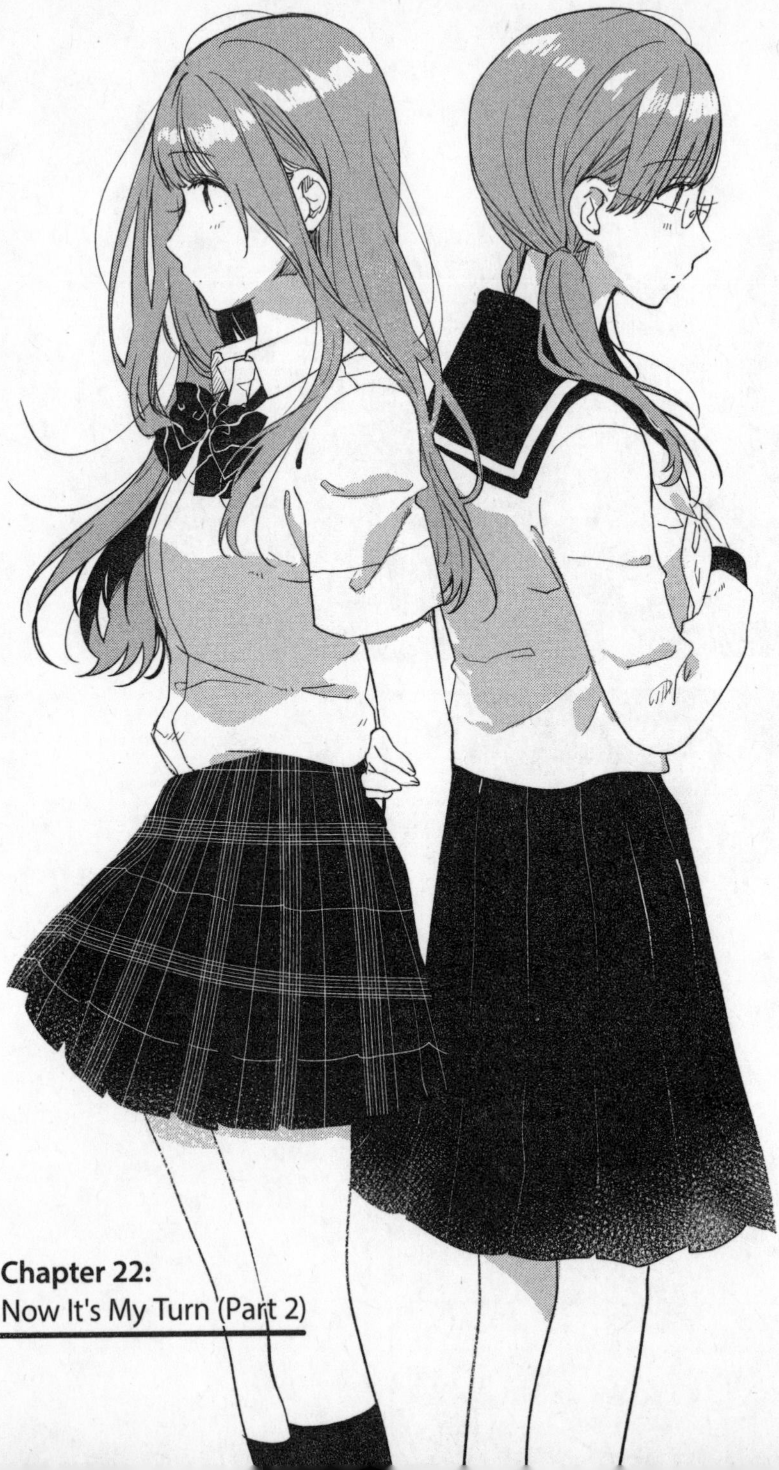

Chapter 22:
Now It's My Turn (Part 2)

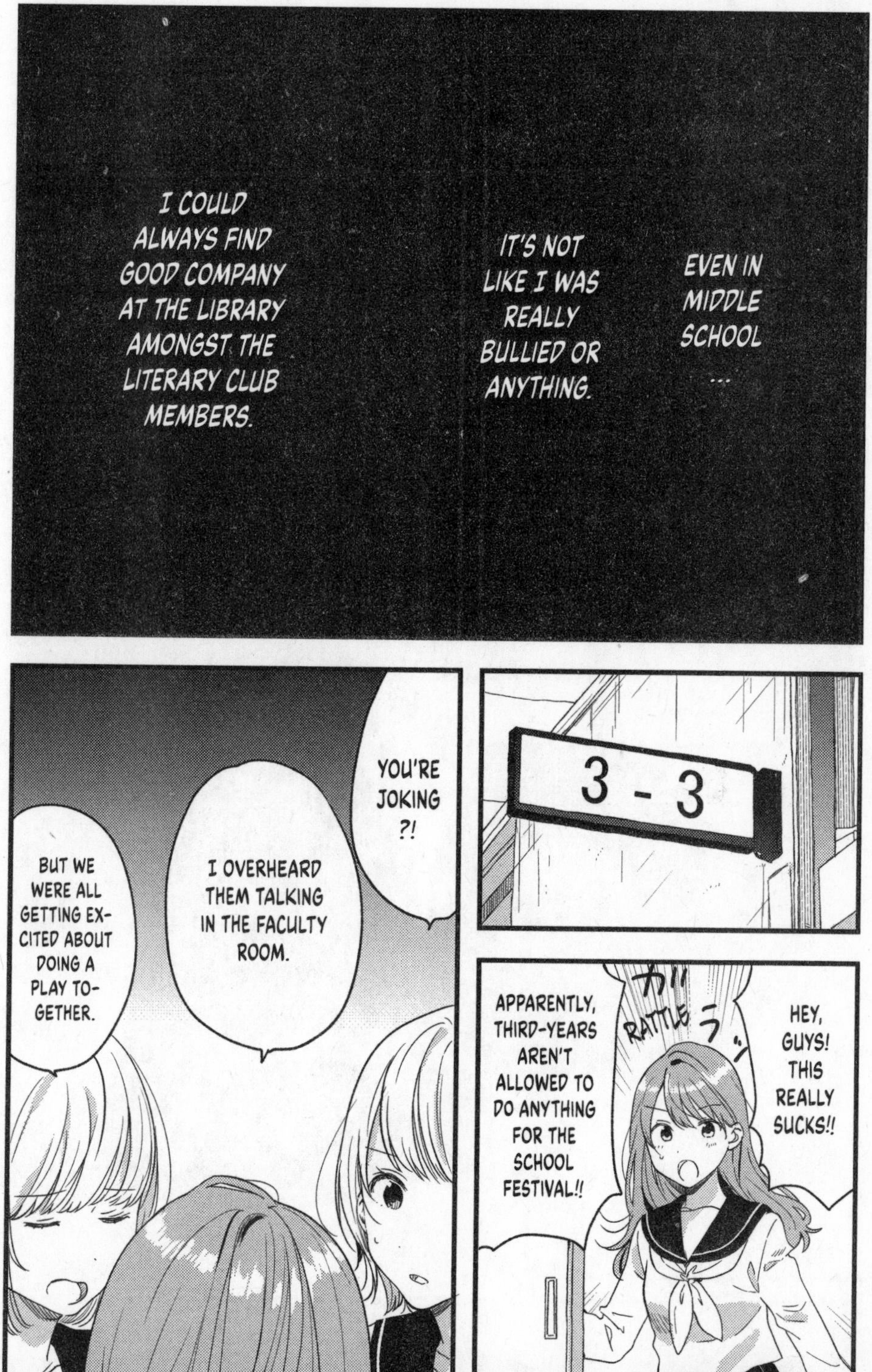
EVEN IN MIDDLE SCHOOL ...
IT'S NOT LIKE I WAS REALLY BULLIED OR ANYTHING.
I COULD ALWAYS FIND GOOD COMPANY AT THE LIBRARY AMONGST THE LITERARY CLUB MEMBERS.
3 - 3
RATTLE
HEY, GUYS! THIS REALLY SUCKS!!
APPARENTLY, THIRD-YEARS AREN'T ALLOWED TO DO ANYTHING FOR THE SCHOOL FESTIVAL!!
YOU'RE JOKING ?!
I OVERHEARD THEM TALKING IN THE FACULTY ROOM.
BUT WE WERE ALL GETTING EX-CITED ABOUT DOING A PLAY TO-GETHER.

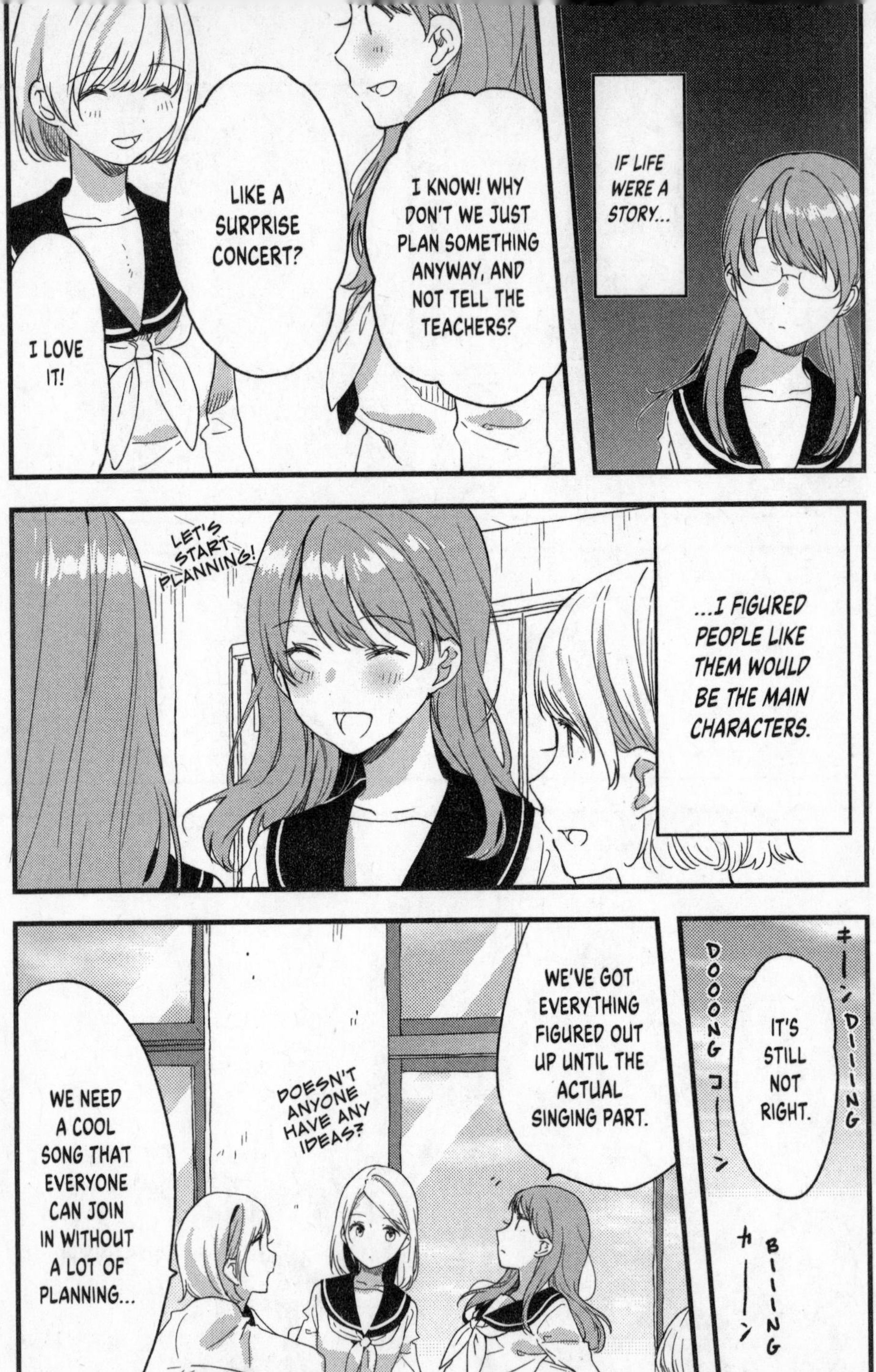
IF LIFE WERE A STORY...
I KNOW! WHY DON'T WE JUST PLAN SOMETHING ANYWAY, AND NOT TELL THE TEACHERS?
LIKE A SURPRISE CONCERT?
I LOVE IT!
...I FIGURED PEOPLE LIKE THEM WOULD BE THE MAIN CHARACTERS.
LET'S START PLANNING!
DIIIING
DOOOONG
IT'S STILL NOT RIGHT.
BIIING
WE'VE GOT EVERYTHING FIGURED OUT UP UNTIL THE ACTUAL SINGING PART.
DOESN'T ANYONE HAVE ANY IDEAS?
WE NEED A COOL SONG THAT EVERYONE CAN JOIN IN WITHOUT A LOT OF PLANNING...

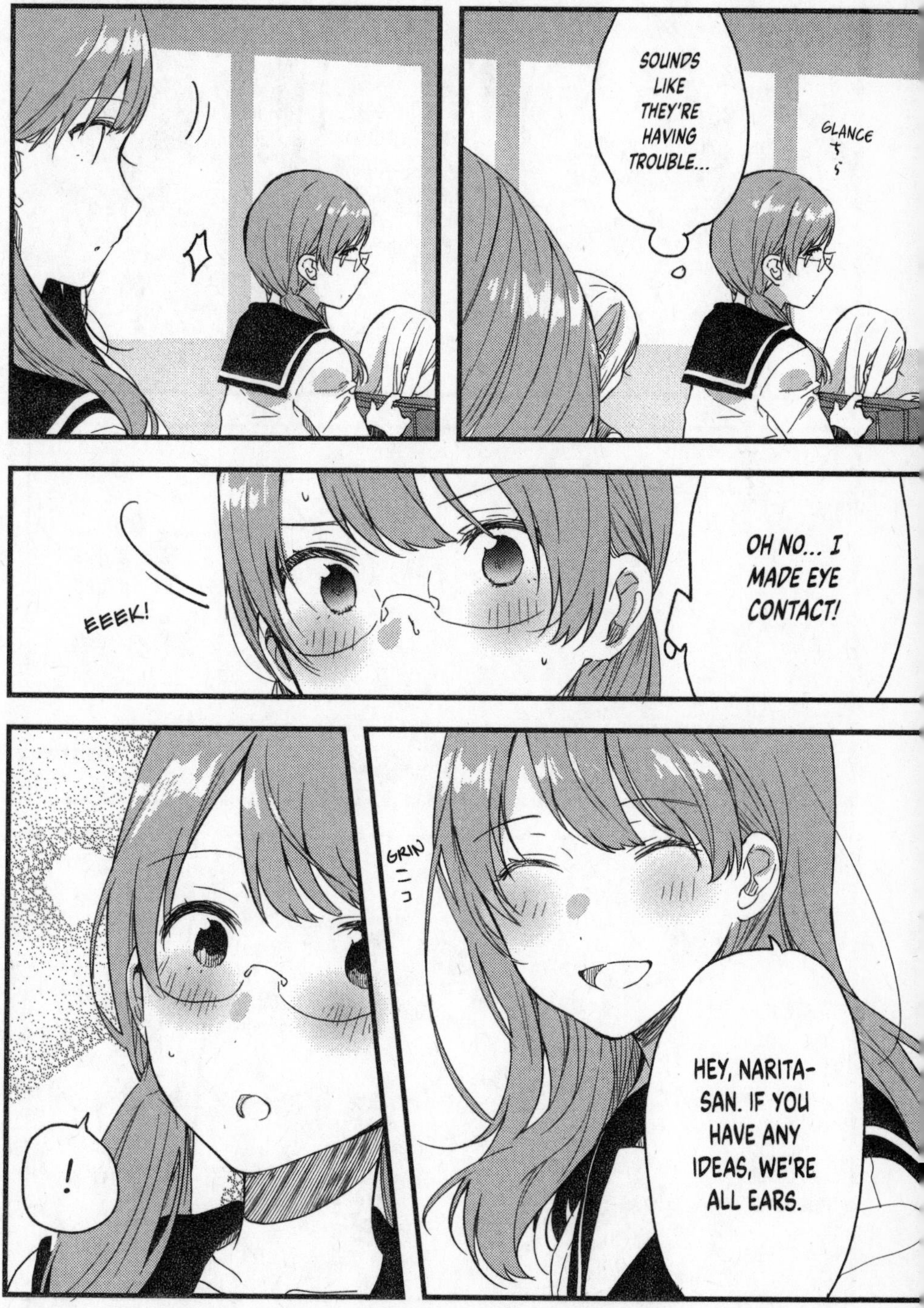
SOUNDS LIKE THEY'RE HAVING TROUBLE...
GLANCE
ちら
OH NO... I MADE EYE CONTACT!
EEEK!
HEY, NARITA-SAN. IF YOU HAVE ANY IDEAS, WE'RE ALL EARS.
GRIN
ニコ
!

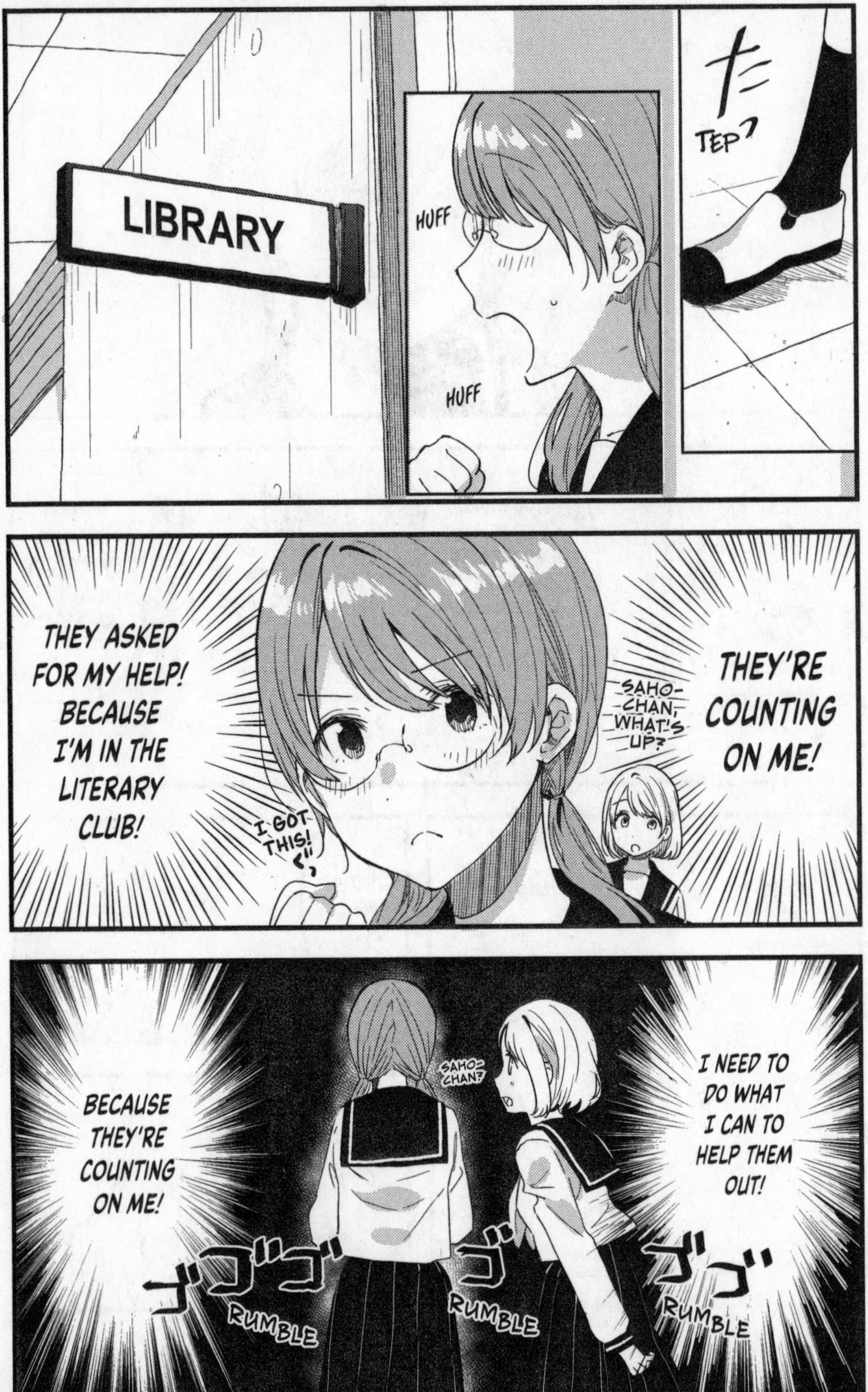
TEP
HUFF
HUFF
LIBRARY
THEY'RE COUNTING ON ME!
SAHO-CHAN, WHAT'S UP?
THEY ASKED FOR MY HELP! BECAUSE I'M IN THE LITERARY CLUB!
I GOT THIS!
I NEED TO DO WHAT I CAN TO HELP THEM OUT!
SAHO-CHAN?
BECAUSE THEY'RE COUNTING ON ME!
RUMBLE
RUMBLE
RUMBLE

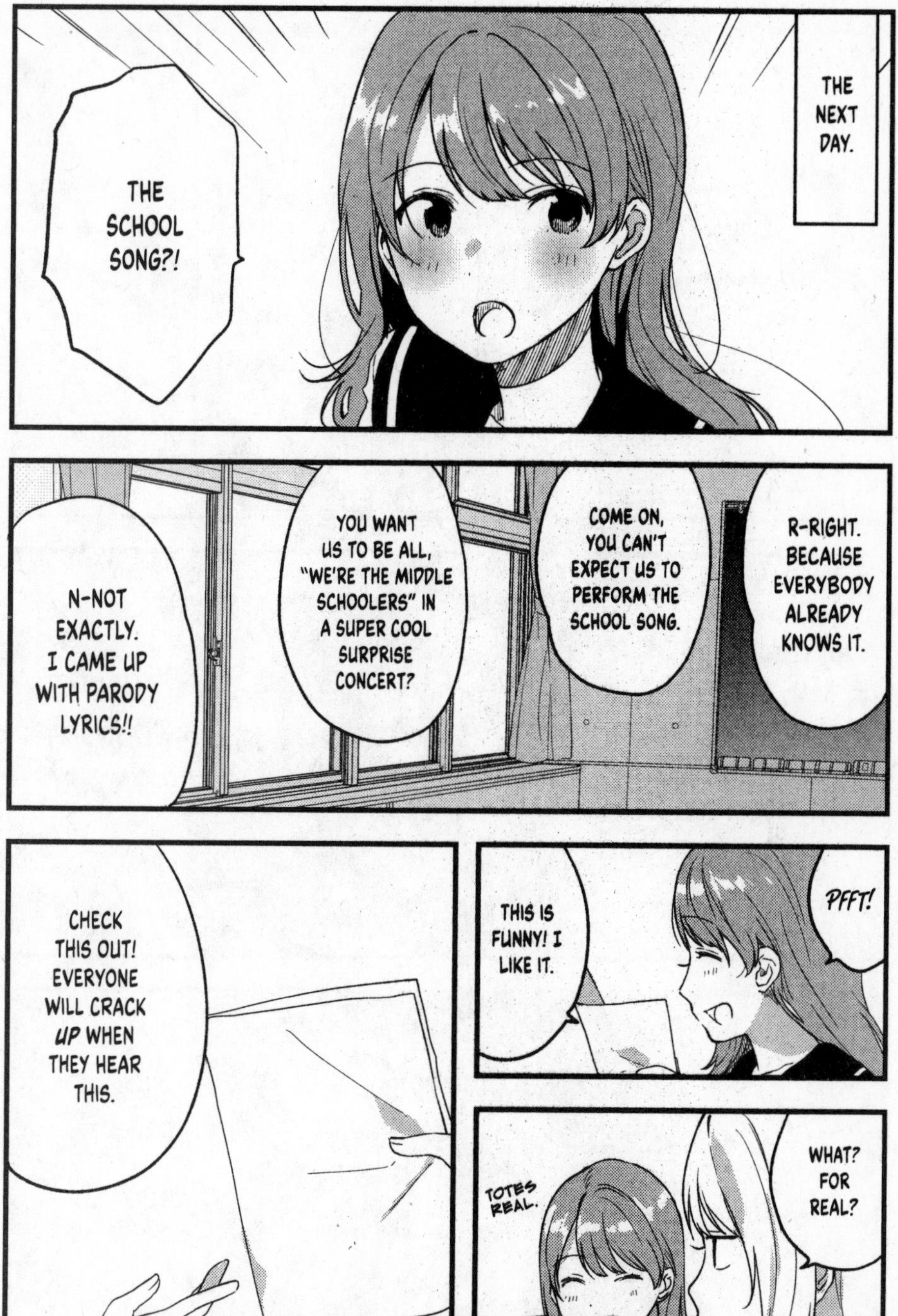
THE NEXT DAY.
THE SCHOOL SONG?!
R-RIGHT. BECAUSE EVERYBODY ALREADY KNOWS IT.
COME ON, YOU CAN'T EXPECT US TO PERFORM THE SCHOOL SONG.
YOU WANT US TO BE ALL, "WE'RE THE MIDDLE SCHOOLERS" IN A SUPER COOL SURPRISE CONCERT?
N-NOT EXACTLY. I CAME UP WITH PARODY LYRICS!!
PFFT!
THIS IS FUNNY! I LIKE IT.
WHAT? FOR REAL?
TOTES REAL.
CHECK THIS OUT! EVERYONE WILL CRACK *UP* WHEN THEY HEAR THIS.

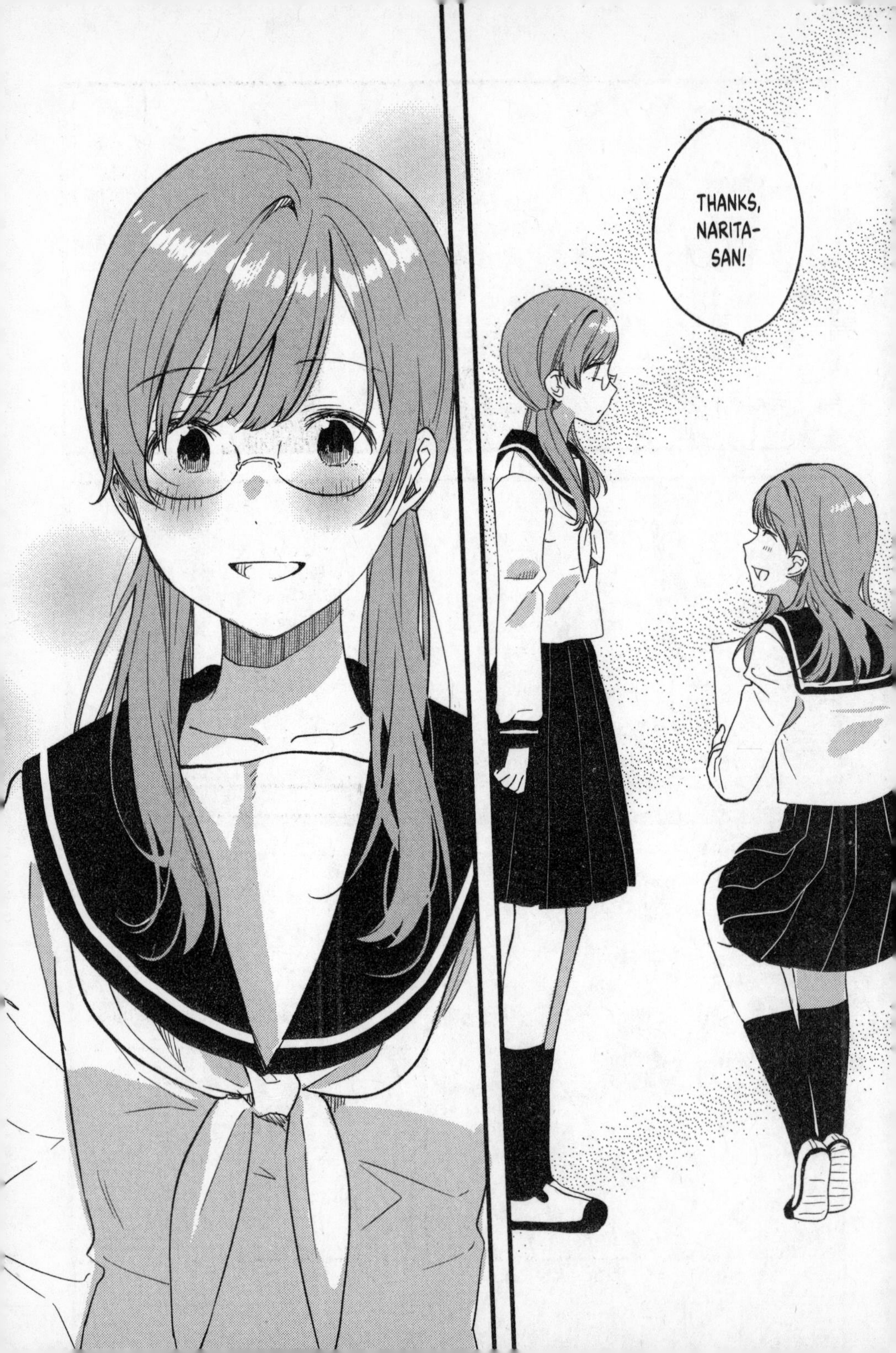
THANKS, NARITA-SAN!

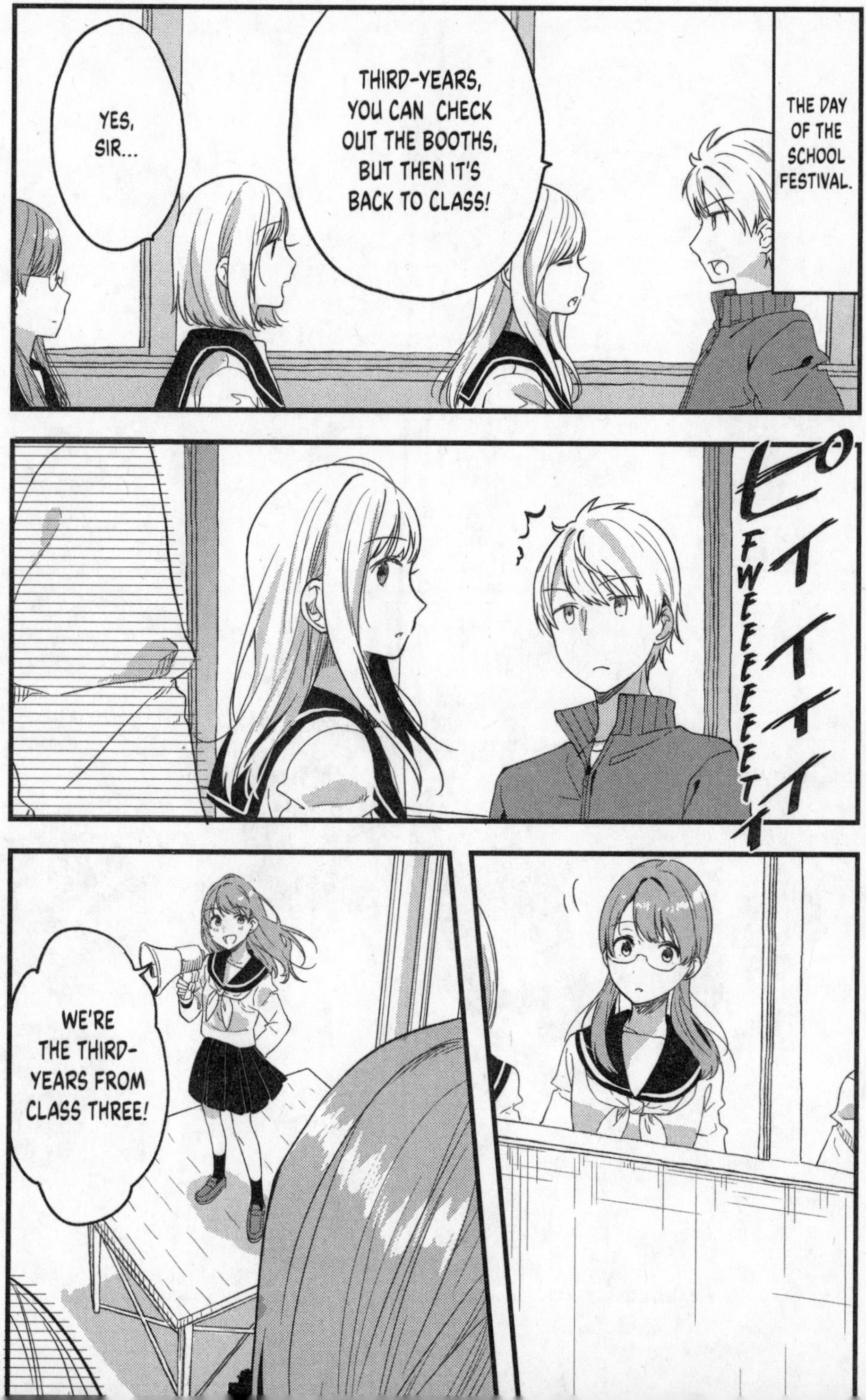
THE DAY OF THE SCHOOL FESTIVAL.
THIRD-YEARS, YOU CAN CHECK OUT THE BOOTHS, BUT THEN IT'S BACK TO CLASS!
YES, SIR...
ピイイイイイ
FWEEEEEEEEET
WE'RE THE THIRD-YEARS FROM CLASS THREE!

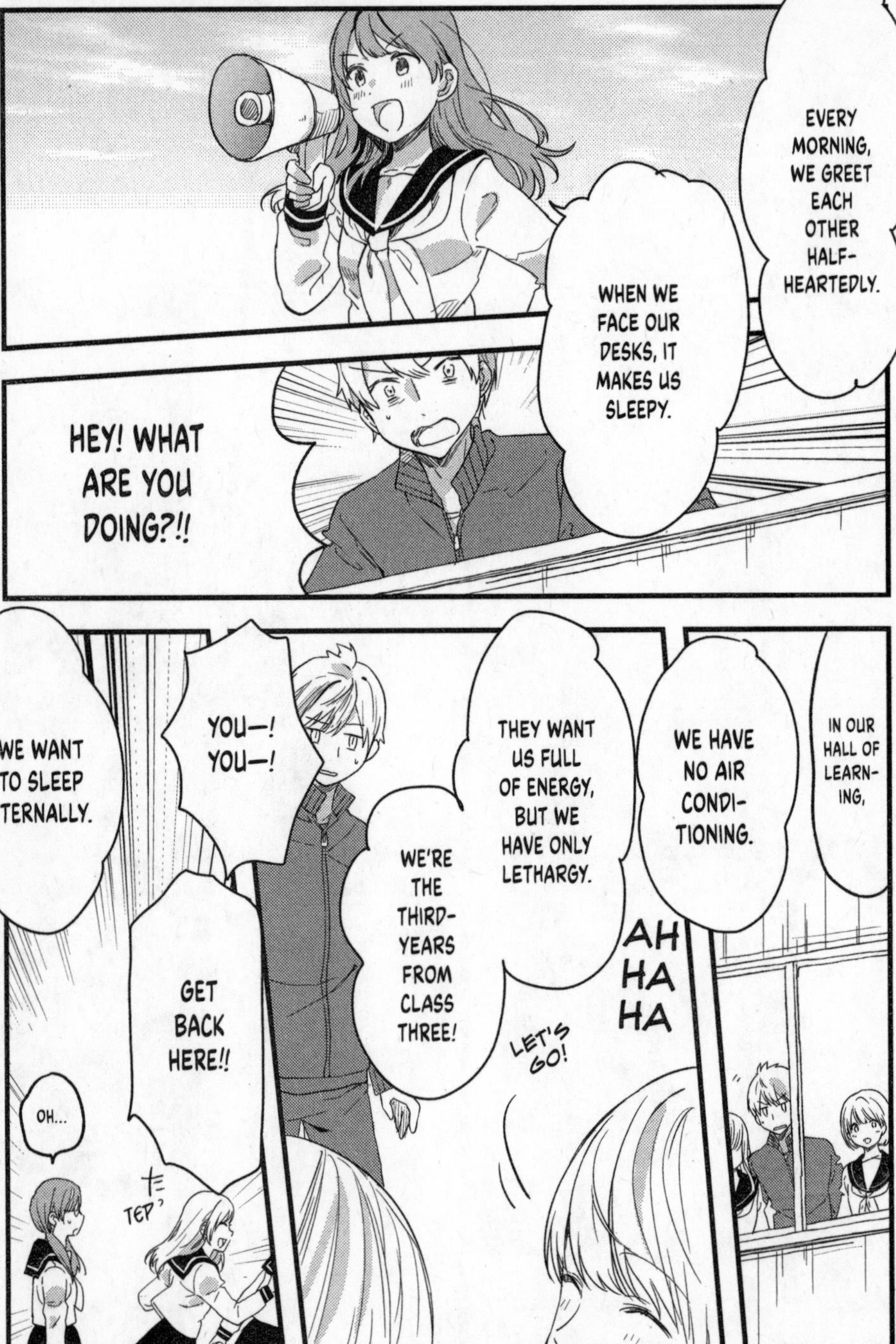
EVERY MORNING, WE GREET EACH OTHER HALF-HEARTEDLY.
WHEN WE FACE OUR DESKS, IT MAKES US SLEEPY.
HEY! WHAT ARE YOU DOING?!!
IN OUR HALL OF LEARN-ING,
WE HAVE NO AIR CONDI-TIONING.
THEY WANT US FULL OF ENERGY, BUT WE HAVE ONLY LETHARGY.
AH HA HA
WE'RE THE THIRD-YEARS FROM CLASS THREE!
LET'S GO!
YOU—! YOU—!
GET BACK HERE!!
WE WANT TO SLEEP ETERNALLY.
OH...
TEP

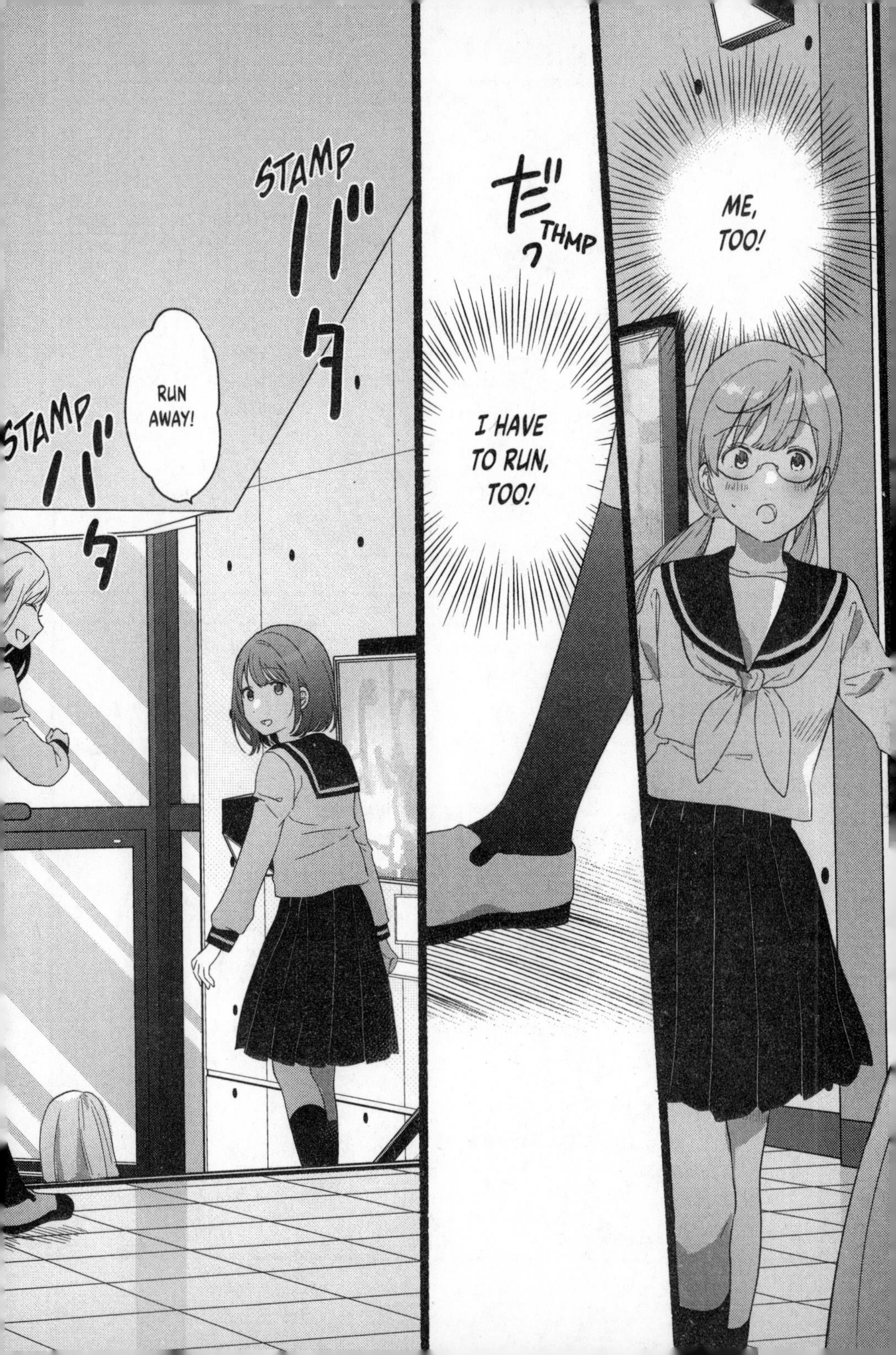
ME, TOO!
だっ
THMP
I HAVE TO RUN, TOO!
STAMP
バタ
RUN AWAY!
STAMP
バタ

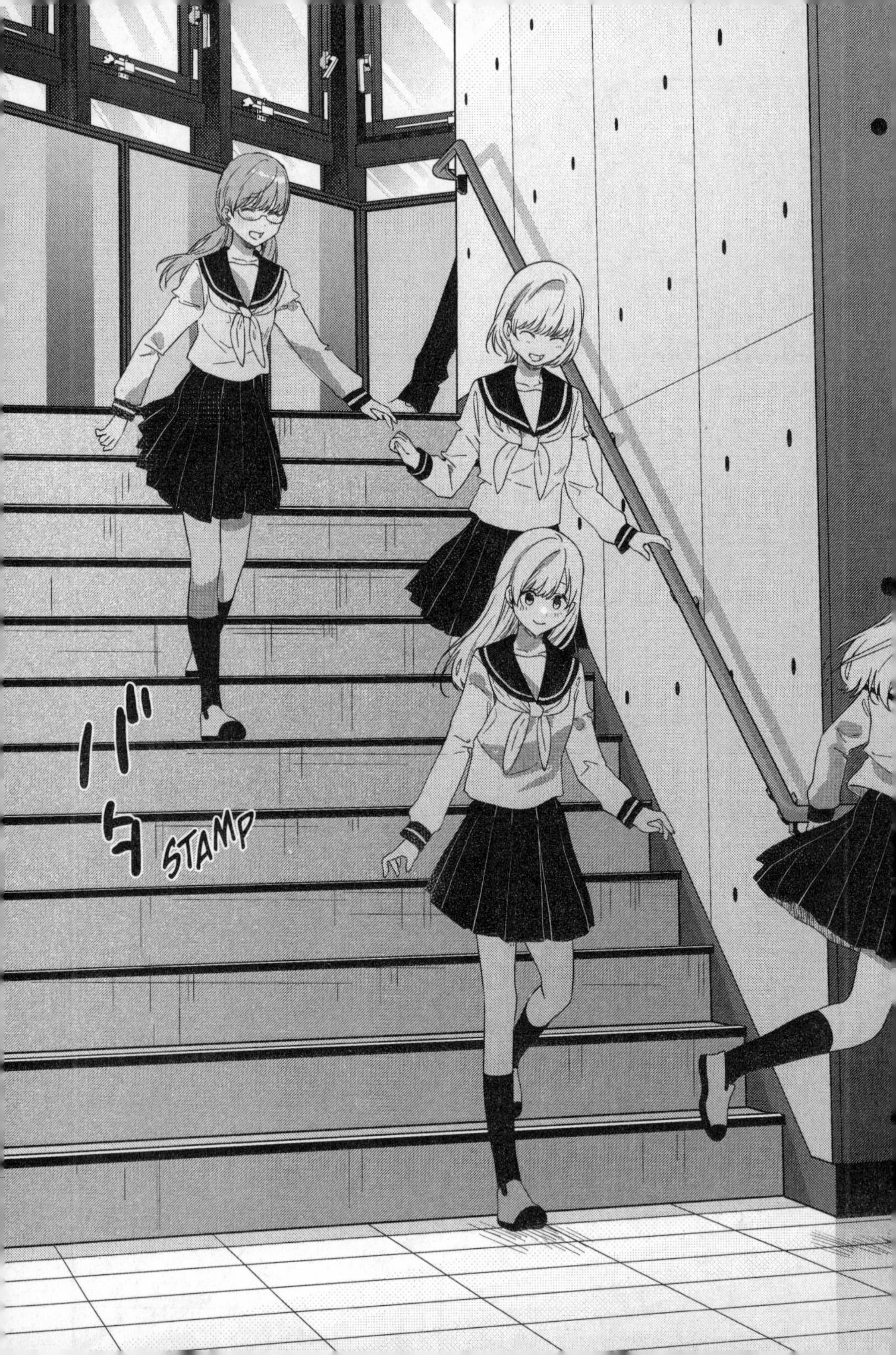
バタ
STAMP

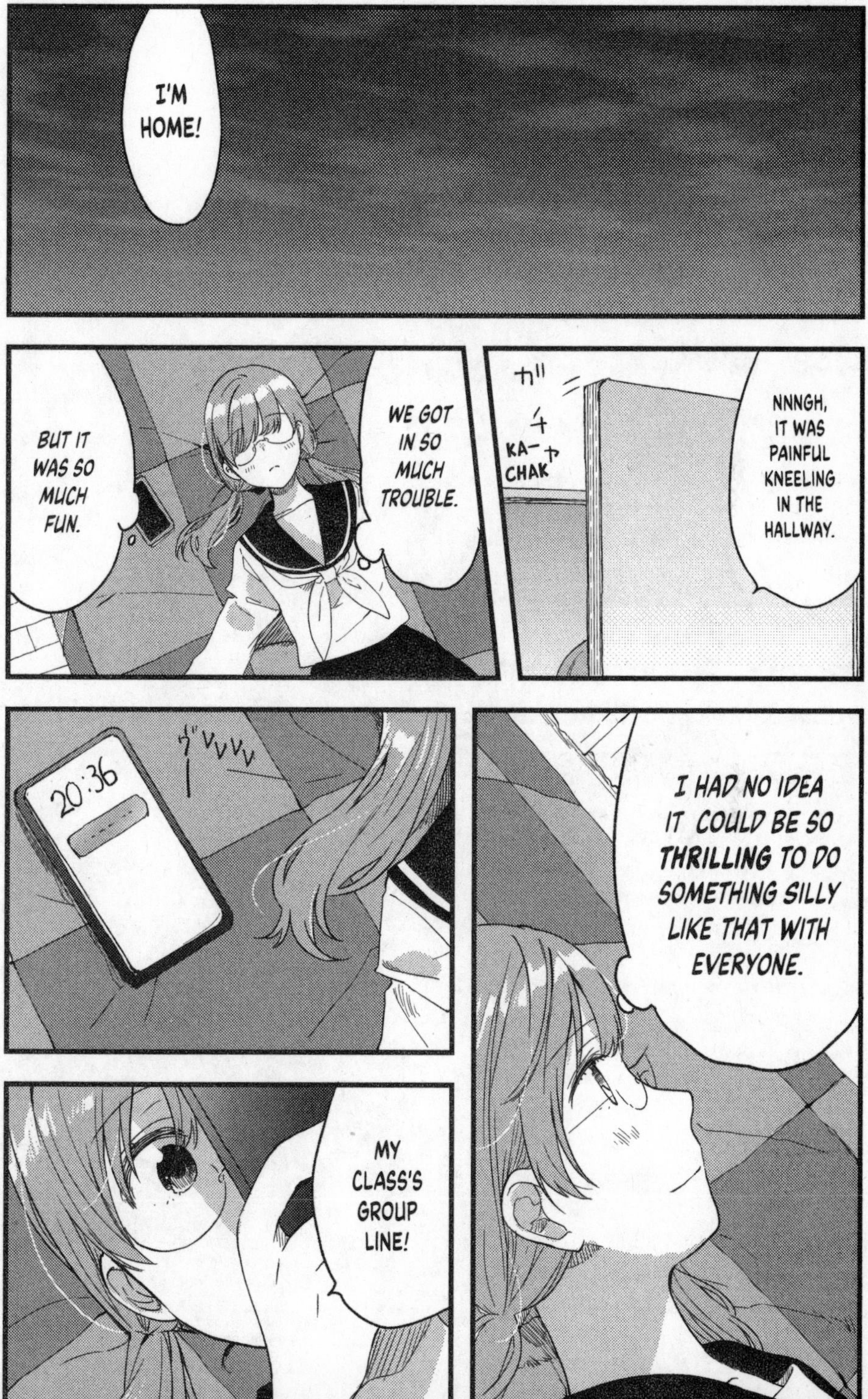
I'M HOME!
NNNGH, IT WAS PAINFUL KNEELING IN THE HALLWAY.
ガチャ
KA-CHAK
WE GOT IN SO MUCH TROUBLE.
BUT IT WAS SO MUCH FUN.
I HAD NO IDEA IT COULD BE SO **THRILLING** TO DO SOMETHING SILLY LIKE THAT WITH EVERYONE.
20:36
MY CLASS'S GROUP LINE!

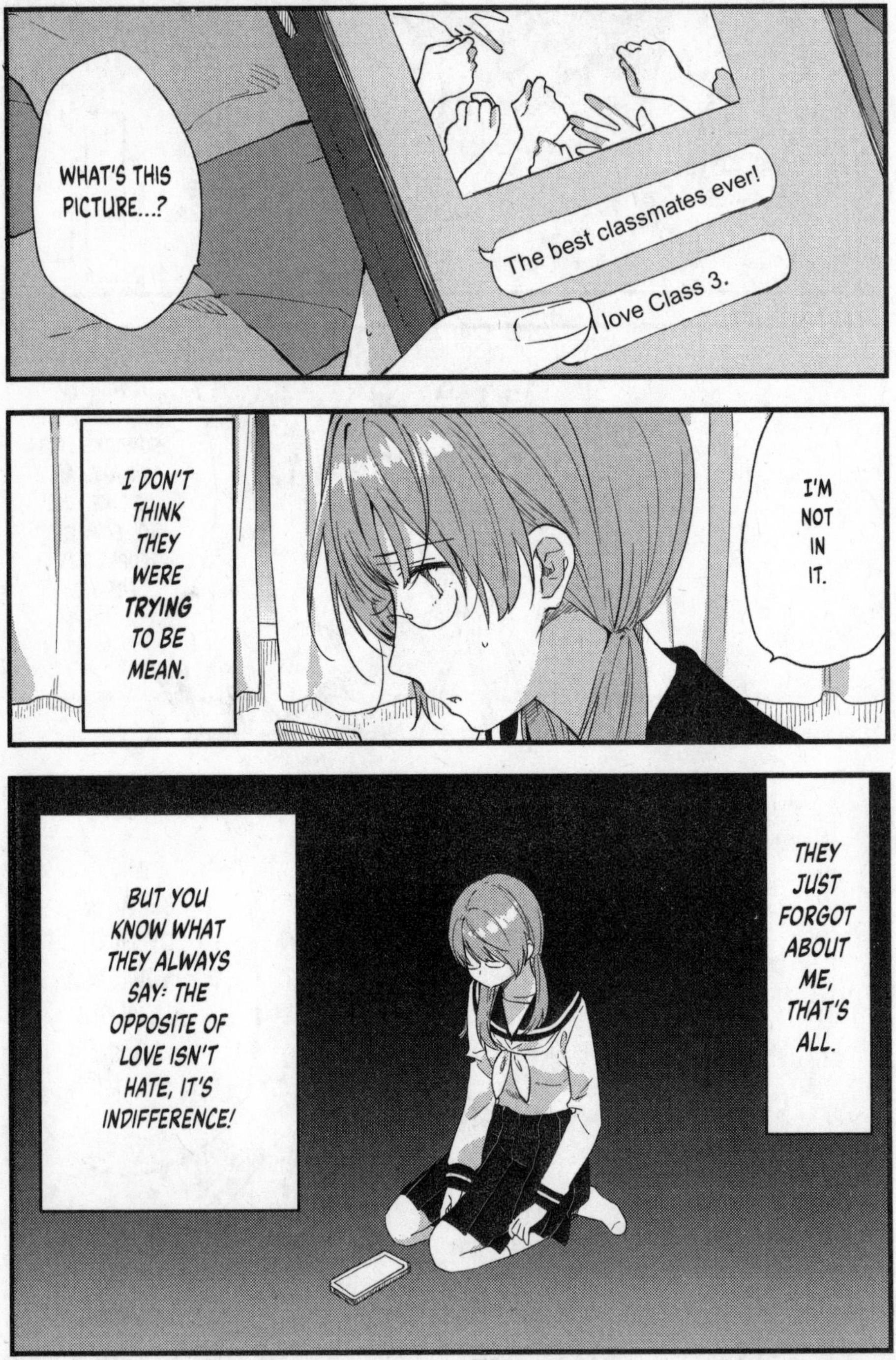
The best classmates ever!
I love Class 3.
WHAT'S THIS PICTURE...?
I'M NOT IN IT.
I DON'T THINK THEY WERE TRYING TO BE MEAN.
THEY JUST FORGOT ABOUT ME, THAT'S ALL.
BUT YOU KNOW WHAT THEY ALWAYS SAY: THE OPPOSITE OF LOVE ISN'T HATE, IT'S INDIFFERENCE!

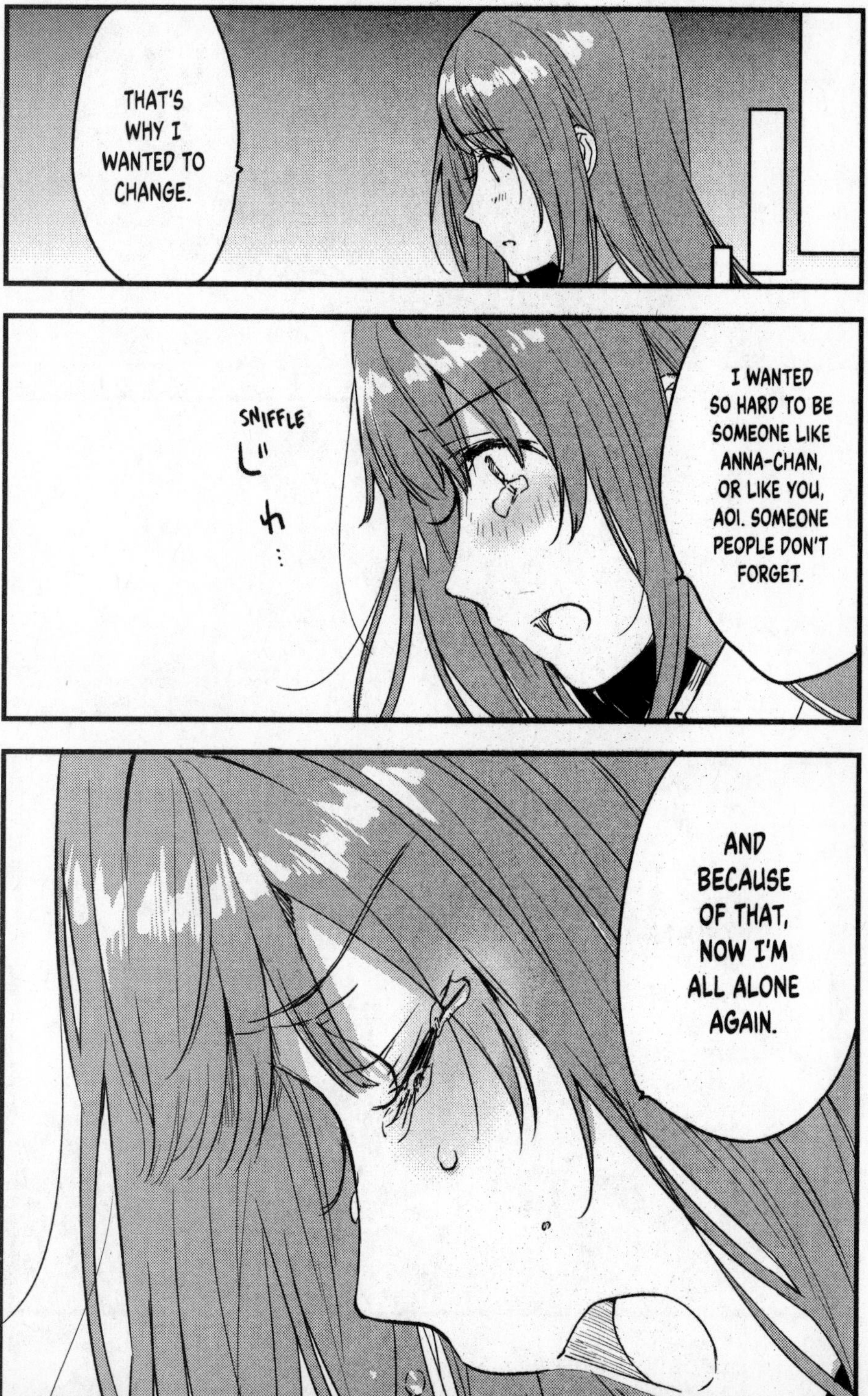

THAT'S WHY I WANTED TO CHANGE.
I WANTED SO HARD TO BE SOMEONE LIKE ANNA-CHAN, OR LIKE YOU, AOI. SOMEONE PEOPLE DON'T FORGET.
SNIFFLE
じわ…
AND BECAUSE OF THAT, NOW I'M ALL ALONE AGAIN.

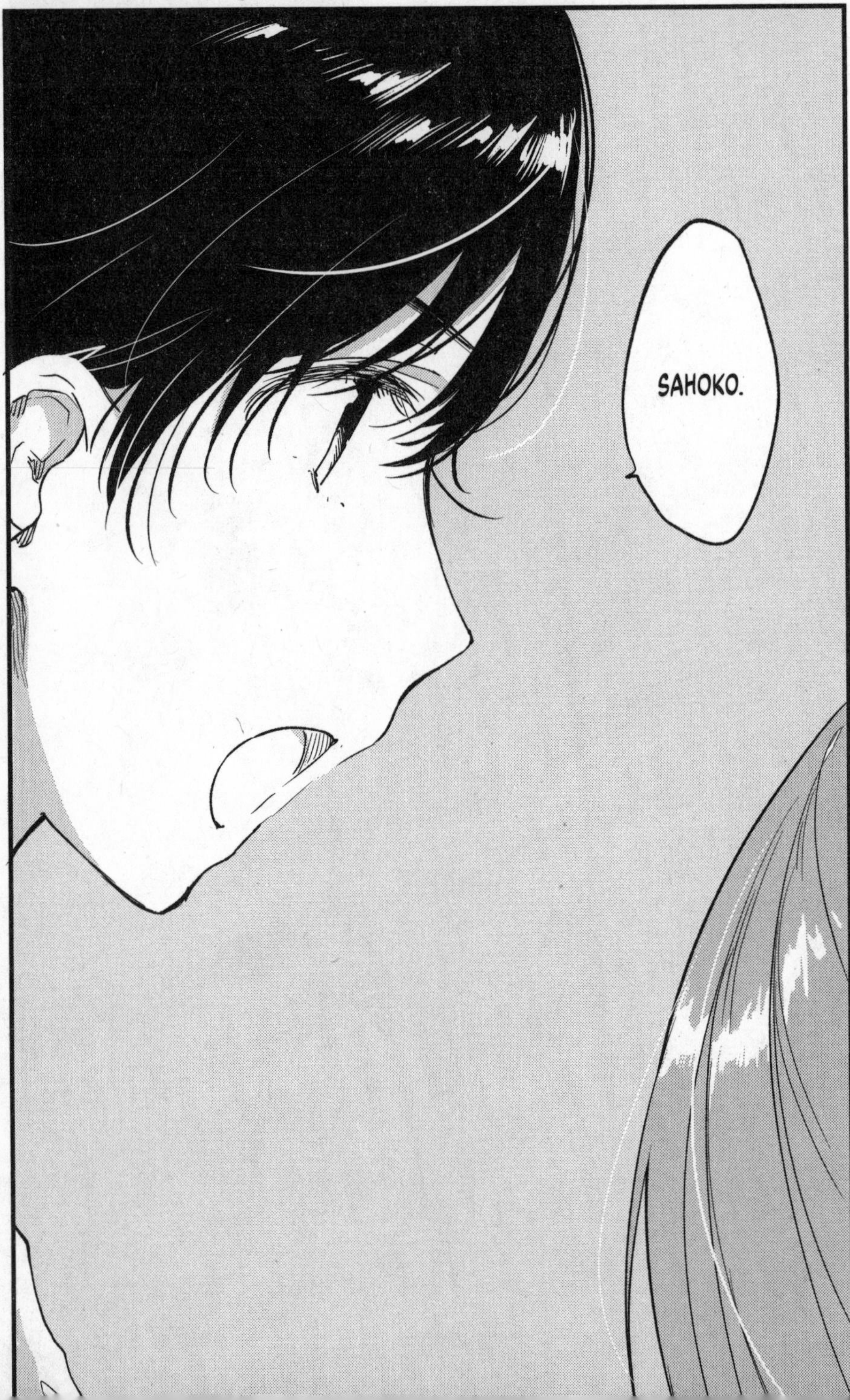
SAHOKO.

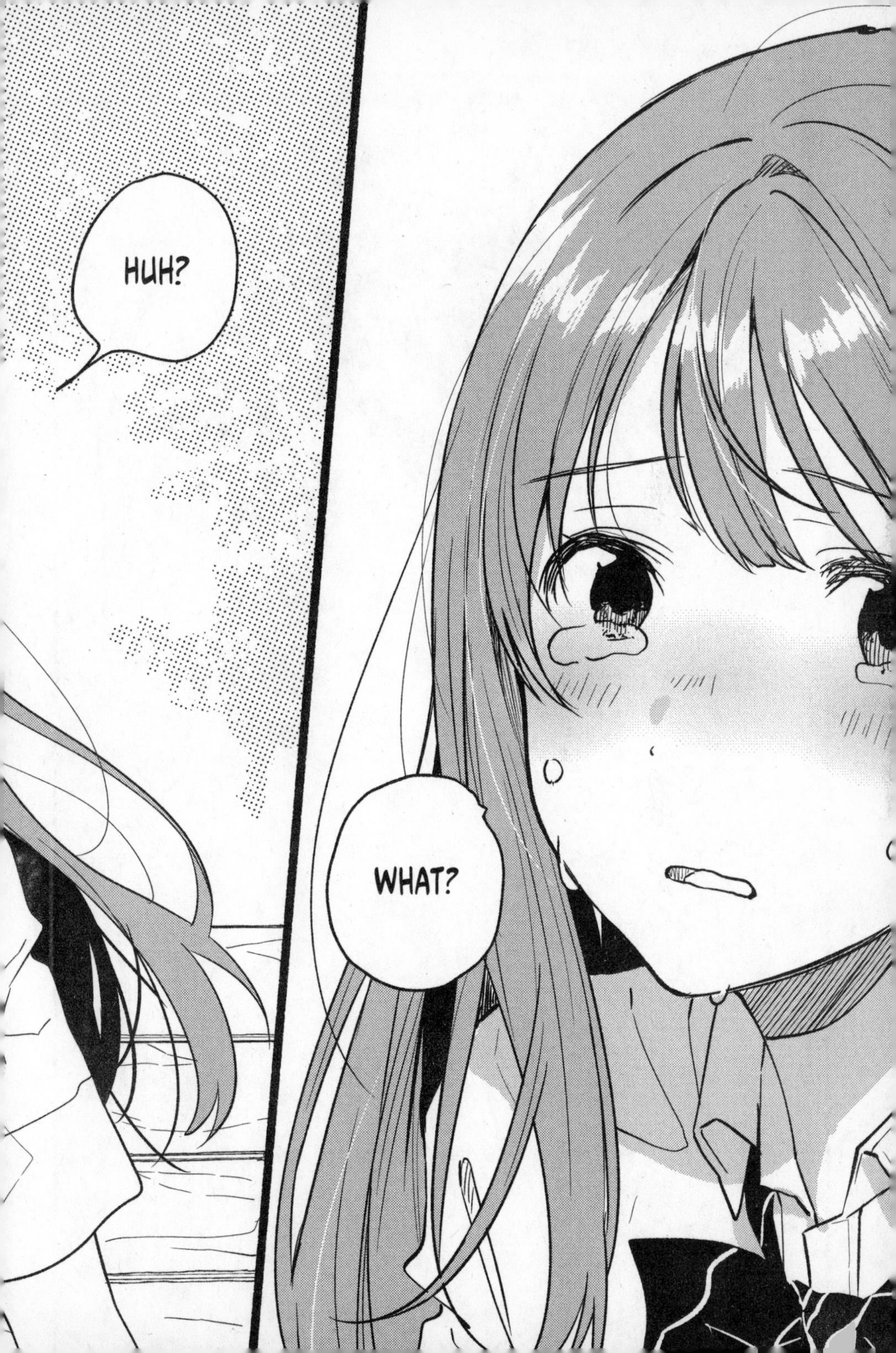
WHAT?
HUH?

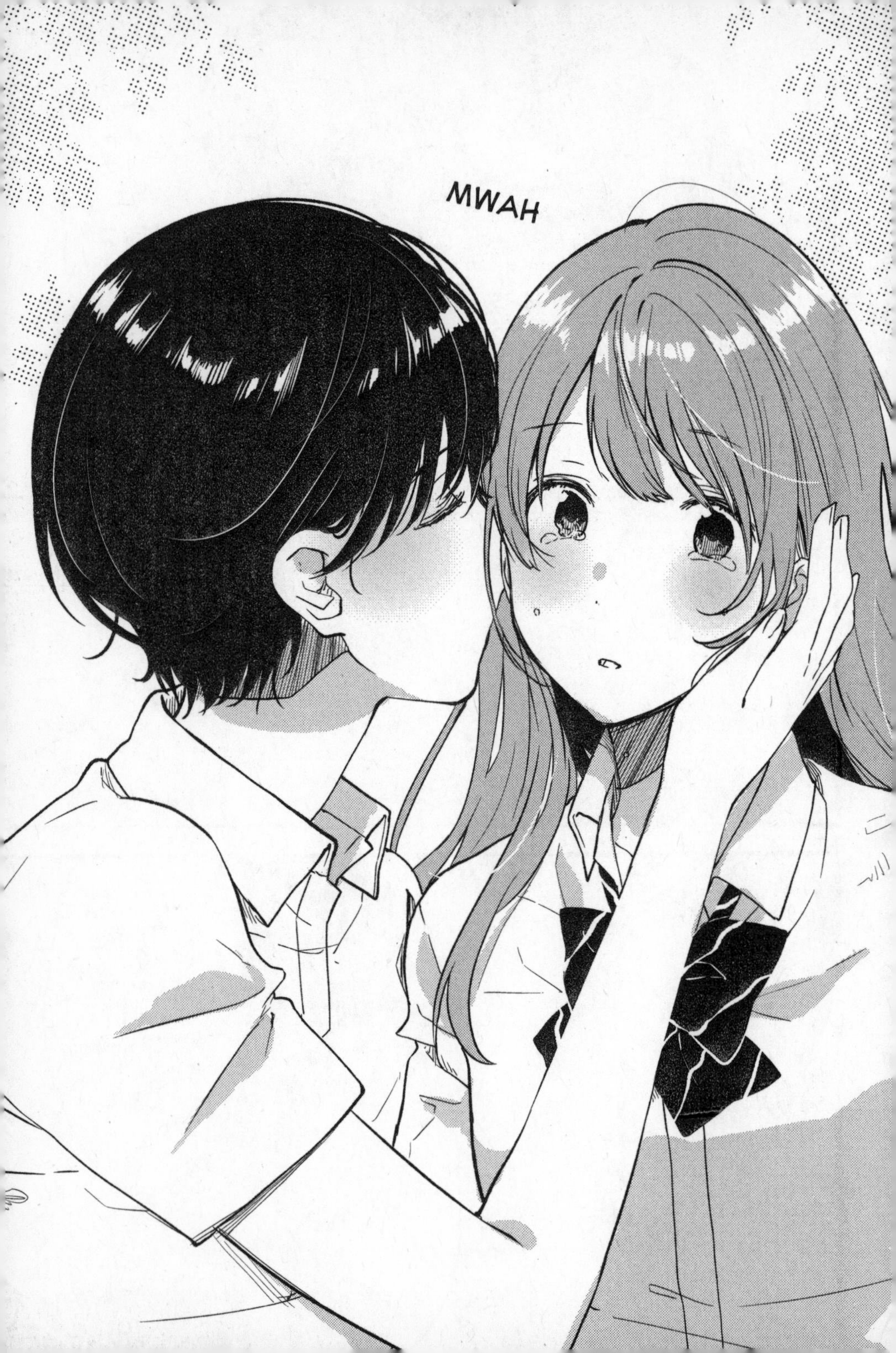
MWAH

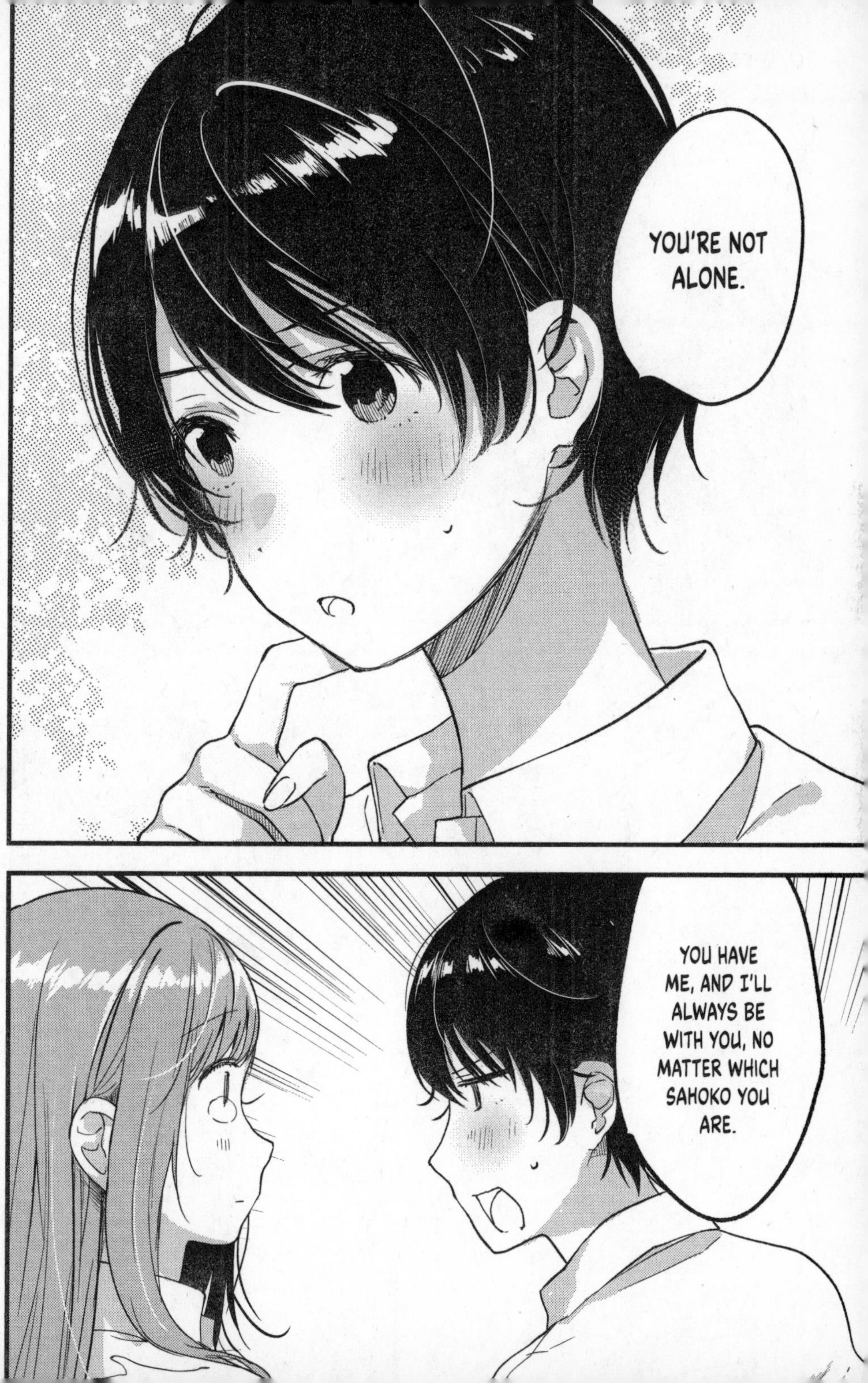
YOU'RE NOT ALONE.
YOU HAVE ME, AND I'LL ALWAYS BE WITH YOU, NO MATTER WHICH SAHOKO YOU ARE.

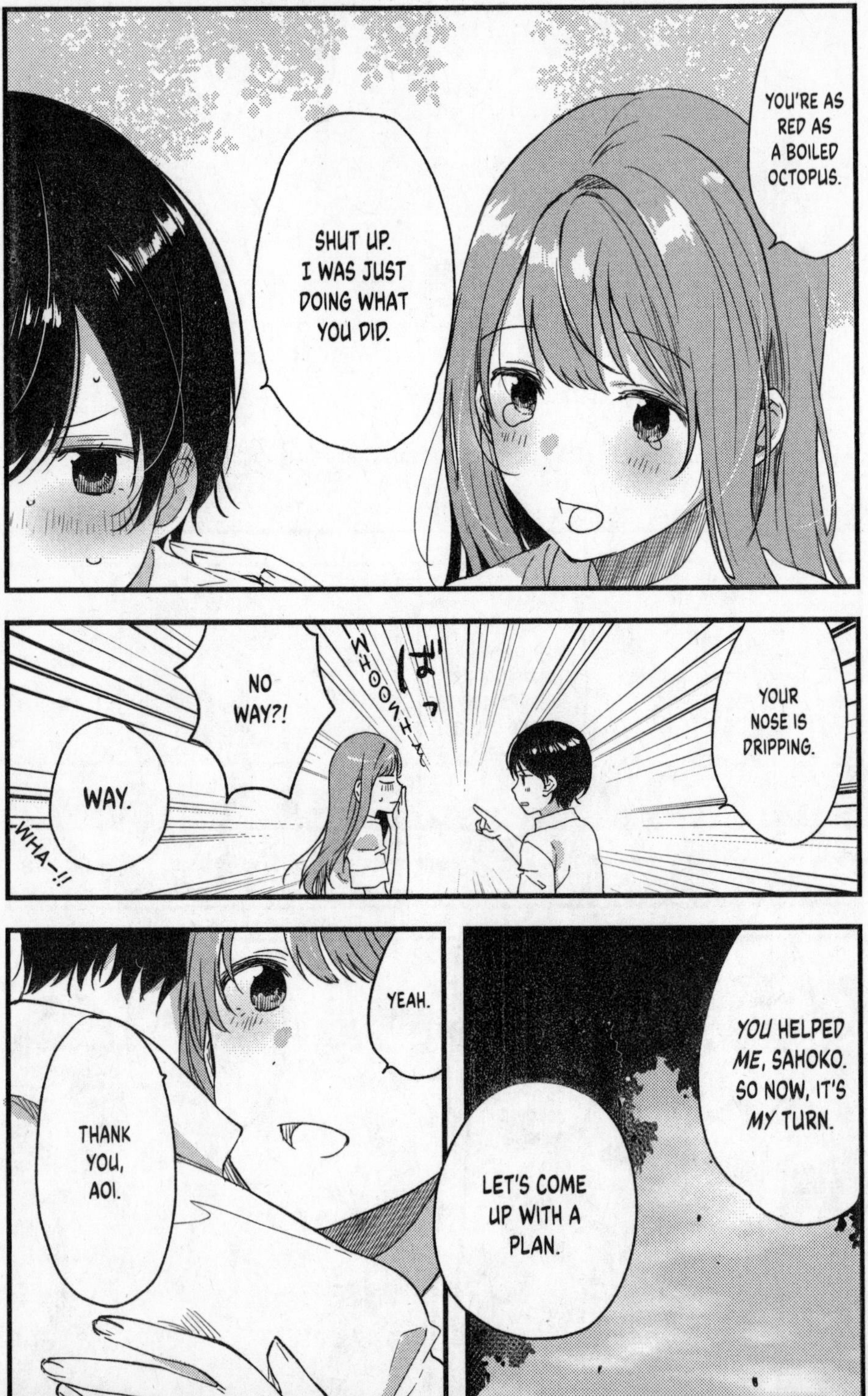
YOU'RE AS RED AS A BOILED OCTOPUS.
SHUT UP. I WAS JUST DOING WHAT YOU DID.
YOUR NOSE IS DRIPPING.
ぱっ
WHOOSH
NO WAY?!
WAY.
WHA—!!
YOU HELPED ME, SAHOKO. SO NOW, IT'S MY TURN.
LET'S COME UP WITH A PLAN.
YEAH.
THANK YOU, AOI.

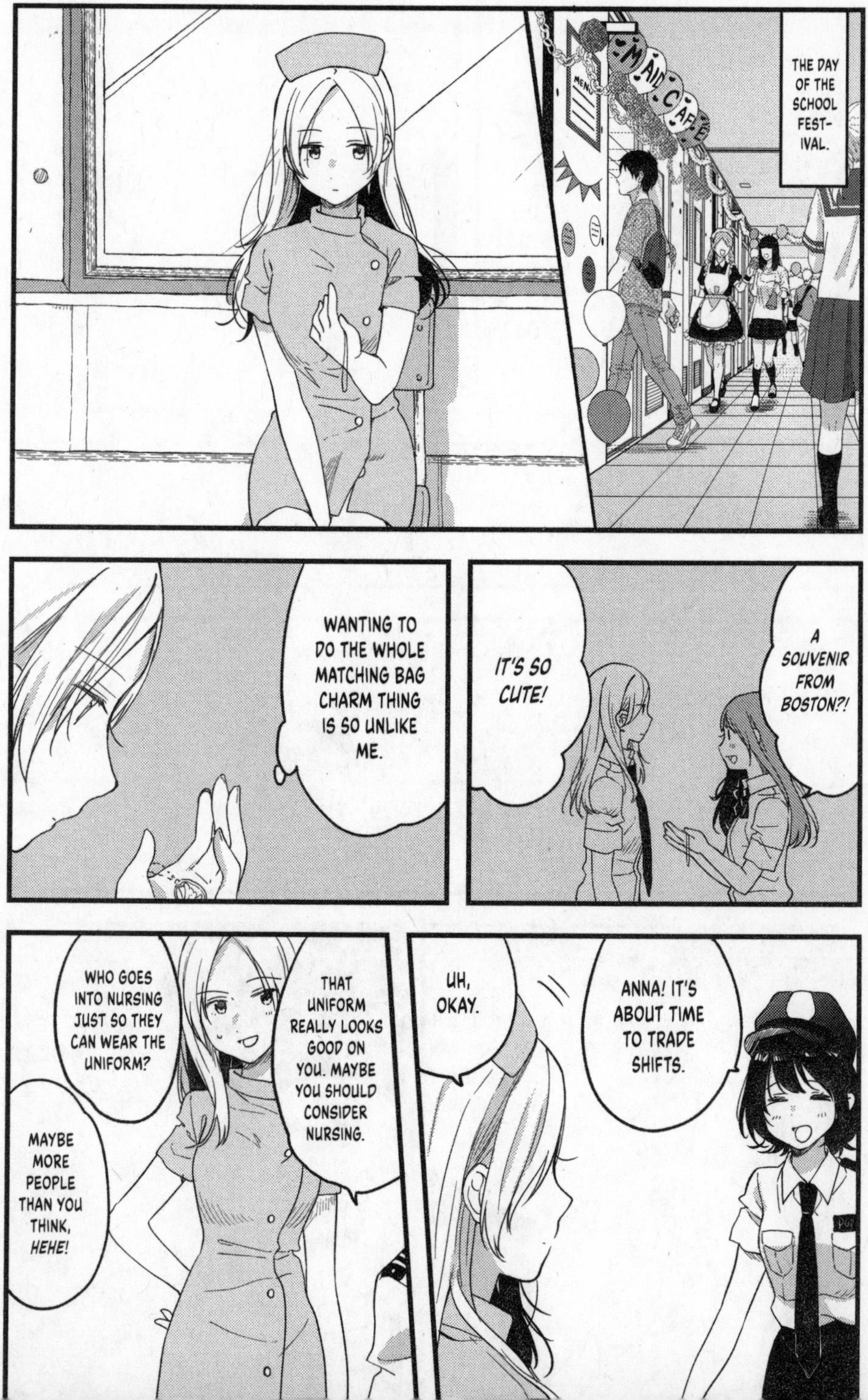
THE DAY OF THE SCHOOL FEST-IVAL.
A SOUVENIR FROM BOSTON?!
IT'S SO CUTE!
WANTING TO DO THE WHOLE MATCHING BAG CHARM THING IS SO UNLIKE ME.
ANNA! IT'S ABOUT TIME TO TRADE SHIFTS.
UH, OKAY.
THAT UNIFORM REALLY LOOKS GOOD ON YOU. MAYBE YOU SHOULD CONSIDER NURSING.
WHO GOES INTO NURSING JUST SO THEY CAN WEAR THE UNIFORM?
MAYBE MORE PEOPLE THAN YOU THINK, *HEHE!*

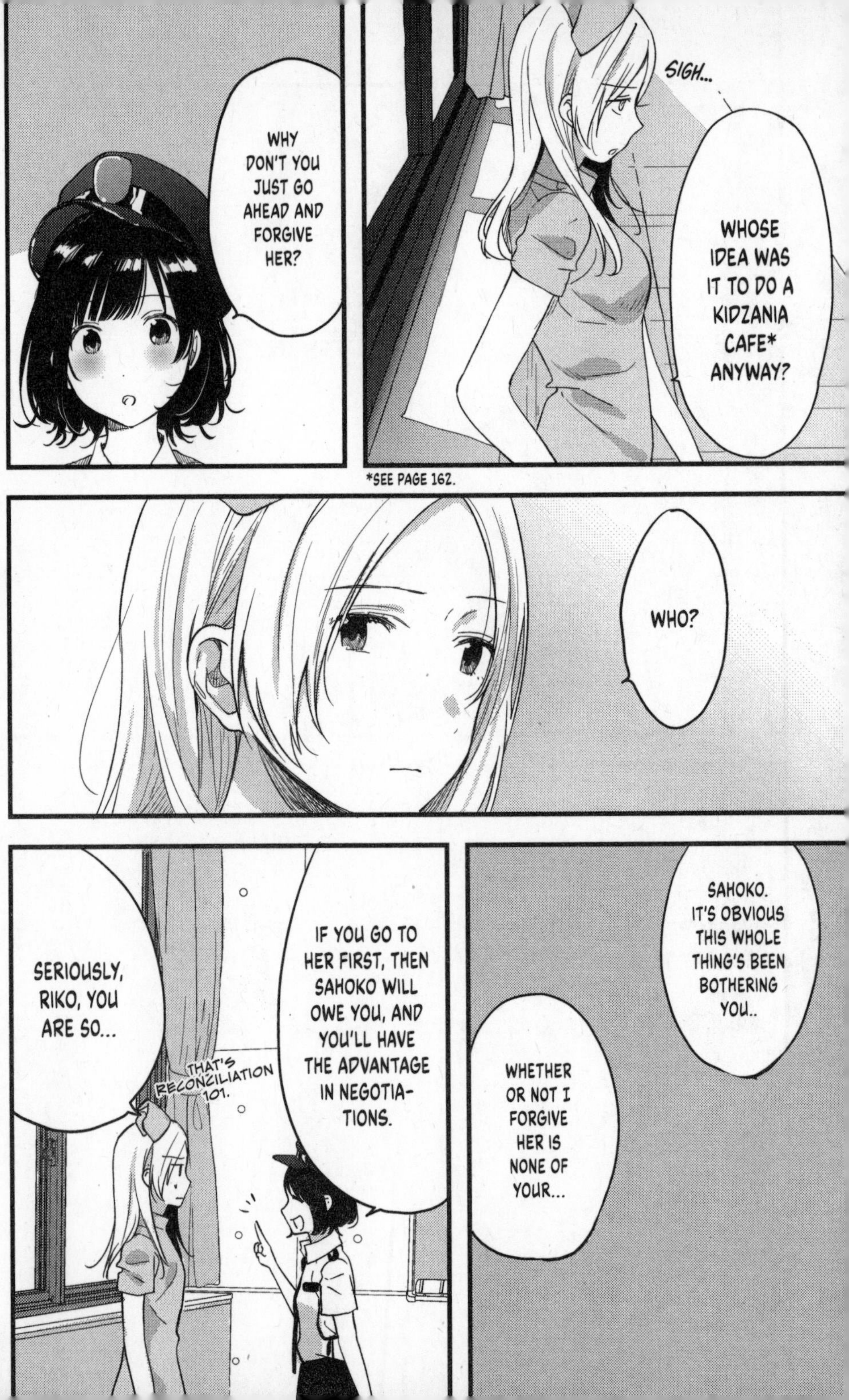
SIGH...
WHOSE IDEA WAS IT TO DO A KIDZANIA CAFE* ANYWAY?
WHY DON'T YOU JUST GO AHEAD AND FORGIVE HER?
WHO?
SAHOKO. IT'S OBVIOUS THIS WHOLE THING'S BEEN BOTHERING YOU..
WHETHER OR NOT I FORGIVE HER IS NONE OF YOUR...
IF YOU GO TO HER FIRST, THEN SAHOKO WILL OWE YOU, AND YOU'LL HAVE THE ADVANTAGE IN NEGOTIA-TIONS.
THAT'S RECONCILIATION 101.
SERIOUSLY, RIKO, YOU ARE SO...

*SEE PAGE 162.

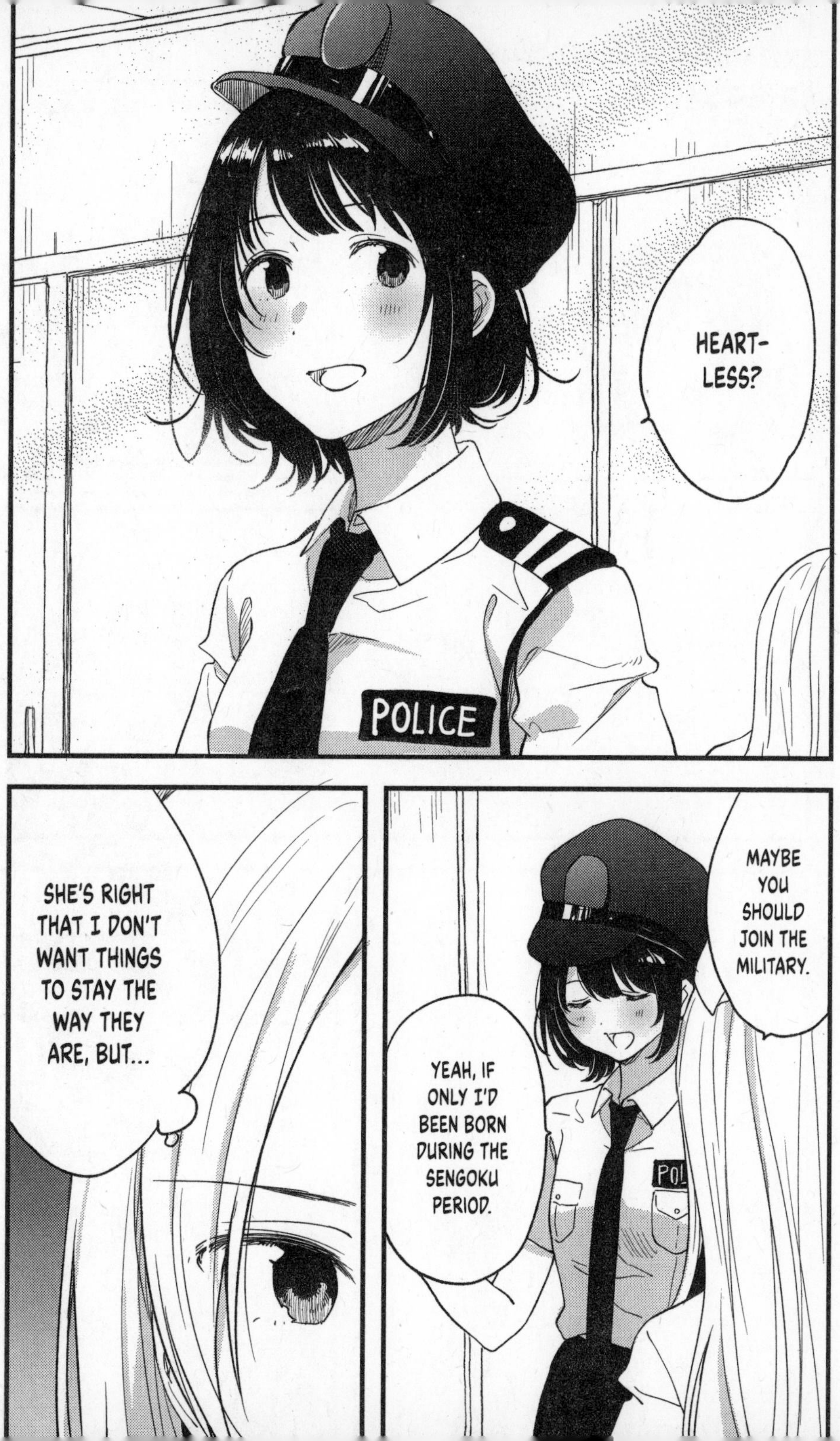
HEART-LESS?
POLICE
MAYBE YOU SHOULD JOIN THE MILITARY.
YEAH, IF ONLY I'D BEEN BORN DURING THE SENGOKU PERIOD.
SHE'S RIGHT THAT I DON'T WANT THINGS TO STAY THE WAY THEY ARE, BUT...

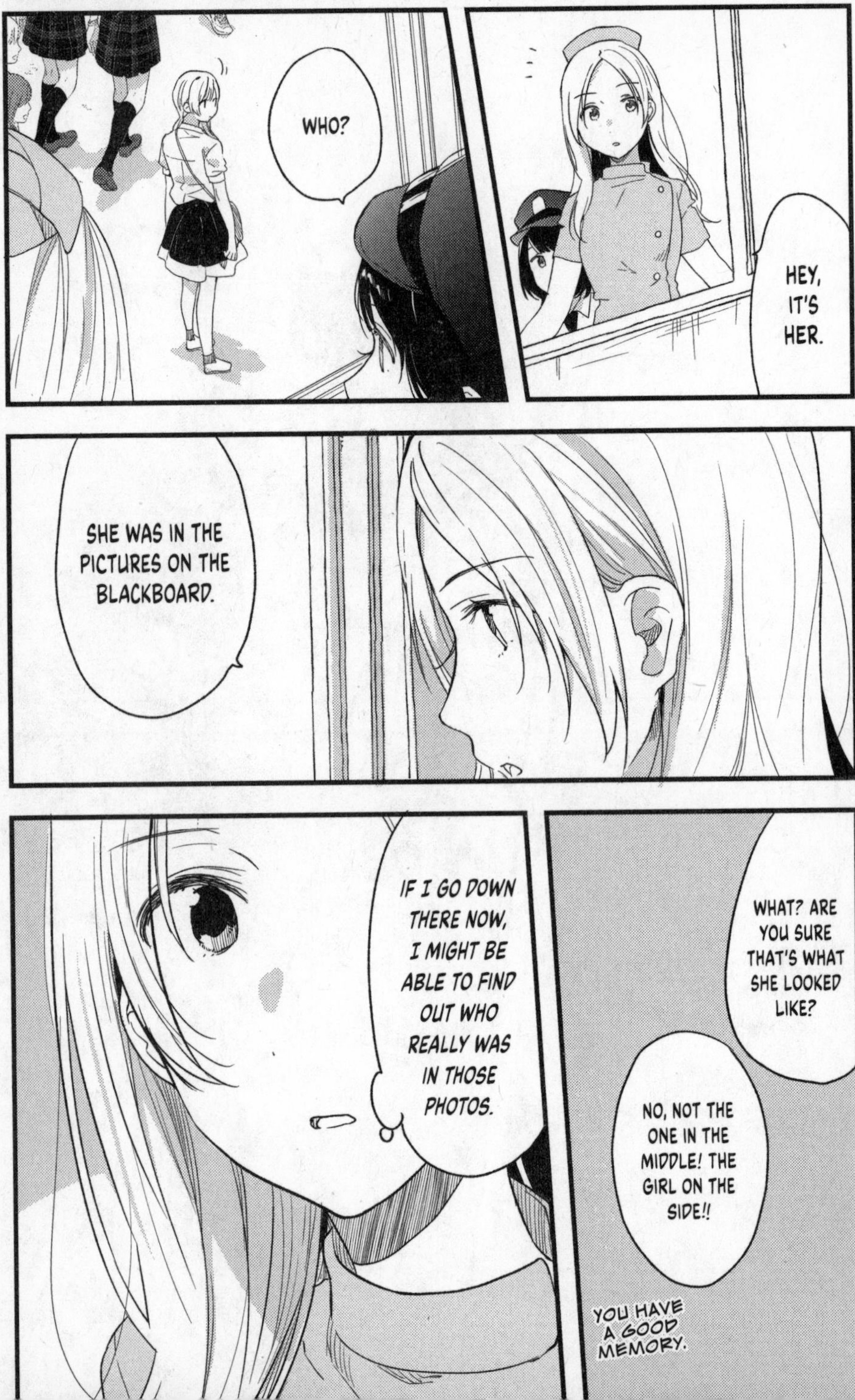
HEY, IT'S HER.
WHO?
SHE WAS IN THE PICTURES ON THE BLACKBOARD.
WHAT? ARE YOU SURE THAT'S WHAT SHE LOOKED LIKE?
NO, NOT THE ONE IN THE MIDDLE! THE GIRL ON THE SIDE!!
YOU HAVE A GOOD MEMORY.
IF I GO DOWN THERE NOW, I MIGHT BE ABLE TO FIND OUT WHO REALLY WAS IN THOSE PHOTOS.

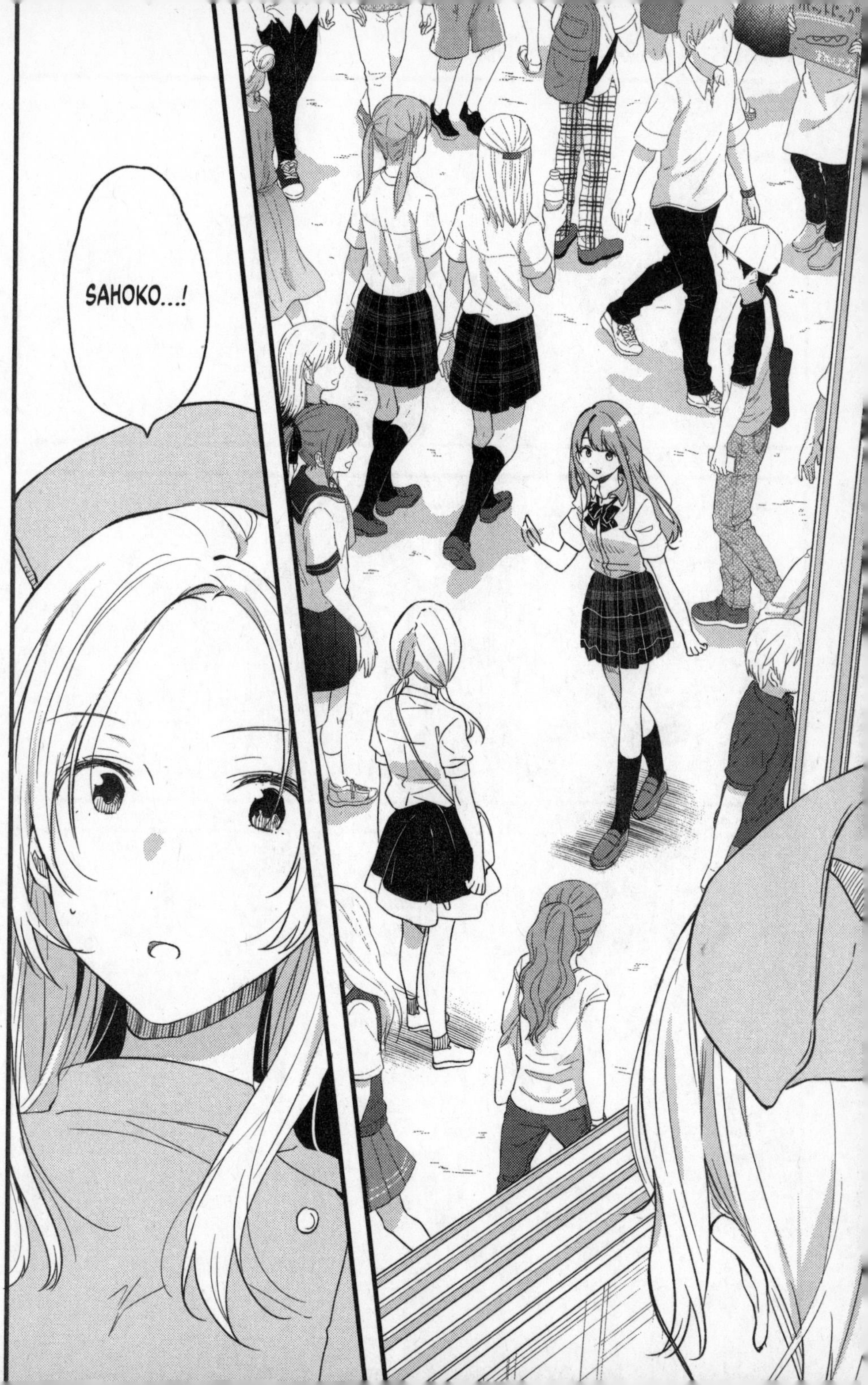
SAHOKO...!

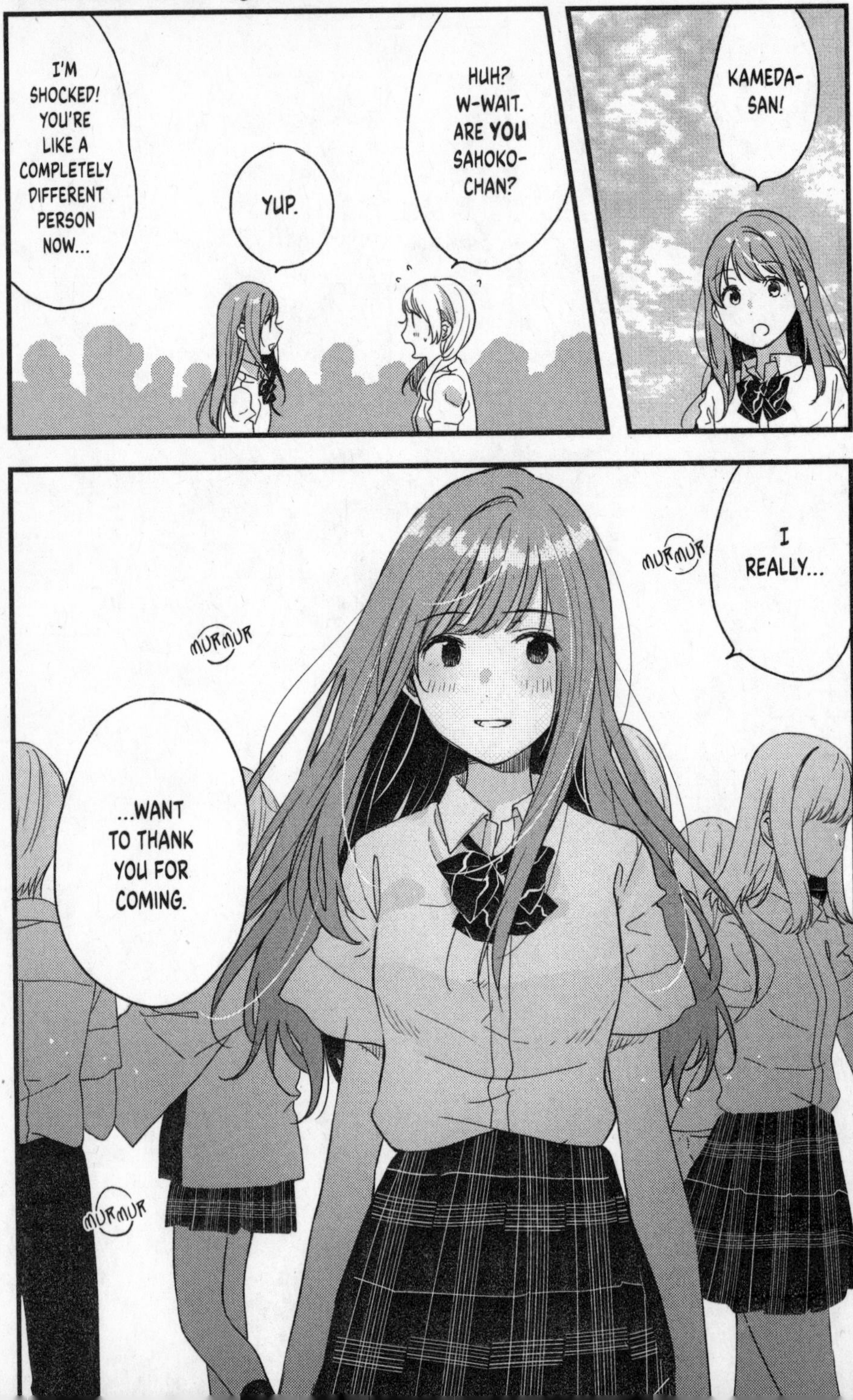
KAMEDA-SAN!
HUH? W-WAIT. ARE YOU SAHOKO-CHAN?
YUP.
I'M SHOCKED! YOU'RE LIKE A COMPLETELY DIFFERENT PERSON NOW...
I REALLY...
MURMUR
MURMUR
...WANT TO THANK YOU FOR COMING.
MURMUR

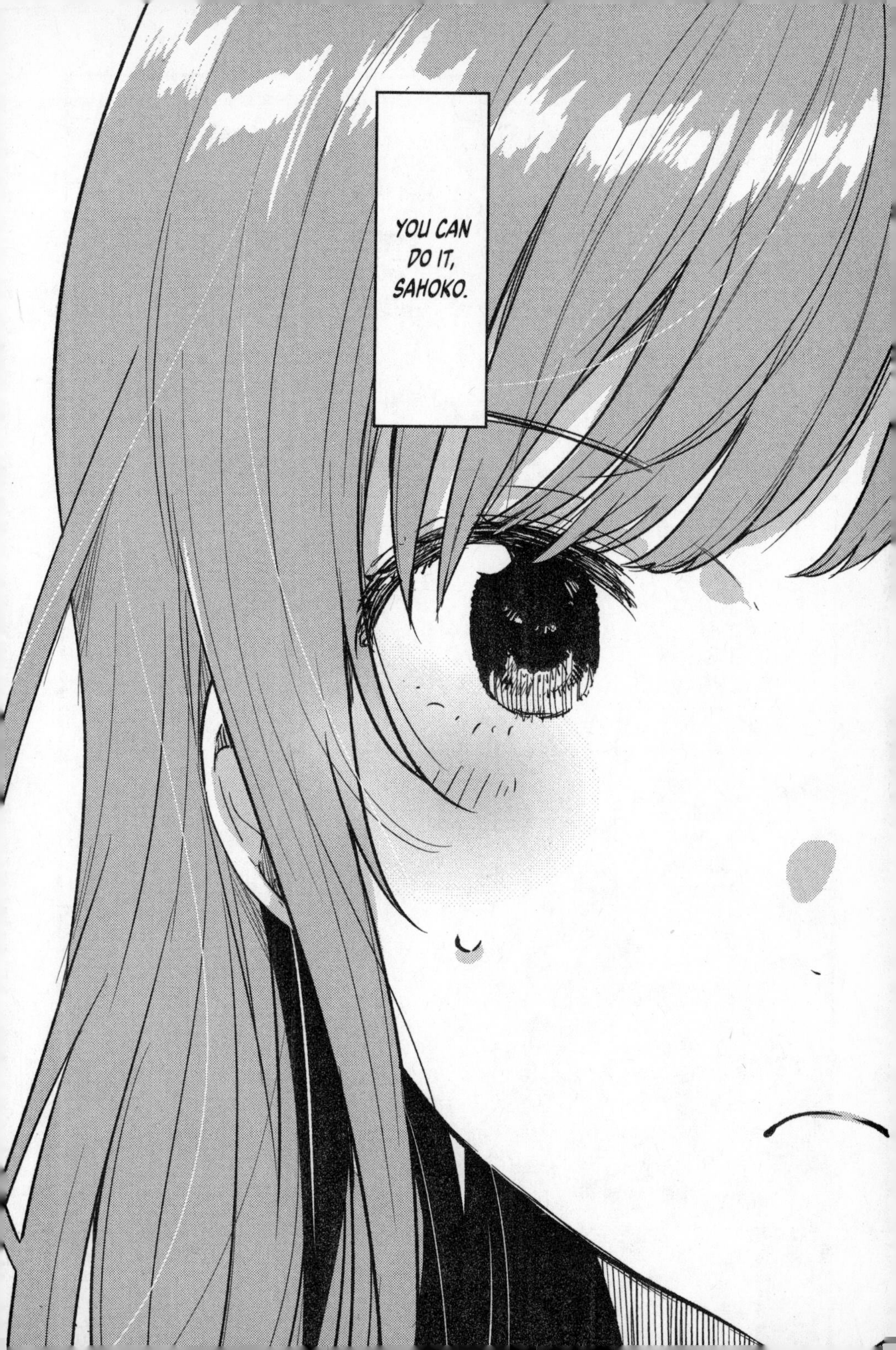
YOU CAN DO IT, SAHOKO.

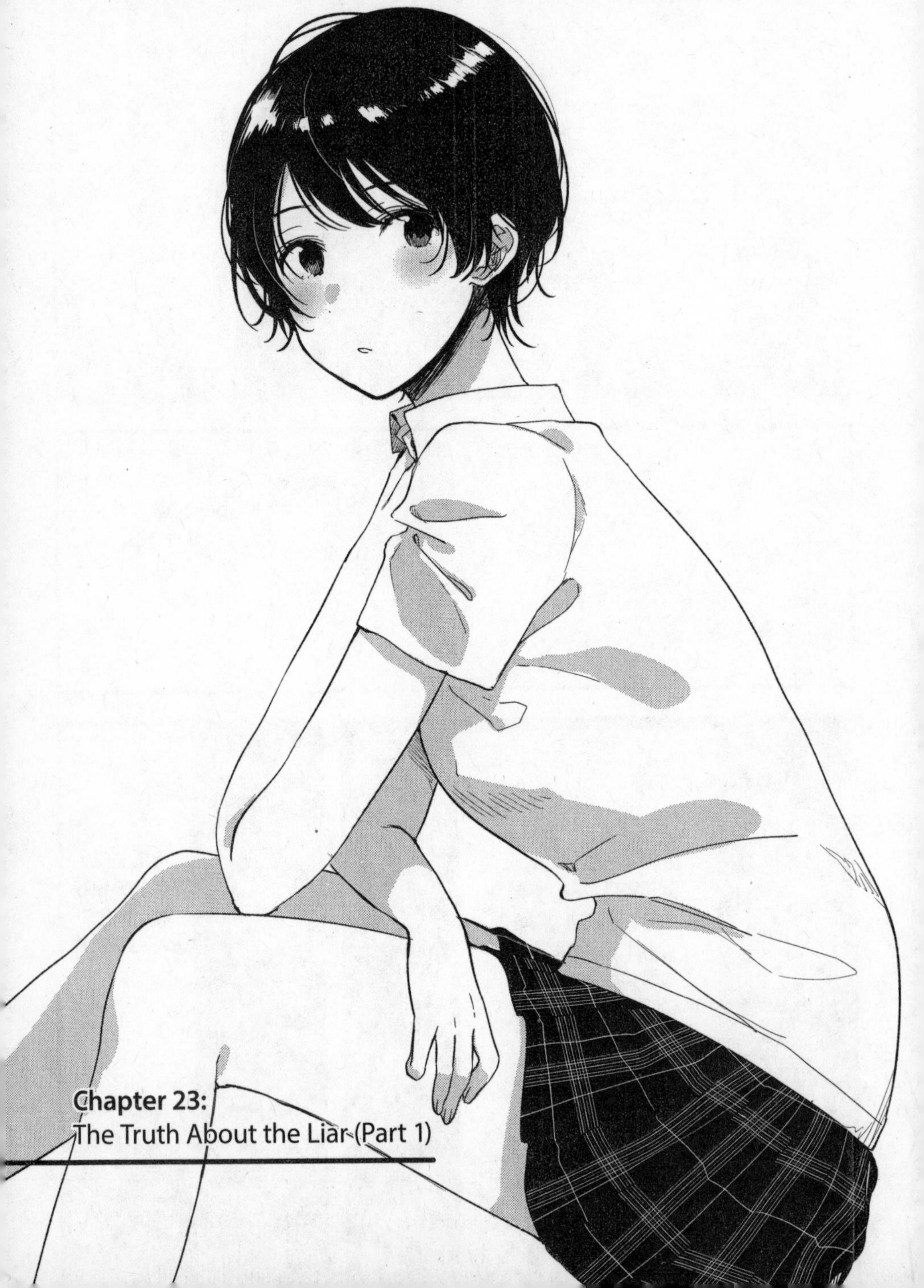

Chapter 23:
The Truth About the Liar (Part 1)

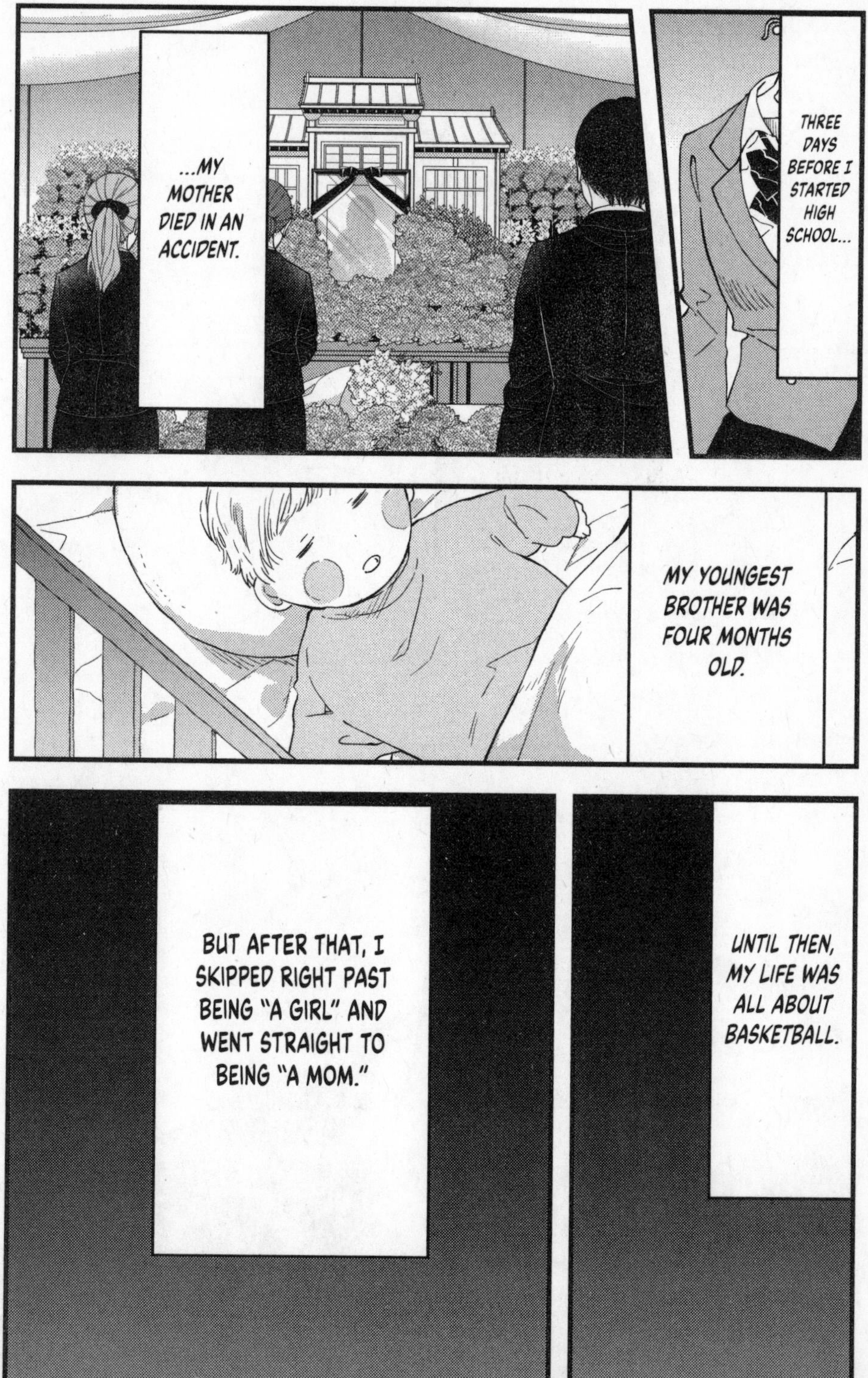
THREE DAYS BEFORE I STARTED HIGH SCHOOL...
...MY MOTHER DIED IN AN ACCIDENT.
MY YOUNGEST BROTHER WAS FOUR MONTHS OLD.
UNTIL THEN, MY LIFE WAS ALL ABOUT BASKETBALL.
BUT AFTER THAT, I SKIPPED RIGHT PAST BEING "A GIRL" AND WENT STRAIGHT TO BEING "A MOM."

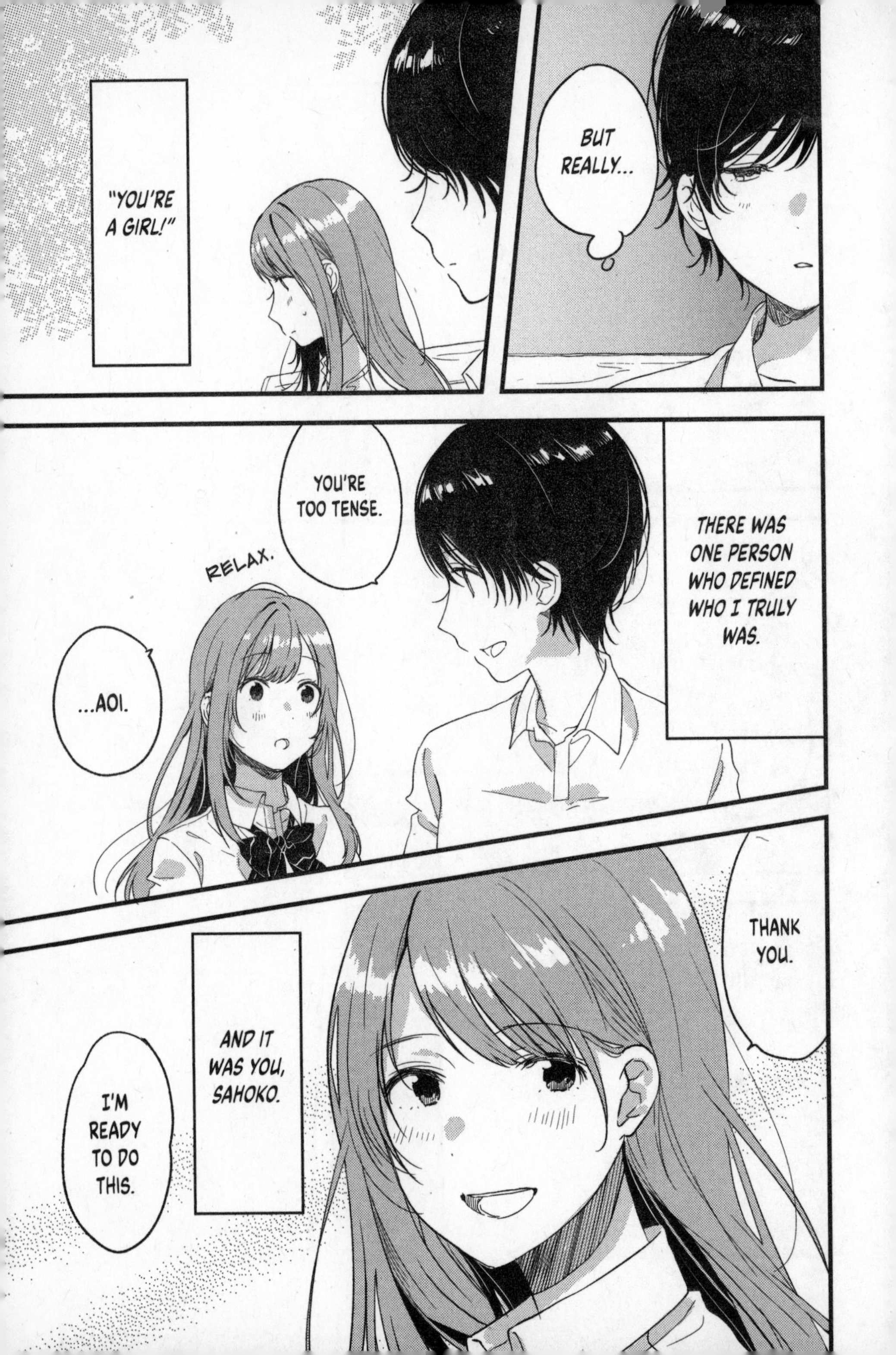
BUT REALLY...
"YOU'RE A GIRL!"
THERE WAS ONE PERSON WHO DEFINED WHO I TRULY WAS.
YOU'RE TOO TENSE.
RELAX.
...AOI.
THANK YOU.
AND IT WAS YOU, SAHOKO.
I'M READY TO DO THIS.

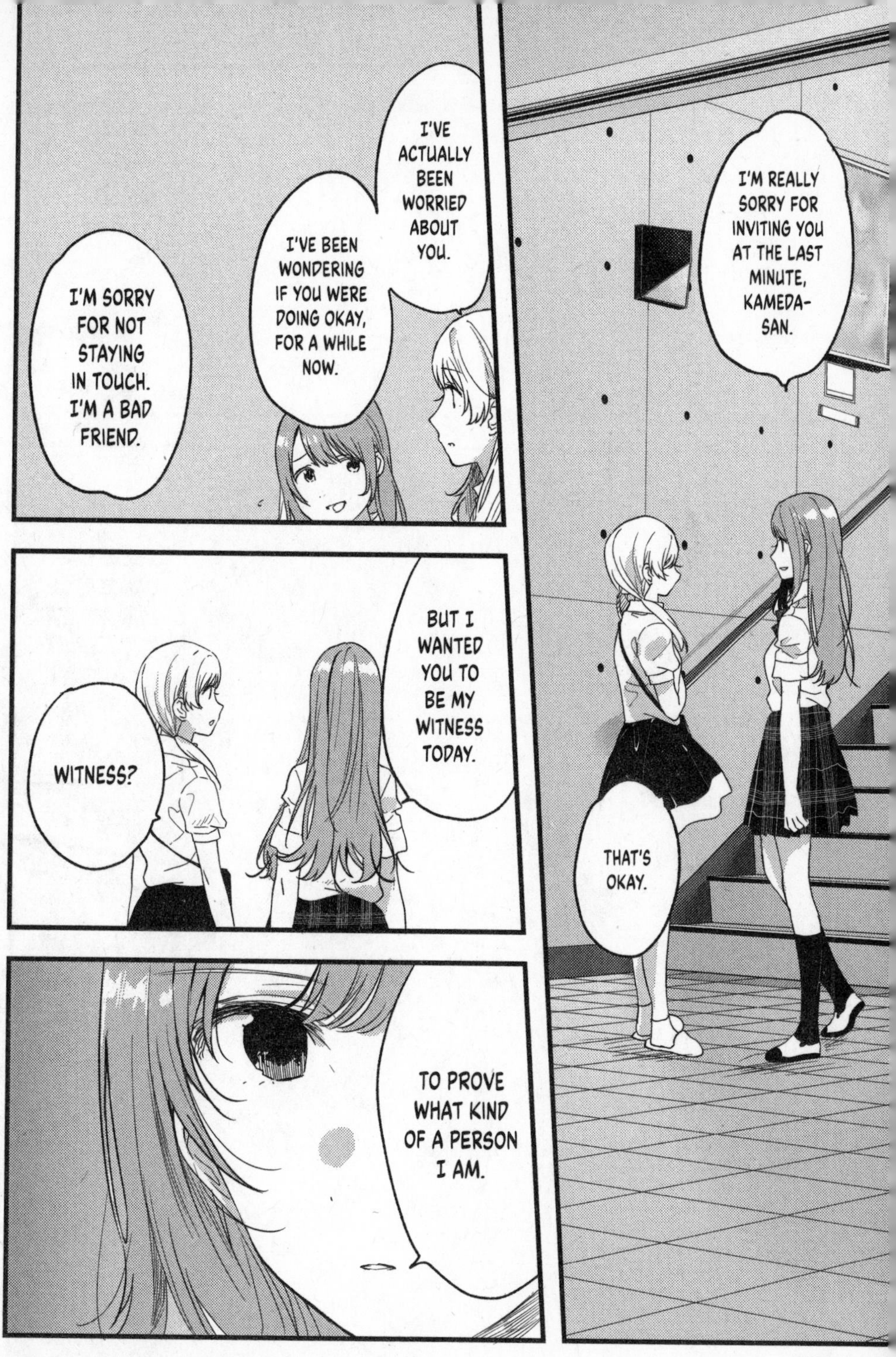
I'M REALLY SORRY FOR INVITING YOU AT THE LAST MINUTE, KAMEDA-SAN.
THAT'S OKAY.
I'VE ACTUALLY BEEN WORRIED ABOUT YOU.
I'VE BEEN WONDERING IF YOU WERE DOING OKAY, FOR A WHILE NOW.
I'M SORRY FOR NOT STAYING IN TOUCH. I'M A BAD FRIEND.
BUT I WANTED YOU TO BE MY WITNESS TODAY.
WITNESS?
TO PROVE WHAT KIND OF A PERSON I AM.

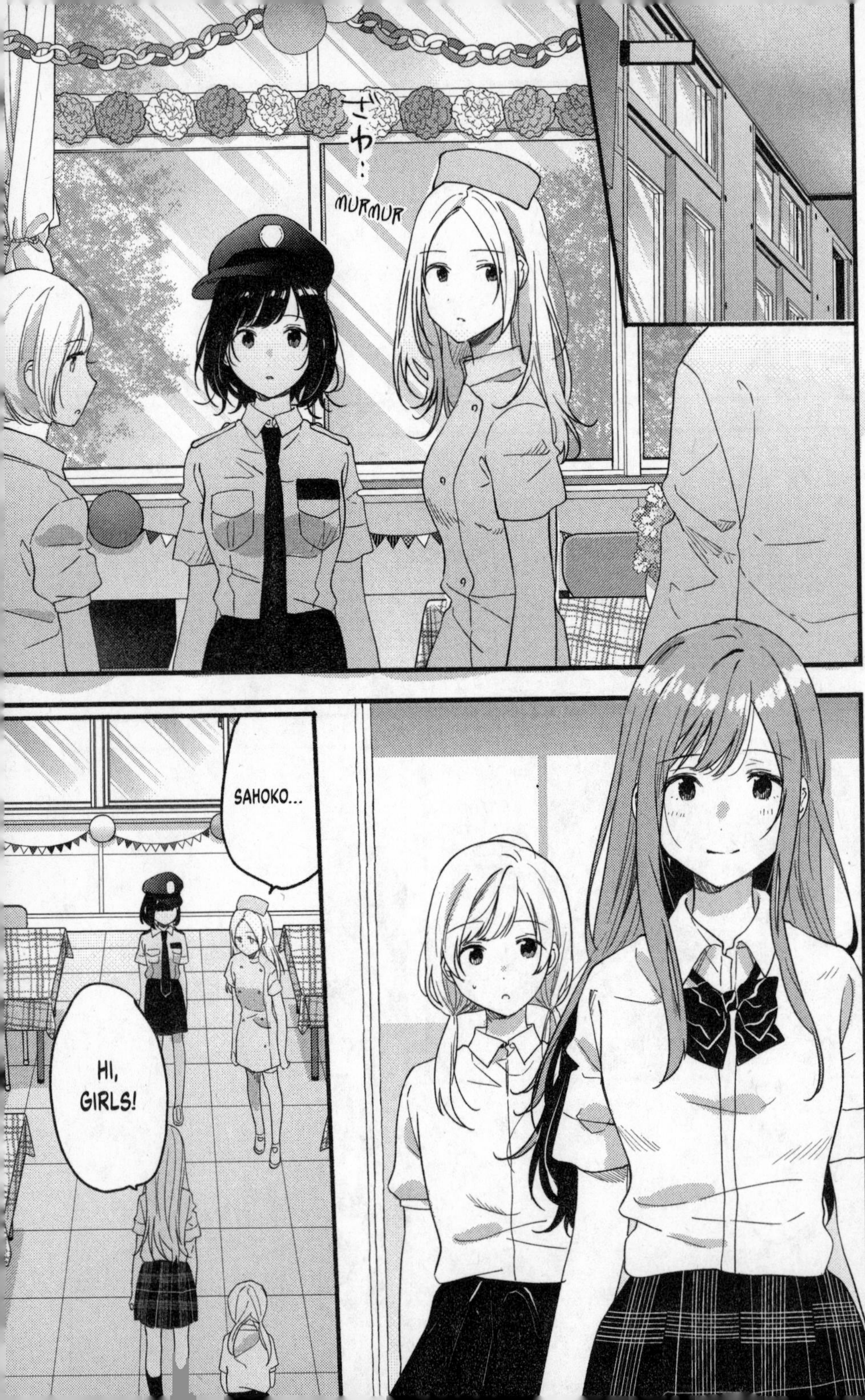
ざや…
MURMUR
SAHOKO...
HI, GIRLS!

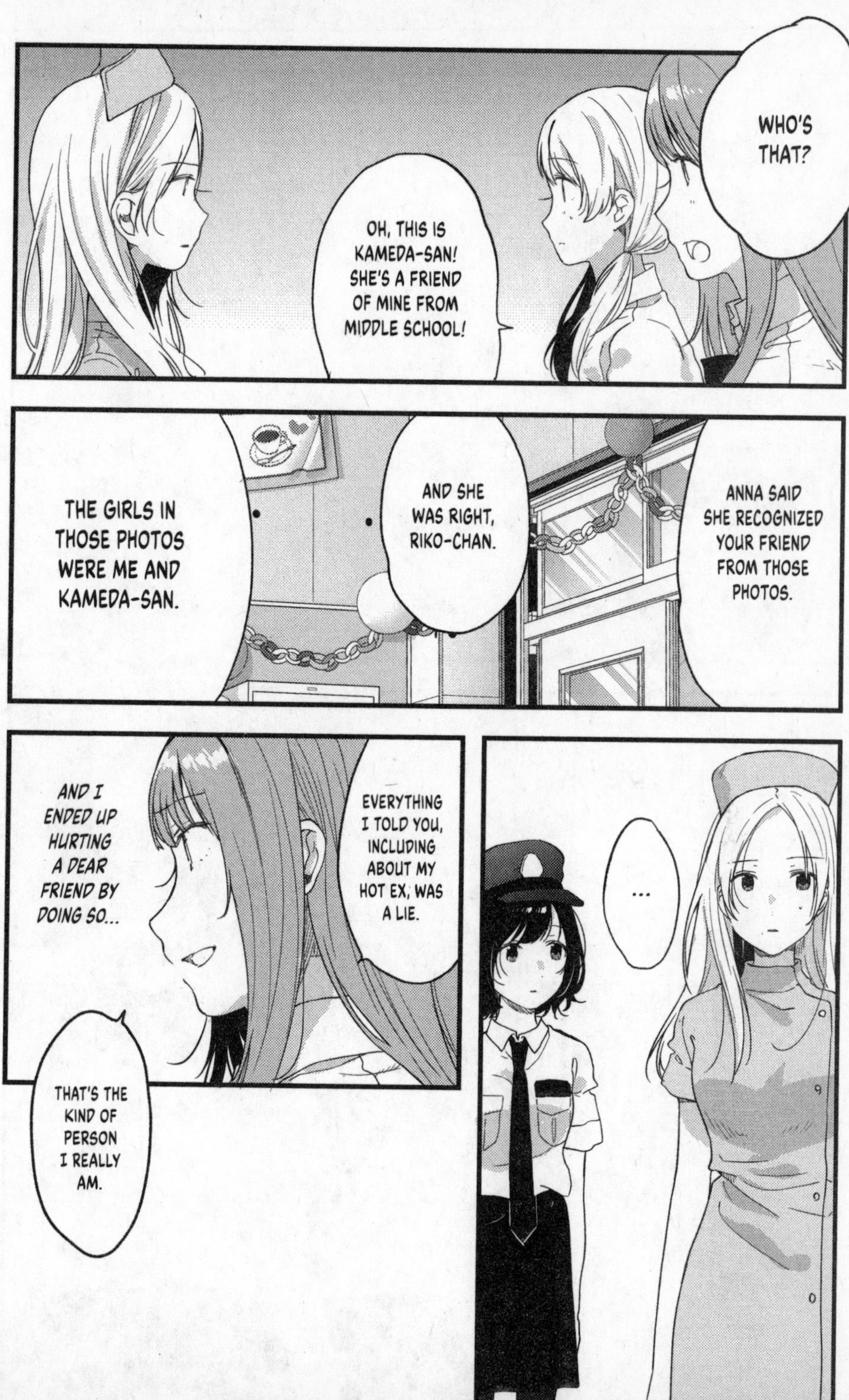
WHO'S THAT?
OH, THIS IS KAMEDA-SAN! SHE'S A FRIEND OF MINE FROM MIDDLE SCHOOL!
ANNA SAID SHE RECOGNIZED YOUR FRIEND FROM THOSE PHOTOS.
AND SHE WAS RIGHT, RIKO-CHAN.
THE GIRLS IN THOSE PHOTOS WERE ME AND KAMEDA-SAN.
...
EVERYTHING I TOLD YOU, INCLUDING ABOUT MY HOT EX, WAS A LIE.
AND I ENDED UP HURTING A DEAR FRIEND BY DOING SO...
THAT'S THE KIND OF PERSON I REALLY AM.

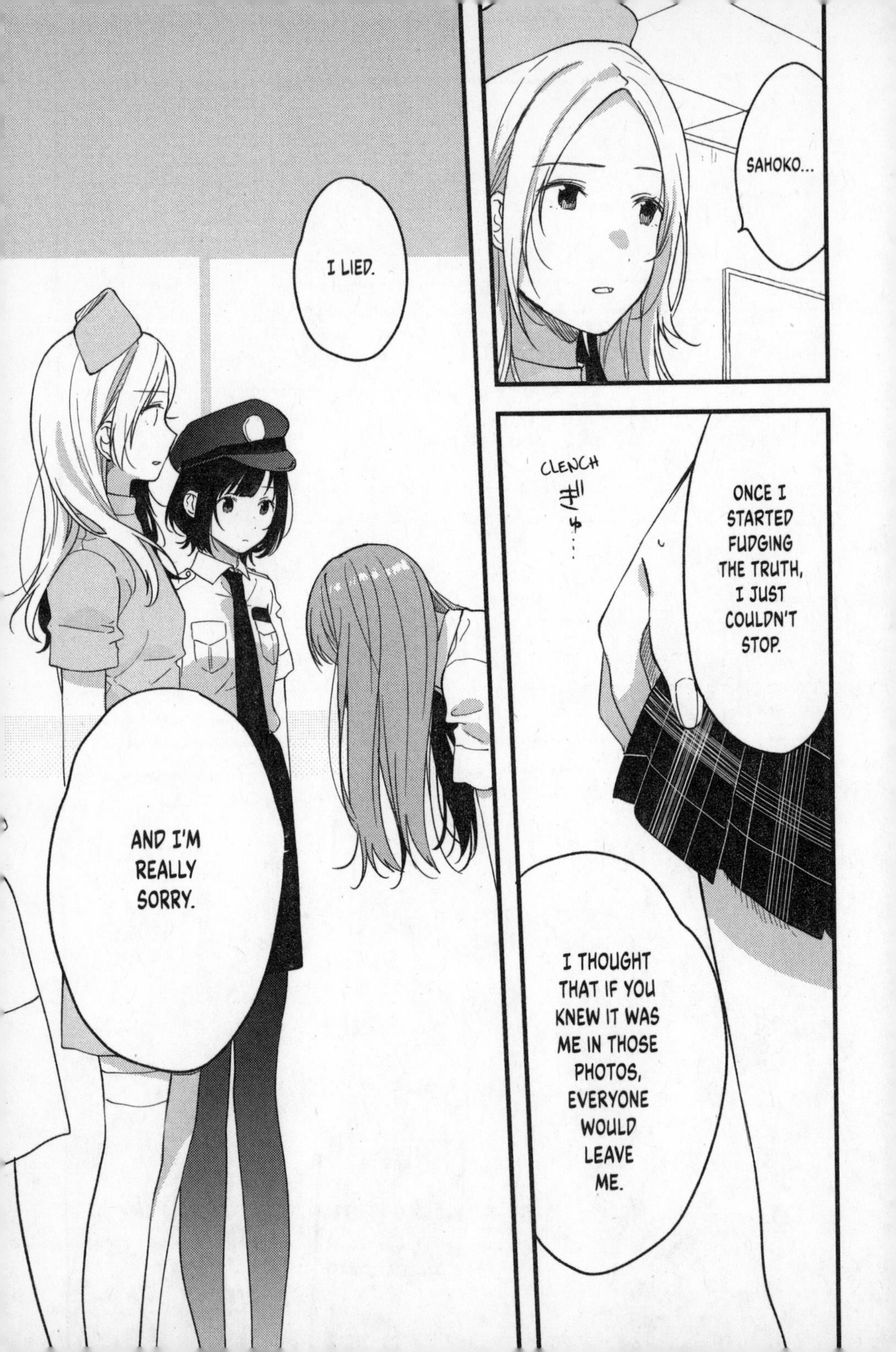
SAHOKO...
CLENCH
ぎゅ…
ONCE I STARTED FUDGING THE TRUTH, I JUST COULDN'T STOP.
I THOUGHT THAT IF YOU KNEW IT WAS ME IN THOSE PHOTOS, EVERYONE WOULD LEAVE ME.
I LIED.
AND I'M REALLY SORRY.

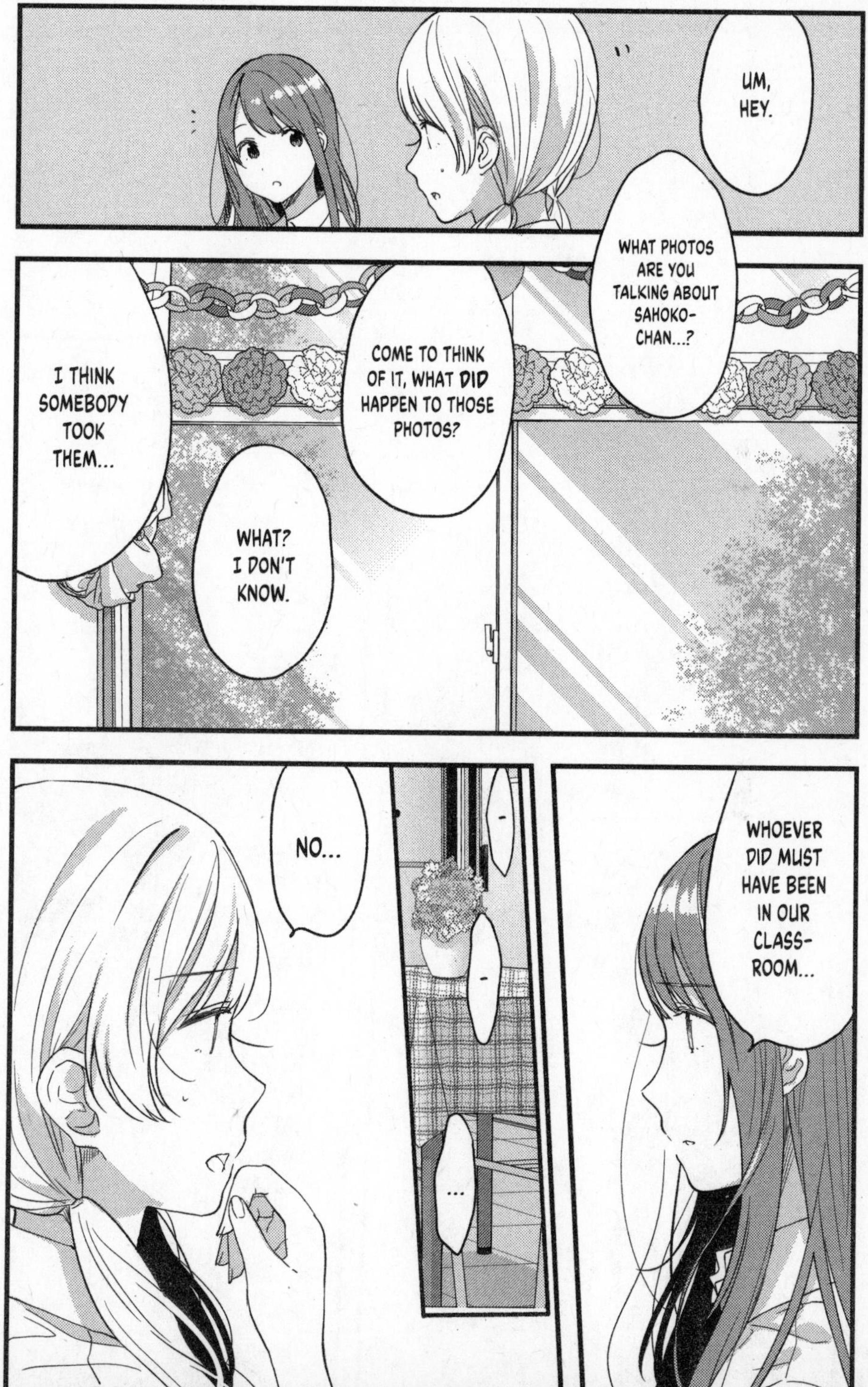
UM, HEY.
WHAT PHOTOS ARE YOU TALKING ABOUT SAHOKO-CHAN...?
COME TO THINK OF IT, WHAT DID HAPPEN TO THOSE PHOTOS?
WHAT? I DON'T KNOW.
I THINK SOMEBODY TOOK THEM...
WHOEVER DID MUST HAVE BEEN IN OUR CLASSROOM...
-
-
...
NO...

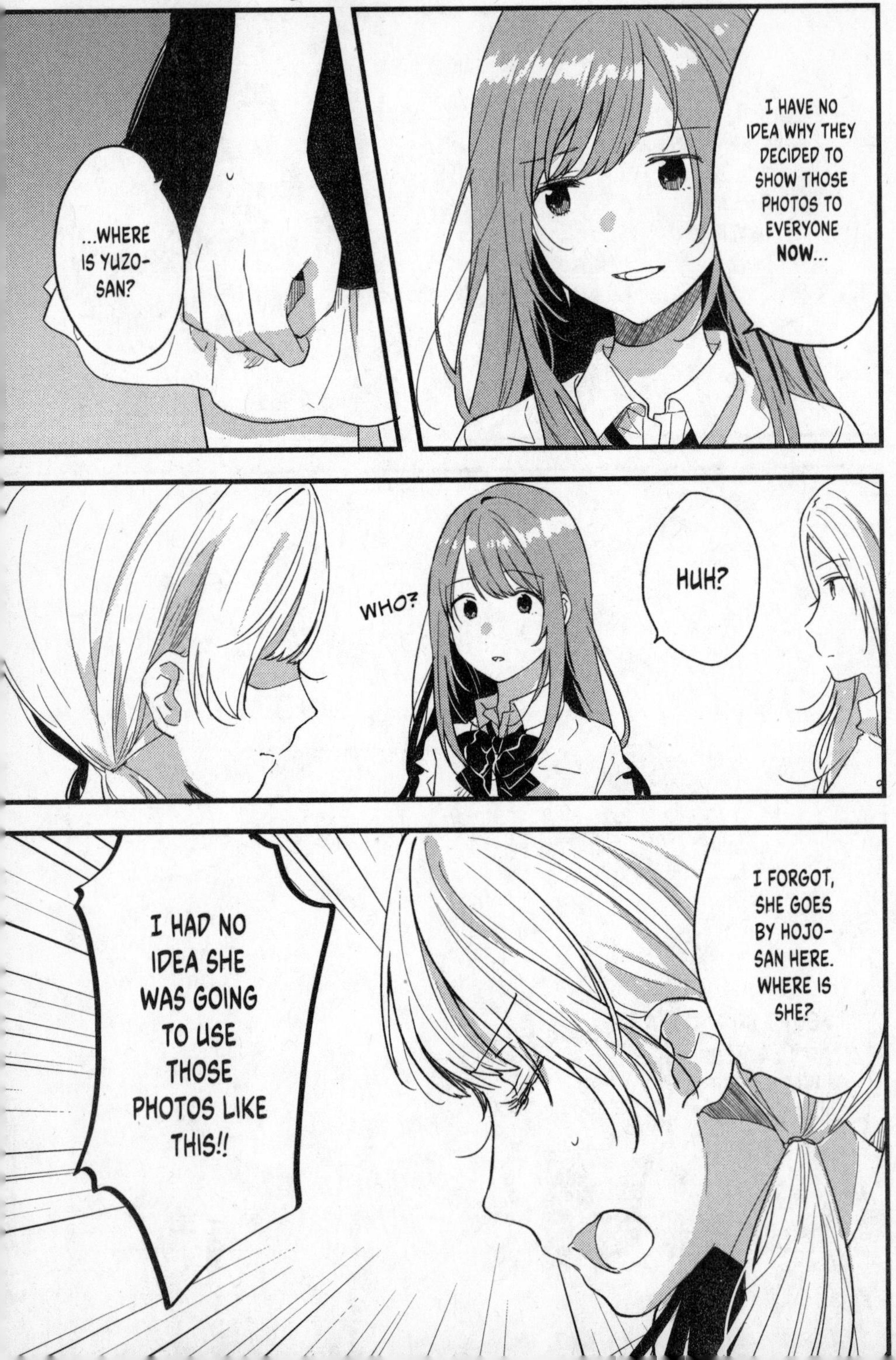
I HAVE NO IDEA WHY THEY DECIDED TO SHOW THOSE PHOTOS TO EVERYONE NOW...
...WHERE IS YUZO-SAN?
HUH?
WHO?
I FORGOT, SHE GOES BY HOJO-SAN HERE. WHERE IS SHE?
I HAD NO IDEA SHE WAS GOING TO USE THOSE PHOTOS LIKE THIS!!

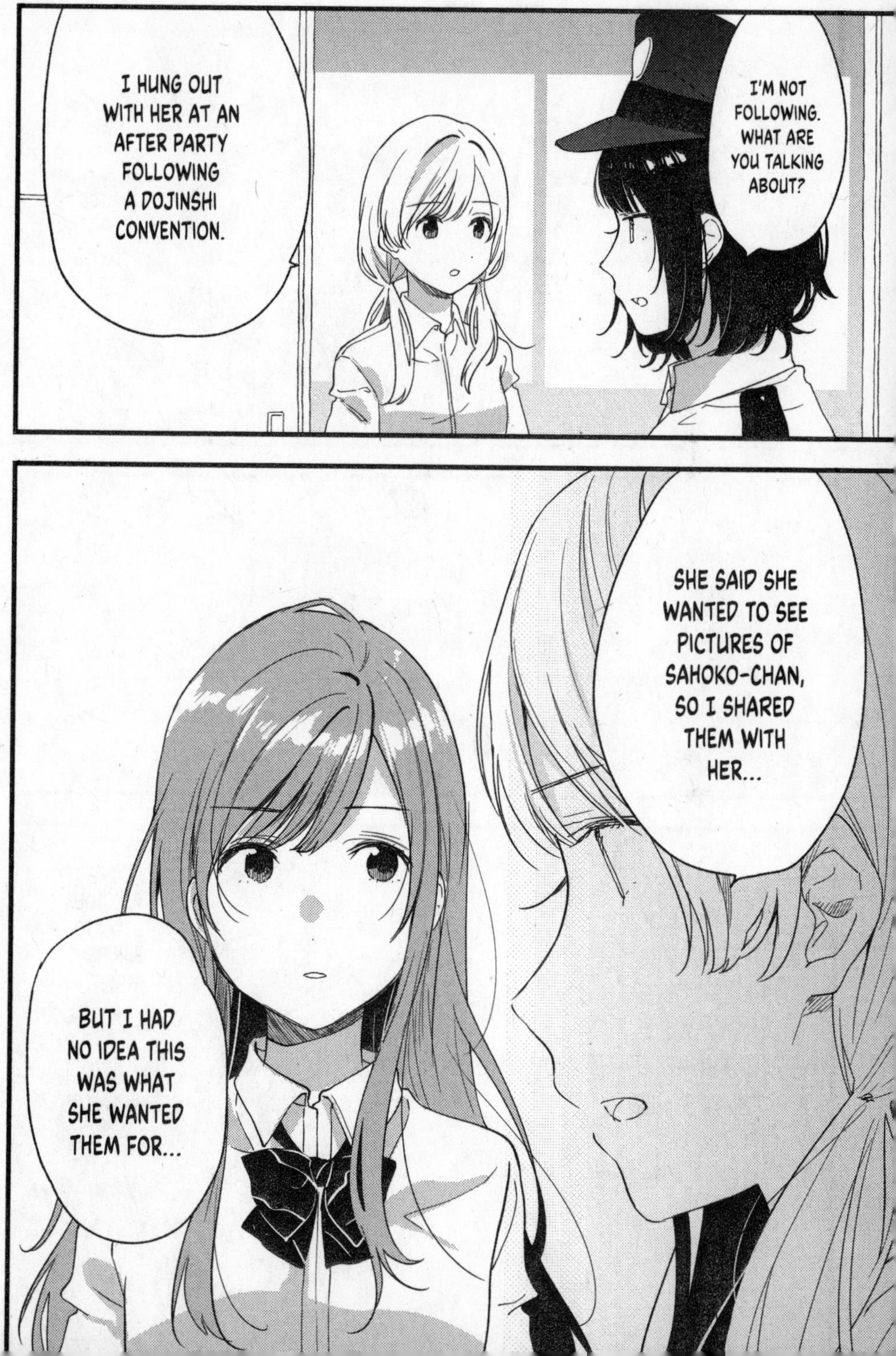
I'M NOT FOLLOWING. WHAT ARE YOU TALKING ABOUT?
I HUNG OUT WITH HER AT AN AFTER PARTY FOLLOWING A DOJINSHI CONVENTION.
SHE SAID SHE WANTED TO SEE PICTURES OF SAHOKO-CHAN, SO I SHARED THEM WITH HER...
BUT I HAD NO IDEA THIS WAS WHAT SHE WANTED THEM FOR...

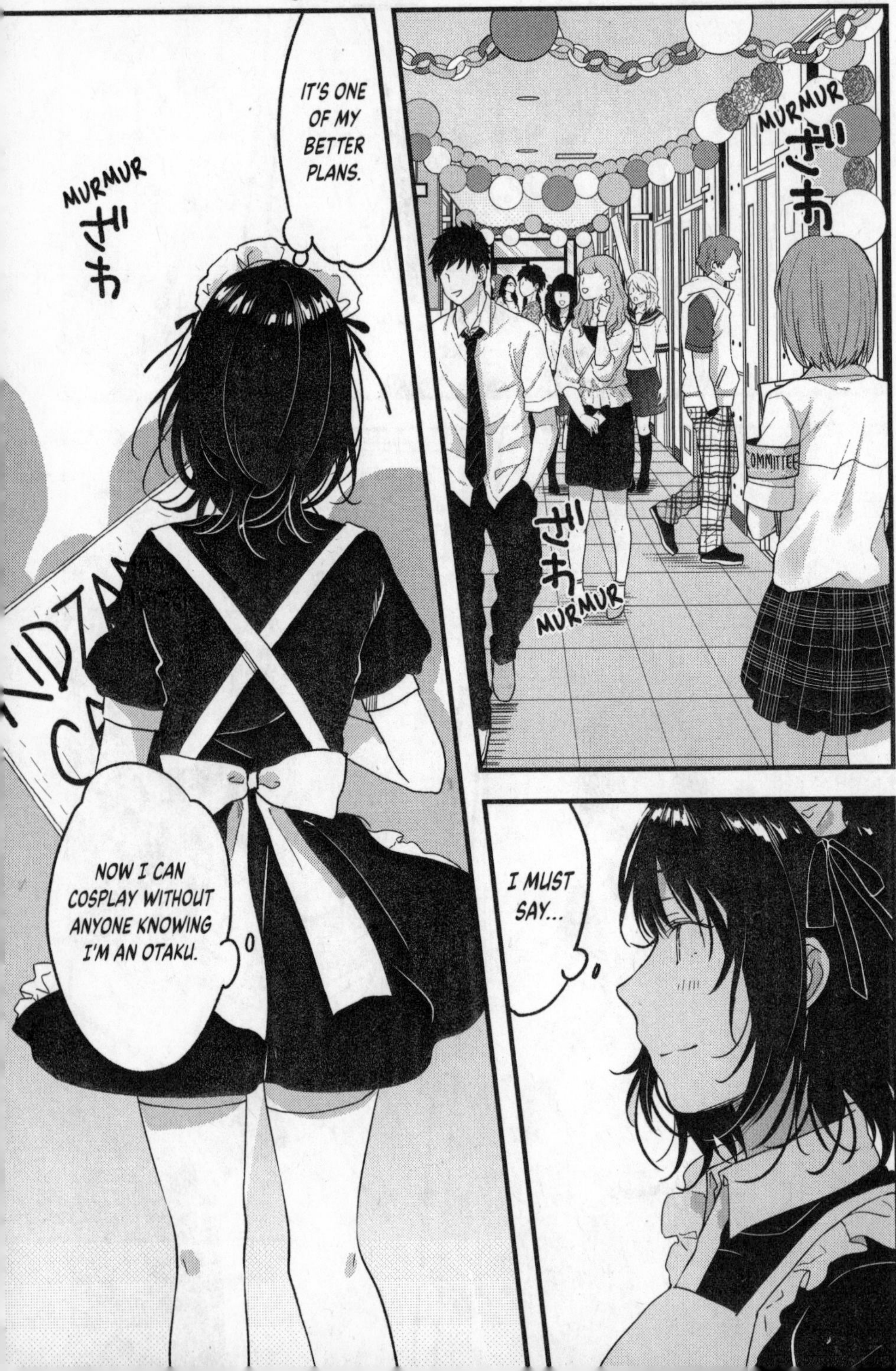
MURMUR
ざわ
ざわ
MURMUR
I MUST SAY...
IT'S ONE OF MY BETTER PLANS.
MURMUR
ざわ
NOW I CAN COSPLAY WITHOUT ANYONE KNOWING I'M AN OTAKU.

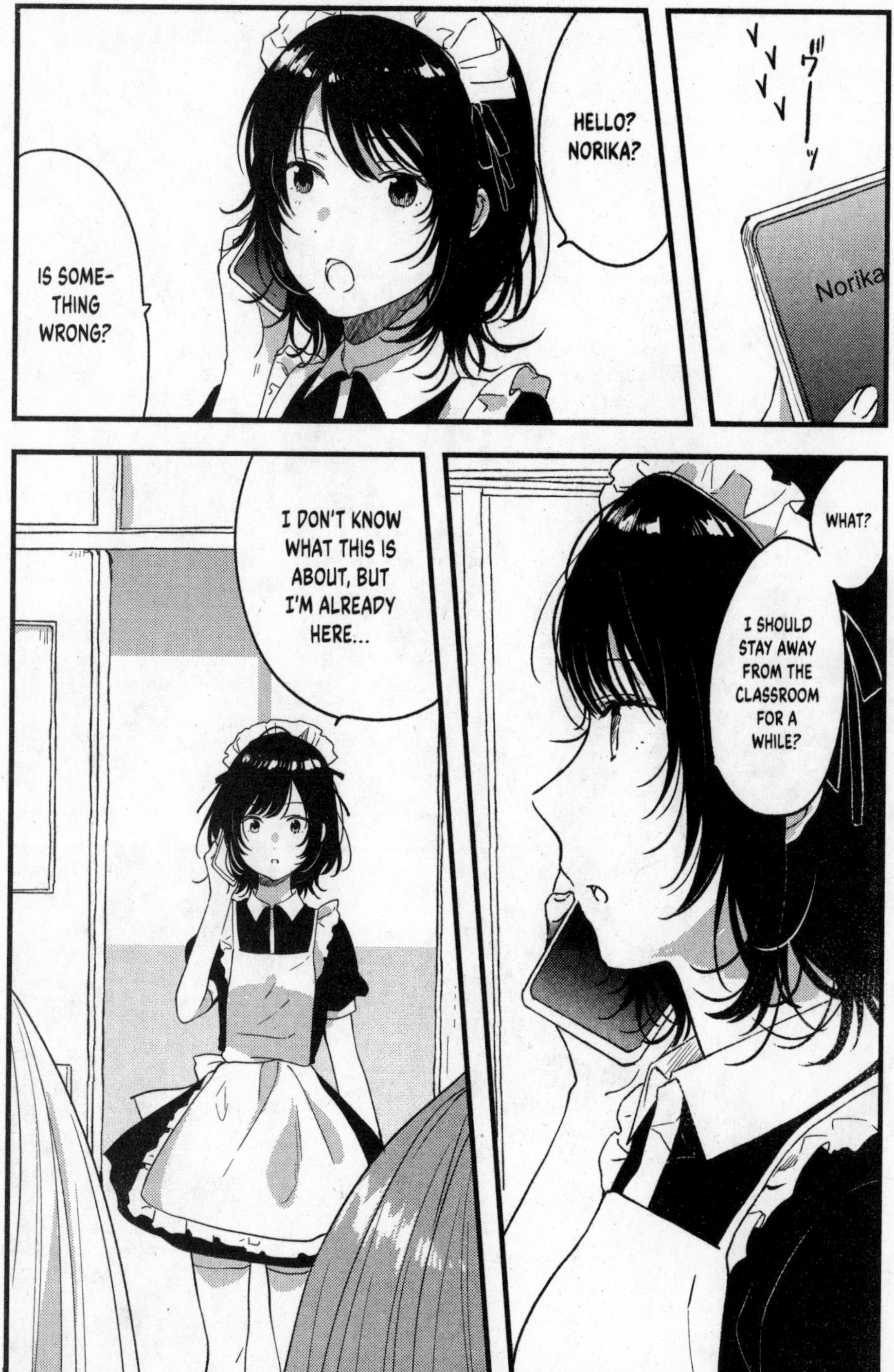
ヴーーッ
Norika
HELLO? NORIKA?
IS SOME-THING WRONG?
WHAT?
I SHOULD STAY AWAY FROM THE CLASSROOM FOR A WHILE?
I DON'T KNOW WHAT THIS IS ABOUT, BUT I'M ALREADY HERE...

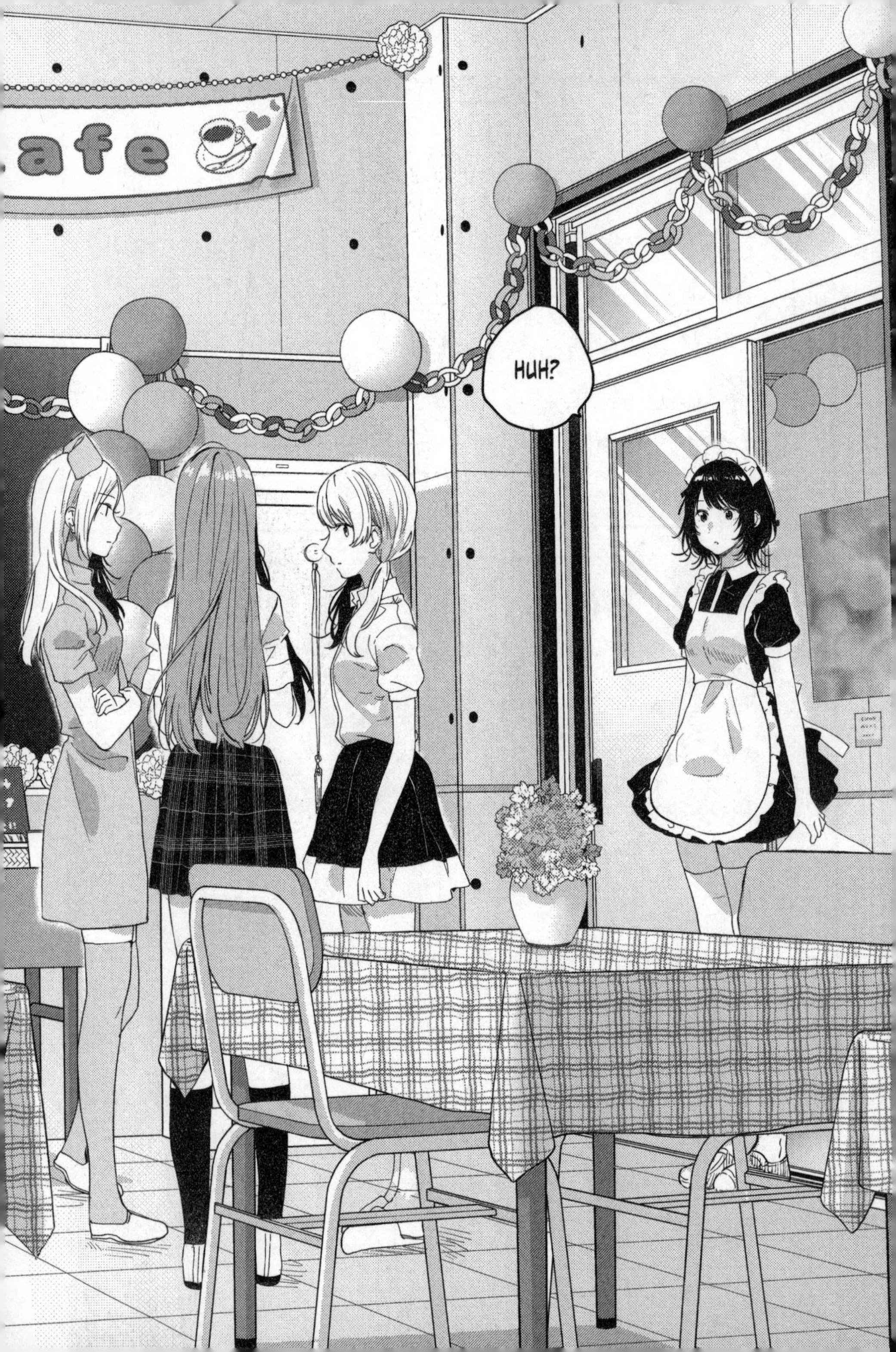
afe
HUH?

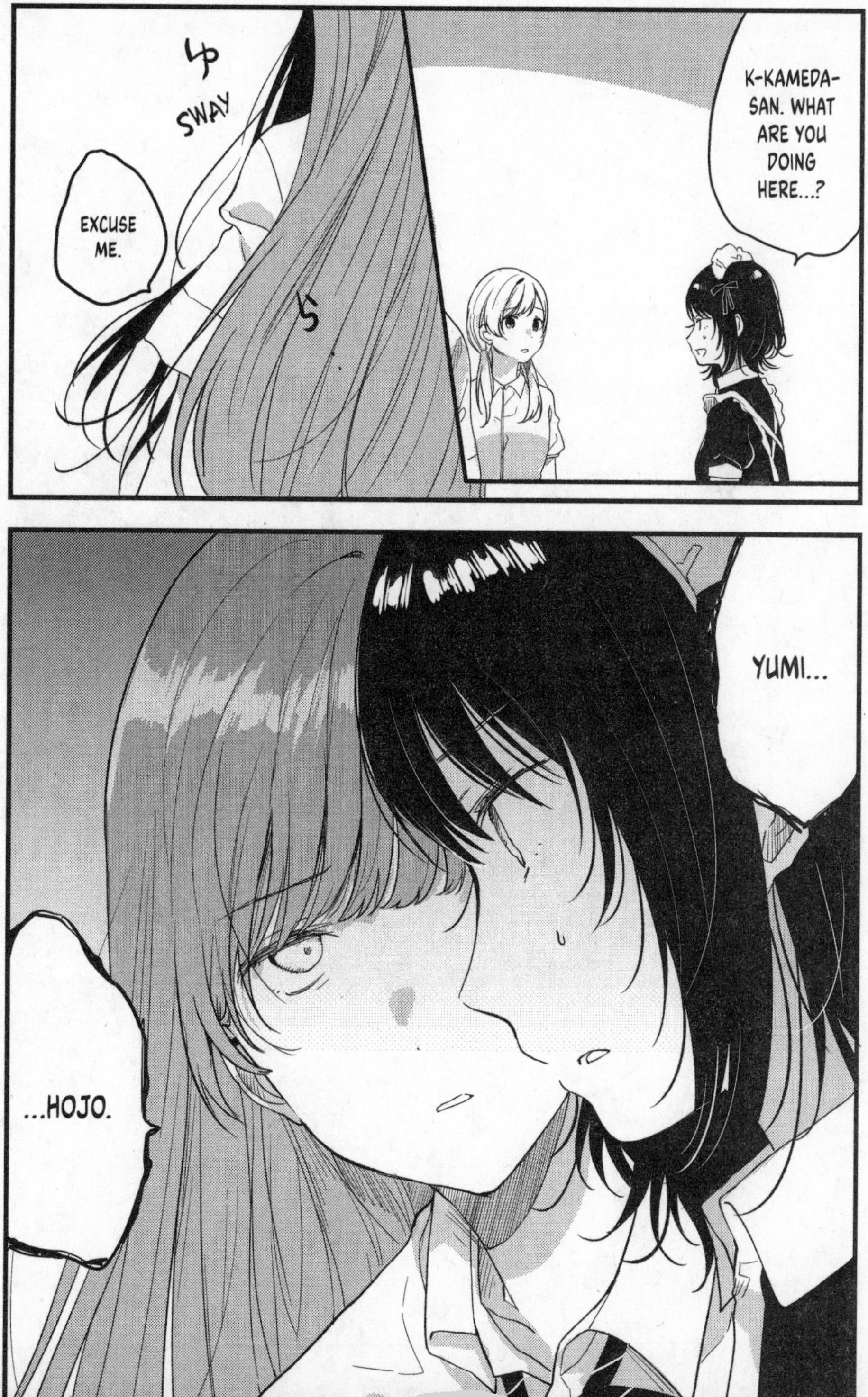
K-KAMEDA-SAN. WHAT ARE YOU DOING HERE...?
SWAY
EXCUSE ME.
YUMI...
...HOJO.

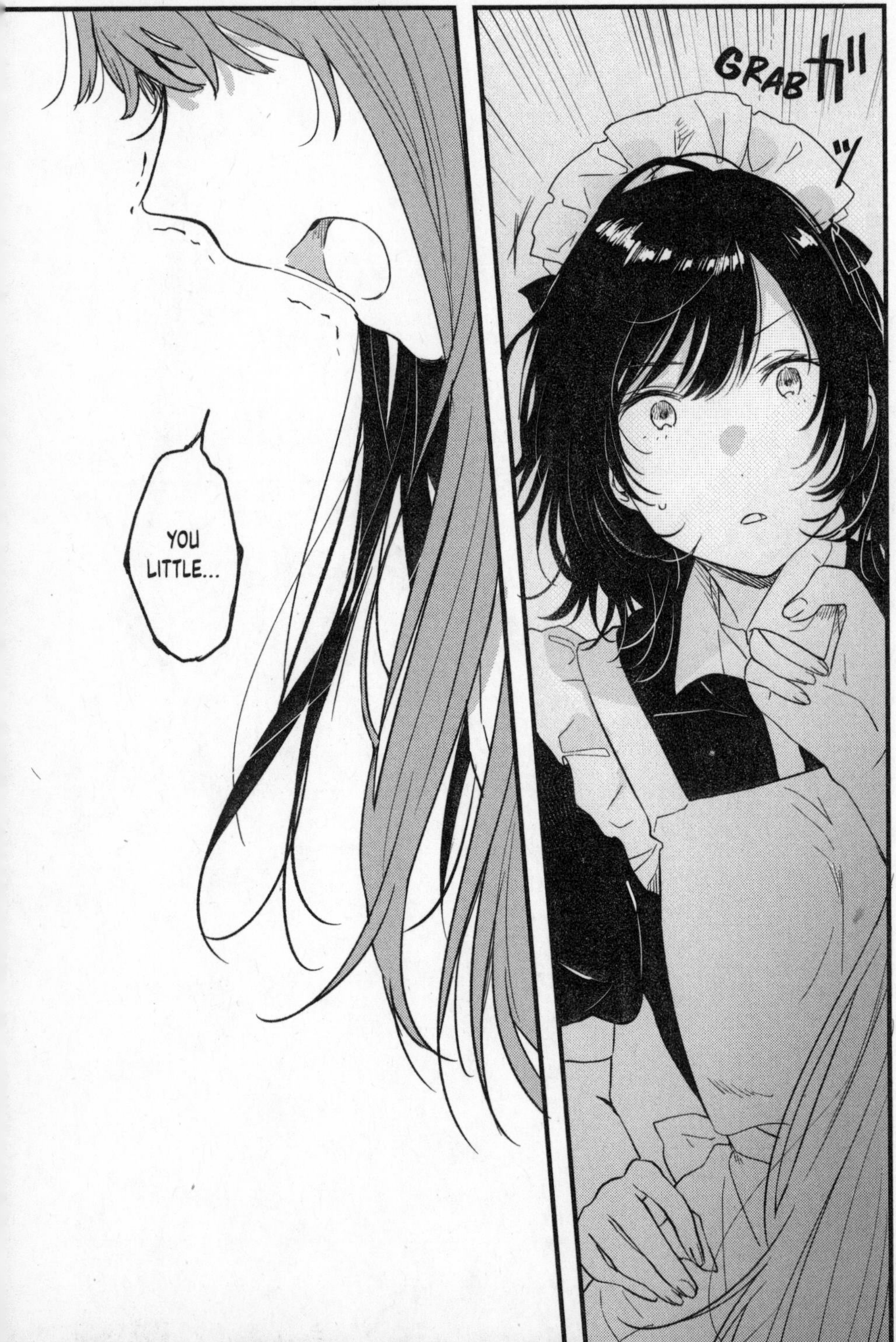
GRAB ガッ
YOU LITTLE...

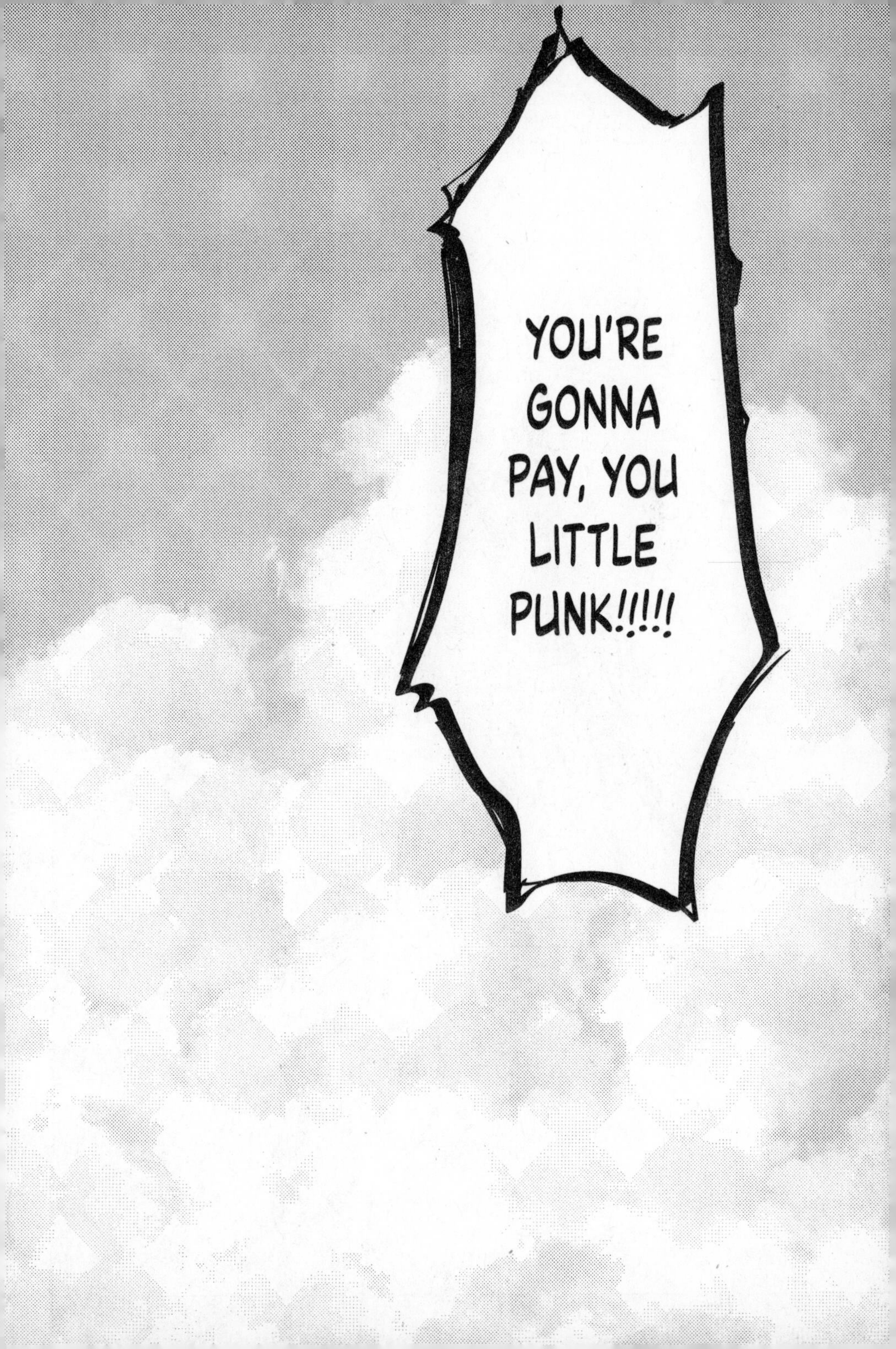
YOU'RE GONNA PAY, YOU LITTLE PUNK!!!!!

Chapter 24:
The Truth About the Liar (Part 2)

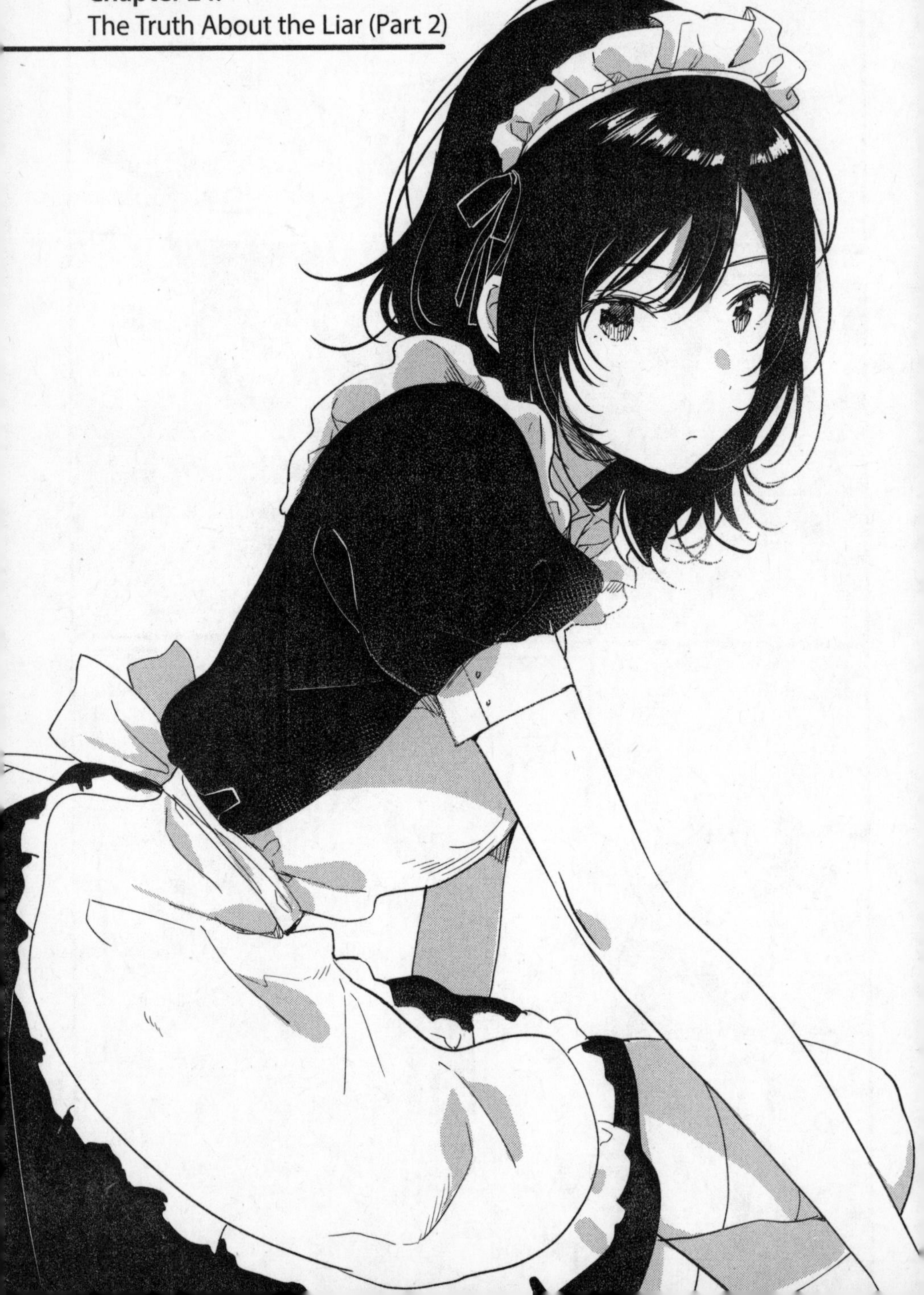

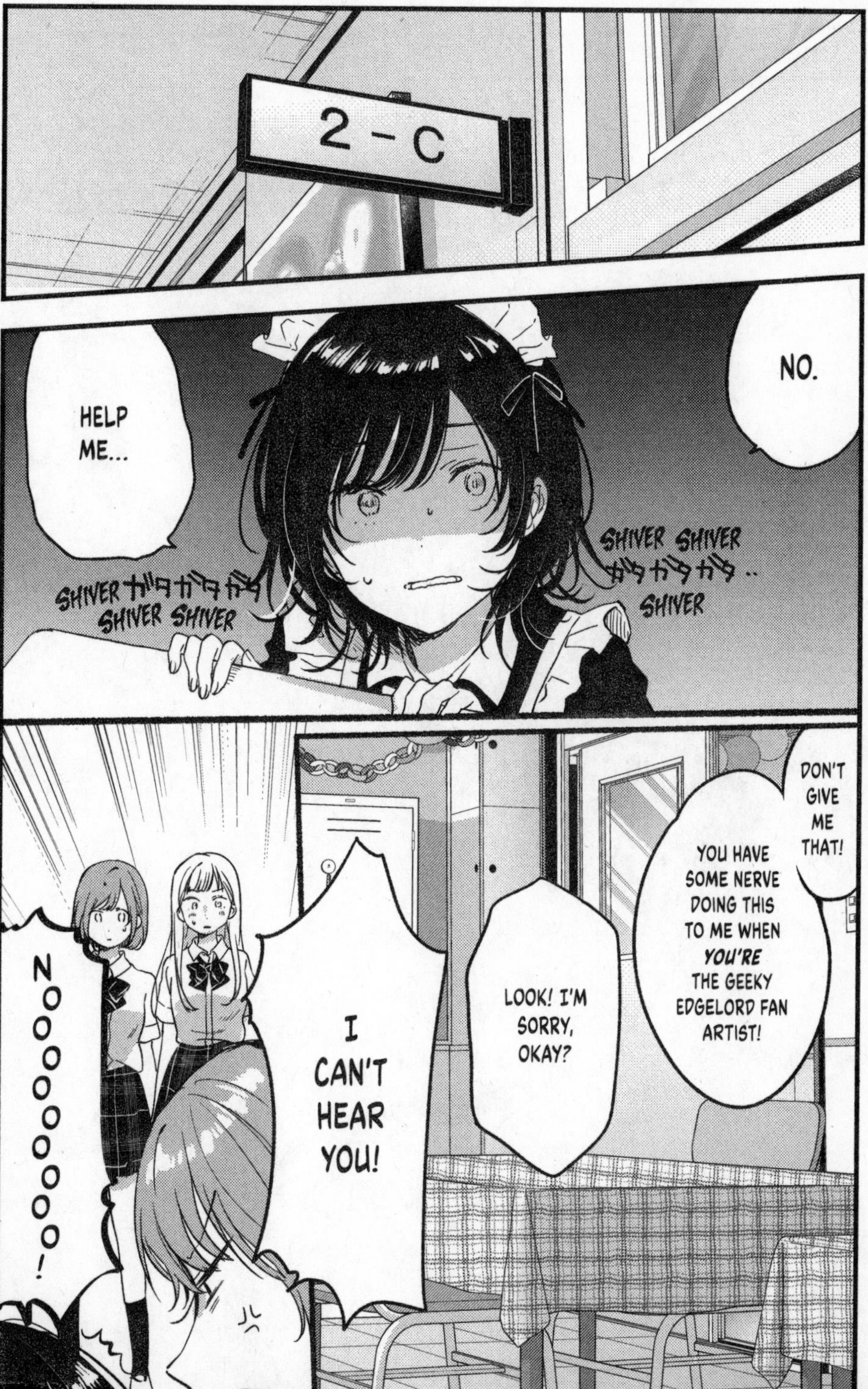
2-C
NO.
HELP ME...
SHIVER SHIVER ガタガタガタ.. SHIVER
SHIVER ガタガタガタ SHIVER SHIVER
DON'T GIVE ME THAT!
YOU HAVE SOME NERVE DOING THIS TO ME WHEN *YOU'RE* THE GEEKY EDGELORD FAN ARTIST!
LOOK! I'M SORRY, OKAY?
I CAN'T HEAR YOU!
NOOOOOOOOOO!

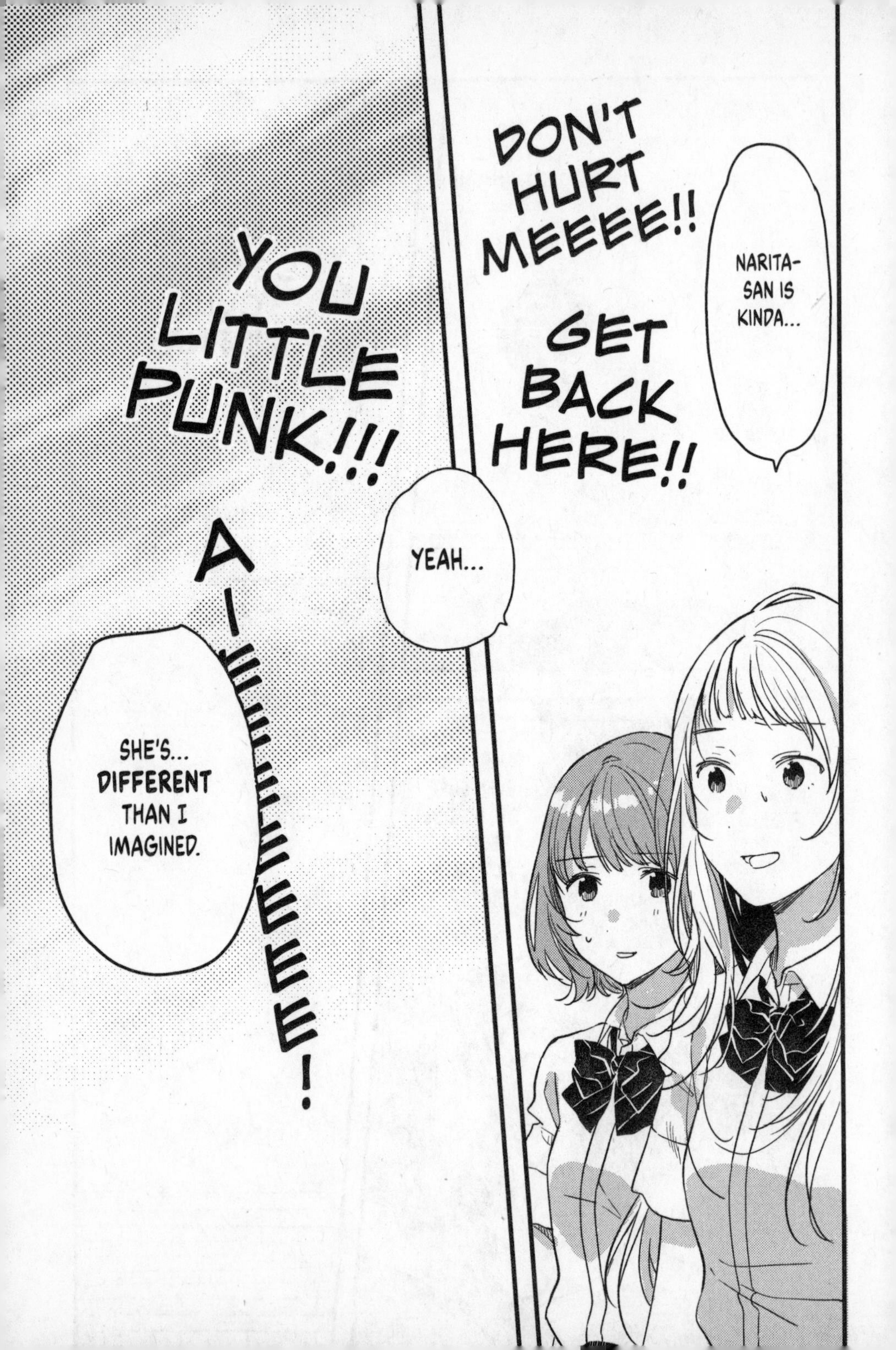
DON'T HURT MEEEEE!!
NARITA-SAN IS KINDA...
GET BACK HERE!!
YEAH...
YOU LITTLE PUNK!!!
A-IEEEEEEEE!
SHE'S... DIFFERENT THAN I IMAGINED.

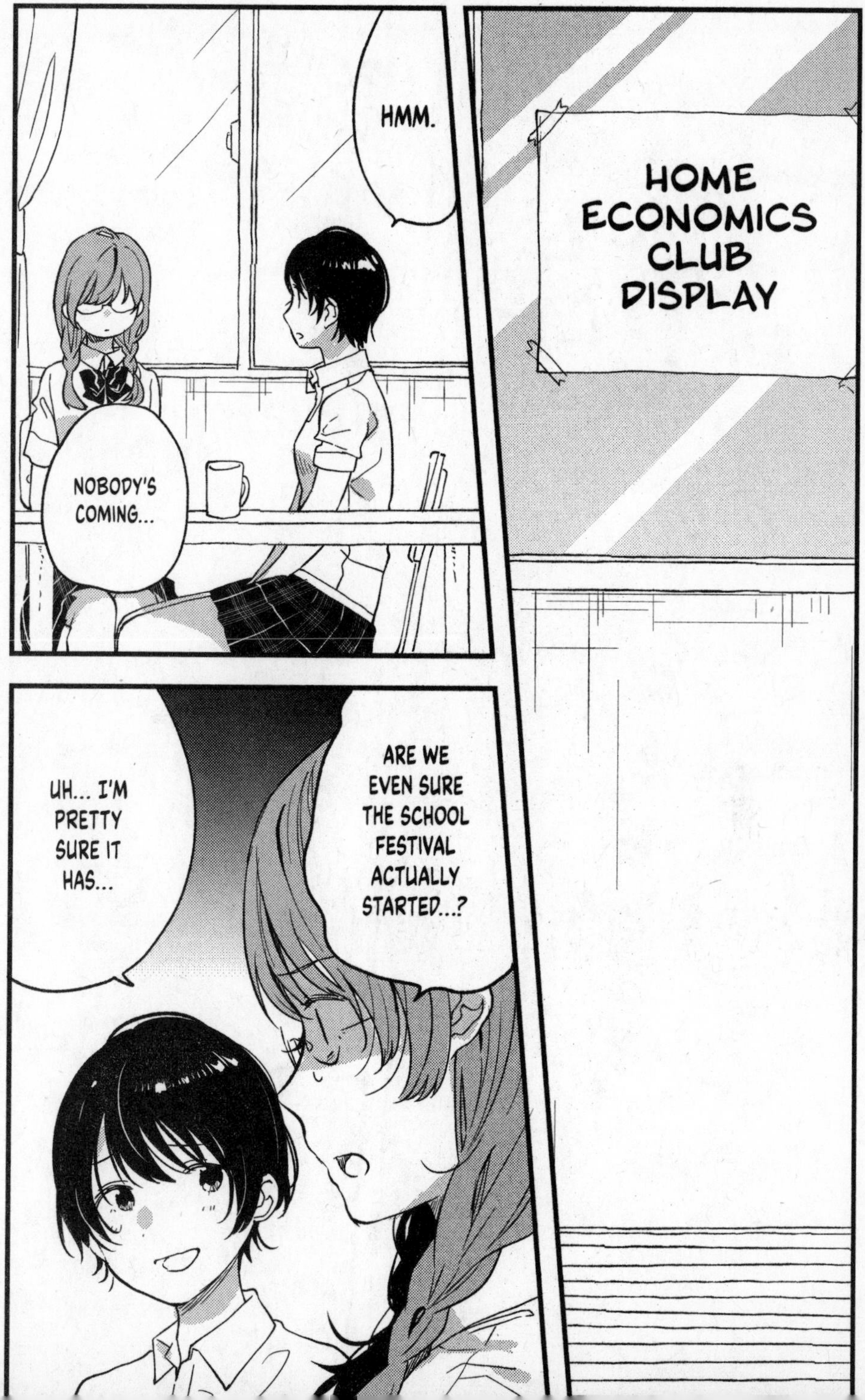
HOME ECONOMICS CLUB DISPLAY
HMM.
NOBODY'S COMING...
ARE WE EVEN SURE THE SCHOOL FESTIVAL ACTUALLY STARTED...?
UH... I'M PRETTY SURE IT HAS...

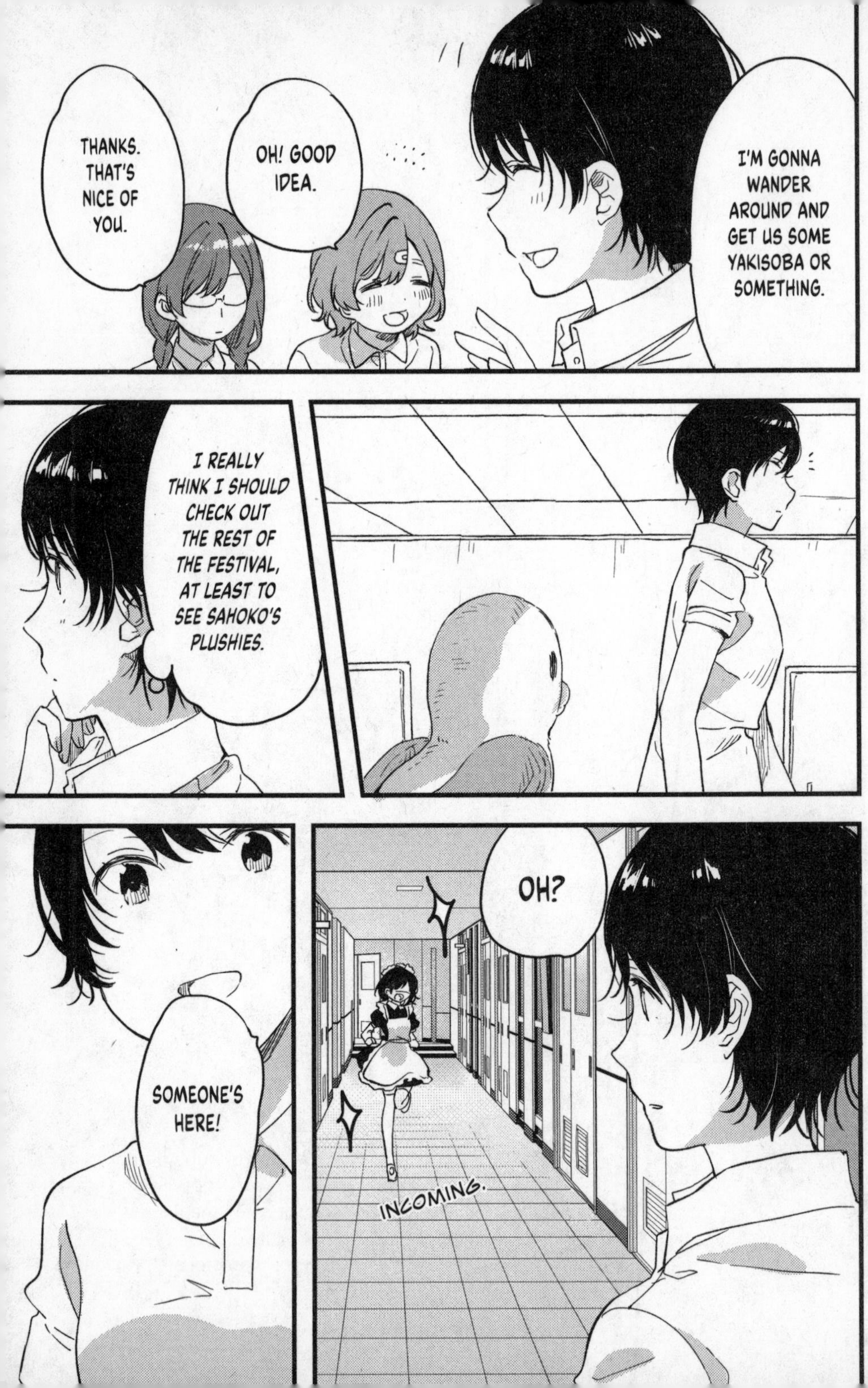
I'M GONNA WANDER AROUND AND GET US SOME YAKISOBA OR SOMETHING.
OH! GOOD IDEA.
THANKS. THAT'S NICE OF YOU.
I REALLY THINK I SHOULD CHECK OUT THE REST OF THE FESTIVAL, AT LEAST TO SEE SAHOKO'S PLUSHIES.
OH?
INCOMING.
SOMEONE'S HERE!

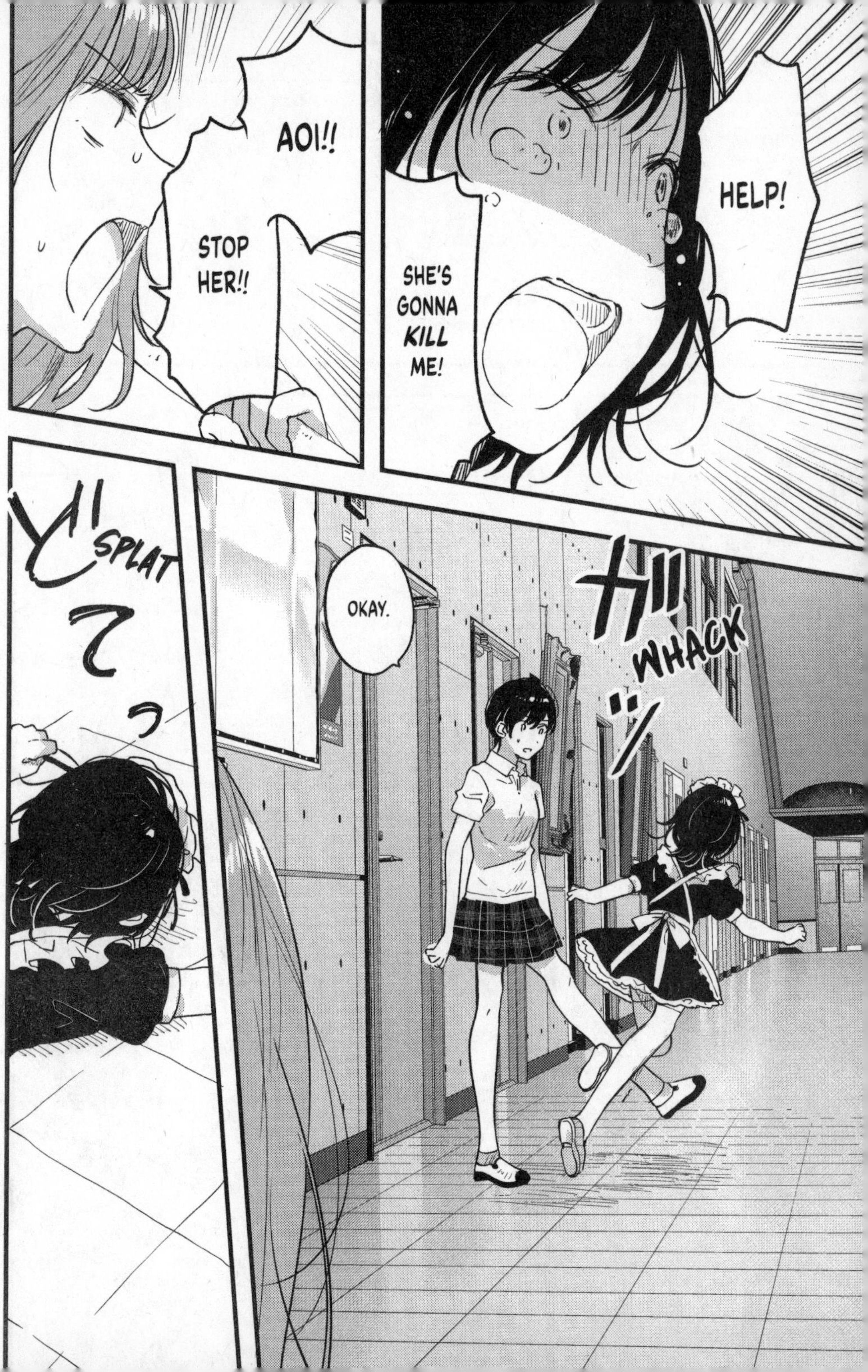
HELP!
SHE'S GONNA KILL ME!
AOI!!
STOP HER!!
OKAY.
WHACK
SPLAT

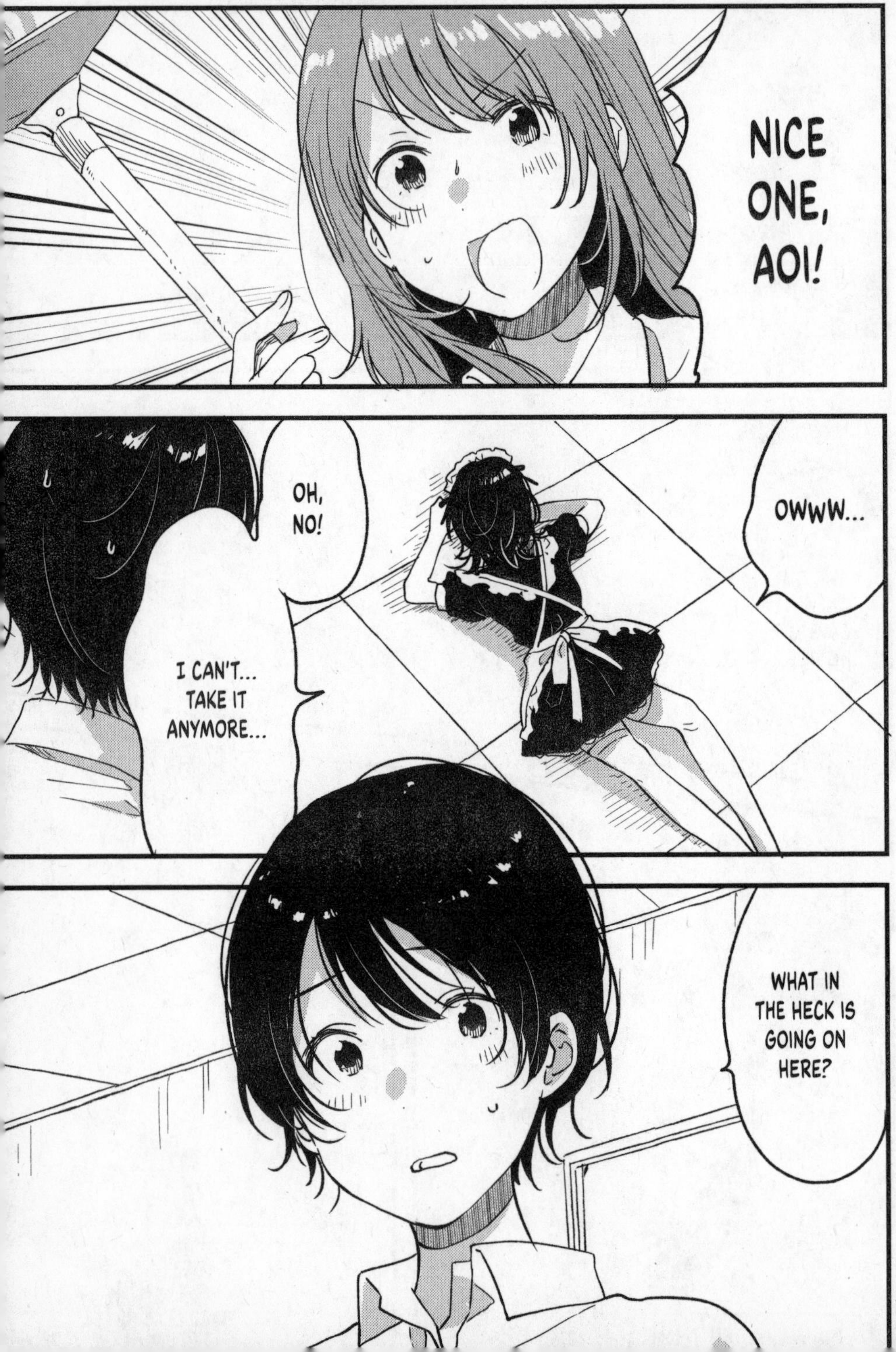
NICE ONE, AOI!
OWWW...
OH, NO!
I CAN'T... TAKE IT ANYMORE...
WHAT IN THE HECK IS GOING ON HERE?

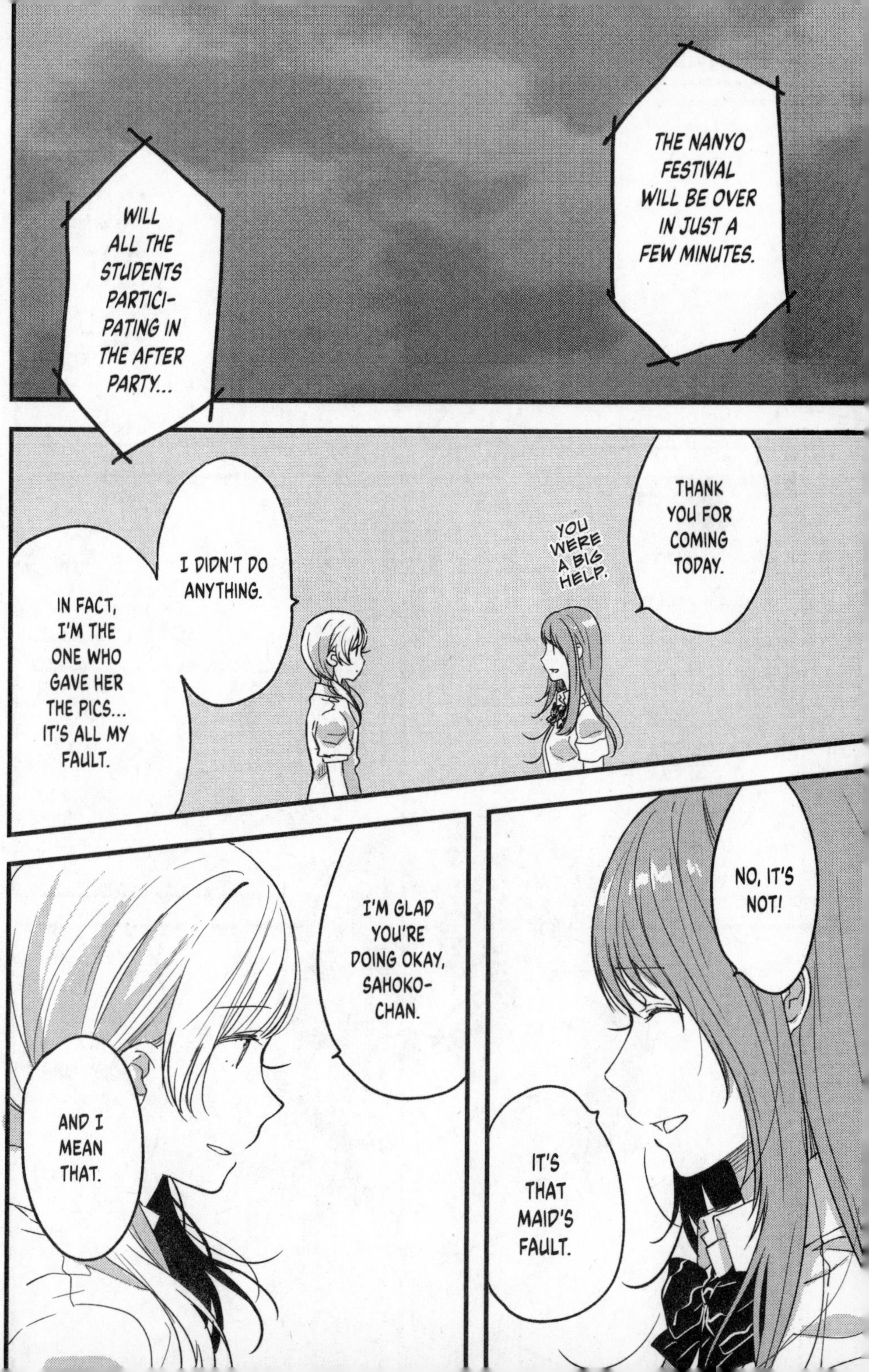
THE NANYO FESTIVAL WILL BE OVER IN JUST A FEW MINUTES.
WILL ALL THE STUDENTS PARTICI-PATING IN THE AFTER PARTY...
THANK YOU FOR COMING TODAY.
YOU WERE A BIG HELP.
I DIDN'T DO ANYTHING.
IN FACT, I'M THE ONE WHO GAVE HER THE PICS... IT'S ALL MY FAULT.
NO, IT'S NOT!
IT'S THAT MAID'S FAULT.
I'M GLAD YOU'RE DOING OKAY, SAHOKO-CHAN.
AND I MEAN THAT.

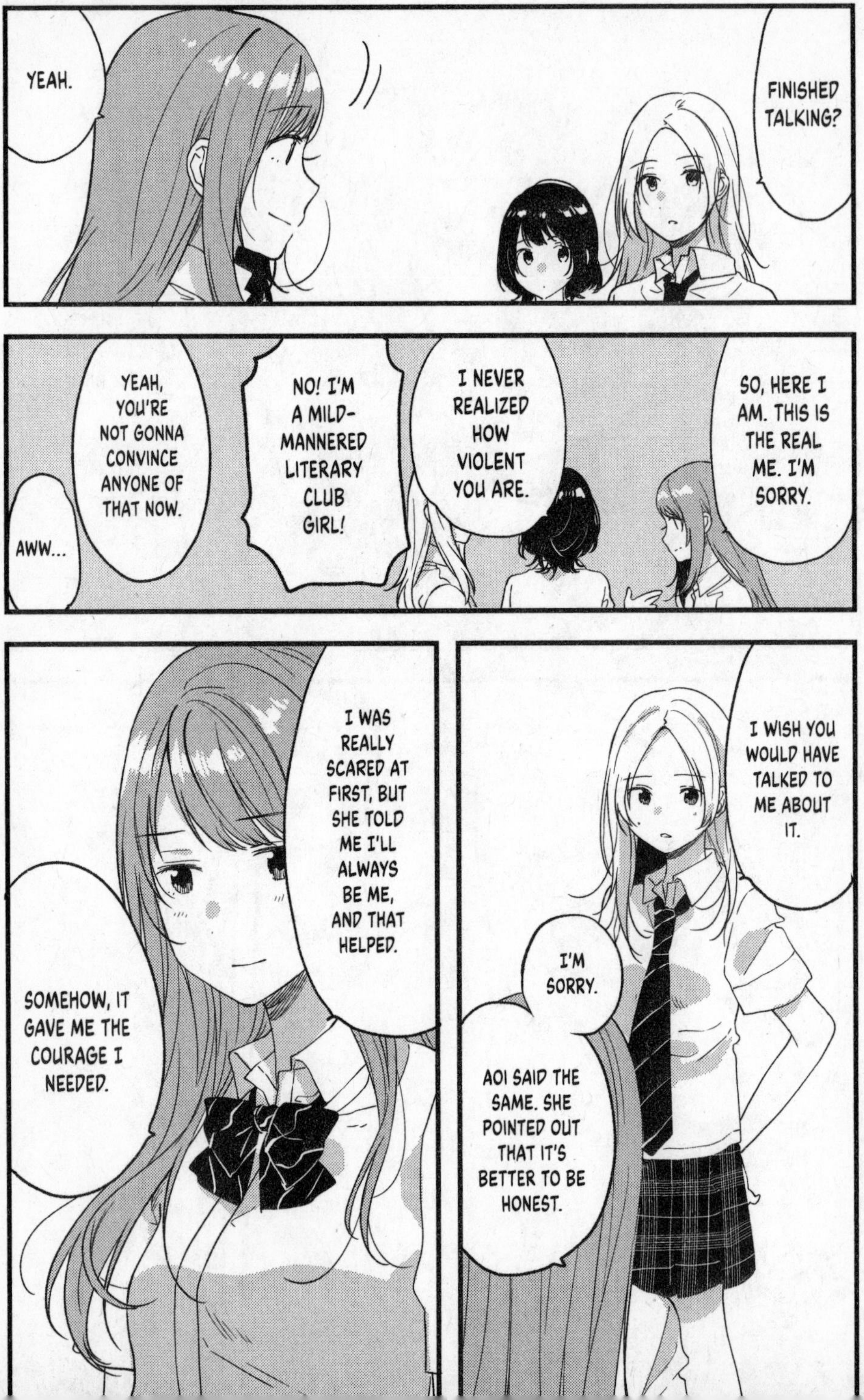
FINISHED TALKING?
YEAH.
SO, HERE I AM. THIS IS THE REAL ME. I'M SORRY.
I NEVER REALIZED HOW VIOLENT YOU ARE.
NO! I'M A MILD-MANNERED LITERARY CLUB GIRL!
YEAH, YOU'RE NOT GONNA CONVINCE ANYONE OF THAT NOW.
AWW...
I WISH YOU WOULD HAVE TALKED TO ME ABOUT IT.
I'M SORRY.
AOI SAID THE SAME. SHE POINTED OUT THAT IT'S BETTER TO BE HONEST.
I WAS REALLY SCARED AT FIRST, BUT SHE TOLD ME I'LL ALWAYS BE ME, AND THAT HELPED.
SOMEHOW, IT GAVE ME THE COURAGE I NEEDED.

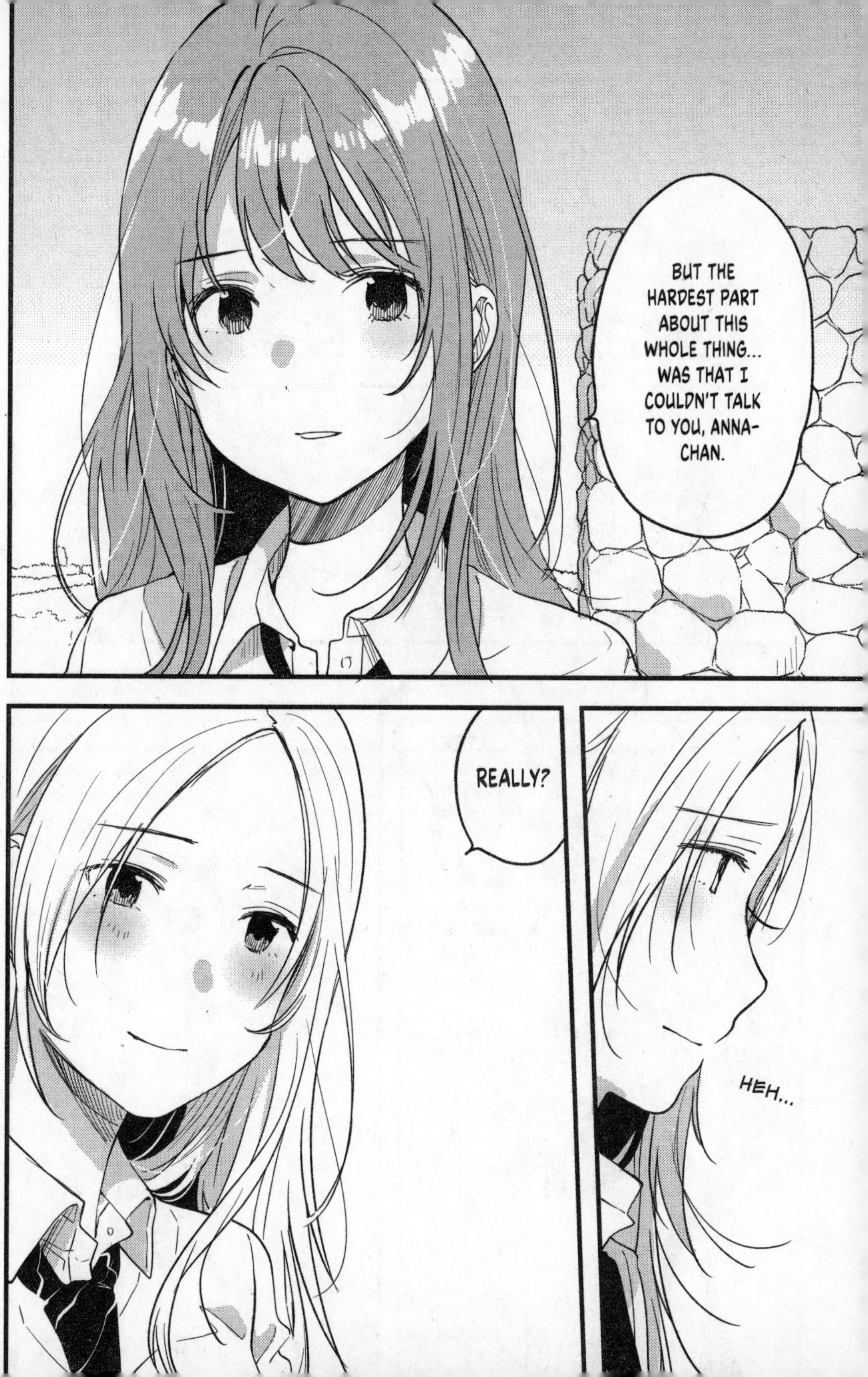
BUT THE HARDEST PART ABOUT THIS WHOLE THING... WAS THAT I COULDN'T TALK TO YOU, ANNA-CHAN.
HEH...
REALLY?

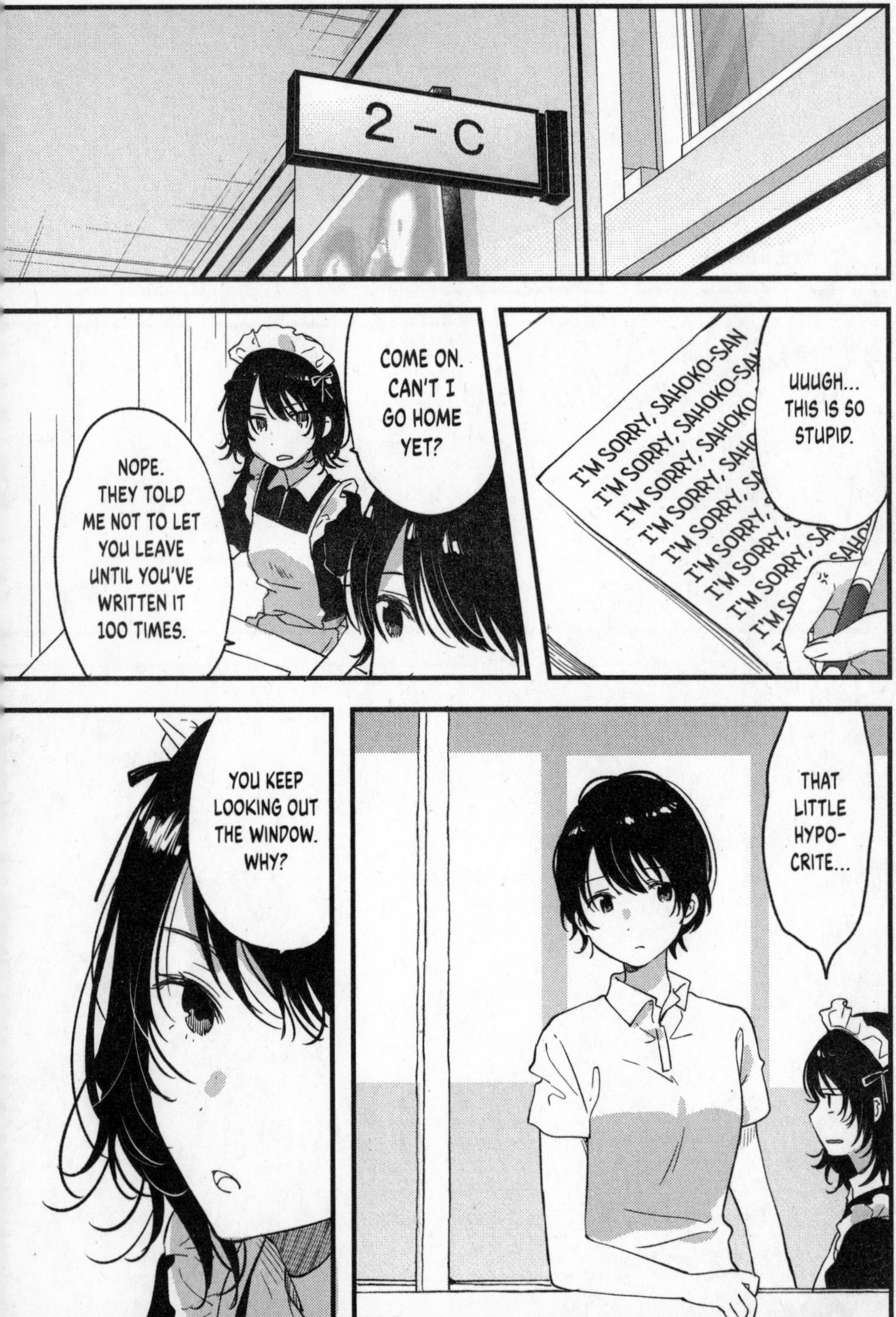
2-C
UUUGH... THIS IS SO STUPID.
I'M SORRY, SAHOKO-SAN
COME ON. CAN'T I GO HOME YET?
NOPE. THEY TOLD ME NOT TO LET YOU LEAVE UNTIL YOU'VE WRITTEN IT 100 TIMES.
THAT LITTLE HYPO- CRITE...
YOU KEEP LOOKING OUT THE WINDOW. WHY?

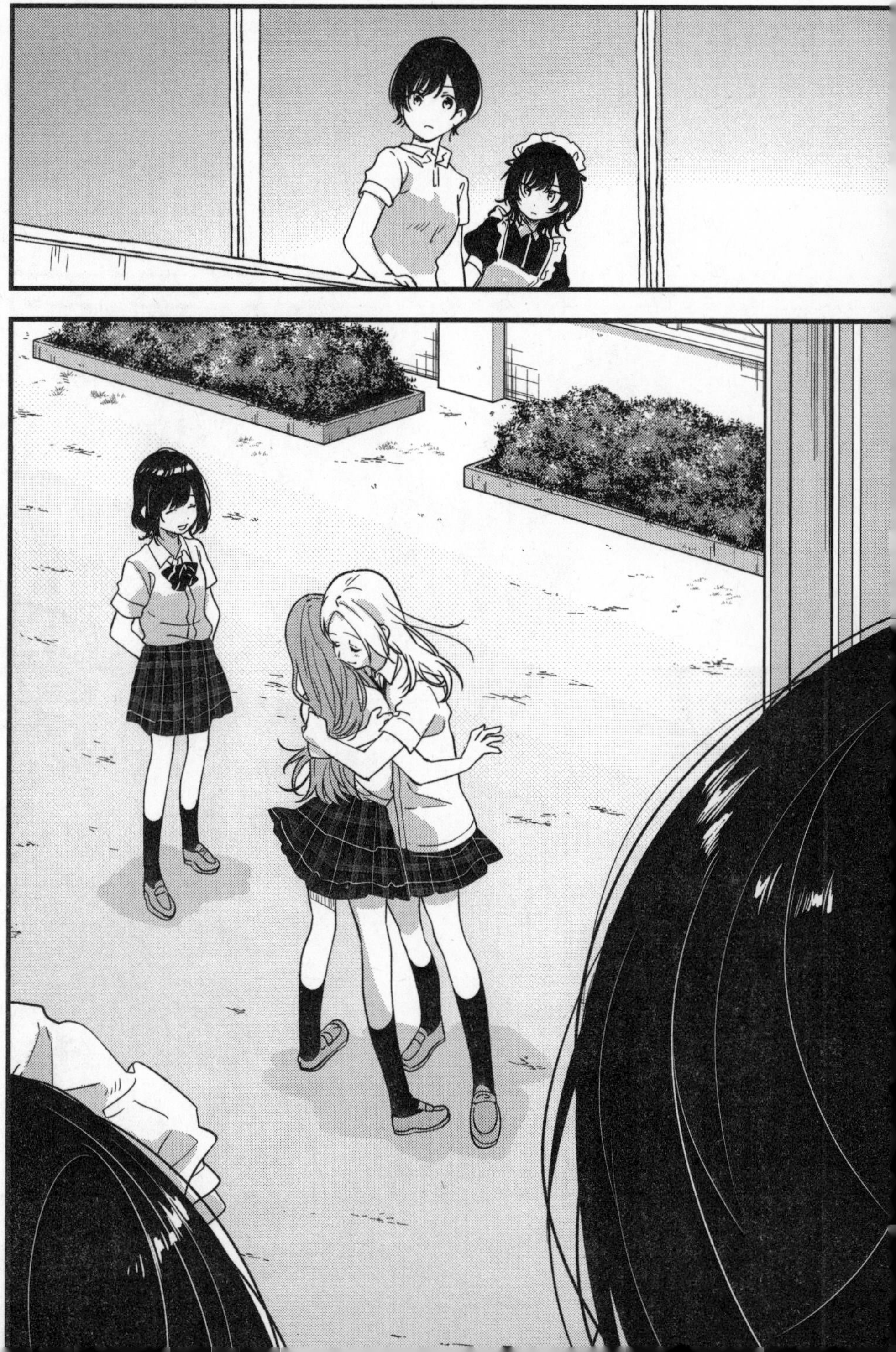

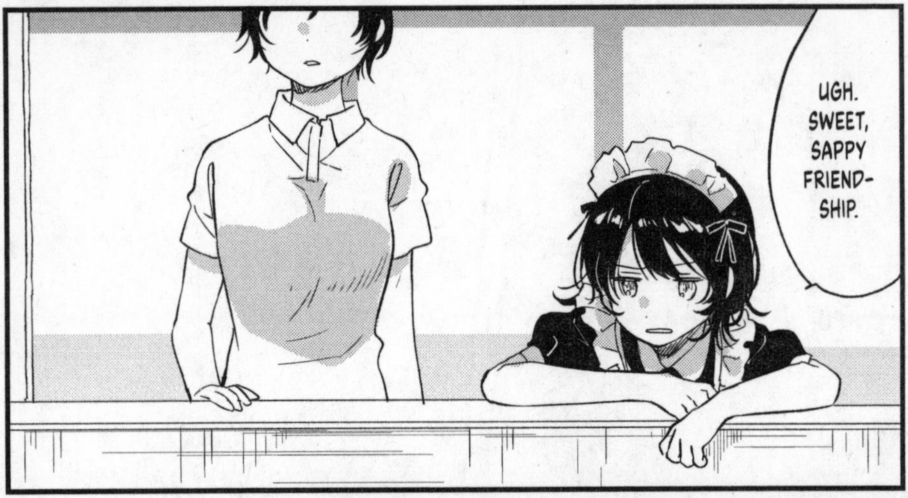
UGH. SWEET, SAPPY FRIEND-SHIP.

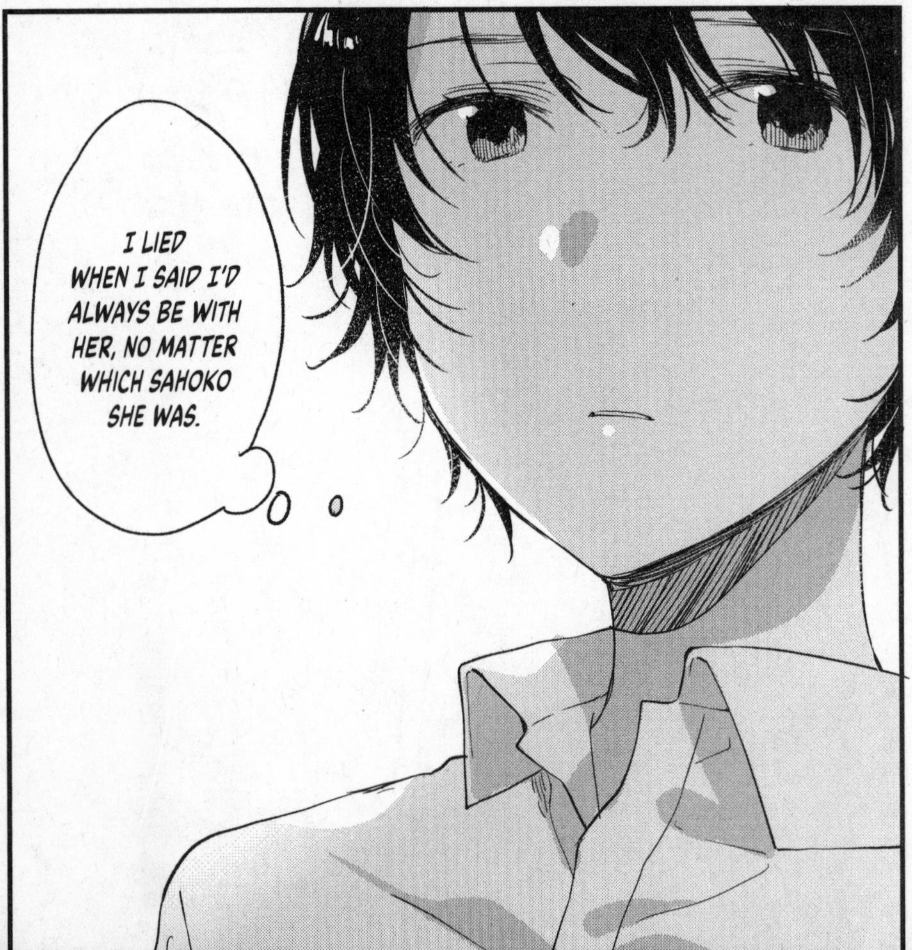
I LIED WHEN I SAID I'D ALWAYS BE WITH HER, NO MATTER WHICH SAHOKO SHE WAS.

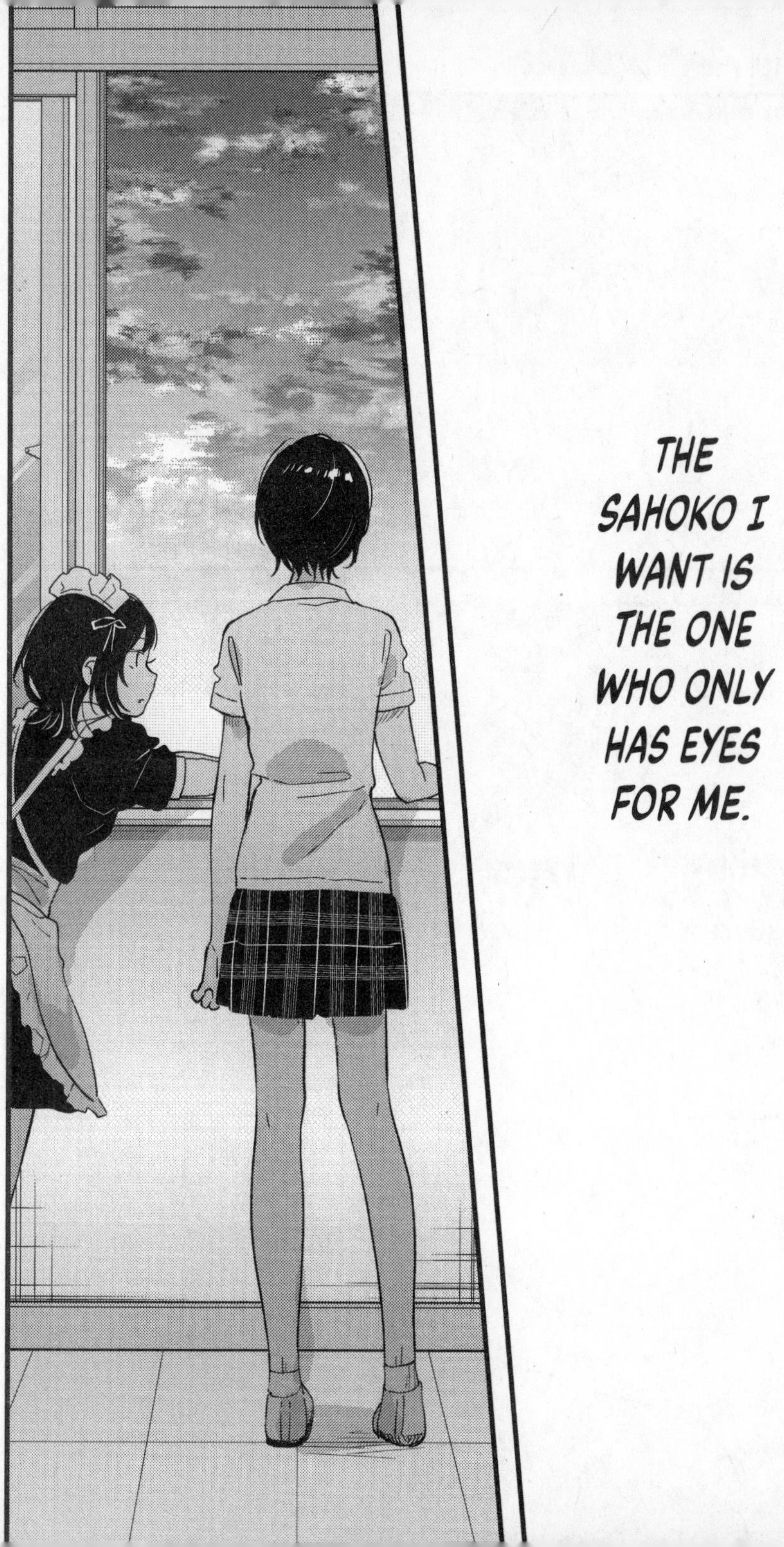
THE SAHOKO I WANT IS THE ONE WHO ONLY HAS EYES FOR ME.

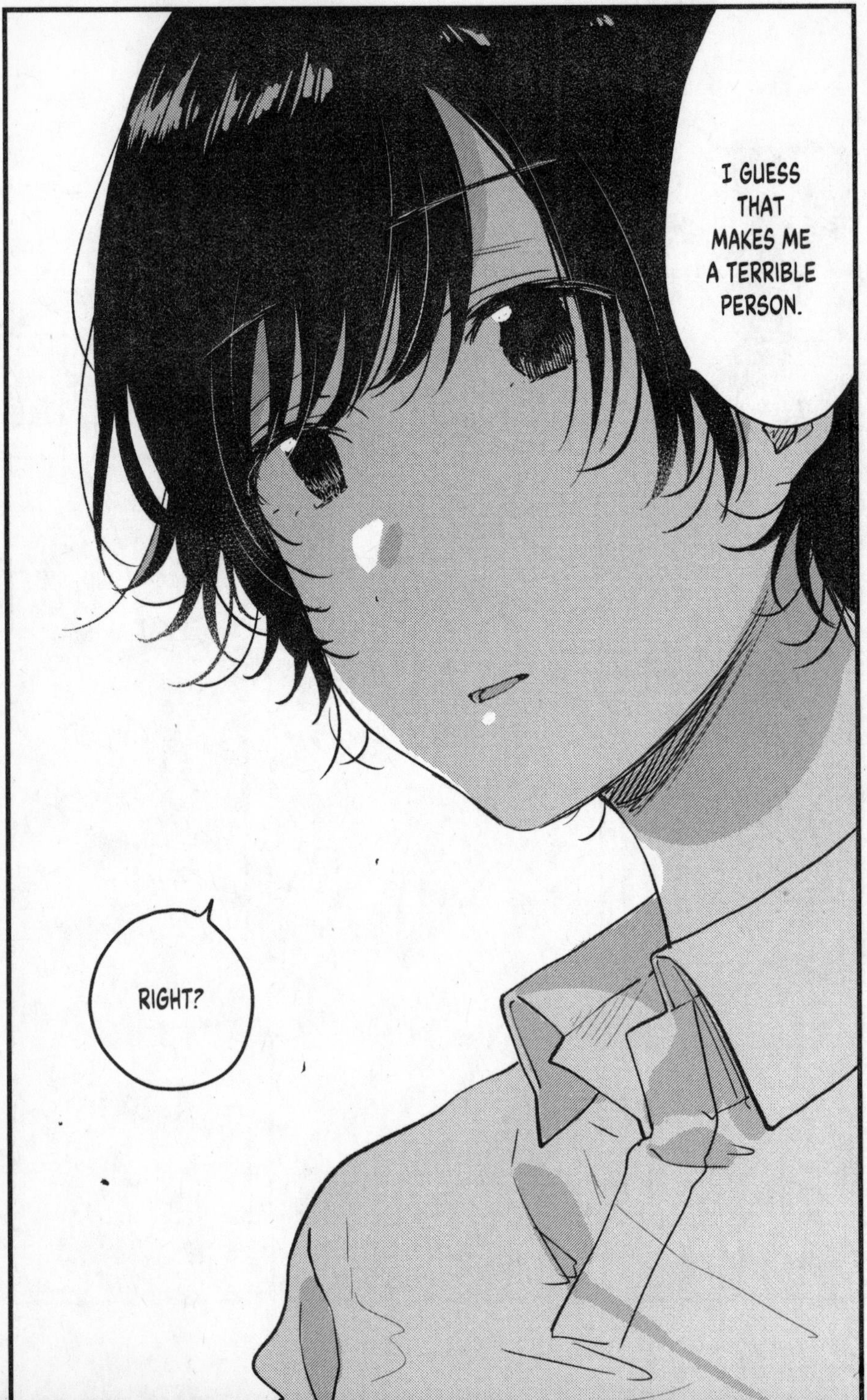
I GUESS THAT MAKES ME A TERRIBLE PERSON.
RIGHT?

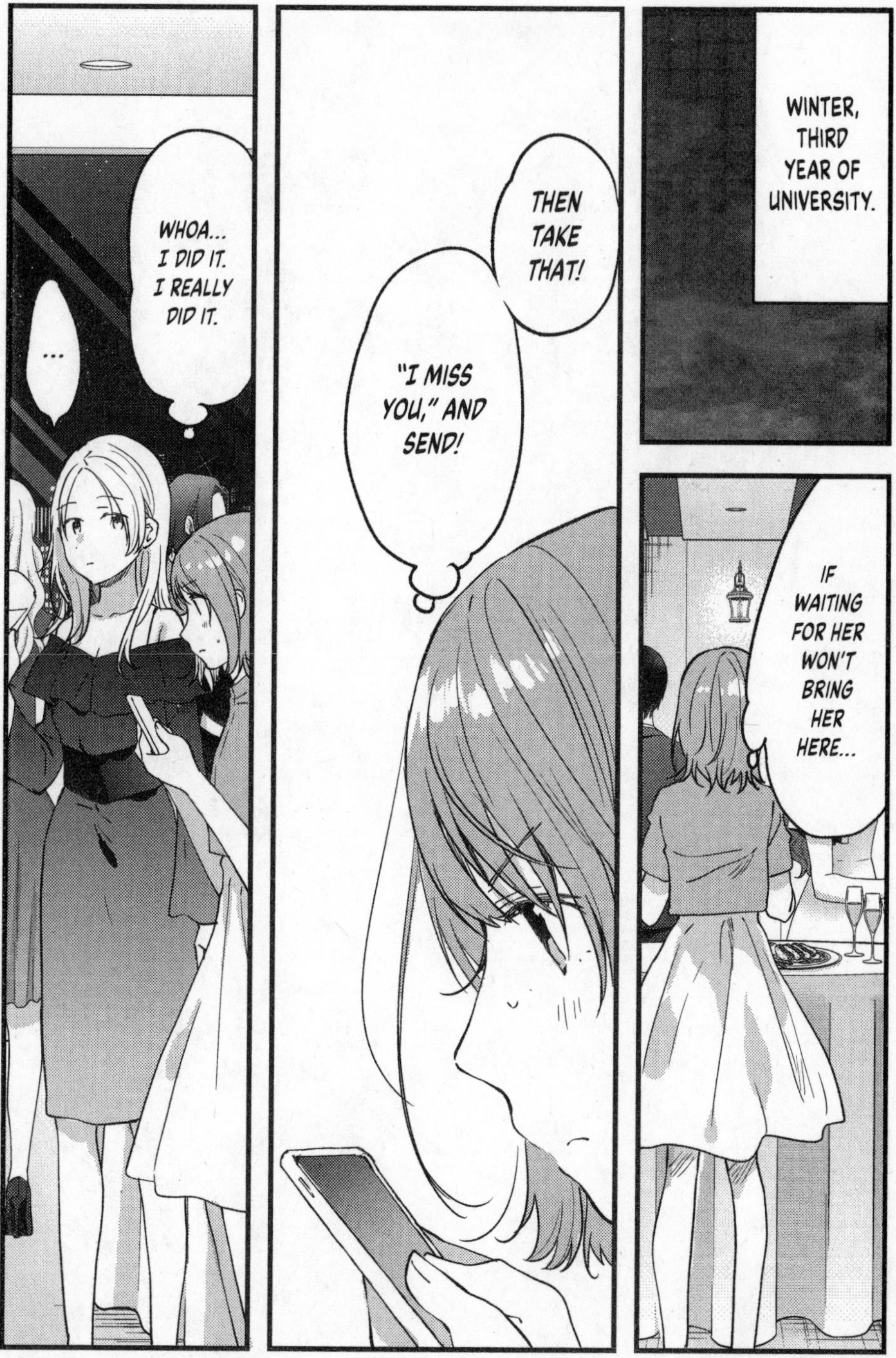
WINTER, THIRD YEAR OF UNIVERSITY.
IF WAITING FOR HER WON'T BRING HER HERE...
THEN TAKE THAT!
"I MISS YOU," AND SEND!
WHOA... I DID IT. I REALLY DID IT.
...

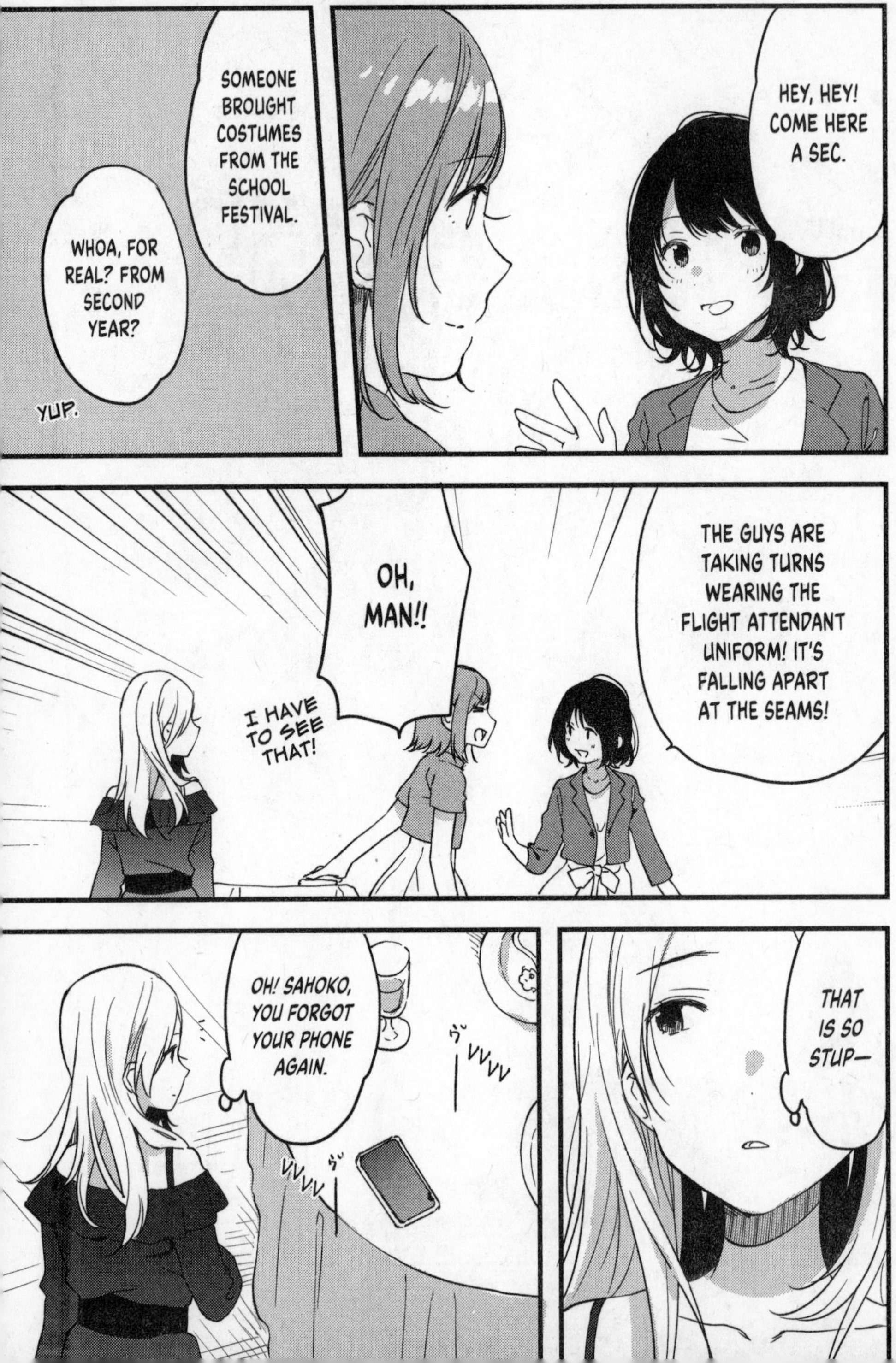
HEY, HEY! COME HERE A SEC.
SOMEONE BROUGHT COSTUMES FROM THE SCHOOL FESTIVAL.
WHOA, FOR REAL? FROM SECOND YEAR?
YUP.
THE GUYS ARE TAKING TURNS WEARING THE FLIGHT ATTENDANT UNIFORM! IT'S FALLING APART AT THE SEAMS!
OH, MAN!!
I HAVE TO SEE THAT!
THAT IS SO STUP—
ヴ VVVV
OH! SAHOKO, YOU FORGOT YOUR PHONE AGAIN.
ヴ VVVV

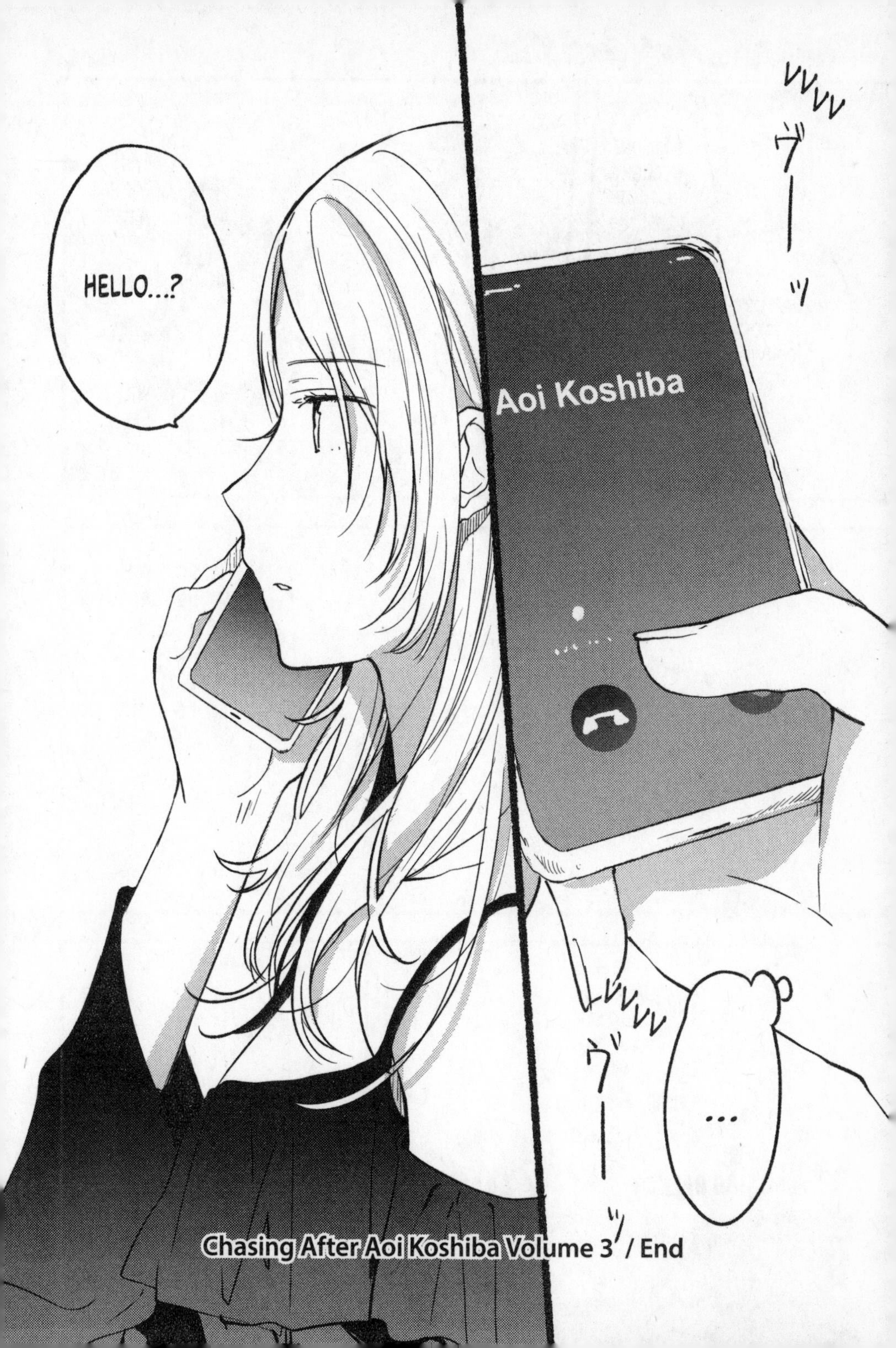
VVVVV
ヴーッ
Aoi Koshiba
VVVVV
ヴーーッ
...
HELLO...?

Chasing After Aoi Koshiba Volume 3 / End

CHASING AFTER *Aoi Koshiba*

Winter, Third Year of University

Translation Notes:

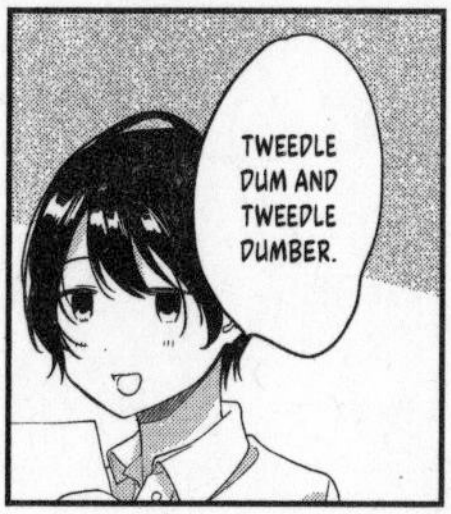
TWEEDLE DUM AND TWEEDLE DUMBER.

Tweedle Dum and Tweedle Dumber, page 20

In the original Japanese, Aoi likens herself and Sahoko to eye boogers and nose boogers. This comes from a Japanese saying that translates roughly to, "Eye goop laughing at nose snot," which means the same thing as "the pot calling the kettle black." In other words, both of them have shown the same flaw. Sahoko's original response is, "Don't be so vulgar, Aoi-san," with a teasing use of the honorific.

Amateur model, page 33

Specifically, these girls call Riko a *dokumo*, short for *dokusha* model or "reader model." This is a term used for models that don't model full-time—they haven't quit their day job, so to speak. They are called "reader models" because originally they were models chosen from a fashion magazine's readership.

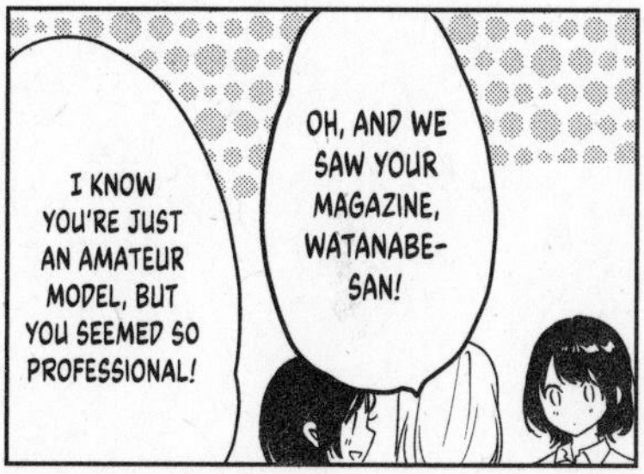
OH, AND WE SAW YOUR MAGAZINE, WATANABE-SAN!
I KNOW YOU'RE JUST AN AMATEUR MODEL, BUT YOU SEEMED SO PROFESSIONAL!

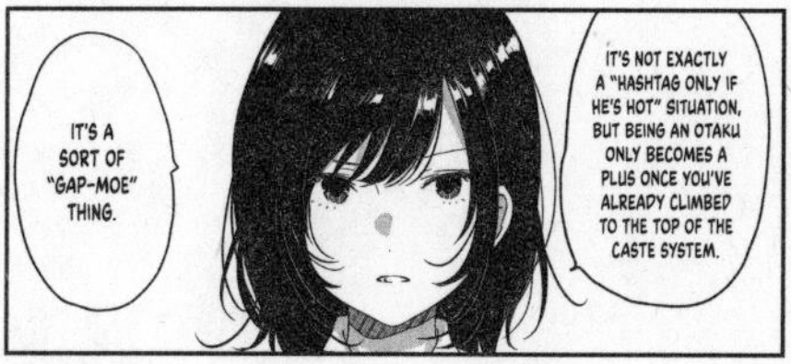
IT'S NOT EXACTLY A "HASHTAG ONLY IF HE'S HOT" SITUATION, BUT BEING AN OTAKU ONLY BECOMES A PLUS ONCE YOU'VE ALREADY CLIMBED TO THE TOP OF THE CASTE SYSTEM.
IT'S A SORT OF "GAP-MOE" THING.

Gap-moe, page 36

Moe refers to feelings of love and affection (and sometimes lust) that are inspired by certain characteristics. For example, someone with a glasses moe might feel an instant attachment to anyone wearing spectacles. A gap moe generally refers to the "gap" between contradictory characteristics. For example, is you were to see someone who, based on outward appearance, seems to be a hit man, eating a cute flavor of ice cream such as strawberry, you might be struck by the seeming contradiction of expectations and reality. If this sight creates inexplicable pleasure for you, that would be gap moe.

KidZania, page 121

KidZania is a family entertainment center built like an interactive miniature city, where kids up to age 14 can role-play adult jobs and earn play money. The very first KidZania opened in Mexico in 1999, and the franchise has since expanded to locations around the world, with the third one opening in Tokyo in 2006.

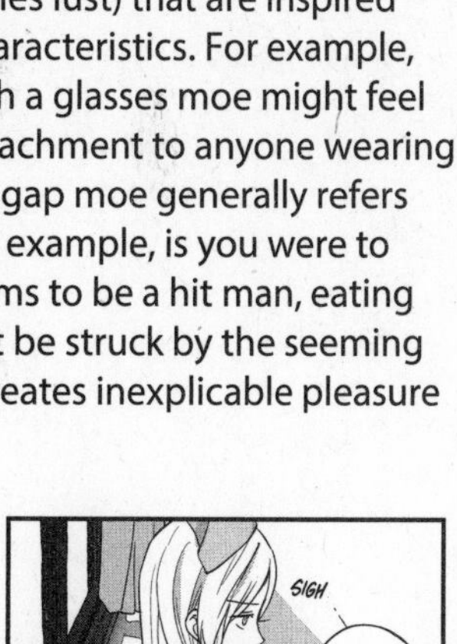
SIGH
WHOSE IDEA WAS IT TO DO A KIDZANIA CAFE...?

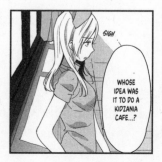

Young characters and steampunk setting, like *Howl's Moving Castle* and *Battle Angel Alita*

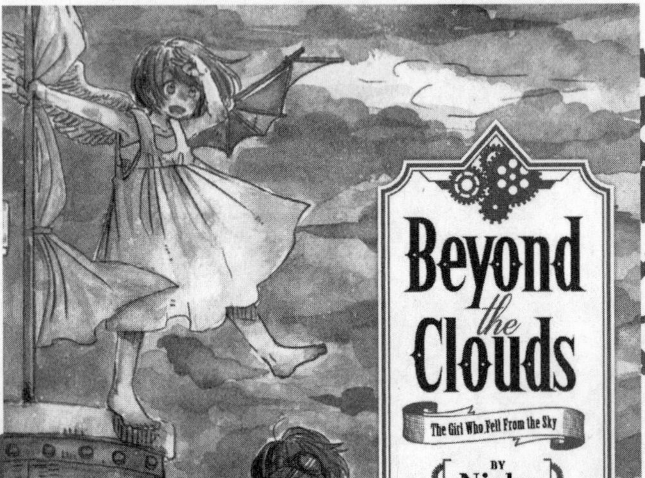
Beyond the Clouds
The Girl Who Fell From the Sky
BY Nicke
VOLUME 01

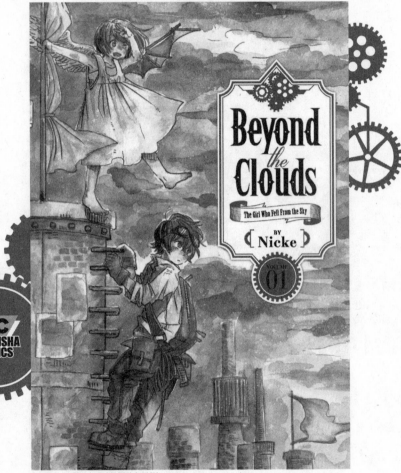

Beyond the Clouds © 2018 Nicke / Ki-oon

KC KODANSHA COMICS

A boy with a talent for machines and a mysterious girl whose wings he's fixed will take you beyond the clouds! In the tradition of the high-flying, resonant adventure stories of Studio Ghibli comes a gorgeous tale about the longing of young hearts for adventure and friendship!

THE SWEET SCENT OF LOVE IS IN THE AIR! FOR FANS OF OFFBEAT ROMANCES LIKE *WOTAKOI*

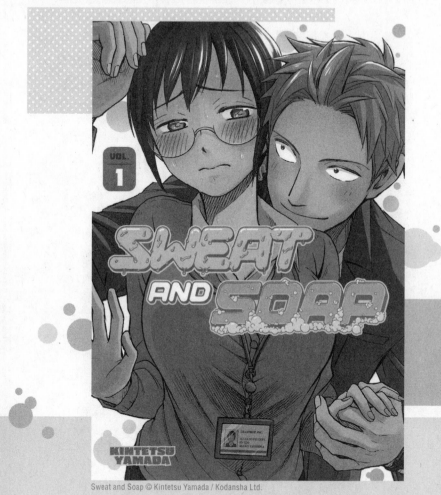

Sweat and Soap © Kintetsu Yamada / Kodansha Ltd.

In an office romance, there's a fine line between sexy and awkward... and that line is where Asako — a woman who sweats copiously — meets Koutarou — a perfume developer who can't get enough of Asako's, er, scent. Don't miss a romcom manga like no other!

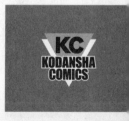

KC KODANSHA COMICS

Something's Wrong With Us

NATSUMI ANDO

The dark, psychological, sexy shojo series readers have been waiting for!

A spine-chilling and steamy romance between a Japanese sweets maker and the man who framed her mother for murder!

Following in her mother's footsteps, Nao became a traditional Japanese sweets maker, and with unparalleled artistry and a bright attitude, she gets an offer to work at a world-class confectionary company. But when she meets the young, handsome owner, she recognizes his cold stare...

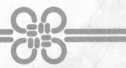

The boys are back, in 400-page hardcovers that are as pretty and badass as they are!

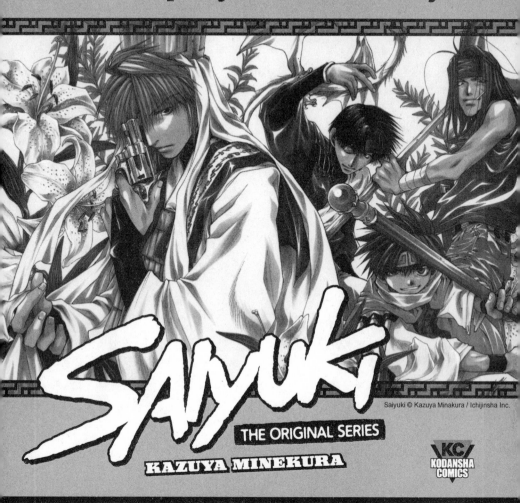

Saiyuki © Kazuya Minekura / Ichijinsha Inc.

SAIYUKI

THE ORIGINAL SERIES

KAZUYA MINEKURA

"AN EDGY COMIC LOOK AT AN ANCIENT CHINESE TALE." —YALSA

Genjo Sanzo is a Buddhist priest in the city of Togenkyo, which is being ravaged by yokai spirits that have fallen out of balance with the natural order. His superiors send him on a journey far to the west to discover why this is happening and how to stop it. His companions are three yokai with human souls. But this is no day trip — the four will encounter many discoveries and horrors on the way.

FEATURES NEW TRANSLATION, COLOR PAGES, AND BEAUTIFUL WRAPAROUND COVER ART!

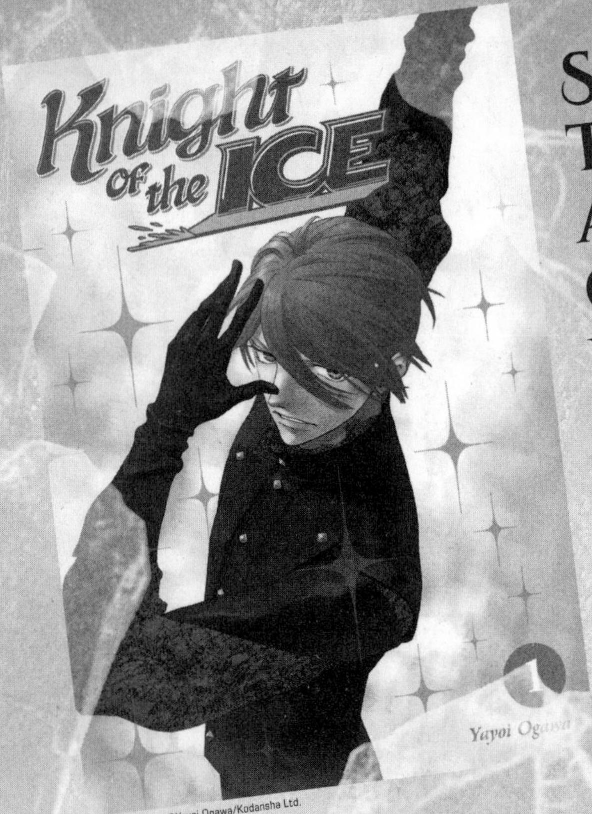

Knight of the ICE

Yayoi Ogawa

SKATING THRILLS AND ICY CHILLS WITH THIS NEW TINGLY ROMANCE SERIES!

A rom-com on ice, perfect for fans of *Princess Jellyfish* and *Wotakoi*. Kokoro is the talk of the figure-skating world, winning trophies and hearts. But little do they know... he's actually a huge nerd! From the beloved creator of *You're My Pet* (*Tramps Like Us*).

Chitose is a serious young woman, working for the health magazine *SASSO*. Or at least, she would be, if she wasn't constantly getting distracted by her childhood friend, international figure skating star Kokoro Kijinami! In the public eye and on the ice, Kokoro is a gallant, flawless knight, but behind his glittery costumes and breathtaking spins lies a secret: He's actually a hopelessly romantic otaku, who can only land his quad jumps when Chitose is on hand to recite a spell from his favorite magical girl anime!

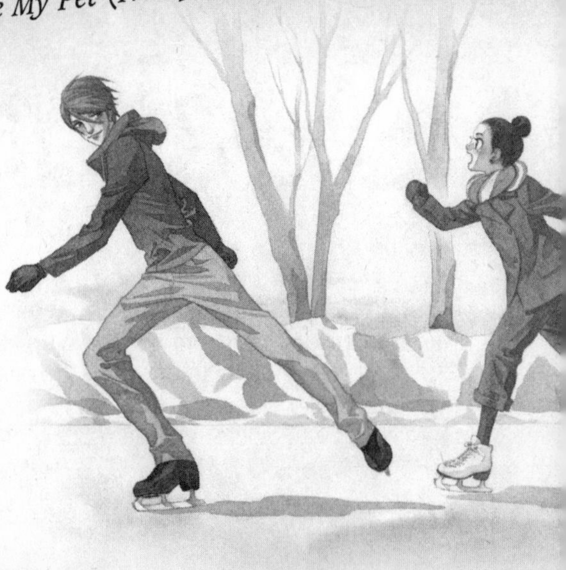

KC KODANSHA COMICS

The adorable new odd-couple cat comedy manga from the creator of the beloved *Chi's Sweet Home*, in full color!

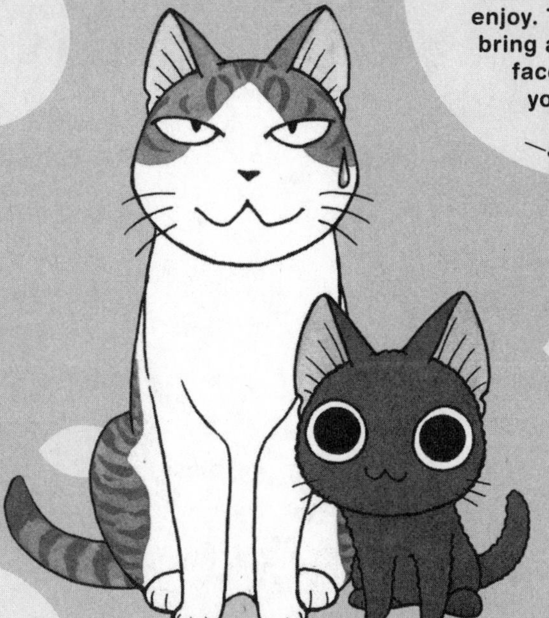

Sue & Tai-chan

Konami Kanata

Sue is an aging housecat who's looking forward to living out her life in peace... but her plans change when the mischievous black tomcat Tai-chan enters the picture! Hey! Sue never signed up to be a catsitter! *Sue & Tai-chan* is the latest from the reigning meow-narch of cute kitty comics, Konami Kanata.

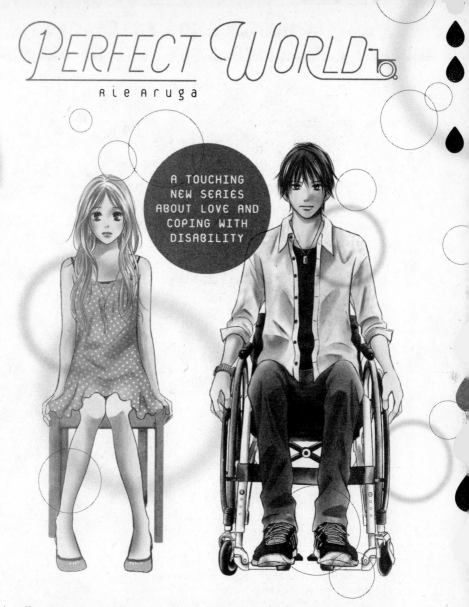

PERFECT WORLD

Rie Aruga

1

A TOUCHING NEW SERIES ABOUT LOVE AND COPING WITH DISABILITY

An office party reunites Tsugumi with her high school crush Itsuki. He's realized his dream of becoming an architect, but along the way, he experienced a spinal injury that put him in a wheelchair. Now Tsugumi's rekindled feelings will butt up against prejudices she never considered — and Itsuki will have to decide if he's ready to let someone into his heart...

"Depicts with great delicacy and courage the difficulties some with disabilities experience getting involved in romantic relationships... Rie Aruga refuses to romanticize, pushing her heroine to face the reality of disability. She invites her readers to the same tasks of empathy, knowledge and recognition."
—Slate.fr

"An important entry [in manga romance]... The emotional core of both plot and characters indicates thoughtfulness... [Aruga's] research is readily apparent in the text and artwork, making this feel like a real story."
—Anime News Network

KC KODANSHA COMICS

A SMART, NEW ROMANTIC COMEDY FOR FANS OF *SHORTCAKE CAKE* AND *TERRACE HOUSE!*

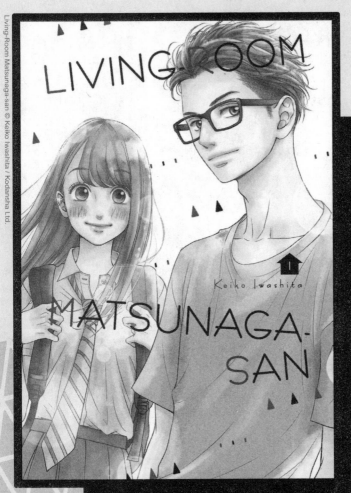

A romance manga starring high school girl Meeko, who learns to live on her own in a boarding house whose living room is home to the odd (but handsome) Matsunaga-san. She begins to adjust to her new life away from her parents, but Meeko soon learns that no matter how far away from home she is, she's still a young girl at heart — especially when she finds herself falling for Matsunaga-san.

One of CLAMP's biggest hits returns in this definitive, premium, hardcover 20th anniversary collector's edition!

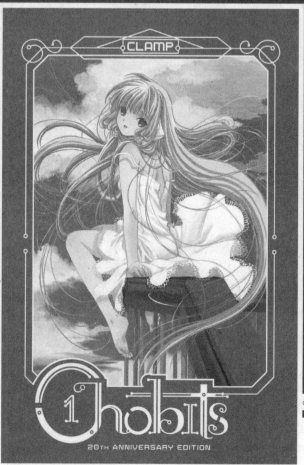

CLAMP

1 Chobits

20TH ANNIVERSARY EDITION

"A wonderfully entertaining story that would be a great installment in anybody's manga collection."
— Anime News Network

"CLAMP is an all-female manga-creating team whose feminine touch shows in this entertaining, sci-fi soap opera."
— Publishers Weekly

Poor college student Hideki is down on his luck. All he wants is a good job, a girlfriend, and his very own "persocom"—the latest and greatest in humanoid computer technology. Hideki's luck changes one night when he finds Chi—a persocom thrown out in a pile of trash. But Hideki soon discovers that there's much more to his cute new persocom than meets the eye.

KC
KODANSHA
COMICS

THE WORLD OF CLAMP!

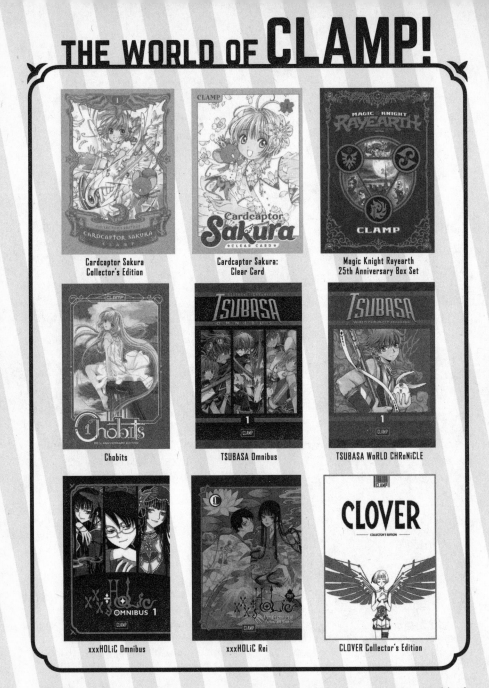

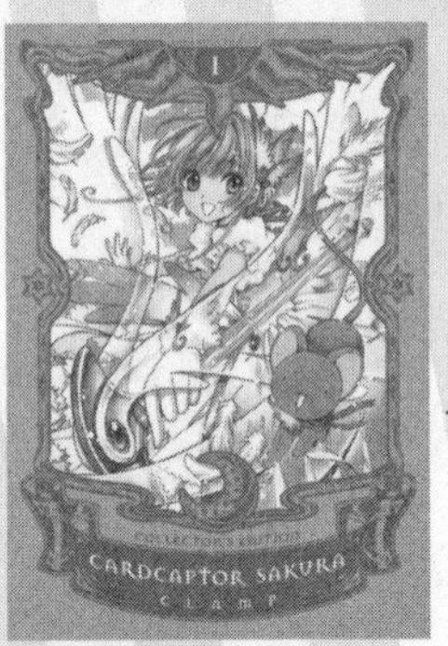
CARDCAPTOR SAKURA
CLAMP

Cardcaptor Sakura
Collector's Edition

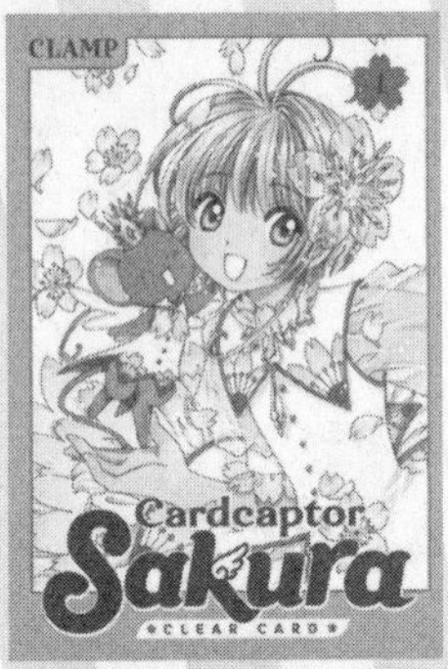
CLAMP
Cardcaptor Sakura
CLEAR CARD

Cardcaptor Sakura:
Clear Card

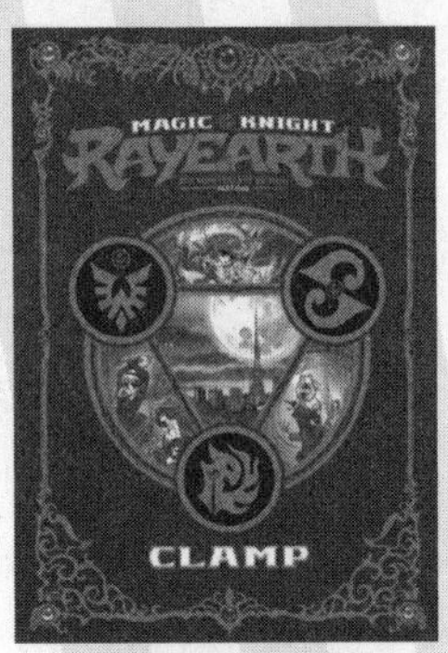
MAGIC KNIGHT
RAYEARTH
CLAMP

Magic Knight Rayearth
25th Anniversary Box Set

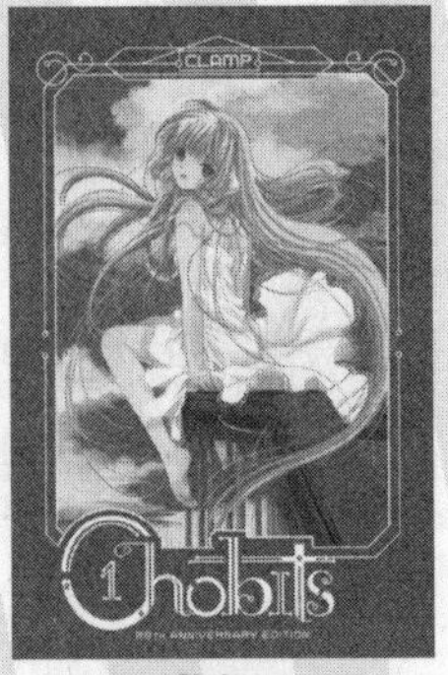
CLAMP
Chobits

Chobits

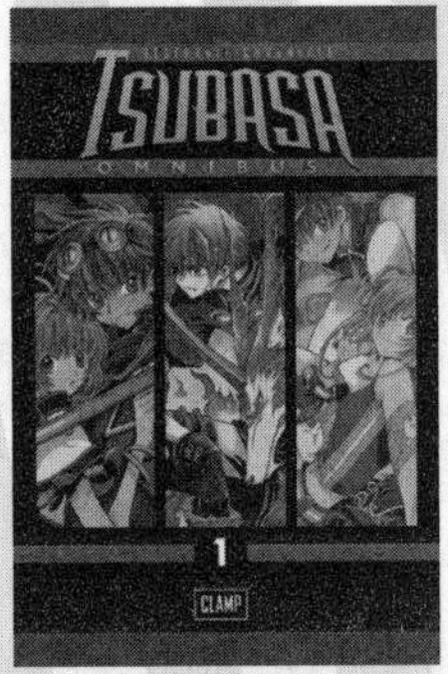
TSUBASA
OMNIBUS
1
CLAMP

TSUBASA Omnibus

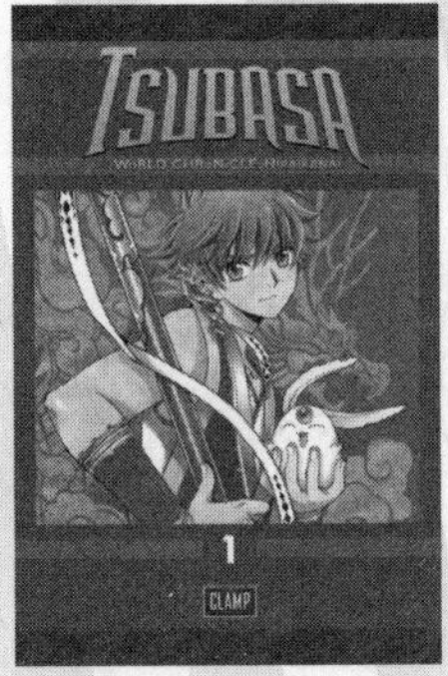
TSUBASA
1
CLAMP

TSUBASA WoRLD CHRoNiCLE

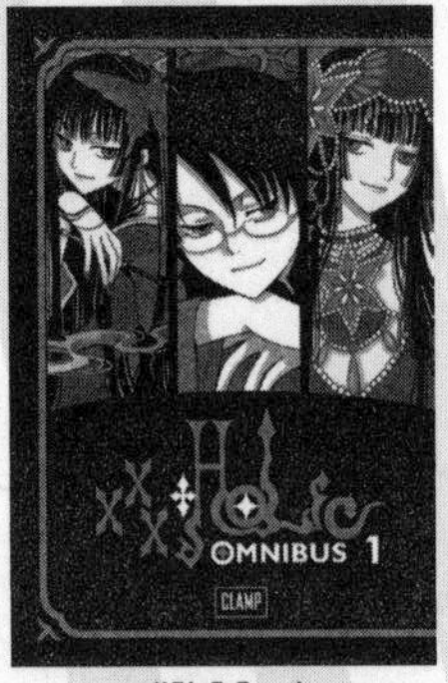
xxxHOLiC
OMNIBUS 1
CLAMP

xxxHOLiC Omnibus

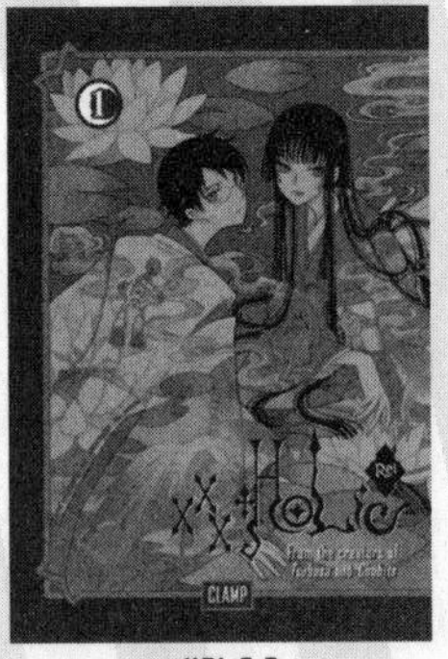
xxxHOLiC
CLAMP

xxxHOLiC Rei

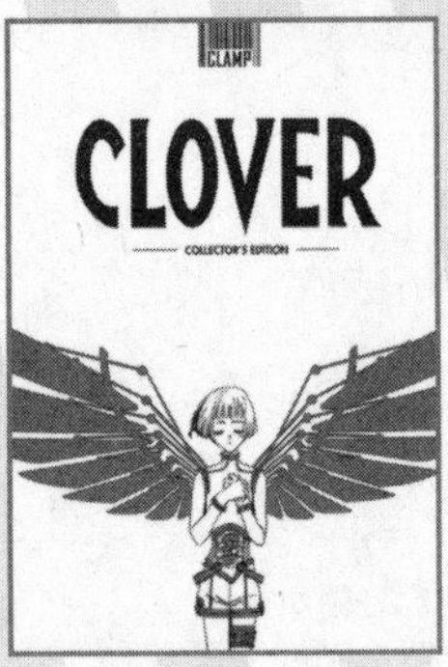
CLAMP
CLOVER
COLLECTOR'S EDITION

CLOVER Collector's Edition

KC KODANSHA COMICS

Kodansha Comics welcomes you to explore the expansive world of CLAMP, the all-female artist collective that has produced some of the most acclaimed manga of the century. Our growing catalog includes icons like *Cardcaptor Sakura* and *Magic Knight Rayearth*, each crafted with CLAMP's one-of-a-kind style and characters!

"Clever, sassy, and original....*xxxHOLiC* has the inherent hallmarks of a runaway hit."
—NewType magazine

Beautifully seductive artwork and uniquely Japanese depictions of the supernatural will hypnotize CLAMP fans!

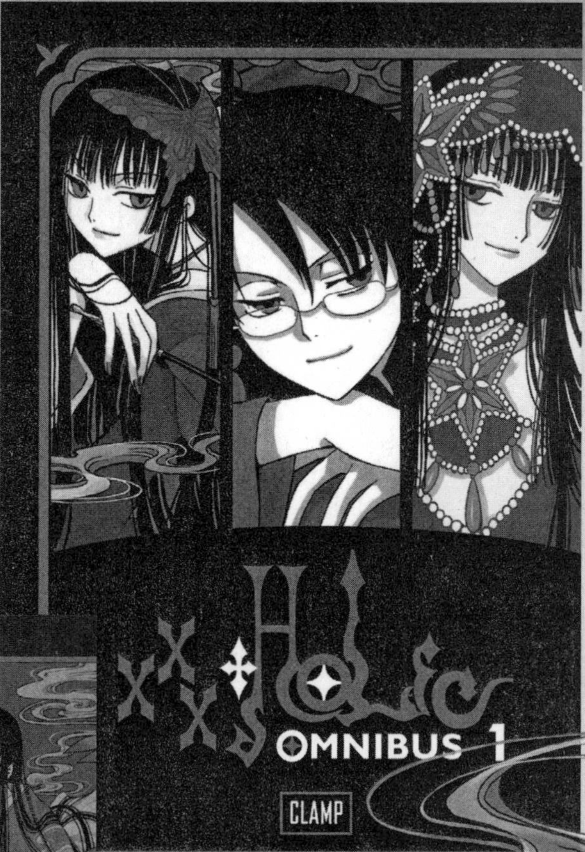

xxxHOLiC OMNIBUS 1

CLAMP

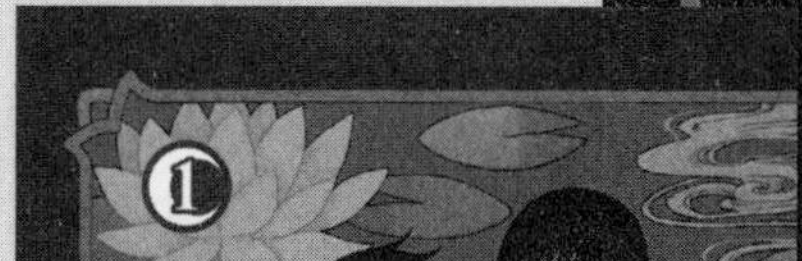

Kimihiro Watanuki is haunted by visions of ghosts and spirits. He seeks help from a mysterious woman named Yuko, who claims she can help. However, Watanuki must work for Yuko in order to pay for her aid. Soon Watanuki finds himself employed in Yuko's shop, where he sees things and meets customers that are stranger than anything he could have ever imagined.

KC
KODANSHA COMICS

The art-deco cyberpunk classic from the creators of *xxxHOLiC* and *Cardcaptor Sakura*!

"Starred Review. This experimental sci-fi work from CLAMP reads like a romantic version of *AKIRA*."
—Publishers Weekly

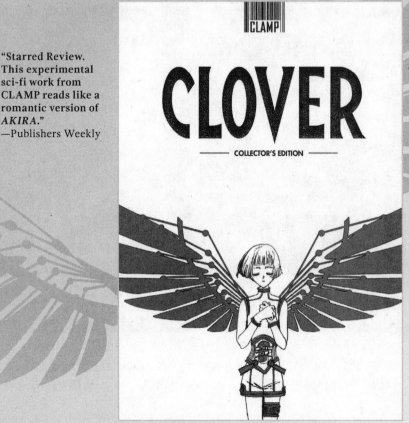

CLOVER © CLAMP-ShigatsuTsuitachi CO.,LTD./Kodansha Ltd.

Su was born into a bleak future, where the government keeps tight control over children with magical powers—codenamed "Clovers." With Su being the only "four-leaf" Clover in the world, she has been kept isolated nearly her whole life. Can ex-military agent Kazuhiko deliver her to the happiness she seeks? Experience the complete series in this hardcover edition, which also includes over twenty pages of ravishing color art!

The beloved characters from *Cardcaptor Sakura* return in a brand new, reimagined fantasy adventure!

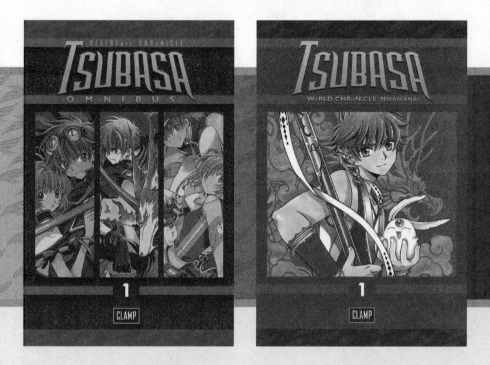

"[*Tsubasa*] takes readers on a fantastic ride that only gets more exhilarating with each successive chapter." —Anime News Network

In the Kingdom of Clow, an archaeological dig unleashes an incredible power, causing Princess Sakura to lose her memories. To save her, her childhood friend Syaoran must follow the orders of the Dimension Witch and travel alongside Kurogane, an unrivaled warrior; Fai, a powerful magician; and Mokona, a curiously strange creature, to retrieve Sakura's dispersed memories!

Tsubasa Omnibus © CLAMP © CLAMP·ShigatsuTsuitachi CO.,LTD./Kodansha Ltd.   Tsubasa: WoRLD CHRoNiCLE © CLAMP·ShigatsuTsuitachi CO.,LTD./Kodansha Ltd.

A Kodansha Comics Trade Paperback Original
Chasing After Aoi Koshiba 3 copyright © 2021 Hazuki Takeoka/Fly
English translation copyright © 2021 Hazuki Takeoka/Fly

All rights reserved.

Published in the United States by Kodansha Comics, an imprint of Kodansha USA Publishing, LLC, New York.

Publication rights for this English edition arranged through Kodansha Ltd., Tokyo.

First published in Japan in 2021 by Ichijinsha Inc., Tokyo.

ISBN 978-1-64651-245-4

Printed in the United States of America.

www.kodansha.us

1st Printing
Translation: Alethea Nibley & Athena Nibley
Lettering: Paige Pumphrey
Editing: Michal Zuckerman
Kodansha Comics edition cover design by Adam Del Re

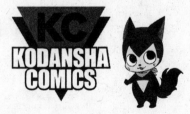

Publisher: Kiichiro Sugawara

Director of publishing services: Ben Applegate
Associate director, publishing operations: Stephen Pakula
Publishing services managing editors: Madison Salters, Alanna Ruse
Production managers: Emi Lotto, Angela Zurlo
Logo and character art ©Kodansha USA Publishing, LLC